WITHDRAWN
FROM THE RECORDS OF THE
MID-CONTINENT PUBLIC LIBRARY

REF. 920 B976BC FEB.
Butler, Alban.
Butler's lives of the saints

MID-CONTINENT PUBLIC LIBRARY

Parkville Branch
Parkville Heights Shopping Ctr.
8815 NW 45 Highway
Parkville, MO 64152

PV

BUTLER'S
LIVES OF THE SAINTS

NEW
FULL EDITION

FEBRUARY

BUTLER'S
LIVES OF THE SAINTS

NEW FULL EDITION

Patron

H. E. CARDINAL BASIL HUME, O.S.B.
Archbishop of Westminster

EDITORIAL BOARD

General Consultant Editor
DAVID HUGH FARMER

General Consultant, U.S.A.
ERIC HOLLAS, O.S.B.

Specialist Consultants
PHILIP CARAMAN, S.J.
JOHN HARWOOD
KATHLEEN JONES, PhD
DANIEL REES, O.S.B.
RICHARD SHARPE, MA, PhD
AYLWARD SHORTER, W.F.
ALBERIC STACPOOLE, O.S.B., MA, FRHS
HENRY WANSBROUGH, O.S.B., MA, STL
BENEDICTA WARD, SLG, MA, DPhil

Managing Editor
PAUL BURNS

BUTLER'S LIVES OF THE SAINTS

NEW
FULL EDITION

FEBRUARY

Revised by
PAUL BURNS

BURNS & OATES

THE LITURGICAL PRESS
Collegeville, Minnesota

First published 1998 in Great Britain by
BURNS & OATES
Wellwood, North Farm Road,
Tunbridge Wells, Kent TN2 3DR

First published 1998 in North America by
THE LITURGICAL PRESS
St John's Abbey, Collegeville,
Minnesota 56321

Copyright © Burns & Oates/Search Press Limited 1998

Butler's *Lives of the Fathers, Martyrs and other principal Saints* ... first published
1756-9. First revised edition, *Butler's Lives of the Saints*, ed. Herbert Thurston,
S.J., 1926-38, copyright © Burns, Oates & Washbourne Limited. Second revised
edition, ed. Herbert Thurston, S.J., and Donald Attwater, 1954-8, copyright ©
Burns & Oates Limited.

All rights reserved. No part of this publication may be reproduced in any form, by
print, photoprint, microfilm, microfiche, mechanical recording, photocopying,
translation, or any other means, known or as yet unknown, or stored in an
information retrieval system, without written permission obtained beforehand from
Burns & Oates/Search Press Limited or The Liturgical Press.

ISBN 0 86012 251 4   Burns & Oates
ISBN 0-8146-2378-6   The Liturgical Press

The emblems appearing at the foot of some pages are taken from W. Ellwood Post,
Saints, Signs and Symbols: A Concise Dictionary. © Copyright 1962, 1974 by
Morehouse Publishing, with the permission of the publishers.

Library of Congress Catalog Card Number: 95-81671

MID-CONTINENT PUBLIC LIBRARY

Parkville Branch
Parkville Heights Shopping Ctr.
8815 NW 45 Highway
Parkville, MO 64152

MID-CONTINENT PUBLIC LIBRARY

3 0000 11795145 3

Typeset by Search Press Limited
Printed in the United States of America

CONTENTS

(Entries in capital letters indicate that the saint or feast is commemorated throughout the Roman Catholic Church with the rank of Solemnity, Feast, Memorial or Optional Memorial, according to the 1969 revised Calendar of the Latin [Roman] Rite of the Catholic Church, published in the Roman Missal of 1970, or that the saint is of particular importance for the English-speaking world. These entries are placed first on their dates. All others are in chronological order, by date of death.)

Contents

Contents

PREFACE

"The people's admiration for its favourites is always unmeasured (and sometimes unjustified)" as Fr Delehaye remarked many years ago in his *The Legends of the Saints*. In recent years there has ben an increasing tendency across the world to make popular secular figures as well as well-known religious personalities the objects of the sort of canonization by popular acclaim that had been the norm for more than a thousand years of the Church's history. After the death in 1997 of Diana, Princess of Wales, for example, "a post-Christian, post-Protestant nation found itself praying for the dead" (Eamon Duffy in *The Tablet*). The day before this article was published, Mother Teresa died, and commentators just geting used to this "very un-English fact" had to grapple with the distinction between praying *for* the dead and praying *to* those dead officially recognized as intercessors in heaven. Those Reformers who had driven "a wedge between the living and the dead," cutting the latter off from "the great web of mutual love and support which was the Church," had "struck the Church dumb at the graveside of sinners" (Duffy). In 1997 it seemed as if the people had rediscovered a voice at the graveside of sinner and saint alike.

Of course some commentators condemned the popular mood as an orgy of self-castigating grief. Nevertheless, a shift in postmodern secular Western attitudes appeared to have become visible, even if the shift was from "secular" to "pagan." That could be a revindication of the perennial religious instinct also evident in the cult of saints, by which the Catholic Church has—implicitly and explicitly—accomodated the insights of other religions.

These volumes seek to approach the saints and their cult in a way consistent—as far as possible—with contemporary insights into personality and motivation and with the appropriation, at a fairly popular level, of historical knowledge gained in recent times, with what Prof. Owen Chadwick (Regius Professor of Modern History at Cambridge University) has defined as "the need to be inside their minds, and to forget the future which they could not know, and to come towards them with the openness of mind, the readiness to listen, which a man gives to his friend." As St Augustine said: *Nemo nisi per amicitiam cognoscitur*: you cannot understand anyone except out of friendship.

This effort is often hampered by sheer lack of information. Moreover, as Prof. Chadwick notes, one ought to suspect "societies of the past, even documents in the archives," of being "sure to mislead you vilely unless your critical sense is ever alert" (*The Making of the Benedictine Ideal*, Washington, D.C., 1951, p. 31). Occasionally it is hampered by the sheer impossibility of "forgetting the future," especially in relation to societies in which intolerance, bigotry, and injustice (after being understood) have to be condemned if we are not to fall into the trap of relativism. How can one not hear future echoes of Eichmann in Topcliffe's excuses for his treatment of Robert Southwell (21st; see p. 215)?

It is not always the persecutors of the saints who show the intolerance and cruelty of their times. Sometimes it is the saints themselves. The saints and blessed of February, while mercifully relatively lacking in figures who pose this problem to an acute degree, raise a number of other issues. The first of these—how to treat obvious legend—is posed by the first entry on the first day: St Brigid of Kildare. I have opted for the generally (though not universally) held view that a historical existence should be claimed for her, and that she was abbess of a double monastery at Kildare at some time in the early sixth century. Beyond that, however, any account has to fall back on legend and myth, and whether these ultimately reveal anything of an individual personality rather than a type is open to question. What can be said is that the individual or type is an extremely attractive one, embodying qualities of mercy, justice, compassion, and earthy humour that none of us would reject. "Historicity" is again raised by St Scholastica (10th). Can anything really be known of her other than that St Gregory in his *Dialogues* provides "the learned woman" as a suitable sister for "the blessed man," Benedict? It is raised again, in a different form, by the feast of Our Lady of Lourdes (11th): here again, different world-views will give different verdicts (and, as with Brigid, the shadows of pagan goddesses again appear). In the end, one is left with the effects of Lourdes, some negative but others, on balance, overwhelmingly positive. This verdict cannot always be applied to Marian centres of pilgrimage—to some of which the Church has been less ready to grant official sanction. Time and again, in this and other months, a "vision" finds its, or a "visionary" finds his or—more often—her significance in the outcome of a life dedicated to the poorest and most disadvantaged, and this aspect is stressed in the beatification process. Cases in point in February include St Catherine dei Ricci (2d), St Adelaide of Villich (5th), St Margaret of Cortona (22d), and the almost unbelievably ill treated Bd Eustochium of Padua (13th). Other remarkable women commemorated in this month laid no claim to special visions; they include a number of nineteenth-century foundresses who achieved great things against all obstacles raised by the society of their time. Among them, Bd Mary of Providence (Eugénie Smet; 7th) has been singled out (perhaps disproportionately).

Women have prompted the initial reflections here, and a woman martyr is the first of those whom in this month the Church honours with a feast-day in its Universal Calendar: St Agatha (5th). The account of her *passio* and, to a greater degree, its reception mainly by male commentators and artists, have raised a number of questions, especially with the rise of Christian feminist commentary in recent decades. Their detailed examinination is beyond the scope of this volume, and readers are referred to the bibliographies and to the primary sources as well as specialized commentaries listed there. Martyrs—apart from Agatha mostly men—feature largely in February, with St Polycarp (23d) pre-eminent among those universally commemorated; indeed, he provided the pattern for most subsequent accounts of martyrs and so for their liturgical commemoration.

Groups of martyrs account for several lengthy entries. How to treat these in a work such as this is a vexed question, and the solution adopted will not please everyone. It follows the principle laid down in the Preface to January in the new Roman Martyrology being prepared by the Congregation for Divine Worship, that the country of martyrdom is the determinant factor rather than the date of beatification. So February gives general consideration to the martyrs of Vietnam (2d), Japan (16th), and China (21st), bringing together several entries in the previous editions of this work and taking account of more recent findings, beatifications, and canonizations. (In the case of China, the more familar spellings of names according to the "Wade-Giles" system have been used in preference to the newer "pinyin" style now in official use in China.) Inevitably, more is known individually of Europeans, usually through records kept and sent back by religious Orders to which they belonged, than of the natives of these countries, who suffered in hundreds and thousands. Patient research into all of these continues, in Rome and elsewhere, and one day they may all have their individual story told, but that day has not yet come, and much information remains stored (resolutely, it seems at the time of writing) within the walls of the Congregation. Where a date of death is known for such individuals, their name and brief details are given in the paragraph headed "*R.M.*" (for Roman Martyrology) at the end of each day's entries. Some outstanding figures have been given separate entries: St Théophane Venard (2d), whose date of death has determined that of the entry on Vietnam, and BB Aloysius Versaglia and Augustus Chapdelaine (25th).

The purpose of giving a brief *eulogium* of each in the new Roman Martyrology will be, at least in part, "to enable local churches to compile their own martyrologies." *Butler's Lives*, as the only major compilation of its kind originating in the English-speaking world, would be failing in its purpose were it not to concentrate on martyrs of that world, which means largely those who suffered in Britain during the Elizabethan period and later, each of whom is given an individual or "small group" entry. Foremost among these on any count is St Robert Southwell (21st), whose literary work helped form the conscience of a generation of Catholics and whose brutal death finally turned off the public appetite for such spectacles. February also has the remarkable St Anne Line (27th), one of the very few women among the canonized martyrs of England.

Beatifications and canonizations of recent times have, however, set out to make the company of saints truly universal, and this is reflected in this edition of *Butler's*. A representative figure from the New World in this month is St

Miguel Febres Cordero (9th), from Ecuador, whose achievements in Spanish grammar and literature, and in education, led him to his death in Barcelona—evangelization from the New World to the Old.

February is rich, too, in reformers: St Benedict of Aniane (12th) and St Peter Damian (21st) are perhaps foremost among them. It also has its share of spiritual writers, including St Evagrius Ponticus (11th), who makes a first appearance as a saint in the West. Popular devotions are well represented by St Blaise (3d), whose crossed candles are still widely used to invoke his aid against sore throats, and of course St Valentine (14th), whose cards have enjoyed a massive increase in popularity since the previous edition of this work. At the risk of Eurocentrism, perhaps the final mention should be made of SS Cyril and Methodius (14th), nominated by Pope John Paul II as patrons of Europe, in addition to St Benedict, and figures of great relevance at a time when the European Union is planning its eastward expansion.

David Hugh Farmer and Fr Eric Hollas have exercised a mainly benign oversight; Peter Doyle has given up St Burchard and Sarah Fawcett Thomas some Vietnam martyrs with good grace; Kathleen Jones has been ready with sage advice and parted with work on the martyrs of Japan with only faint mutters of "pirate"; Sr Clare Wilson provided sources for Bd Mary of Providence (Eugénie Smet) and Sr Francis Willis for Bd Mary Kasper; David Baldwin, Serjeant of the Vestry at The Queen's Chapel, allowed me to use unpublished material that made St Claude La Colombière a much more interesting figure than in his conventional portrayals; Jean Olwen Maynard has been an invaluable mentor, critic, and source-finder for all the far-eastern martyr entries; Dom Gerard McGinty and Dom Bonaventure Dunne alerted me to the pitfalls of St Brigid on a delightful visit to Glenstal Abbey some time ago and have been kind about the result; John Harwood has again helped with saints of the Eastern Church: to all these, and any I have overlooked, my sincere thanks. My wife, Penny, has once again put up with books and paper everywhere and shared my enthusiasm for at least some of the figures to whom I hope to have done some justice.

Paul Burns

16 November 1997, St Margaret of Scotland

Abbreviations and Short Forms

A.A.S.	*Acta Apostolicae Sedis, Commentarium officiale.* Rome, 1908-.
AA.SS.	*Acta Sanctorum.* 64 vols. Antwerp, also Rome and Paris, 1643-. (Page and volume numbers vary in different editions.)
A.C.M.	H. Musurillo, S.J. *Acts of the Christian Martyrs.* Oxford, 1972.
Anal. Boll.	*Analecta Bollandiana.* 1882-.
Anstruther	G. Anstruther, O. P. *The Seminary Priests,* 4 vols. Ware, Ushaw, and Great Wakering, 1968-77.
Auréole Séraphique	Léon de Clary, O.F.M., *Auréole Séraphique,* Eng. trans., *Lives of the Saints and Blessed of the Orders of St Francis,* 4 vols. Taunton, 1887.
Bede, *H.E.*	The Venerable Bede. *Historia Ecclesiastica.* Various editions.
Bibl.SS.	*Bibliotheca Sanctorum,* 12 vols. Rome, 1960-70; Suppl. 1, Rome, 1987.
B.G.	S. Baring Gould. *Lives of the Saints,* 12 vols. London, 1872-9; rp. 1907.
B.H.G.	Society of Bollandists. *Bibliotheca Hagiographica Graeca.* 3d ed., Brussels, 1957.
B.H.L.	Society of Bollandists. *Bibliotheca Hagiographica Latina,* 2 vols. Brussels, 1898-1901.
B.H.O.	Society of Bollandists. *Bibliotheca Hagiographica Orientalis.* Brussels, 1910; rp. 1970.
Bibl.SS.	*Bibliotheca Sanctorum,* 12 vols. Rome, 1960-70; Suppl. 1, Rome, 1987.
B.T.A.	H. Thurston and D. Attwater (eds.). *Butler's Lives of the Saints,* 4 vols. London & New York, 1956 (the previous edition of the present work).
C.M.H.	*Commentarius Perpetuus in Martyrologium Hieronymianum,* ed. H. Delehaye, P. Peeters et al.: in *AA.SS.,* vol. 64. 1940.
C.R.S.	Publications of the Catholic Record Society. 1905-.
D.C.B.	W. Smith and H. Wace (eds.). *Dictionary of Christian Biography,* 4 vols. London, 1877-87.
D.H.G.E.	A. Baudrillart *et al.* (eds.). *Dictionnaire d'histoire et de géographie écclésiastique.* Paris, 1912-.
Dict.Sp.	M. Viller *et al. Dictionnaire de spiritualité.* Paris, 1937.
D.N.B.	Leslie Stephen *et al.* (eds.). *Dictionary of National Biography.* London, 1885-.
D.T.C.	A. Vacant, A. Mangenot, and E. Amann (eds.). *Dictionnaire de théologie catholique,* 15 vols. Paris, 1903-50.

Duchesne, *Fastes*	L. Duchesne. *Fastes épiscopaux de l'ancienne Gaule*, 3 vols. 4th ed., Paris, 1908.
E.H.R.	*English Historical Review.* 1886-.
E.M.C.A.	Edward G. Tasker. *Encyclopedia of Medieval Church Art.* Ed. J. Beaumont. London, 1993.
España Sagrada	Enrique Florez. *España Sagrada: Indice.* Madrid, 1877; 2d ed. 1946.
Eusebius, *H.E.*	Eusebius of Caesarea. *Historia Ecclesiastica.* Various editions.
F.B.S.	Marion A. Habig. *The Franciscan Book of Saints.* Rev. ed., Chicago, 1979.
Gillow	J. Gillow (ed.). *A Literary and Biographical History, or Bibliographical Dictionary of the English Catholics from the Breach with Rome in 1534 to the Present Day*, 5 vols. London and New York, 1881-1903 (plus Index vol. added by J. Bevan, 1985).
H.C.S.	L. Bouyer *et al. A History of Christian Spirituality*, 3 vols. London and New York, 1963-8.
Hefele-Leclercq	C. J. Hefele. *Histoire des Conciles d'après les documents originaux*, ed. H. Leclercq *et al.* Paris, 1907-.
H.S.S.C.	F. Chiovaro *et al.* (eds.). *Histoire des saints et de la sainteté chrétienne*, 12 vols. Paris, 1972-88.
Irish Saints	D. Pochin Mould. *The Irish Saints.* Dublin and London, 1964.
Jedin-Dolan	H. Jedin and J. Dolan (eds.). *History of the Church*, Eng. trans., 10 vols. London & New York, 1965-81.
Jedin-Holland	H. Jedin and J. Dolan (eds.), abridged by J. Larrimore Holland. *History of the Church*, 3 vols. New York, 1993. (Text of Jedin-Dolan abridged; notes, indexes, and bibliographies removed.)
J.T.S.	*Journal of Theological Studies.* 1900-.
K.S.S.	A. P. Forbes (ed.) *Kalendars of Scottish Saints.* Edinburgh, 1872.
L.E.M. 1	Bede Camm (ed.). *Lives of the English Martyrs*, first series., 2 vols. London, 1904-5.
M.G.H.	G. Pertz *et al.* (eds.). *Monumenta Germaniae Historiae, Scriptores*, 64 vols. Hanover, 1839-1921. Sub-series include *Auctores Antiquissimi, Epistolae Selectae*, and *Scriptores Rerum Merovingicarum.*
M.M.P.	R. Challoner. *Memoirs of Missionary Priests.* New ed. by J. H. Pollen. London, 1924.
Mortier	D. A. Mortier. *Histoire des maîtres généraux O.P.*,4 vols. Paris, 1923.

N.C.E.	*New Catholic Encyclopedia*, 14 vols. New York, 1967.
N.L.A.	C. Horstmann (ed.). *Nova Legenda Angliae*, 2 vols. Oxford, 1901.
N.P.N.F.	P. Schaff and H. Wace (eds.). The Nicene and Post-Nicene Christian Fathers, 1887-1900: 2d series rp., Grand Rapids, Michigan, 1979. Vol. 1, Eusebius of Caesarea, *Historia Ecclesiastica*; vol. 2, Socrates, *Historia Ecclesiastica*; Sozomen, *Historia Ecclesiastica*; vol. 3, Jerome, *Viri Illustri*; Rufinus, *Historia Ecclesiastica*; vol. 4, Theodoret, *Historia Ecclesiastica*; vol. 10, Ambrose, *Principal Works and Letters*.
N.S.B. 1	Thierry Lelièvre. *100 nouveaux saints et bienheureux de 1963 à 1984*. Paris, 1983.
N.S.B. 2	Thierry Lelièvre. *Nouveaux saints et bienheureux de 1984 à 1988*. Paris, 1989.
O.D.C.C.	F. L. Cross and E. A. Livingstone (eds.). *The Oxford Dictionary of the Christian Church*. 2d ed., Oxford, 1974; 3d ed. 1997 (refs. to 3d ed.).
O.D.P	J. N. D. Kelly (ed.). *The Oxford Dictionary of Popes*. Oxford, 1986.
O.D.S.	David H. Farmer. *The Oxford Dictionary of Saints*. 3d ed., Oxford, 1992; 4th ed. 1997 (refs. to 3d ed.).
P.B.	F. Guérin (ed). *Vie des Saints des Petits Bollandistes*, 17 vols. Paris, 1880.
P.G.	J. P. Migne (ed.). *Patrologia Graeca*, 112 vols. Paris, 1857-66.
P.L.	J. P. Migne (ed.). *Patrologia Latina*, 221 vols. Paris, 1844-64.
Plummer, *V.S.H.*	C. Plummer. *Vitae Sanctorum Hiberniae*, 2 vols. Oxford 1910, 2d ed., 1968.
Procter	J. Procter (ed.). *Short Lives of the Dominican Saints*. London, 1900.
Propylaeum	H. Delehaye (ed.). *Propylaeum ad Acta Sanctorum Decembris*. Brussels, 1940.
Rev.Bén.	*Revue Bénédictine*. 1885-.
R.S.	Rolls Series: *Rerum Britannicum Medii Aevi Scriptores*, H. M. Stationery Office. London, 1858-.
Saints in Italy	Lucy Menzies. *The Saints in Italy*. London, 1924.
S.C.	*Sources chrétiennes*. Paris, 1940-.
Socrates, *H.E.*	See N.P.N.F. 2.
Sozomen, *H.E.*	See N.P.N.F. 2.
Stanton	R. Stanton. *A Menology of England and Wales*. London, 1892.
Theodoret, *H.E.*	See N.P.N.F., 2.

VIETNAM
See *The Martyrs of Vietnam*, pp. 22-8
and *St Théophane Vénard*, pp. 28-30

JAPAN
See *The Martyrs of Japan*, pp. 57-63

Maps show significant place names mentioned in the text.

CHINA
See The Martyrs of China, pp. 175–84
and
BB Aloysius Versaglia
and
Callistus Caravario,
pp. 248–51

Significant place names mentioned in the text

xvii

ST BRIGID OF KILDARE
Red lamp and green wreath on white field.
The lamp is for her good works; the oak wreath
for Kildare—Cill dara, "church of the oak."

1

ST BRIGID OF KILDARE, *Abbess* (*c.* 452–*c.* 524)

Veneration of Brigid, or Bride (Bríd), in Ireland is second only to that of St Patrick (17 Mar.). In many ways she is the type of figure who undoubtedly had a historical existence but whose life has been transmitted only in forms designed to enhance her reputation rather than to record facts. Other aspects of her cult, however, are more individual and link her figure, possibly through the root of her name—*Brig*—to the deities of pre-Christian Ireland.

The date of her birth was probably around the middle of the fifth century, and one tradition assigns Faughart, near Dundlak in Co. Louth as her birthplace. Traditional dates assigned to her and Patrick would make her about six years old at the time of his death. It is probable that she followed a widespread custom and consecrated herself to God as a virgin at an early age. There are many accounts of her "being veiled" by other saints and even being consecrated bishop, or given the *pallium*, but the former are merely conventional and the latter one more example of the desire to pay her, or rather her church of Kildare, the maximum of honour.

She is known as abbess of Kildare, which lies some forty miles south-west of Dublin and was a double monastery, for both women and men, of the type that arose in France, Spain, and Britain as well as in Ireland in the fifth century, after the death of St Patrick. Such was the abbey of Whitby in Yorkshire, of which St Hilda (17 Nov.) was abbess. It was quite usual for the abbess to be the superior of both halves; this, rather than being an interesting indication of the status of women in the Celtic church, reflected the higher social standing of the nuns, who required monks to perfom manual labour to provide them with food and also to perform liturgical services. There would thus have been nothing very unusual in Brigid being superior of the double monastery at Kildare. The foundation should be accepted as historical fact and as the significant achievement in her life, even though no exact date can be assigned to it. It is treated as such in the earliest and most "biographical" of her Lives, that by Cogitosus written in the seventh century, though not in other and more fanciful accounts.

Early Lives of Brigid show her exercising influence on a scale peculiar to the Celtic churches, which drew on pagan tribal structures and were thus further removed from the influence of Mediterranean and Middle Eastern cultures, which, then as now, conditioned the structures of the Western Church and were more reluctant to give such status to women. In the provinces of the Roman Empire (which never extended to Ireland), the Church tended more to imitate and inherit the pomp and circumstance of imperial court life, so that its heroes were garbed in the trappings of wealth and power in their Lives, whereas more pastoral qualities were brought to the fore in the Lives of Celtic saints. So the story of Brigid giving her father's sword to a leper signifies that her spiritual authority lay not in power and aggressivity but in mercy and compassion. The proportion of women saints to men is notably greater in early Irish martyrologies, such as that of Gorman, than in those of other countries. Women were also associated in ministry, to a degree that scandalized continental bishops in the sixth century; these called the fact that women "take the chalice and administer the blood of Christ to the people," "an innovation, an unheard-of superstition."

Accounts of her life tend, as do so many Celtic and other medieval Lives, to follow a pattern drawn from the gospel accounts of Jesus' life. So her birth is foretold by a Druid; she has early saintly mentors, in the persons of St Maccaille and St Mel, as Jesus is announced by John the Baptist and is guided by the Holy Spirit and angels; in time she becomes a spiritual mentor herself and a leader of others, gathering followers around her, corresponding to Jesus' pastoral ministry; miracles are attributed to her—in her case, as in Jesus', these are, to a remarkable extent, responses to human need rather than demonstrations of divine power. She is even attributed her own "marriage feast at Cana," in local terms, when in Meath she "supplied beer out of one barrel to eighteen churches, which sufficed from Maundy Thursday to the end of paschal time" (*Aberdeen Breviary*). This is reflected in the delightful "Brigid's prayer":

> I should like a lake of ale for the King of Kings
> I should like the household of heaven to be there
>   drinking it for eternity. . . .
> I should like cheerfulness to be in their drinking
> I should like Jesus here also.

These stages, as recounted in the Lives, make up a pattern of kinship with Jesus: their expression may be conventional, but the underlying aim is constant and meaningful.

Symbols are used to underline this message: her association with fire means that she is seen to have lived in the presence of God—fire is said to have risen to heaven from the place where she slept as a child. Her emblem contains a flame, reflecting the tradition of the perpetual fire in an enclosure within the abbey tended by her and her nuns at Kildare: after her death, so the legend goes, she returned every twentieth night to take her place in the rota of watchers. This was described by Gerald of Wales in the twelfth century: "Although in the time of Brigid there were twenty servants of the Lord here, Brigid herself being the twentieth, only nineteen have ever been here after her death. . . . They all, however, take their turns, one each night, in guarding the fire. When the twentieth night comes, the nineteenth nun puts the logs beside the fire and says, 'Brigid, guard your fire. This is your night.' And in this way the fire is

2

left there, and in the morning the wood, as usual, has been burnt and the fire is still alight."

Special numbers are also associated with her (and other Celtic saints): three angels appear at her baptism, representing special strength and intimacy with God; she cures four sick people at a church, signifying wholeness, as in the four seasons or the four cardinal points of the compass. Animals, too, feature in her legends in the same way as they do in Celtic folklore: in perhaps the best known incident, a traditional story involving a fox—symbol of cleverness and ingenuity—is turned to show her mercy and compassion. A foolish man kills the king's tame performing fox; the king threatens him with death and his family with slavery unless the fox can be replaced with one as clever. The man's fate comes to the ears of Brigid, who hastens to the court in her chariot. On the way, a fox jumps in and settles in her clothing. Arrived at the court, the fox shows itself capable of the same skills as the dead one; the king relents and spares the man's life. The theme of mercy extends, happily, even to the fox, which escapes back to the woods and is spared further artificial performance.

Kindness and mercy mitigate her attitude to rules, and in this she parallels St Patrick. Cogitosus tells that when she went to visit Bishop Ibar, "St Ibar rejoiced with great gladness at the arrival of St Brigid, but he had no food for the arrival of the guest except dry bread and the flesh of a pig. So Bishop Ibar and St Brigid ate bread and bacon during the Lenten fast before Easter." He also relates that two of Brigid's nuns refused to eat meat during the Lenten fast, whereupon their portions were turned into snakes to rebuke them for their rigorous attitude. Her help is also sought in improving marital relations: "There came a married man asking St Brigid to bless some water which he might sprinkle on his wife, for she held him in hatred. So Brigid blessed water, and while his wife was out he sprinkled their house and food and drink and bed, and from that day his wife loved him greatly as long as she lived." Her blessing was also powerful protection against danger: when a bishop had been riding at speed in his chariot, he "looked down at the chariot [and] saw it had no linchpins. Then he leapt from the chariot, and, landing on the ground, he thanked God and blessed St Brigid, for he recalled that she had blessed the chariot."

The perpetual flame which the nuns at Kildare cultivated for many centuries in honour of the fire surrounding Brigid's sleeping place perhaps has its origin in the goddess Brigid, whose cult was observed by female druids (whose leader was named after the goddess) on the same spot long before Brigid arrived. The goddess Brigid, was the goddess of knowledge and life, also of fire, wisdom, and hearth, and known as the mother of poets; she had two sisters, also named Brigid, who were patrons of healing and metalwork. All these attributes came to be associated with the abbess Brigid, whose feast is celebrated on the same day as that of the goddess, the date being that of *Imbolg*, the pagan festival of spring. A peaceful spot with a spring outside the town of Kildare, now adorned with Stations of the Cross, is known as St Brigid's Well and was probably a

3

place sacred to the druids. In many ways she marks a transitional point between paganism and Christianity, taking over much of the old religion without intolerance or persecution, incorporating its roots in the land and the seasons. It has been suggested that the "nuns and holy women" of Kildare were descendants of a college of women who formerly attended the shrine of the goddess Brigid there. Kildare, *Cill dara*, means "church of the oak"; it had an altar resting on a massive wooden beam to which miraculous healing powers were attributed; Cogitosus described it as "fresh and green to the present day."

Other aspects of the legends associated with her place her as part of the unknown origins of Christianity in Ireland, on a par with the Irish sages who were on Golgotha "in spirit," so that there was never a time when Christianity was not part of the culture. So Brigid is supposed to have been brought up by Druids. One day she is led by a white dove to a desert place, where she assists as midwife at the birth of a Holy Child, placing three drops of water on his brow to unite him with the earth. Animals come into this story, too: the cows are parched and can give no milk, so Brigid sings "runes of Paradise" to them and their milk flows freely for the child. In this, she is being assimilated partly to the goddess Artemis, who was midwife to Leto at the birth of Apollo, partly to the northern goddess Brigantia, and partly to the Celtic Brigid. She is also given a future incarnation in which, unique among saints, she will return, to bind Christ's hair and wash his feet, perhaps even to be his bride; in this she appears to take on the characteristics of Sophia, Wisdom. In other ways she is seen as a reincarnation of the Virgin Mary: called "Mary of the Gael," she is hymned in terms redolent of the woman clothed with the sun in Revelation 12, popularly taken as an allusion to Mary: "Brigid ever-excellent woman / Golden sparkling flame / Lead us to the eternal kingdom / The dazzling sparkling sun."

Besides the presence of fire in her emblem she is depicted with a four-armed cross woven from straw or rushes, the *Crosóg Brigde*, which was believed to protect buildings from fire. The story behind this also emphasizes her kindness and compassion: she was acting as nurse to a pagan chieftain who was sick, and made a cross from the rushes covering the floor. When he awoke, the chieftain asked the reason for the cross, and she told him the story of Calvary, which made such an impression on him that he was converted as well as returned to health. St Brigid's Crosses are still made widely throughout Ireland and on the eve of her feast are placed in houses and outbuildings.

In the mid-ninth century Donatus, the Irish bishop of Fiesole just outside Florence (from *c.* 826 to *c.* 877) wrote a Life of Brigid in Latin hexameters. He was one of the many Irish pilgrims who settled in one of the shrines on the route to Rome. He granted a church in Piacenza to the monastery of Bobbio and then added a hospice for Irish pilgrims, which was the forerunner of the well-known church of St Brigid in the city. To judge from manuscripts, the circle of Sedulius "Scotus" of Liège (ninth century), who came from Ireland, had a particular devotion to St Brigid. Churches dedicated to her were known in Fosses, Liège, Cologne, Henndorf (near Salzburg), and throughout Brittany, as well as in Piacenza. There are still pilgrimages held in her honour in Fosses and Amay in Brittany. Writing in the late nineteenth century, Mgr Guérin states that at Fosses, in the diocese of Namur, peasants took blessed *baguettes* on 1 February and touched the sick with them. The Irish *Liber hymnorum* contains two Latin and two Irish hymns in her honour. In the twelfth-century *Black Book of Carmarthen* there is an invocation in Welsh: *Sanffreid suynade ni undeith,* "St Brigid, bless us on our journey." Oengus the Culdee has the following couplet (cited in *The Irish Saints*): *Brigid bán, bale núalann, / Cenn cáid caillech n Érenn,* "Brigid the fair, the strong, the praiseworthy, / Chaste head of Erin's nuns."

The Lives are of relatively late composition, attributed to (1) Bishop Ultan MacConcubar (d. 662); (2) the monk Chilian (d. 740); (3) "Cogitosus" (n.d.); (4) a late anonymous source, possibly Donatus. They are ed. Jean Bolland in *AA.SS.,* Feb., 1, pp. 99-185; that by Cogitosus is also ed. J. Colgan in *Trias Thaumaturga* (1647); trans. by J. Connolly in *Journal of the Royal Society of Antiquaries of Ireland* 119 (1989), pp. 5-49; the citations above are from R. Sharpe (ed. and trans.), *Adomnán of Iona: The Life of St Columba* (1995), pp. 287, 341, 344, who makes the point that similar stories are told of St Columba. See also *Bibl.SS.,* 3, 430-7; *N.L.A.,* 1, pp. 153-60; *D.H.G.E.,* 10, 717-8; *B.H.L.,* 1, pp. 217-8; Heist, *V.S.H.,* 1, pp. 1-37. Modern lives by S. Atkinson (1907); J. A. Knowles (1927); J.-J. Gaffney (1931); A. Curtayne, *St Brigid of Ireland* (1931, n.e. 1954); F. O'Briain (1938); D. Pochin Mould (1964). See also: T. Hayden, *St Brigid and Kildare Cathedral* (for Co. Kildare Vocational Education Committee, 1980); J. L., "St Brigid and Glastonbury," *Journal of the Royal Society of Antiquaries of Ireland* 83 (1953); *Irish Saints,* pp. 41-7; C. Plummer *et al.* (eds.), "The Old Irish Life of St Brigid," *Irish Historical Studies* 1 (1938), pp. 121-34, 343-53; K. Hughes, "The Celtic Church and the Papacy," in C. H. Lawrence (ed.), *The English Church and the Papacy in the Middle Ages* (1965); E. MacNeill, *Celtic Ireland* (1981), esp. p. 93 on her birthplace. The account of the legend of the past and future Brigid is taken from C. Bamford, "Holiness and Ecology," in R. O'Driscoll (ed.), *The Celtic Consciousness* (1981); information on Donatus and the churches on the Continent from J. P. Mackey (ed.), *An Introduction to Celtic Christianity* (1989, n.e. 1995), pp. 120, 124, 134. On the significance of trees and fire see Mary Low, *Celtic Christianity and Nature: Early Irish and Hebridean Traditions* (1996), esp. pp. 157ff., citing Gerald of Wales, p. 157. *N.C.E.,* 2, p. 803, has a picture of her being clothed as a religious, from the fifteenth-century Breviary of the duke of Bedford (Bib. Nat., Paris, Ms. Lat. 17294, f. 410v).

St Sigebert (632-56)

He was the brother of Clovis and son of the Merovingian king Dagobert I, who lived a dissolute life until prompted by the birth of this son to mend his ways. He wanted Sigebert to be baptized by the holiest man in the Frankish kingdom and sent for St Amandus (6 Feb., below), whom he had previously banished for admonishing him on his ways. Amandus relented and baptized the boy with great pomp and ceremony in Orleans. Sigebert's education was entrusted to Pepin of Landen, mayor of the palace and effectively regent. Dagobert died in 638, and Sigebert inherited the eastern part of the kingdom, Austrasia, at the age of six or seven, ruling for the rest of his life as King Sigebert III, while Clovis ruled the western part.

Under the guidance of Pepin both brothers ruled in harmony, and Sigebert's reign was generally peaceful, marred by one revolt in Thuringia. He was known as a man of prayer and for his beneficence in endowing hospitals, monasteries, and churches. He founded twelve (or twenty, according to Sigebert d'Usuard) monasteries, the major ones at Stavelot and Malmédy. He died at the age of only twenty-four, but as the previous edition of this work comments, "a life filled with good works and devoted to God can never be called short."

P. Vincent of Nancy, O.F.M., *Histoire fidèle de saint Sigebert, douzième roi d'Austrasie, et troisième du nom* (1702). His Life was written by Sigebert of Gembloux, in *AA.SS.*, Feb., 1, pp. 206-44; also *M.G.H., Scriptores Merov.*, 2, pp. 215-328. There is a biography in the series "Les Saints" by the abbé Guise (1920). *Bibl.SS.*, 11, 1035-7.

Bd Raymund of Fitero, *Abbot* (1163)

Raymund is honoured in Spain as a hero of the wars of reconquest and founder of the military Order of Calatrava. He was the Cistercian abbot of Fitero, in the region of Toledo, then capital of Christian Spain, in late 1157 or early 1158, when King Sancho I of Castile was in Toledo. The Moors were threatening the outpost town of Calatrava, which was defended by the Templars, who sent word to the king that their numbers were too few to hold it and entreated the king to send reinforcements. With Raymund was a fellow-monk, Diego de Velázquez, who had been schooled as a knight. He persuaded the king, against the advice of his ministers, to give the town to the abbey of Fitero. Its defence then became a church matter: Raymund approached the archbishop of Toledo for help and was promised all the reinforcements he needed, with the archbishop declaring a crusade. There was an immense mobilization of men and materials in Toledo, and the Moors refrained from attacking Calatrava.

Raymund used the opportunity of this flocking of recruits to what was his abbey's possession and kept the best of the volunteers as the nucleus for what developed into the military Order of Calatrava, which was soon waging offensive wars against the Moors. His cult was approved in Spain in 1719.

AA.SS., Feb., 1, pp. 254-7; *Bibl.SS.*, 11, 11-15; *B.G.*, Feb., pp. 29-31, citing Cistercian Breviary and Radez, *Crónica de las Ordines de Santiago, Calatrava y Alcántara*; *España Sagrada*, 1, pp. 37-48; on the Order of Calatrava see also *N.C.E.*, *s.v.*

St John of the Grating, *Abbot and Bishop* (c. 1170)

John was born in Brittany to relatively poor parents but managed to receive a good education. Drawn as a young man to the Cistercian Order, then in its first flush of dramatic expansion, he went to see St Bernard (20 Aug.), who personally welcomed him into his original community at Clairvaux. A Breton count named Stephen de Pentièvre and his wife wanted to establish a monastery on their estate and approached Bernard, who sent John to make the foundation at Bégard in the diocese of Tréguier (on an estuary on the north coast of the

Côtes d'Armore department of central Brittany). He then founded another monastery at nearby Buzay, which he ruled as abbot for some years. He apparently ruled it well, as his monks were distressed when he was elected bishop of Aleth some thirty miles to the east. Seeing that the population on the isle of Aaron at the mouth of a major estuary, was increasing, John transferred his see there, and renamed the place Saint-Malo. It is today a bustling fishing and ferry port.

His episcopate was marred by ecclesiastical quarrels. Following the trend of the time, he replaced the monks who originally staffed his cathedral, from the abbey of Marmoutier in Tours, with canons regular. The monks objected and appealed to the French hierarchy, who upheld their objection and ordered that they should be reinstated. John appealed to Bernard, who advised a direct appeal to the pope. John travelled to Rome and made his case to the pope, who decided in his favour. But the monks continued to find legal pretexts for further quarrels, and the affair dragged on for eighteen years, involving John in further journeys to Rome. All this time he was known for the personal austerity of his life and his charitable dealings with others—including the monks—and while his quarrels with them may appear to reflect badly on his administrative ability, he founded and reformed other religious houses in Brittany.

He died in about 1170 and was buried in the cathedral of Saint-Malo. His *sobriquet* "of the grating" (*de craticula*) derives from the iron railings surrounding his tomb.

AA.SS., Feb., 1, pp. 250-4; B.G., Feb., pp. 26-8, citing letters of St Bernard and Nicholas of Clairvaux; A. Le Grand, *Vie des saints de la Bretagne Armorique*; Lobineau, *Saints de Bretagne*, 2, pp. 393-410.

Bd Reginald of Orleans (1183-1220)

He was born at Saint-Gilles, near Arles in the Languedoc region of southern France, and embarked on a distinguished academic career. He taught canon law at the university of Paris from 1206 to 1211 and was then appointed dean of the collegiate chapter of Saint-Aignan at Orleans. In 1218 he went on pilgrimage to Rome, where he met St Dominic (8 Aug.), whom he identified as the spiritual leader who had been revealed to him in a vision by Our Lady. He applied to join the Order of Friars Preachers, established by Dominic two years earlier. Dominic immediately welcomed him and made him his vicar during his travels to Spain to oversee foundations there. He was already establishing a Dominican presence in the great universities and appointed Reginald to oversee the foundation of a Dominican house of studies at Bologna. The following year he was sent to Paris for the same purpose; in both he won a great reputation with his preaching and was succesful in gaining large numbers of recruits to the new Order. This promising career was cut short by his untimely death the following year—the earliest death of a Dominican subsequently proposed for veneration, though his cult was not confirmed till 1875. He died in Paris on 1 February 1220 and was buried in the church of Notre-Dame-des-Champs.

Early accounts in chronicles of the Dominican Order: Gérard de Frachet, *Vitae Fratrum*; Bartholomew of Trent, *Liber Epilogorum;* see also Mortier, 1, pp. 96-100, 118-9; *Bibl.SS.*, 11, 74-5; *N.C.E.*, 12, 203-4, with illustration.

Bd Antony the Pilgrim (1267)

Antonio Manzi (or Manzoni) came from a distinguished family of Padua and was left an orphan in his youth on the death of his father. He promptly gave his whole inheritance to the poor, which outraged his fellow-citizens and his family, in particular his two sisters, who were thereby deprived of dowries. Reviled in the streets of Padua, he left the city dressed as a pilgrim and eventually settled at Bazano, near Bologna, to care for a sick elderly priest. They spent three years there, both living on the alms Antony begged. When the old priest died, Antony embarked on a course of pilgrimages to all the major centres of Europe: Rome, Loreto, Compostela, Cologne, and Jerusalem. He finally returned to Padua to find he had not been forgotten and was as unpopular as ever, especially with his sisters, who had both become nuns. He was forced to shelter in the colonnade of a church outside the city walls, and he soon died there. Miracles began to be reported at his tomb, and the citizens who had mistreated him now sought to have him canonized; the pope refused, saying that one St Antony (13 June) was enough for Padua. But his cult persisted there, though he is known as Blessed—unusual for the Middle Ages—indicating that there was no official cult.

AA.SS., Feb., 1; see also *Anal.Boll.* 13 (1894), pp. 417-25; 14 (1895), pp. 108ff.

Bd Andrew of Segni (1302)

He was born to a noble family, as Andrea dei Conti di Segni, but is also known as Andrea d'Agnani (or of Cignani) from his birthplace or, as in the Franciscan supplement to the Roman Martyrology (which commemorates him on 17 Feb.), simply *de Comitibus*, "of the counts." He was the nephew of Rainaldo Conti, who was to become Pope Alexander IV (1254-61, himself in turn a nephew of Pope Gregory IX, 1227-41), and a close relative of another native of Anagni and future pope, Benedetto Caetani, Pope Boniface VIII (1294-1301).

With such connections, a distinguished ecclesiastical career would have been open to him, but he renounced all such ambitions and joined the Order of Friars Minor, in which he remained a simple lay brother for the rest of his life. He joined the monastery of San Lorenzo, founded by St Francis (4 Oct.) himself, and obtained permission to live as a solitary. His distinguished relatives were reluctant to accept this: in 1295 his uncle, Alexander IV, came to see him and placed a cardinal's hat on his head; "our saint immediately took it off, declaring that he refused the dignity" (*Auréole Séraphique*). His nephew, Boniface VIII, later sent him the cardinal's insignia, but again he declined to accept the honour.

He was a gifted man of letters and wrote a book on the Virgin Mary, said to have been "prized by the Doctors of the Church" but now lost. Beyond this little is known of his life except that he was held in great esteem for holiness during it and for miracles both during and after it, and that he "was troubled in life by demons [and] became celebrated for his assistance to those who invoked his aid against them" (*The Book of Saints*). He died on 1 February 1302, and his cult was confirmed in 1724.

For legends and miracles attributed to him, see *Auréole Séraphique*, 1, pp. 132-4; also Mazzara, *Leggendario Francescano*, 1 (1676), pp. 155-6; *Saints in Italy*, pp. 25-6.

St Henry Morse, *Martyr* (1595-1645)

Henry was born in Brome in Suffolk in 1595, the sixth of nine sons of Robert M. Morse, a Protestant landed gentleman from Tivetshall St Mary in Norfolk, and his wife, Margaret Collinson. Henry's father died in 1612, leaving him an annuity. He is said to have decided to become a Catholic while reading law at Barnard's Inn in London, but there is no record of him having belonged to any of the Inns of Court, though there is a record of his elder brother Robert being admitted to Gray's Inn in 1617. In June 1614 he went to Douai to begin his studies for the priesthood. He seems to have interrupted these and returned to England, since he was in the New Prison awaiting banishment in June 1618. He was back in Douai that August and proceeded to the English College in Rome in December. He was ordained deacon in July 1620, but there is no record of his ordination to the priesthood. He went back to Douai and from there was sent on the English mission in September 1620 but was arrested soon after he landed at Newcastle. He was imprisoned in York Castle, where he found the Jesuit John Robinson a fellow-prisoner. He had declared his intention of joining the Society of Jesus while still in Rome, and his superiors had agreed. He devoted the three years spent in prison in York to making the Jesuit novitiate and at the end of this time made his simple vows. He was then released and banished and went to Flanders, where he acted as chaplain to English Catholic mercenaries fighting for Spain. He was certainly a priest by May 1624.

He returned to England at the end of 1633 under the alias of Cuthbert Claxton and carried on his ministry in London. A plague epidemic hit the capital in 1636-7; at great risk to his health he brought spiritual and material comfort to four hundred families, which made such an impression that nearly one hundred families were reconciled to the Catholic Church in a year. He caught the disease three times but each time recovered. His superiors eventually persuaded him to lessen his efforts in view of the risk to his life. He was re-arrested and charged with "perverting" Protestants as well as with being a priest. He was acquitted on the first charge but condemned on the second. Queen Henrietta Maria intervened on his behalf, and he was released against payment of bail of ten thousand florins. In 1641 a royal proclamation ordered all priests to leave the country; for the sake of those who had put up the bail he obeyed and returned to ministering to English soldiers in Flanders.

Two years later he was again sent back to England, and he worked for eighteen months in the north of the country, until he was arrested on the borders of Cumberland. His captors took him in the direction of Durham; they stayed overnight at the house of one of them, whose wife was a Catholic and who enabled him to escape during the night. He was rearrested some six weeks later, taken to Durham jail, and from there to London. There he was sentenced to death on the strength of his conviction of being a priest at the trial held years earlier. He was executed on 1 February 1645 at Tyburn, where the French, Spanish, and Portuguese ambassadors with their staffs were present in his honour. The Spanish ambassador took several of his relics to the Continent. He was beatified as one of the large group of martyrs so honoured in 1929 (see the general entry for 4 May) and selected from among them as one of the Forty Martyrs of England and Wales canonized on 25 October 1970 (see the entry for that day).

His Life was written in Latin with that of BB Ralph Corby and Thomas Holland, executed in 1644 and 1642 respectively, by Fr Ambrose Corby, brother of Bd Ralph, as *Certamen Triplex*. This formed the basis for the account in *M.M.P.* An Eng. trans. was published as *The Threefold Conflict* in 1858. There is a biography by P. Caraman, S.J., *Henry Morse* (1957). Anstruther, 1, p. 27, gives the date of his execution as 22 January. *N.C.E.*, 9, p. 1152; *O.D.S.*, p. 348.

Bd Anne Michelotti, *Foundress* (1843-88)

Anna Michelotti was born at Annecy in France on 29 August 1843. Her father was Piedmontese, her mother French. From childhood she showed a marked devotion to the Eucharist and a desire to help the sick poor. She joined the Salesian Sisters founded by St John Bosco (31 Jan.), the Daughters of Mary Help of Christians, taking the religious name Joanna Francis of the Visitation. (She is here referred to as "Anne," since this is the name used in the beatification documents.) Her loving concern for the poor led to the foundation of the Congregation of the Little Servants of the Sacred Heart in Turin in 1874. Its object was care for the poorest and most abandoned sectors of the population.

She had a great veneration for Don Bosco and declared that she hoped to meet him in Paradise. She seems to have been misunderstood and calumnied during her short and dedicated life. She died on 1 February 1888, at the age of forty-four, and was beatified by Pope Paul VI on 1 November 1975.

N.C.E., 17 (Suppl. 2), p. 36; *A.A.S.* 68 (1976), pp. 253-6; *Bibl.SS.*, 9, 471; *N.S.B.*, 1, p. 134.

R.M.

St Trypho, martyr in Nicaea (third century)

St Severus, bishop of Ravenna (*after* 342)

St Felix, martyr of Salerno (fourth century)

St Bendinian, hermit in Bithynia (fifth century)

St Praecordius, hermit in Belgium (sixth century)

St Sorus, hermit in Gaul (sixth century)

St Paul, bishop of Trois-Châteaux (Vienne) (*c.* 780)

Bd Viridiana, recluse in Castel Fiorentino (1236 or 1242)

Bd Marie-Anne Vaillot and forty-six Companions, martyrs of Angers—see "Martyrs of the French Revolution," 2 Jan.

SS Paul Hong, John Yi, Peter Maubert, and Barbara Tchoi, martyrs (1840)—see "Martyrs of Korea," 21 Sept.

2

St Cornelius the Centurion (First Century)

All that we know about Cornelius derives from Acts 10 and 11, but he is one of those figures who are wonderfully brought to life by Luke in a few sentences and whose brief story is made to encapsulate an important lesson, as he becomes the vehicle through whom Peter is convinced that the gospel message must be taken to the Gentiles.

He is the commander of a hundred soldiers of the "Italian Cohort, as it was called," living in Caesarea, belonging to a victorious army in a conquered land, hardly the sort of situation likely to be conducive to a pious and charitable disposition. Yet, without explanation, he is presented as "a devout man who feared God with all his household; he gave alms generously and prayed constantly to God" (Acts 10:1-2). For this he is rewarded by a vision of an angel, who tells him that his prayers and generosity have touched God and that he is to send some of his men for "a certain Simon who is called Peter" (10:5). The scene shifts to Peter, who is "lodging in the house of Simon the tanner" in Joppa. He too has a vision, whose purport he does not immediately understand, as it seems to be telling him he should eat the sort of meat forbidden to the Jews, at which he protests that he has never eaten anything profane, only to be told that "what God has made clean, you must not call profane" (10:15).

While Peter is puzzling over what to make of this, the men sent by Cornelius arrive. Peter is told by the Spirit to listen to what they have to say, and they tell him that Cornelius, "a centurion, an upright and God-fearing man, who is well spoken of by the whole Jewish nation" (10:22), has been directed by an angel to ask Peter to come to his house so that he can listen to what he has to say. Peter, as a Jew, is forbidden by the Law to visit a Gentile but on the strength of the message from the Spirit agrees. He invites them to stay the night, and they set out the next day, to find Cornelius expecting them, having gathered all his relatives and close friends to listen to Peter. Cornelius falls at Peter's feet, treating him as though he were a god, but Peter makes him stand up, assuring him that he is "only a mortal" (10:26). He then explains that he would not be there unless God had given him permission and asks Cornelius why he asked him. Cornelius explains his own vision, in which he was assured that his prayers were being answered, and so convinces Peter that "his" God communicates with the Gentiles as well as with the Jews. He tells them that he now knows that God has no favourites (or "shows no partiality": 10:34) and briefly relates the history of Jesus' preaching and death.

At this, the Holy Spirit is poured out on all who are listening, Jew and as yet unbaptized Gentile alike, so that "the circumcised believers who had come with Peter were astounded that the gift of the Holy Spirit had been poured out even on the Gentiles" (10:45). In view of this, Peter feels he has no option but to baptize Cornelius and his household immediately, and he then stays for several days in his house. In this, Peter is in advance of the "apostles and believers who were in Judea," who criticize him for his actions when he returns to Jerusalem. Peter tells them the story of the two visions and the coming of the Holy Spirit on Jew and Gentile alike while he was speaking. The brethren are convinced—first silenced, and then moved to praise God, saying, "Then God has given even to the Gentiles the repentance that leads to life" (11:18).

Even if one regards the choice of an officer of the imperial army to convey a message that Christianity is no threat to the Roman Empire as "politically motivated," a centurion could hardly have been presented in this way, with a name and place, if he had no verifiable historical existence, and so the balance of probability is that he did exist and was a good man as he is presented in this vivid sketch.

AA.SS., Feb., 1, pp. 281-7; *P.G.*, 114, 1287-312, including a Life by the Metaphrast; *Lib. Pont.*, 1, pp. 150-2; 3, p. 74. *P.B.*, 2, pp. 217-9, has an essay on the biblical story, stating that Cornelius is honoured on this day as the first pagan converted to Christianity. In the East he is commemorated on 13 Feb.

In art he is generally shown being baptized by St Peter; *N.C.E.*, 4, 334-5, reproduces a sixth-century fresco from the cemetery of St Callistus in Rome showing him holding a Bible.

St Laurence of Canterbury, *Bishop* (619)

Laurence was one of the monks from the monastery of Sant'Andrea al Monte Celio in Rome who accompanied St Augustine of Canterbury (27 May) on his mission to England. Pope St Gregory (the Great; 4 Sept.) had chosen Kent as the springboard for the mission deliberately: in 589 (or earlier) King Ethelbert of Kent had married the Merovingian princess Bertha, who had brought a Frankish bishop named Liuthard to Ethelbert's court at Canterbury, where a Roman burial basilica had been converted into a church, dedicated to St Martin of Tours (11 Nov.), thereby facilitating the possibility of a mission based on Canterbury. Queen Bertha is said to have informed Gregory that the Angles wished to become Christians but had no bishop to oversee their conversion; Gregory may have planned to lead such a mission himself in the years before he became pope and in the event found it difficult to persuade anyone to undertake what appeared a very dangerous journey to a distant and pagan land. Those who were eventually persuaded to make it went armed with letters of recommendation to ecclesiastical and secular rulers along the way. They landed on the isle of Thanet, which belonged to the kingdom of Kent, in the spring of 597.

Virtually all that is known about Laurence derives from books 1 and 2 of Bede's *Ecclesiastical History*. Augustine sent him back to Rome to report on the relative success of the mission in Kent and to receive further instructions from Pope Gregory the Great (3 Sept.). He returned to England in 601 with answers to questions about how the church at Canterbury should be organized (*H.E.*, 1, 27). Ethelbert was converted and baptized, probably in 601, and the mission made good progress in Kent, but the organization planned by Gregory, plus Augustine's imperious manner, impeded its progress beyond the confines of this kingdom. Augustine died in around 604, having already nominated Laurence to succeed him in the see of Canterbury. He consecrated the "church dedicated to the blessed apostles Peter and Paul [where] the bodies of Augustine and all the archbishops of Canterbury and of the kings of Kent were to rest" (1, 33). He continued Augustine's policy of consolidation among the Anglo-Saxons in the south-east of England but, like him, failed to make headway in cooperating with the Irish or the British bishops in the west of the country, who clung to what were already insular ways, refusing to accept the Roman date of Easter and other measures of standardization. He addressed to the former (with Mellitus; 24 Apr., and Justus; 10 Nov.) a letter expressing an attitude that was to find an echo in England down the centuries: "Until we realized the true situation, we had a high regard for the devotion both of the Britons and of the Irish. . . . On further acquaintance with the Britons, we imagined that the Irish must be better. We have now, however, learned . . . that the Irish are no better in their practices. . . ." He wrote in similar vein to the British bishops, but as Bede remarks, "the present state of affairs shows how little he succeeded" (2, 4).

He was then faced with a worsening situation even in Kent. Ethelbert died in 616 and was succeeded by his son Edbald, who refused to embrace Christianity as his father had done and married his father's widow—which Laurence condemned as incest. Two of the monks who had come over with him, Mellitus and Justus, retired to Gaul, fearing the destruction of the church at Canterbury and preferring to "serve God in freedom, rather than remain impotently among heathen who had rejected the Faith" (2, 6). Laurence thought of doing the same but then stood firm and faced up to Edbald. According to Bede, relating local legend, his mind was changed when St Peter appeared to him in a vision, of such physicality that he was able to show Edwald the bruises Peter had inflicted on him for his intended cowardice: "Christ's servant Laurence sought audience with the king early next morning, and removing his garment, showed him the marks of the lash" (2, 6). Edbald was so impressed by this demonstration of supernatural power that he became a Christian, and the progress of the Church in Kent was able to resume, with Mellitus and Justus returning to resume their offices.

Laurence died on 2 February 619 and was buried in the monastery church of SS Peter and Paul (later St Augustine's) in Canterbury, next to Augustine. The tomb was opened in 1091 by Abbot Wido for the relics to be translated to a more eminent place, and Goscelin, who wrote an account of the ceremony, records that "a mighty blast of fragrance" came out and swept through the whole monastery. The tomb was opened again in 1915, and a full record of the findings was made by the archaeologist Sir William St John Hope. His early cult is attested by the Irish Stowe Missal, which records his feast-day as 3 February, the date on which it was kept until the new draft Roman Martyrology revised it to the actual date of his death.

Bede, *H.E.*, 1, 27, 33; 2, 4-7; Goscelin, *Historia translationis S. Augustine*, of which two MSS are in the British Library: see T. D. Hardy, *Catalogue of Materials, History of Great Britain and Ireland* (R.S. 26, 1, 217-8). The account by W. St John Hope is in *Archaeologia Cantiana* 22 (1916), pp. 1-26. See also N. Brooks, *The Early History of the Church of Canterbury* (1984); *N.C.E.*, 8, p. 567; F. M. Stenton, *Anglo-Saxon England* (2d ed. 1947), pp. 106-13, 125, 127; Stanton, pp. 46-7; *O.D.S.*, pp. 290-1; Jedin-Holland, 1, pp. 426-9; R. Gem (ed.), *St Augustine's Abbey, Canterbury* (1997).

St Burchard of Würzburg, *Bishop* (*c.* 764)

Burchard was born in Wessex and became a monk at Malmesbury. After his ordination he became one of the group of Englishmen who went to Germany in around 732 to join St Boniface (5 June) in his mission of evangelization. Boniface soon appointed him bishop of Würzburg, in Franconia, where the Irish St Kilian (8 July) had worked and been martyred some fifty years earlier and whose relics Burchard translated to his cathedral. He took part in the first Frankish reform council, summoned by Boniface on 21 April 743, which sought restoration of law and order in the Frankish Church as well as renewal of moral and religious order among clergy and laity, all of which required guarantees from the secular power.

In 747 Pepin the Short, second son of Charles Martel, controlled the Frankish kingdom, but had not been elected by the people or anointed by the bishops as king. He sent his chaplain, Fulrad, together with Burchard, to Rome, to consult Pope St Zachary (15 Mar.) on the question of the succession, asking "*de regibus in Francia, qui illis temporibus non habentes regalem potestatem, si bene fuisset an non,*" whether the kings of Franconia, who had not received royal power, should have it or not. The pope returned the answer that it was better for those who actually held the power to be called king than those who ruled without power. This paved the way for Pepin's accession and anointing and marked the end of the Merovingian dynasty. Burchard, like Boniface, worked in close cooperation with the civil rulers to advance the cause of the Church.

He had the reputation of being an energetic bishop and founded a school and a monastery in Würzburg; the monastery was originally dedicated to St Andrew, but this was later changed to St Burchard himself. He is said to have resigned his see in 753, but this is dismissed (by P. L. Hug) as "mere legend." He died at Homburg-am-Main, probably in 754, and was buried, at his request, near the remains of St Kilian, to whom he had a deep devotion.

Two medieval Lives survive: the second, written some centuries after his death and attributed to the monk Englehard of Saint-Berchard, has more details, especially about his relics. The first is in *AA.SS.*, Oct., 6, pp. 573-94; the second is ed. F. J. Bendel, *Vita sancti Burkardi* (1912); both are ed. Holder-Eggar in *M.G.H., Scriptores*, 15, pt. 1, pp. 47-62. See also *Bibl.SS.*, 3, 608-10; W. Levison, *England and the Continent in the Eighth Century* (1945); *O.D.S.*, pp. 74-5; Jedin-Dolan, 3, pp. 16-19

In art he is usually represented with the attributes of a bishop: staff, book, and coat of arms. There is a remarkable wood reliquary figure of him in the National Gallery of Art, Washington, D.C.; this is the work of Tilman Riemenschneider (fourteenth or early fifteenth century): illus. in *N.C.E.*, 2, p. 887. His figure on the tomb at St Kilian's Altar in the New Minster of Würzburg shows him with a bishop's crozier.

Bd Simon of Cascia, (*c.* 1295-1348)

Materials for his actual life are scarce and confined for the most part to generalities about his character. He was born into the Fidati family at Cascia in Umbria around 1295 and seems to have been gifted with above normal intelligence. He joined the Augustinian friars and began preaching around 1318, after what must have been an unusually short novitiate. He is said to have preached effectively without preparation, trusting in the Spirit to inspire him with the necessary words. He acquired a large circle of dependent penitents and would sit up all night writing as many as thirty or forty letters to them. As a young man he mortified himself severely, but he was forced to abandon this régime with advancing years. He was reputed to be extremely strict in reproving offenders, which had the effect of making them even more devoted to him. He was a prominent figure in the Umbrian cities of Florence, Perugia, and Siena but avoided all posts of authority within his Order and in the Church at large, devoting himself as far as posible to a life of prayer, reading, writing, and solitude. He founded a house of refuge for "fallen women" and one for young girls. He died, possibly in Florence, on 2 February 1348.

He is best known to history as the author of certain published works, including *De gestis Domini Salvatoris,* which have occasioned both literary and theological debate. The literary one revolves around whether some works written in pure fourteenth-century Tuscan and generally attributed to the Dominican Dominic Cavalca were actually the work of Simon. The claim for his authorship is based on internal evidence relating to their content, but it is also argued that even if the ideas are his, he would have expressed them in Latin and that it was probably his companion for seventeen years, disciple, and biographer, John of Salerno, who put them into the vernacular. The theological debate is over the orthodoxy or otherwise of the *De gestis*, and whether it could have been a major source of inspiration for his fellow-Augustinian Martin Luther. The work was first printed at Strasbourg in 1480 and so could well have come into Luther's hands; it aroused some controversy in Simon's lifetime, being called incautious by some and hypocritical by others, as John of Salerno records. Both debates remain unresolved. The relative frequency of editions of his works between

1527 and 1540 suggests that he enjoyed a theological vogue until the works of Luther himself overtook him, since when interest in him declined.

The cause for confirmation of Simon's cult was introduced in 1833 in terms that, according to the previous edition of this work, show the promoter as "very imperfectly acquainted with the facts of his history."

The biography by John of Cremona and some of Simon's letters are printed in N. Mattioli, *Il b. Simone di Cascia* (1898). His influence on Luther is advanced in A. V. Müller, *Una Fonte ignota del sistema di Lutero* (1921). See also *Bibl.SS.*, 5, 674–5, *s.v.* Fidati.

Bd Peter of Ruffia, *Martyr* (*c.* 1320-65)

Pietro was born into the noble family of Cambiani at Ruffia in Piedmont and entered the Dominicans at the age of sixteen. He was a brilliant scholar in scripture, theology, and law and so was enlisted by the Order in the struggle against the Waldensians in Piedmont. This movement, somewhat like the Cathars in southern France (see St Dominic; 8 Aug.), had started as an evangelical campaign for holy poverty and later developed heretical overtones. Its founder was a wealthy merchant of Lyons named Valdes, who in 1173 renounced all his possessions and began preaching the ideal of poverty, inviting other laypeople to do the same. They were initially regarded reasonably favourably by the church authorities, though they were told that laymen were not allowed to preach without official sanction. Then attitudes hardened, and they were expelled from Lyons and declared heretics. After a period of coexistence with a similar movement, the *Humiliati*, they split into factions, most of which sought reconciliation with orthodoxy and official recognition of their communal way of life. Their ideas spread rapidly throughout the thirteenth century, and by 1320 they had moved into the valleys of Piedmont, converting most of the inhabitants. This is where Peter encountered them.

By the end of the twelfth century their radical peaceful ideals had already developed into a contempt for the power of the Church. They declared priests to have no authority, church buildings to be useless, the cult of saints futile, purgatory a deception, and indulgences a disgrace. They were pursued by the Inquisition but survived, eventually to transfer their allegiance to Protestant bodies at the Reformation. Peter, on account of his local knowledge, was appointed inquisitor general in Piedmont by Pope Innocent VI in 1351. He worked in the diocese of Turin for fourteen years and then began a tour of the Alpine valleys leading up toward the Swiss border. He was assassinated by two Waldensians at the Franciscan friary of Susa on 2 February 1365.

His body was recovered and taken for burial in the church of St Dominic in Turin, where it remains. His cult was approved by Pope Pius IX in 1865, five hundred years after his death. The Dominicans commemorate him on 7 November.

AA.SS., Nov., 3, pp. 684–6; *N.C.E.*, 11, p. 228, and for the Waldensians, 14, pp. 770–1, with bibliography.

St Catherine dei Ricci, (1522-90)

She is known, to an extent that completely overshadows other aspects of her life, for her extraordinary display of what Fr Thurston called "the physical phenomena of mysticism"—ecstatic trances in which she re-enacted the passion of Christ, stigmata, bilocation, and the mark of "mystical espousals," a ring on her finger given her by Christ. The value and the details of the testimony of witnesses to these vary considerably, but the overall impression cannot be dismissed as hysteria, whatever the cause of the phenomena is judged to be. Both in the nature of her experiences and in the detailed records kept of them she resembles the slightly later St Mary Magdalen de' Pazzi (1566-1607; 25 May), also from Florence.

She was born into a prominent family of Florence and christened Alexandrina. At the age of thirteen she entered the religious life as a Dominican nun, in the convent of St Vincent at Prato, of which her uncle, Timoteo dei Ricci, was director. The next two years were filled with a succession of complicated diseases, which no one could treat successfully. Obviously, the question of how far these adolescent sufferings underlay the later phenomena has to be raised, even though it is not possible to essay a retrospective diagnosis. She bore her sufferings with great patience, "offering them up" through constant meditation on the passion of Christ. She progressed rapidly in the religious life, becoming successively novice-mistress and subprioress, and was then elected prioress in perpetuity at the age of thirty.

From February 1542, when she was twenty years old, she underwent a series of ecstatic trances every week for twelve years, lasting from midday on Thursday to four o'clock on Friday afternoon. During these she would recover sufficiently to receive Communion with great devotion on the Friday morning, and her body would assume the posture dictated by her meditation on the successive phases of Christ's passion: standing at the pillar, bowing her head to receive the crown of thorns, and so on. News of these manifestations brought crowds of devout, or at least curious, onlookers, and eventually she begged all the nuns to pray that they should cease, which they did.

Her bilocation is reported as attested by none other than St Philip Neri (26 May), far from the most credulous of men. They had corresponded, and then she appeared to him in Rome without ever leaving her convent. Five witnesses in Rome confirmed this under oath, but it seems that St Philip himself never actually did so. When we come to the other manifestations, the physical marks on her body, the evidence is more confusing. The stigmata were recalled in very different forms by those who made depositions at the introduction of her cause, which did not start till twenty-four years after her death. The most convincing testimony is that provided by Sr Mary Magdalen, who left a manuscript account and who was sensible enough to tell Catherine that the fame surrounding it was doing the convent no good and to try various methods of washing the signs off, all to no avail. Catherine apologized for the trouble she was causing, but she could do nothing about it.

At the examination of the depositions of witnesses before the Congregation of Rites, the promoter of the faith, or "devil's advocate," was none other than Prosper Lambertini, later to become Pope Benedict XIV. He raised a number of awkward questions concerning the phenomena, but eventually the testimony of witnesses, the chief of whom was a Dominican, Fr Neri, prevailed. It has to be said that Catherine did nothing consciously to encourage her phenomena—rather the reverse—and that they and their attendant fame did not prevent her from being a good administrator and most assiduous and seemingly happiest in caring for the sick. She in fact lived an uncommonly effective life, advising bishops, cardinals, no fewer than three future popes, and generals of religious Orders—not only her own. Her spirituality has been described as "that of a Savanarola, softened by her optimism and compassion" (*N.C.E.*). As did St Teresa of Avila (15 Oct.), who was both born and died a mere seven or eight years before her, she got on with her life despite, not on account of, her mystical experiences. Both mystics lived at a time when reforms of religious life and a more emotional devotion to the person of Christ could produce an overcharged atmosphere, especially in convents of nuns. Her letters show her as a person of down-to-earth common sense. To a lay friend, Filippo Salviati, for example, she wrote (in terms reminiscent of Teresa herself): "Now that you are . . . at Florence, I am sure no one will offer you soup and biscuits at supper, so I am sending you a basket of chestnuts, and order you to eat at least four each night. We must look to life not death as our goal. . . . I am sure that this weather is really bad for your health, so I beg you to take care of yourself. . . . Do it out of love of our Lord, and to gain time to work for God: that should be our real aim."

Catherine died after a long illness on 2 February 1548 and was finally canonized in 1747, not on account of the physical phenomena but for her heroic virtue.

F. M. Capes, *St Catherine dei Ricci: Her Life, her Letters, her Community* (1905); C. Guasti, ed., *Le lettere spirituali e familiari di S. Caterina de'Ricci* (1861). See also H. Thurston, S.J., "Tokens of Espousal," in *The Physical Phenomena of Mysticism* (1952); J. Petrie, *St Catherine de'Ricci: Sources* (1985), Eng. trans. of G. di Agresti, *S. Caterina de'Ricci: Fonti* (1963). *N.C.E.*, 3, p. 258; *O.D.S.*, p. 415, and *Bibl.SS.*, 3, 1044-5, for further bibliography. *D.H.G.E.*, 11, 1516-7, points out that much of her correspondence remains unedited.

There is a portrait of her attributed to Nardini in the Pinacoteca of Montepulciano in Umbria.

St Joan de Lestonnac, *Foundress* (1556-1640)

Joan (Jeanne) was born to a distinguished family of Bordeaux. There was a religious division in her family, as her mother, Jeanne Eyquem de Montaigne, who was a sister of the famous essayist Michel de Montaigne (1533-92), es-

poused Calvinism, then spreading rapidly in the region, while her father remained staunchly Catholic. (Her uncle Michel, though sceptical and humanist,
eventually died reconciled to the Catholic Church.) Her mother tried to persuade her to embrace Calvinism, but she refused. In 1573 she made a Catholic
marriage to Gaston de Montferrant, who was related to the royal houses of
France, Aragon, and Navarre; this brought the title of *baronnesse de Landiras*.
Their happy marriage was ended by Gaston's death in 1597. Joan was left to
bring up four children and devoted herself to them until they were grown up.
Two daughters became nuns and the other two children, a son and a daughter,
eventually married.

Relatively freed from family responsibilities, Joan became a Cistercian nun,
joining the convent of Les Feuillantes in Toulouse. This was in 1603, when she
was forty-seven years old. This step was opposed by her son and made despite
the fact that her adored younger daughter was still unmarried. The austere
Cistercian régime proved too harsh for her, and she was forced to leave after
six months, despite her pleas to be allowed to stay and die in the convent. She
left apparently with the idea of somehow founding a religious Congregation.

She returned to Bordeaux and then went to the Périgord, where she gathered
several young women round her as the nucleus of her future Congregation,
which was, however, not to come into being just yet. After two years spent
quietly at her country estate of La Motte she went again to Bordeaux, which
was then struck by an outbreak of plague. She nursed its victims heroically,
again with a band of young women whom she inspired to do the same. She
received spiritual direction from two Jesuits, Frs Jean de Bordes and Raymund,
who were inspired with the idea that a Congregation of women was needed to
counteract the growing influence of Calvinism in the area, through teaching
girls according to the same principles the Jesuits applied in their schools for
boys, and that Joan de Lestonnac should be its first superior. The first house
was opened in the former Priory of the Holy Ghost in Bordeaux with the
sanction of the archbishop, Cardinal de Sourdis, who clothed her and her
companions in 1608. Joan was elected superior in 1610, and the Congregation
grew rapidly, despite the difficulty of holding back the advance of Calvinism in
the district and campaigns of calumny and intrigue mounted against her personally. Schools flourished in the region, with foundations made first in
Périgueux, followed by several other towns.

This happy and peaceful endeavour was disrupted by a disagreement between the Congregation and the archdiocese over freedom of action. A nun
named Blanche Hervé and the director of one of the houses spread discreditable
stories about Joan, which prompted the archbishop to remove her from her
position as superior, appointing Blanche Hervé in her place. Blanche then treated
her with contempt, showering insults and even physical violence on her. After
three years, perhaps unnerved by Joan's inexhaustible patience, she repented,
but by this time Joan was elderly and declined to be re-appointed as superior.

She did, however, visit all twenty-six houses of what was then called the Company of Mary Our Lady between 1625 and 1631, when she returned to Bordeaux to spend her remaining years in retirement. She died on 2 February 1640, the feast of the Purification. Miracles were reported at her tomb, but the cause of her beatification failed to advance. When the French Revolution came, her body was lost and the nuns of her Congregation scattered. The body was found in the early nineteenth century and solemnly reinterred at the motherhouse in Bordeaux. She was finally beatified in 1900 and canonized in 1949. The Work of her Congregation is still carried on in seventeen countries by some 2,500 nuns.

Two Lives were written in French around the time of her beatification, and Paula Hoësl provided a further one at the time of her canonization: *Ste Jeanne de Lestonnac* (1949; Eng. trans. *In the Service of Youth*, 1951). See also *Bibl.SS.*, 6, 587-8; *N.C.E.*, 8, pp. 678-9. Lives in French by V. Mercier (1891); Testore (1949); L. Entreaygues, *Une nièce de Montaigne: La bse. Jeanne de Lestonnac* (1938). The Company of Mary Our Lady has a house in Essex and one in the U.S.A.

Bd Stephen Bellesini (1775-1840)

His life was one of quiet devotion rather than outstanding achievement. He was born at Trent (Trento), in northern Italy, and entered the Order of Hermits of St Augustine at the age of sixteen. He studied in Rome and Bologna but was forced to return to Trent when Napoleon annexed the Papal States of Emilia and Romagna. With the community dispersed by the revolutionary government of the period 1796-9, Stephen devoted himself to preaching and instructing children. He was so succesful in the latter role that he was appointed government inspector of all schools in the Trentino region. With the restoration of the Papal States agreed by the Congress of Vienna (1814-5), he insisted on rejoining his community in Bologna despite opposition from the government. He was appointed master of novices first in Rome and then at Città della Pieve, and then parish priest at the Augustinian church of Gennazzano, south-east of Rome near Palestrina, which held the supposedly miraculous icon of Our Lady of Good Counsel. (The Augustinians had first been allowed to celebrate a feast of this title in 1779, and it was to be declared a feast of the whole Church in 1876.) He nursed the sick devotedly during an epidemic of cholera in the region in 1839, caught the disease himself, and died from it on 2 February 1840. He was beatified in 1904.

The documents in the beatification process gave rise to two Lives in Italian, by F. Balzofiore and P. Billeri (both 1904). See also *N.C.E.*, 2, 253; *AA.SS.*, Feb., 2, pp. 199-212; *Bibl.SS.*, 1, 1082-3.

The Martyrs of Vietnam (Seventeenth to Nineteenth Centuries)

Martyrs who suffered in various persecutions, mainly between 1745 and 1862, were beatified in groups in 1900, 1906, 1909, and 1951. Of these, 117 were canonized together in 1988. Ninety-six of the 117 were Vietnamese, thirty-seven of them priests, and fifty-nine laypeople, including catechists and tertiaries; the others were European: ten French priests including one bishop, and eleven Spaniards, bishops, priests, and laymen. Only one of the 117 was a woman, Agnes De (d. 12 July 1841). Inevitably, more is known of the Europeans as individuals than of the Vietnamese. (They are grouped together here following the principle laid down in the new draft Roman Martyrology that the country of martyrdom is of more significance than groupings for beatification. St Andrew Dung-Lac and Companions are commemorated separately on 21 December, while the following entry gives an account of the best known of all, Théophane Vénard.)

As with all the great "expansionary" missionary endeavours that brought Christianity into contact and generally conflict with—and colonization of—other, often older civilizations—China (see 17 Feb.), Japan (see 6 Feb.), not to mention South America—the "history" of the Martyrs of Vietnam has been written by the victors and tinged with their nationalisms. So earlier French and Spanish accounts are undergoing radical revision by the current Vietnamese government, which takes the line that the martyrs were simply political agents of the colonial powers. As with the other missionary endeavours, the background is too complex to be dealt with in other than the most summary fashion here; the missionaries were inevitably conditioned by their time but, equally, were often outstanding individuals who worked single-mindedly for Christ and the Church and cannot be held responsible for the actions of their governments. The ex-colonial view is also generally expressed by current rulers, who by no means always represent that of the people.

The present territory of Vietnam was first evangelized some time in the sixteenth century. Christianity failed to take root at this stage, however, and when the French Jesuit Alexandre de Rhodes arrived in southern Vietnam in 1623 it was to all practical purposes virgin territory. The Portuguese referred to the whole country as Cochin China. In de Rhodes' time it was divided into two, under the Trinh lords in the north (the region of Tonkin) and the Nguyen in the south (the regions of Annam and Cochin China). De Rhodes worked virtually alone and was not always in the country. He was brilliantly effective in planting the Church as a largely self-managing evangelizing community through training native catechists. These were vowed to celibacy, lived in community, and were quite capable of working independently. De Rhodes devised the *quoc ngu* system (still in use) of writing Vietnamese in the Roman alphabet instead of Chinese characters, which gave ordinary people access to literacy and helped them to see Christianity as a liberating influence in an excessively hierarchical society.

With his mission, which moved to the north in 1627, the faith now spread rapidly, and despite persecution—the "protomartyr," a nineteen-year-old catechist, André Trung, died during this period—the number of Christians in Tonkin had grown to about 300,000 in less than fifty years and to perhaps 800,000 in the whole of the country. Missionaries had to work clandestinely, but this did not prevent them from coming, with the Dominicans providing the greater number. So great was the number of converts that the Sacred Congregation for the Propagation of the Faith (created in 1622 by Gregory XV in the Bull *Inscrutabili Divinae*) decided to divide the area into two vicariates apostolic, named Tonkin in the northern part and Cochin China in the southern. Persecution flared up again in 1696; it has been claimed that about 100,000 people may have been martyred between then and the 1860s, but this figure is probably a considerable exaggeration and may include reprisal killings for essentially political reasons. All historical records for the majority of these have unfortunately been lost.

The earliest European martyrs for whom there are records are two eighteenth-century Spanish Dominicans, Francisco Gil de Federich and Alonzo Lenziana. The former is known to have carried out a fruitful apostolate during the nine years he spent in prison; the latter, who for thirteen years managed successfully to evade capture by the authorities, ministered faithfully though clandestinely to Christians in the region. These two men died in 1745. In 1773 two more Dominicans, Jacinto Castaneda and Vincent Liem, lost their lives. Castaneda, a Spaniard, had served for several years as a missionary in the Philippines and in China before being deported to Vietnam, where he spent three years in prison. Liem was the earliest Vietnamese martyr to be canonized; he had spent fourteen years taking the gospel to the people of his country when he was arrested and, like Castaneda, beheaded. Twenty-five years later, in 1798, Jean Dat and Emmanuel Nguyen became the first Vietnamese diocesan priests to suffer martyrdom.

In 1802 the first Nguyen emperor, Gia Long, established himself with the aid of the Jesuit vicar general for Cochin China, Pigneau de Béhaine, ensuring that Christianity in the area enjoyed a period of calm during which many converts were made, in the first quarter of the nineteenth century. This came to an abrupt end, however, with the succession of the emperor Minh Mang (1820–41), who, believing that attempted revolts against him were inspired by the missonaries, instituted a persecution of Christians and also brought in strict laws against Buddhism and Taoism. In 1832 Minh Mang banned all foreign missionaries and ordered all Vietnamese Christians to renounce their faith by trampling on the crucifix (in much the same way as Japanese Christians had been ordered to trample on images two centuries earlier); existing churches were to be destroyed, and it became an offence to teach Christianity. Many people suffered as a result of these laws. Minh Mang then ordered the arrest of all priests; most escaped, but François-Isidore Gagelin, who had previously been a cartographer at the imperial court, was captured. He was taken to the imperial capital, Hue in central Vietnam, condemned to death for "preaching the religion on Jesus," and slowly strangled on a scaffold. The date was 17 October 1833. Three days later the emperor had his body dug up to check that he had not been resurrected.

Among those arrested in this wave of persecutions, which lasted to 1840, were two Spanish Dominicans, Bishop Ignacio Delgado and Bishop Domingo Henárez, both of whom had worked in the region for about fifty years. Bishop Ignacio was placed in a cage, where he died from hunger, thirst, and exposure before he could be beheaded; he was seventy-six years old. Bishop Domingo, who must have been about the same age, was beheaded together with his southern Vietnamese catechist, François Chien. Vietnamese priests who were martyred at this time include Pierre Tuan, Bernard Due, and Joseph Nien; we also know the names of two Vietnamese laymen, Joseph Cahn, a doctor, and Thomas De, a tailor, who suffered in the same way. Some of the victims seem to have made temporary retractions under the influence of drugs, but many endured appalling tortures, including having their limbs severed joint by joint. In 1835 a number of French missionaries were arrested, including Fr Jean-Charles Cornay and Fr Joseph Marchand. The latter, whom the emperor believed to have been responsible for instigating a serious uprising in Gia Dinh, was arrested in Saigon and died as St Bartholomew (24 Aug.) is reputed to have done, by being flayed alive; his flesh was stripped from his body with red-hot tongs. This was on 30 November 1835. Fr Cornay was set up by the authorities, who buried weapons in the plot of land he cultivated. He was imprisoned in a series of cages and, because he was young and had a fine voice, forced to sing to his captors. Finally, on 20 September 1837, the sentence of the supreme tribunal was carried out—"that he is to be hewn in pieces and that his head, after being exposed for three days, is to be thrown into the river." In 1839 a Vietnamese priest named Andrew Dung (who had changed his name to Lac to avoid recognition and is known as Andrew Dung-Lac) was executed on 21 December together with another Vietnamese priest, Peter Thi. He was canonized with others as "St Andrew Dung-Lac and Companions."

In 1840 Minh Mang attempted a reconciliation with France and sent two mandarins as ambassadors but, as a result of protests by Catholic activists, Louis Philippe refused even to receive them. The concessions forced on China by the British after the Opium War of 1841 led to an increase in French intervention in South-East Asia. After a slight lull persecution in Vietnam began again in earnest in 1847. Several French missionaries were placed in prison and sentenced to death, including a priest named Lefèbvre, who had really been plotting against the emperor, Thieu Tri. Not knowing that he had actually been released, the French navy blockaded and bombarded the port of Danang (near Hue), infuriating the emperor, who threatened reprisals against the missionaries but did not carry them into effect. But he did execute a Vietnamese sea captain, Matthew Gam, who had been arrested for smuggling foreign priests into the country. He died on 11 November 1847 and is numbered among the 117 canonized martyrs.

The emperor Tu Duc issued decrees against Christianity in 1848 and 1851. Native Catholics were branded and had their property confiscated. Many—native clergy and laity as well as foreign missionaries—died in the years that followed, including Frs Augustin Schöffler and Jean-Louis Bonnard, both of whom had studied at the college for foreign missionaries in Paris. Fr Schöffler was a native of Lorraine. He came to Tonkin in 1848 and soon learned enough of the language to hear Confessions and give simple instruction. He was arrested on 1 March 1851. Although he was not tortured, strictly speaking, the fact that, with his legs in fetters and a great wooden frame (*cang*) round his neck, he was thrown on the mercy of the other prisoners (not to mention the rats and mice) in the common gaol, effectively amounted to torture. His execution was a very public affair, during which his courage and dignity impressed even the most hardhearted and anti-Christian of those present. Fr Bonnard reached Tonkin in 1850 at the height of a cholera epidemic. He immediately set about helping those stricken by the disease while continuing his efforts to learn the language. He seems to have been a man of great personal warmth: the vicar general under whom he served wrote about him in terms that showed great affection as well as admiration; a touching letter he wrote to his family while he was under sentence has been preserved. He was beheaded on 1 May 1852; his heavily-weighted remains, which had been thrown as was customary into the river, were recovered by local Christians.

Among the Vietnamese priests executed was Philip Minh, on 3 July 1853. He had been a priest for six years, was highly respected for his zeal, and had been given facilities for administering Confirmation, which involved him in frequent travel and increased danger of arrest. When he was captued, the officers bound his hands behind his back with his own hair. He received civilized treatment from the mandarins, however, and was expecting to be exiled to a distant province. In the early years of Tu-Duc, this was the legal penalty for native priests, only foreign missionaries being exiled. But Tu Duc had recently changed the law. When the—completely unexpected—death sentence arrived from the capital, Philip was led out for execution the same day. He had only a few hours notice to prepare himself but remained very calm. After the execution the mandarins immediately left the spot, so the Christians were able to retrieve his body. They laid it in a coffin, dressed in priestly vestments, and took it back to his native village, Cai-Mong, for an elaborate funeral, at which about a thousand people were present.

Senior missionaries began appealing to France for protection, and the vicar apostolic, Pellerin, went to France to request the government specifically to establish a permanent presence in Vietnam by acquiring territorial concessions as the British and French had been doing in China. In 1856 French warships again bombarded Danang, and two years later an expeditionary force, mainly French but with token Spanish participation, attacked the port. The French, on the basis of information provided by Pellerin, expected Vietnamese Catholics to rally to their support, but they did not, and the conflict dragged on for several years, during which eight Vietnamese priests, eight Vietnamese laymen, one French bishop and two priests, and two Spanish bishops and one priest, from among the 117 canonized, were martyred.

The French bishop was Etienne-Théodore Cuénot. Unlike Frs Schöffler and Bonnard, who had been in the region for so short a time before being arrested, Fr Cuénot had left France for Vietnam in 1829. During the period of persecution that started in 1833 he was directed by his superiors to take some of the native students for the priesthood and seek refuge in Siam (modern Thailand). Despite the discouraging reverses that met him at every turn he showed such courage and resourcefulness that in 1835, while he was in Singapore, he was consecrated episcopal coadjutor to the local bishop. After this he returned to southern Vietnam, where his work was hampered by the fact that the persecution was still raging and he had to remain in hiding. His zeal, however, was contagious: he inspired the demoralized native priests and catechists with fresh courage, and many converts were made. He managed, moreover, to reorganize the scattered Christian communities; within fifteen years he had established three separate vicariates in Cochin China, each served by about twenty priests: when he had arrived as vicar apostolic there were scarcely more than twelve priests, most of them old and infirm, in the entire country. Then in 1861 during a particularly violent outbreak of persecution in the province of Binh-Dinh, where until then Christians had been left in comparative peace, Bishop Cuénot, who by this time was fifty-nine years old, took refuge in the house of a sympathetic non-Christian, "who concealed him in a double cell adroitly built in the thickness of a double wall." Two days later, exhausted and ill, he ventured out in order to assuage his terrible thirst. He was seized immediately, thrown into a low, narrow cage, and transported to the principal town of the district. Here he was given some measure of liberty in the prison, but a few days later, on 14 November, he died of dysentery, just as the order for his beheading arrived from the capital.

Of the Spanish bishops put to death in 1861, Jerónimo Hermosilla, a Dominican, had succeeded Ignacio Delgado as vicar apostolic of eastern Tonkin. When the persecution started up again, he was arrested, but he managed to escape and to continue his ministry in secret until he was betrayed by a soldier. He was then imprisoned with two other missionaries: Valentín Berrio-Ochoa, a Basque, had joined the Dominicans with the idea of becoming a missionary, left Spain for Tonkin in 1858 when Bishop Melchior Sampedro was martyred, and succeeded him as bishop; Pedro Almatò, a Catalan, had worked as a missionary in the region for six years, always under the handicap of ill health. These three were beheaded on 1 November 1861, Pedro's thirty-third birthday. Five weeks later Joseph Khang, an Indochinese secular tertiary, was put to death in the same place.

In January 1862 the pro-vicar wrote from Saigon: "Half the clerical students, all the pupils of the junior college, all the nuns, altogether a band of 250, have fallen into the hands of the persecutors and are branded on the face with the letters TA DAO (false religion) as a badge of infamy. They either have a *cang* or a chain round their necks, some have both; they are divided into small parties and distributed among the different villages where they are crowded into wretched hovels. . . . The rumour has now spread that two villages have burned Christians in order to save their guards the trouble of watching them, and when called to account by the mandarins, they pretended the fire was accidental." The methods adopted by the persecutors were clearly defined: "All Christians shall be scattered among the non-Christian villages, wives separated from their husbands, and children from their parents. Christian villages must be destroyed and their possessions distributed elsewhere. Every Christian shall be marked on the face with the words 'false religion.'" Vietnamese who had suffered death included three priests, Laurence Hunh (1856), Paul Lok (1859), and Jean Hoan (1861); a catechist, André Nam-Thung (1855); and a high-ranking official, Michel Ho-Dinh-Hy (1857). In 1859 the Dominican tertiary Dominic Cam was savagely executed. He had been brought up at the mission in Cam-Chuong in Tonkin and ministered for many years, coming out of hiding to administer the sacraments. He was delated to the mandarin, who ordered him to be arrested and taken to the provincial capital, Hung-yen. He was offered his life if he would trample on the cross, but declared that he would suffer any torment rather than do so. After many months imprisoned in a *cang*, he was taken out to be beheaded. Three blows of a sword failed to sever his head from his body, and the job was finished off with a saw. The laymen who died included a judge, Vincent Thuong, and two fishermen, Pierre Thuan and Dominique Toai, who, with Pierre Da, were burned alive in their bamboo hut in 1862. Their names are among the 117 canonized.

By 1862, however, Emperor Tu Duc was also facing a rebellion (fomented by the French) in the north and could not fight on two fronts. He signed a humiliating treaty, ceding three provinces to the French and thereby commencing the colonial takeover of Vietnam, completed with the formation of the Indochinese Union in 1887. Tu Duc failed to honour treaty commitments guaranteeing religious freedom and carried out large-scale massacres in the 1870s and 1880s, treating Catholics as collaborators when France resumed hostilities, but their victims have not been recognized as martyrs.

Biographical material on the Vietnamese martyrs is scattered and hard to come by. The Catholic Truth Society pamphlet issued to commemorate the canonization of the 117 (1988) gives a full list of their names. On the background see K. S. Latourette, *History of the Expansion of Christianity* (1944); D. R. SarDesai, *Southeast Asia* (1997), pp. 125-6; S. Karnow, *Vietnam: A History* (1994), pp. 68-100. A. de Rhodes' memoirs are trans. S. Hertz, *Rhodes of Vietnam* (1966). The current Vietnamese government's position (that the martyrs were all agents of imperialism) was presented at a seminar in Ho Chi Minh City (formerly Saigon) in March 1988: a French translation of the proceedings was published as *Autour de l'affaire de canonisation des 117 bienheureux martyrs du Vietnam* (1988). On the martyrdom of Philip Minh and Matthew Gam see *The New Glories of the Catholic Church* (trans. Fathers of the London Oratory, 1870); on that of Auguste Schöffler and Jean-Louis Bonnard see *Annals of the Propagation of the Faith* (1852-3); for Etienne Cuénot, *ibid.* (1862), pp. 250-60. See also A. Lannay, *Les bienheureux martyrs de la Société des Missions Etrangères* (1921). On the Dominicans see G. Clementi, *Gli otto martiri Tonchinesi O.P.* (1906); A. Bianconi, *Vita e martirio dei beati Domenicani* (1906). See also *Bibl.SS.*, 12, 616-22; T.-M. Tiet, *Histoire des persécutions au Viet-Nam* (1961); L. Huy, *L'An-Nam Martire 1615-1885* (1945).

St Théophane Vénard, *Martyr* (1829-61)

His startling, almost feminine good looks, preserved in a number of photographs; his exuberant charm, expressed in letters published after his death; and perhaps above all else, the fact that St Thérèse of Lisieux (1 Oct.) saw in him a kindred spirit, another "little saint," have combined to make Théophane Vénard the best-known martyr of the nineteenth century.

His father, Jean Vénard, was a village schoolmaster at Saint-Loup-sur-Thouet, in the Deux-Sèvres department, west of Poitiers. He and his wife, Marie Guévet, had six children, of whom the four eldest—christened Mélanie, Théophane, Henri, and Eusèbe—survived infanthood. She died giving birth to the last, when Théophane was thirteen. He was then at school at Doué-la-Fontaine, from where he progressed in 1847 to the minor seminary of Montmorillon and then to the major seminary in Poitiers the following year. It was here that his thoughts turned to a missionary vocation, as he confided in a letter to his sister Mélanie, but asking her to keep it a secret, as he was not yet a sub-deacon, a condition for entry into the Seminary for Foreign Missions. He entered this in March 1851 and was ordained priest in June 1852.

With four companions he left Paris on 19 September 1852; they took ship in Antwerp and sailed to Hong Kong. He had originally been assigned to a mission in China, but for various reasons was diverted to western Tonkin in Vietnam, which he reached in July 1854. He found the region undergoing a fresh wave of persecution, with forty-nine Christians put to death since 1837. But there was still a strong and well-organized missionary presence, grouped mainly under the Institute known as *La Maison Dieu*, which ran schools and hospitals.

He learned the language from two native catechists assigned to him as helpers but was prevented from carrying out an effective ministry for two and a half years owing to a succession of illnesses—asthma, typhoid, and tuberculosis—from which he was cured by a ferocious administration of blistering jars (candles set in jars and applied to various pressure-points of the body, on much the same principle as acupuncture). He then spent a period of convalescence at Ke-Vinh, brought to an end when two mandarins ordered the destruction of the *Maison Dieu* college there. Warned in time, he fled by boat toward Hoang-

Nguyen, where his friend Fr Theurel was acting head of the school. In 1857 Theurel was appointed pro-vicar and Théophane district head of missions. He spent the next year working to spread the gospel further among the 300,000 population of his district, of whom some 12,000 were already Christian. Then on 10 June 1858 Hoang-Nguyen was also destroyed. Again the alarm had been raised in time; the missionaries fled into a clandestine existence, often having to hide in pits infested with spiders, toads, and rats. From one of these, he wrote cheerfully enough to a priest friend: "One has to be ever watchful. If the dog barks, or any other stranger passes, the door is instantly closed, and I prepare to hide myself in a still lower hole. . . . This is how I have lived for three months. . . . What do you think of our position? Three missionaries, one of whom is a bishop, lying side by side, day and night, in a space of about one and a half yards square, our only light and means of breathing being three holes, the size of a little finger, made in the mud wall. . . ." Yet he made light of his physical sufferings; for him, the worst part was that he was unable to bring consolation or the sacraments to his scattered flock. Under such conditions he managed to translate the New Testament into Vietnamese.

He was betrayed to the authorities, arrested on 30 November 1860, put in a wooden cage, and taken to Hanoi to be interrogated. There he was repeatedly ordered to trample on a cross. He refused and after two months of delay was beheaded, on 2 February 1861. Between his arrest and his execution, kept continually in his cage, he was able to write eleven letters to his family. In one, dated 2 January 1861, he describes the impression he made on the crowds who came to stare at him: "What a lovely fellow that Westerner is! He's as jolly and cheerful as someone going to a feast! He doesn't seem at all afraid. That one hasn't sinned! He only came to Annam to do good, and yet he's being put to death. . . ."

In fact everyone, from mandarin to peasant, seems to have treated him kindly and with respect, expressing regret that the law of the kingdom was forcing them to do what they were. "I have not had to endure tortures as so many of my bethren have. One light blow from a sabre will separate my head from my body like a spring flower which the Master of a garden picks for his pleasure. We are all flowers planted on this earth, which God picks in his time, some earlier, some later." To his brother Eusèbe he wrote less than two weeks before his death: "I have loved and still love this Annamite people with a burning love. If God had given me long years, I believe I would have devoted myself completely, body and soul, to building up the Church of Tonkin."

His Life and letters were published in 1864, and a copy of the book was later brought to Thérèse of Lisieux by a missionary, Fr Roulland, who came asking for the Carmelites' prayers. Thérèse was struck by the book's revelation of a kindred spirit and was inspired to volunteer to go to the Carmelite monastery in Hanoi. She copied out some of the letters written by this "sister soul" and composed a poem in his honour, "To the Venerable Théophane Vénard," for the thirty-sixth anniversary of his death, 2 February 1897. In March she sent a copy of this to Fr Roulland. The poem picks up the image of the flower from the letter quoted above: "O Virgin Lily! in your springtime days / The King heard your desires and answered them— / You were a bloom, of whitest fire ablaze: / The Lord desired to pick you off the stem." She, of course, referred to herself as "The Little Flower." She clung to a picture and a relic of Théophane as her final illness progressed and she was no longer able to speak.

Théophane's body was transferred to the church of the Foreign Mission Society in Paris, but without his severed head, which remains in Tonkin. He was beatified in 1909 with nineteen other martyrs from Tonkin and canonized in 1988.

The above owes much to *H.S.S.C.*, 8, pp. 22-5, from which some portions of letters are translated; other extracts from J. Cumming (ed.), *Letters from Saints to Sinners* (1995), pp. 239, 243. Life and letters by E. Vénard, *Vie et correspondance de J. Th Vénard* (1864; Eng. trans., *Life of J. Théophane Vénard*, 1888); selected letters republished in 1964. See also J. Guennou (ed.), *Bienheureux Théophane Vénard* (1960); J. Nanteuil, *L'épopée missionaire de T. Vénard* (1950). *N.C.E.*, 14, p. 594; *Bibl.SS.*, 12, 987-91; *O.D.S.*, pp. 476-7. For the background see the previous entry.

Bd Mary Kasper, *Foundress* (1820-88)

The future foundress of the Poor Handmaids of Jesus Christ was born in Dernbach, in the Westerwald on the Rhine in Germany, on 28 May 1820 and christened Katharina. She was the seventh of eight children in a family of poor peasants, and from this humble background, scarcely able to provide her with a formal education, which was made more difficult by her frequent childhood illnesses, she went on to devote her life to educational and social causes.

Her father died when she was twenty-two, and the family was forced to sell their home and move into lodgings; she had to work at a number of menial tasks, even breaking stones for road-building, to help support the family. While engaged in this, she had a vision that caused her to exclaim: "Sisters! Oh, what a large number of Sisters!" She later said this was so clear that she even saw the colour, pattern, and material of the habit of her future Congregation.

She did not join an existing Order but importuned the bishop of Limburg to let her build a small house where she could gather her associates into a community. Eventually the bishop agreed, and with virtually no money but with help from men of the parish, she began building. At one stage the work was brought to a halt through torrential rains; then her mother died, and she herself contracted typhoid. She persevered through thick and thin, however, and on the feast of the Assumption, 1848, she and her companions were able to move in. The house immediately became a centre dispensing charity to the needy of the area. This in turn attracted more helpers, and the bishop, seeing their purpose and permanence, appointed her leader and drew up a set of rules for them to live by. Katherine chose the name for the Congregation, saying; "We should like to be called Poor Handmaids of Jesus Christ, and have for our patroness Mary, the first Handmaid of the Lord."

In 1851 they were allowed to take a religious habit and vows at a ceremony presided over by the bishop in the parish church of Wirges: such was the size of the congregation that the bishop was forced to address them in the open air. On receiving the habit Katherine took the name Mary. Generally known from then on as Mother Mary, she started sending Sisters out on nursing missions, some to their deaths in an epidemic. New missions were founded in neighbouring villages, each deliberately kept as a "Little House" after the pattern of the first in Dernbach. Each would usually contain four Sisters—two nursing, one conducting a kindergarten, and the fourth looking after the house and the pensioners or homeless people who were housed there. She had devised a form of charitable work that exactly fitted the needs of the locality, and requests poured in for her to establish more foundations on the same lines. She was able to do this, as the number of candidates seeking admission was always larger than could be accommodated. The motherhouse was consequently enlarged continually between 1851 and 1861.

By 1853 there were eighteen homeless children living in the original convent, and the need for a qualified teacher was becoming desperate. In answer to prayer, a man named Wilhelm Schwarz came and offered his services in return for board and lodging only, opening an elementary school there in May 1854. A lay woman teacher joined the following year, and the bishop advised Mother Mary to entrust the boys to the Brothers of Mercy at Montabaur. Wilhelm Schwarz left to join that Congregation, taking the boys with him.

The original aims of her Congregation had been to look after poor and abandoned children and to care for the sick and the aged, not to provide and run schools. However, she saw the direction she was being forced to take as God's will, and it was to prove the way the Congregation expanded into other countries. Conditions in Germany became difficult in the 1860s, with increasingly anti-Catholic state legislation that was to blossom into Bismark's *Kulturkampf* in the following decade. In 1859, Mother Mary opened her first mission outside Germany. This was at Lutterade in Holland and comprised a school, a teacher's college, and a novitiate. Other schools in Holland followed; then in 1868 the bishop of Fort Wayne, Indiana, invited her to send Sisters to the United States. Eight took charge of an orphanage in Chicago, and the diocese soon offered them Rockhill House, a failed hotel it had purchased, to run as a hospital. This became St Joseph's Hospital, and the motherhouse for the Congregation in America. Young American women applied to join, and by the time Mother Mary died in 1898, the province in America numbered 226 Sisters.

In 1873 she received a request from a Fr Volk for Sisters to minister to Germans in his parish in the East End of London. At first she refused, but when the request was repeated two years later, backed by a personal plea from Cardinal Manning, she complied. The Sisters visited the sick, then established a kindergarten, followed by a parochial school, which continued until the children and Sisters were evacuated at the outbreak of the Second World War.

Another community was started in Hendon in 1882, providing a boarding school first at Ravensfield House (once the home of Cardinal Wiseman) and then at Norden Court, where it still continues, known as Westminster House. Other foundations in England followed, and then several missions were opened in India in the early 1970s, where the Sisters care for the sick and for orphans and run schools. There are also recent foundations in Brazil and Mexico.

From her humble beginnings Mother Mary had achieved an enormous amount, all carried out with humility and simplicity. She told her Sisters to "be saints, but hidden saints," and attributed all that she achieved to Divine Providence working in her: "God's divine will shall and must be accomplished in me, by me and for me." Nevertheless, the qualities that shine out from her photograph, and which were those most stressed by witnesses in the cause of her beatification, were determination and strength. In 1890 she received the joyful news that the Constitutions of her Congregation had been approved by the Holy See. She outlived most of her contemporary friends and acquaintances as well as four hundred Sisters she had professed. She suffered a heart attack on 27 January 1898 and died early in the morning of 2 February, the feast of Candlemas. At the time of her death her Congregation numbered 1,725 Sisters. Crowds flocked to pay homage as her body lay in its open coffin, and more came to her solemn requiem and funeral procession in Dernbach. Her wooden coffin was placed inside a zinc one with the aim of preserving her remains. Miraculous cures were soon being attributed to her intercession.

Her cause was introduced by the bishop of Limburg in 1928. In 1950 her remains were translated to the chapel of the motherhouse, and her body, which had in fact decomposed, was clothed in a fresh habit. She was re-buried in a vault in the chapel. She was beatified by Pope Paul VI in St Peter's on 16 April 1978. Today some two thousand Sisters carry on her work in Germany, the U.S.A., England, Ireland, the Netherlands, India, Mexico, and Brazil.

The above account is based on *Mother Mary Katherine*, booklet by the Sisters of St Joseph's Convent, Hendon. The most comprehensive study in English is G. Meagher, C.S.C., *With Attentive Ear and Courageous Heart* (1956). See also P.H.J.C. Generalate, *The Spirit moves where It wills* (1965); *History of Dernbach, 1926: 125 Years of PHJC* (1976). Numerous publications in German, mainly for young people, include: W. Meyer, *Heiliges Magdtum vor Gott* (1933); *Wie soll das weitergehen, Katharina* (1980). See also *A.A.S.* 67 (1975), pp. 132-8; *N.C.E.*, 17 (Suppl. 2), p. 35. *Osservatore Romano*, 20 Apr. 1978, no. 17, pp. 1 and 4: *N.S.B.* 1, pp. 146-7, has a French trans. of the address at her beatification ceremony.

Bd Andrew Ferrari, *Bishop and Cardinal* (1850-1921)

Andrea Carlo Ferrari was born in Parma, in Emilia Romagna, halfway between Milan and Bologna, on 13 August 1850. He was consecrated bishop of Guastalla in 1890 and was then bishop of Como before being appointed archbishop of Milan in 1894. As cardinal archbishop—he had been given a cardinal's hat before becoming archbishop—he guided the fortunes of the archdiocese in ways that recalled his great predecessors St Ambrose (7 Dec.) and St Charles Borromeo (4 Nov.), and indeed prefigured those of his distinguished successors Cardinals Schuster (beatified in 1996; see 30 Aug.), Montini (later Pope Paul VI), and Martini.

In 1894 he came to an archdiocese facing a multiplicity of social and religious problems stemming from rapid processes of industrialization and secularization. He found a sure touch in tackling these, seeing above all the importance of involving the laity in making decisions and organization. Modelling himself on the "Good Shepherd," he did not wait for matters to be brought to him, but travelled the huge archdiocese ceaselessly, visiting the most inaccessible places, which had not seen a bishop in centuries, travelling sometimes on a mule and sometimes on foot, getting in close touch with the people and speaking their sort of language. So "St Charles has come back!" was a statement given in evidence for the *Positio super virtutibus* in the process of his beatification.

He developed new forms of practical charity suited to the times: abandoned children and young people, the elderly, and workers were the first objects of his attention. He started an initiative known officially as the Company of St Paul, but generally as the *Opera Cardinale Ferrari,* the Work of Cardinal Ferrari, as an umbrella group for the charitable organizations of the archdiocese, including a "People's Secretariat," soup kitchens, missions to working people, children's homes, and a centre for retraining released prisoners. He also started Catholic newspapers, including the diocesan daily *L'Italia,* organized mass pilgrimages, and was an early supporter of Catholic Action, whose influence spread from Milan throughout Italy with his encouragement. His efforts toward starting the Catholic University of Milan were crowned with the satisfaction of seeing it in being by the time of his death. He saw the problems posed by the diocesan major seminary being situated far from the city and bought land for a new one at Attori, but he had not managed to start building on it by the time of his death. It was later completed by Cardinal Schuster.

His ceaseless activity was fortified by a deep interior spirituality, very much of his time, with deep devotion to the Virgin and to Jesus in the Eucharist and on the cross. He suffered a most painful cancer of the throat for the last few months of his life, making his last diary entry on 20 September 1920: "May God's will be done always and in everything." He died on 2 February 1921 and was beatified by Pope John Paul II on 10 May 1987.

Osservatore Romano (French ed.), 17 May 1987, cited in *N.S.B.* 2; *Bibl.SS.,* 5, 647; *N.C.E.,* 834–5, *s.v.* Milan.

R.M.
St Flosculus (Flou), bishop of Orleans (*c.* 500)
Bd Nicholas Saggio, O.Minim., of Longobardi in Calabria (1709)

3

ST BLAISE, *Bishop and Martyr* (? *c.* 316)

Of St Blaise, nothing can be known with certainty, and very little with any
probability, as his cult seems not to have developed less than five centuries after
his death. Yet in the calendar reform of 1969 he retained his universal commemoration, being demoted merely from Memorial to Optional Memorial. This
is in part a tribute to the continued appeal of his patronage of sufferers from
sore throats and in part perhaps to the influence of France and above all of
Germany, where he was long revered as one of the Fourteen Holy Helpers.

He is said to have been bishop of Sebastea, in Armenia, and to have been put
to death in the persecution of Diocletian by beheading after having his flesh
torn with metal wool combs—hence his patronage also of wool-combers. He
features in the legendary Acts of St Eustratus, supposedly put to death with St
Orestes, a soldier, and others. According to these he received Eustratus' relics
and was punctilious in carrying out the terms of his will. Legendary Lives in
both Greek and Latin make him (in traditional fashion) the son of wealthy
parents who becomes a bishop at an early age. In order to escape persecution
he flees to a cave, where his only companions are wild animals. He cures them
of their wounds and ailments with the result that they flock to him to receive
his blessing. Hunters after the animals find him surrounded by them and,
despite their amazement at the scene, drag him off to be interrogated by the
governor of Cappadocia and Lesser Armenia, Agricolaus. On the way they
meet a poor woman whose pig has been carried off by a wolf; she appeals to
Blaise, and at his command the wolf gives up the pig whole and unharmed.
Later, when he is in prison, this same woman brings him provisions and also
tapers to lighten the gloom: this gave rise to the use of tapers or candles in the
blessing of throats, still widely practised.

His particular association with sore throats results from the legend (perhaps
attributed to him because his feast-day comes at the time of the year when
suffering from this ailment is generally at its highest, at least in Europe) that
while he was in prison, he cured a boy who had a fish bone stuck in his throat.
This and the story of the pig produced the ceremony in which two candles are
held in the form of a St Andrew's cross under the throat of those receiving the
blessing, while the words "Through the intercession of St Blaise may God
deliver you from ills of the throat and other ills" are said. This practice seems
to have arisen in the sixteenth century, a time when his cult as one of the
Fourteen Holy Helpers was at its peak, mainly in the Rhineland. Lists of these

healers vary, but nearly always include St Blaise. Their cult was discouraged by the Council of Trent, but it persisted, with a collective feast-day on 8 August, until it was abolished in 1969. One legend states that before his death he promised that anyone who lit a taper in his memory would be free of infection.

Canterbury claimed to possess relics of him, and processions in his honour were still being held in the eighteenth century, as Parson Woodforde describes in his *Diary of a Country Parson*. S. Baring Gould, writing in the late nineteenth century, says: "It was lately the custom in many parts of England to light bonfires on the hills on St Blaise's night. Some have affirmed that these usages arose from an absurd pun on the saint's name (*sc.* 'blaze'), but this seems clearly erroneous, as they are not peculiar to England. In some parts of Germany, St Blaise's day is called 'Little Candlemas Day' because of the bonfire it was usual (for an uncertain reason) to kindle on that night. At Bradford, Yorkshire, a festival is holden every five years in memory of St Blaise." (This festival has now disappeared from memory, but his association with the centre of the wool industry was presumably due to his patronage of woolcombers.)

France also lays claim to a remarkable number of relics—especially considering that he lived in Cappadocia—at Corbie, Faremoutiers, Notre Dame de Longpré, and elsewhere, and he is still regarded as a most efficacious saint there. There is a chapel dedicated to him at Subiaco. His patronage of wool combers produced his iconographic emblem.

O.D.S., p. 56, with bibliography. For the names of the Fourteen Holy Helpers, see *ibid.*, p. 185; M. Walsh, *A Dictionary of Devotions* (1993), p. 107. The supposed relics at Canterbury are discussed in J. Wickham Legg and W. H. St John Hope (eds.), *Inventories of Christ Church, Canterbury* (1902). Parson Woodeforde's account of the procession is in *Diary of a Country Parson*, ed. J. Beresford (1956), pp. 198-200. B.G., Feb., pp. 47-9. See also *N.C.E.*, 2, pp. 600-1; *Bibl.SS.*, 3, 158-65; *Saints in Italy*, pp. 72-3.

In Western art he usually wears episcopal robes, and holds a woolcomb in reference to his martyrdom and his patronage of woolworkers. He is shown as a bishop and holding a woolcomb on a screen at Ashton in Norfolk; holding a comb on the restored screen at St Mary Steps, Exeter; in glass without an attribute in Malvern Priory and Christchurch Cathedral, Oxford (*E.M.C.A.*, p. 115). In Greek paintings he is depicted as an old man with a pointed beard.

ST ANSKAR, *Bishop* (*c.* 801-65)

There is abundant material for the life of St Anskar, or Anschar, patron saint of Denmark, including the contemporary *Vita Anskarii* by his fellow missionary and successor as archbishop, St Rembert (11 June).

He was born around 801 near Amiens, in northern France, and educated at the nearby monastery of Corbie in Picardy. He entered monastic life there and then moved to Corvey, Corbie's daughterhouse on the river Weser, the first great monastery in Saxony. (The two are also known as Old Corbie and New Corbie.) This monastery, through its abbot, Warin Wala, was to play an important part in the Scandinavian mission organized from northern Germany. In 825 the conflict in Denmark between Horik, son of King Göttrik, and the pretender Harold was brought to an end. Harold came to Ingelheim to do homage to the Frankish king Louis the Pious and was baptized at Sankt Alban in Mainz. Louis invested him with the Frisian county of Hriussi, at the mouth of the Weser, as a Frankish fief.

At Corvey Anskar had begun the preaching ministry that was to become such a distinguishing feature of his apostolic life. Abbot Wala suggested to Harold that he should appoint Anskar as missionary in his territory, and he accordingly went to Denmark, taking with with him a fellow-monk named Autburt, to convert the Danes. Their preaching, under this royal patronage, was immediately succesful, and many converts were made, but in the following year Harold was expelled and Anskar returned to Saxony, taking a number of new converts with him to be educated at Corvey and other monasteries there.

In 829 King Björn of Sweden sent envoys to make contact with the Frankish empire, and Anskar returned with them to Sweden. There again his mission met with initial success. In 831 King Louis appointed him abbot of Corvey and had him nominated to the new see of Hamburg, founded to organize the mission to the Danes and Swedes. He was consecrated bishop by the emperor's brother, Bishop Drogo of Metz, and by the metropolitans of Mainz, Trier, and Reims. Pope Gregory IV (827-44) sent him the *pallium*, raising him to the rank of archbishop, and appointed him legate of the Holy See to the peoples of the North.

He spent thirteen years as archbishop of Hamburg, where he organized the missions to Denmark, Sweden, and Norway and also built churches and founded a library. The Nordic mission, however, was not to achieve a lasting success in his lifetime, largely because of the decline of the Frankish empire, which underpinned its efforts. Its growing weakness encouraged raids by the Vikings, and in 845 they sacked Hamburg, with serious consequences for the mission. King Horik of Denmark was well disposed to Anskar's mission, though he never became a Christian himself. But his death in 854 marked the end of the kingdom of Denmark for the time being and with it the end of the mission. Anskar was appointed to the see of Bremen, a suffragan see of Cologne, by Louis the German, who hoped to strengthen the missions by uniting the sees of Hamburg and Bremen in this way. The union was approved at the Synod of Mainz in 848 and ratified in 864 by Pope St Nicholas I (858-67; 13 Nov.). Anskar and Rembert (who succeeded him as archbishop from 865 to 868) maintained mission stations at Schleswig and Rügen in Denmark and Birka in Sweden, but resources were lacking to enable the missions to expand, and they were to collapse completely in the 880s, not to revive in Sweden until the end of the Viking age in the eleventh century encouraged Scandinavia seriously to seek incorporation within the Christendom of western Europe. Revival came sooner in Denmark, where by the late tenth century the Danish church was expanding again and providing missionaries to Sweden.

Anskar's great talent was for preaching; he was also renowned for his charity to the poor: he took the Gospel counsels literally, washing their feet and waiting on them at table. Personally austere, he wore a hair shirt and lived on bread and water for as long as his health permitted. He devised the practice of adding a short prayer to each psalm in the psalter, which soon became a widespread form of devotion. He died in 865 and was buried in Bremen.

Rembert's *Vita Anskarii* is in *AA.SS.*, Feb., 1, pp. 395-450. It was published in English in the edition by G. Waitz for *M.G.H., Scriptores rerum Germanicarum*, trans. C. H. Robinson (1921). There are modern Lives by E. de Moreau (Fr., 1930) and P. Oppenheim (Ger., 1931). See also C. J. A. Opperman, *English Missionaries in Sweden and Finland* (1937), pp. 38-45; *Bibl.SS.*, 1, 1337-9; *O.D.S.*, p. 24. For the background, Jedin-Dolan 3, 1, esp. pp. 114f. *P.B.*, 2, pp. 230-6, cites "un auteur Protestant, Munter," who praises Anskar's missionary work.

St Werburga, *Abbess* (650-*c.* 700)

Werburga (Werburgh, Werbyrgh, or Werburh) traditionally comes from a family of saints. As the daughter of King Wulfhere of Mercia and his wife, St Ermengild (or Ermenhilda, 13 Feb.), she was the grand-daughter of St Sexburga (6 July) and the great-niece of Sexburga's sister St Etheldreda, the first abbess of Ely (23 June), who was succeeded in that post by her sister.

On Wulfhere's death in 675 Werburga renounced the world and retired to the abbey at Ely. Wulfhere was succeeded as king of Mercia by his brother, Ethelred, who summoned Werburga from Ely and placed her in charge of a group of houses for women religious in the Midlands with the task of establishing strict observance in them. These included Weedon in Nothamptonshire, which was a royal house, where she spent some time and which she may have turned into a nunnery; Threckingham in Lincolnshire, where she died; and Hanbury in Staffordshire, where she was buried at her own request. Her relics were later moved from there to Chester probably to save them from the Danish invaders, and her shrine in the cathedral became a popular place of pilgrimage.

Her popularity derived largely from romantic legend, reproduced in the late-eleventh-century Life by Goscelin, according to which she was a beautiful girl who rejected many suitors including several princes, saying that she had vowed herself to the Lord Jesus Christ. Chief among her suitors was a favourite at her father's court, Werbod. Her father gave his permission for the marriage, provided that Werbod could obtain Werburga's free consent. But Werbod was not a Christian, and Ermenhild and her sons opposed the proposed match. The princes had received religious instruction from St Chad (2 Mar.), the bishop of Lichfield, who lived in a forest, so the princes could disguise their visits to him as hunting expeditions. Werbod slandered them to the king, who had them put to death. Werbod met a miserable death soon after; Wulfhere was stung with remorse, and sought instruction from his saintly queen and St Chad. This emboldened Werburga to ask his permission to enter Ely, which he granted.

37

Another legend recounted by Goscelin, which accounts for her main emblem of a goose, tells that when a flock of wild geese devastated the crops at Weedon, she had them locked up. Next morning one was missing, and she discovered that it had been killed by a servant and cooked. She restored the bird to life, whereupon it flew away with the rest of the flock, which never came back to attack the crops. Her relics were translated again in Chester Cathedral in 1095 (when Goscelin wrote the Life), and this story is depicted on a misericord: Werburga holds a crozier in the centre, while a servant hands her the goose; on the right a man confesses to having stolen the goose; on the left the geese are seen locked up. The story is actually a borrowing by Goscelin from his own Life of St Amelburga (or Amelia, 10 July).

Twelve ancient churches are dedicated to her in England, and the translation of her relics is also commemorated at Chester on 21 June. She is the guardian saint of Chester Cathedral and drew pilgrims from far and wide until her shrine was destroyed during the reign of King Henry VIII.

The Life by Goscelin is in *AA.SS.*, Feb., 1, pp. 386-94; it draws on the earlier *Chronicon ex Chronicis* by Florence of Worcester, 1, p. 32, and the *Liber Eliensis*, which has been ed. E. O. Blake (Camden Series, 1962). The fullest historical discusion is in J. Tait, preface to *Chartulary or Register of the Abbey of St Werburgh, Chester*, 1 (1920), pp. vii-xiv. *N.L.A.*, 2, pp. 422-5; *Bibl.SS.*, 12, 1027-8; *P.B.*, p. 249; P. Grosjean in *Anal.Boll.* 58 (1940), pp. 183-6; *O.D.S.*, p. 491. Stanton, pp. 49-50, mentions another St Werburg on this day (d. *c.* 785): she is clearly a different person, being the wife of Ceolred of Mercia, who retired to an abbey after his death, but she does not feature in the new draft R.M.

The misericord is reproduced in *E.M.C.A.*, p. 168. In a modern stained-glass window in Chester Cathedral she is shown with a crozier and holding a church and with geese in a smaller panel below the main figure. Recent excavations prove the existence of a Saxon minster on the site and have unearthed a mass of bones, which may possibly include hers, believed to have been buried under the floor to save them from the Danish invaders: report and illustration in *The Times*, 3 Mar. 1997, p. 9. What remains of her shrine has been converted into the throne of the bishops of Chester, which "still displays the carved images of Werburga'a ancestors" and is still in use (*N.C.E.*, 14, p. 585).

Bd John Nelson, *Martyr* (*c.* 1533-78)

He was the son of Sir N. Nelson of Skelton, in North Yorkshire, and the brother of Martin and Thomas, both of whom also became priests after studying at Douai and were sent on the English mission, though neither was martyred. John was nearly forty when he was inspired to enter the English College at Douai. He was ordained by the bishop of Cambrai on 16 June 1576 and sent to England in November of the same year. There he met Jesuit priests and was received into the Society of Jesus shortly before being discovered by the authorities. He was arrested in London on 1 December 1577 on suspicion of being a Catholic and imprisined in Newgate. He was tried and condemned to death for refusing to take the oath recognizing Queen Elizabeth as supreme head of the Church, "because he had never heard or read that any lay prince could have that pre-eminence," and for calling her a schismatic and a heretic. He was dragged on a hurdle from Newgate gaol to Tyburn, where he was executed with the usual butchery of being hanged, drawn, and quartered on 3 February 1578.

Anstruther, 1, pp. 245-6; *M.M.P.*, pp. 7-11; *L.E.M.* 2, pp. 223-33; *N.C.E.*, 9, p. 324; *Bibl.SS.*, 9, 974.

St Claudia Thévenet, *Foundress* (1774-1837)

Claudine was born in Lyons on 30 March 1774, the second child of Philibert and Marie-Antionette (*née* Guyot), and was educated at the abbey of Saint-Pierre-les-Nonnais until she was fifteen, when the French Revolution broke out. Lyons suffered exceptionally during the Terror of 1793-4, with widespread massacres. On a January morning in 1794, Claudia, aged nineteen, had the appalling experience of seeing two of her brothers, Louis-Antoine and François-Marie, being led away in a group to be executed. Catching sight of her, they asked her to forgive their executioners, as they had done. These were their last words.

She managed to summon up a spirit of forgiveness, and this incident probably encouraged her in her future vocation, but the experience left her physically scarred for life, with a tremor of the head and breathing difficulties. She began to involve herself in the charitable activities of the parish, alone at first, then in company with other young people who were inspired by her example. This group was guided and supported by the parish priest, Père André Coindre, who recognized Claudia's outstanding qualities.

In 1816 she was instrumental in establishing the Pious Union of the Sacred Heart of Jesus, together with her co-workers in the parish. Two years later she left the family home and founded the Congregation of the Sacred Hearts of Jesus and Mary. Its aims were to bring the message of divine forgiveness to a society torn apart by the Revolution, particularly through educating young women, especially the poor, who were often in a desperate state. Two establishments were begun at Fourvière in Lyons, one for the education of girls of good family, the other to take in orphans and street children, who were taught weaving so as to enable them to find employment in the silk trade, of which Lyons was a major centre.

In 1835 there was a proposal that her Congregation should be merged with the Society of the Sacred Heart founded some thirty years earler by St Madeleine Sophie Barat (25 May). Claudia rejected this idea, and the struggle to retain her foundation's independence exhausted her. From then on her health declined progressively until her death on 3 February 1837. Her foundation continued to flourish, and today some two thousand Sisters carry on her ideal of education with a strong maternal spirit, preparing young women for marriage and motherhood but also enabling them to equip themselves technically and professionally for the world of work. Whatever course they followed, strong Christian ideals were to be the foundation: "There is no greater misfortune," she declared, "than to live and die without knowing God."

Her cause was officially introduced in 1973; she was beatified by Pope John Paul II on 4 October 1981 and canonized by him on 21 March 1993.

A.A.S. 73 (1981), pp. 466-8; *Bibl.SS.*, Suppl. 1, 1369-71, with portrait; *N.S.B.* 1, pp. 180-1; *N.C.E.*, 12, *s.v.* "Religious of Jesus and Mary," and 18 (Suppl. 3), p. 34.

Bd Mary Rivier, *Foundress* (1768-1838)

Almost the exact contemporary of St Claudia Thévenet (above entry), her life followed a remarkably parallel course, as she went through the trauma of the Revolution and founded an educational Congregation of women. She was born in Montpezat-sous-Bauzon in the Auvergne on 19 December 1768. Education of children, taking hold of them "like a mother," seems to have been her passion from an early age. The Congregation she founded, the Sisters of the Presentation, concentrated on poor children, orphans, or those abandoned. She not only took the children but tried to form their mothers into groups, convinced of the evangelizing value of the family, particularly the first impressions of religion that children would naturally pick up from their mothers: "The whole of life lies in one's first impressions!" she declared. Pope Pius IX called her the "female apostle" and said of her that "her spirit is solidly theological and clearly apostolic."

As a child she was generally sickly but was eventually cured through, as she saw it, the intercession of Our Lady on one of her feast-days. But she was left with a permanent growth deficiency and delicate health, which did not prevent her from living to the age of seventy. Besides the physical obstacles she had to overcome there was the general religious apathy and even antipathy with which she had to contend throughout her life. She refused to allow these to depress her, however, preaching that one had to be always full of the spirit of Jesus, "our vocation," to bring his kingdom into being, especially among the young.

She died at Bourg-Saint-Audéol, also in the Auvergne, on 3 February 1838. She was beatified by Pope John Paul II on 23 May 1982.

Osservatore Romano 24 (14 June 1982), p. 7; *N.S.B.* 1, pp. 187-8; *N.C.E.*, 11, p. 759, *s.v.* "Anne-Marie Rivier"; 18 (Suppl. 3), p. 34, *s.v.* "Rivier"; *Bibl.SS.*, 11, 222-6.

R.M.

St Celerinus, martyr of Carthage (third century)

St Leo, disciple of St Hilary of Poitiers (fourth century)

SS Tigides and Remedius, successive bishops of Gap in the French Alps (fourth-fifth centuries)

St Lupicinus, bishop of Lyons (end fifth century)

St Hadelin, abbot, founder of Chelles (Liège) (*c.* 696)

St Berlinda, nun and then recluse at Meerbeke (Belgium) (*c.* 702)

Bd Helinand, O.S.B. Cist., monk of Froidmont (1237)

4

ST GILBERT OF SEMPRINGHAM, *Abbot and Founder*
(*c.* 1083-1189)

Gilbert was born physically handicapped, and so he was unable to follow in the footsteps of his father, a Norman knight named Jocelin. He instead joined the ranks of the clergy and went to pursue his higher studies in France. On his return to England he started a school in which both boys and girls could be educated, an unusual step for the age in which he lived.

The gift of the livings attached to the churches of Sempringham and West Torrington in Lincolnshire belonged to his father's estates, and Jocelin gave them to his son. Gilbert did not content himself with the relatively easy life the gift could have entailed. Though in minor orders, he was not an ordained priest, so he employed a priest to conduct the services, while he lived in poverty in the vicarage. His care, teaching, and example made his parish a model of its kind, with his parishioners notable for their devotion and sober way of life. In 1122 the bishop of Lincoln, Robert Bloet, appointed Gilbert his household clerk. Bishop Bloet died the following year, but Gilbert stayed on under his successor, Alexander. He was still a "pluralist," enjoying the livings of two churches, but he gave all the revenues from West Torrington to the poor. He was also still unordained, but Alexander ordained him priest and offered him a rich archdeaconry. Gilbert refused this and returned to his parish sometime before 1131. His father had died, so he inherited the position of squire as well as parish priest of Sempringham.

The parishioners included a group of seven young women who had sought his guidance in living a communal religious life. He had a house built for them next to the church, where they lived in strict enclosure under a rule he devised for them based on the Rule of St Benedict. The foundation grew, and acting on the advice of William, the first abbot of Rievaulx (see St Aelred of Rievaulx, 12 Jan.), Gilbert added first lay sisters and then lay brothers to work the land, following the pattern established by the Cistercians. Growth continued, and Gilbert saw the need for a more permanent form of guidance for their way of life than could be provided by him personally. Accordingly, in 1147 he travelled to Cîteaux to ask the Cistercian general chapter to take over the foundation, ruling it through English Cistercian abbots. The Cistercians, however, had just accepted jurisdiction of the Savignac Order and felt unable to accept this further responsibility. Pope Eugenius III (1145-53; Bd, 8 July) was attending the chapter and persuaded Gilbert to carry on with the responsibility himself.

St Bernard of Clairvaux (20 Aug.) helped him to draw up a series of Institutes for what was originally called the Order of Sempringham, of which Pope Eugenius appointed Gilbert master; the Order was generally known as the Gilbertines. It was the only medieval religious Order of English origin. Gilbert added canons regular to act as chaplains and help in the direction of the nuns, who remained the major part of the Order. The situation with regard to a Rule was somewhat complicated, as the nuns followed the Rule of St Benedict and the canons that of St Augustine. The monasteries were double, for both women and men, and the master general was a canon, but the men did not rule the women; their function was rather to minister to their spiritual and temporal needs. Discipline was strict, on the lines established by the Cistercians, and to encourage a spirit of humility the divine office was chanted in monotone rather than the more usual and elaborate plainchant. Most of the houses were in Lincolnshire and Yorkshire, and Gilbert, as master, visited them frequently, between visits continuing to lead an austere life and working as a copyist, carpenter, and even builder. His abstemiousness was typified in his custom of having "the plate of the Lord Jesus" on his table, on which he placed all the best morsels. These were then given to the poor. He wore a hair shirt and spent large portions of the night in prayer.

The nuns incurred the displeasure of King Henry II (reigned 1154-89), who accused them of aiding Thomas Becket (29 Dec.) in his escape to France after he had been condemned, for opposing the king in matters that Thomas saw as church prerogatives, at a council held in Northampton in 1164. Thomas, disguised as a Sempringham lay brother, had eluded the king's officers and taken refuge in the Order's houses in Lincolnshire before making his way south again to Kent and from there to France, where he was to spend six years in exile before returning to Canterbury and martyrdom. Gilbert had made no secret of his support for Thomas; he was summoned to the king to answer for his part in the affair but managed to obtain a pardon and immunity for himself and the Order.

He eventually accepted the post of master general of the Order, but his old age—and his old age is said to have been extreme, reaching the age of 106 (though allowance has to be made for errors of ignorance)—was blighted both by failing sight and by a revolt of the lay brothers, who complained of overwork on too little food. When he was nearly ninety, two of the lay brothers drew up a series of slanderous indictments against him, for which they obtained support and funds from dignitaries of both Church and State. They took their complaints to Rome, but the pope declared in favour of Gilbert, who took the rebels back, making some concessions in the matters of food and clothing. He delegated much of the adminstration of the Order to Roger of Malton in the years before his death.

By the time he died, there were some fifteen hundred members in thirteen houses of the Order, of which nine were double monasteries and the other four for canons only. Their number was to increase to twenty-six, all in England except for one in Scotland. All were dissolved under Henry VIII, when the Order died out.

His cult developed on a wide scale immediately after he died, and he was canonized a mere thirteen years later by Pope Innocent III (1198-1216). Some of his relics were supposedly taken by King Louis VIII to the basilica of Saint-Sernin in Toulouse, but in reality these were of a Cistercian, Gilbert of Cîteaux.

His Life was written by John Capgrave, in *Bulletin of the John Rylands Library* 55 (1972-3), pp. 112-87; also edited by J. J. Munro for the Early English Text Society (1910). See also R. Graham, *St Gilbert of Sempringham and the Gilbertines* (1901); D. Knowles, *The Monastic Order in England* (1949), pp. 205-7; "The Revolt of the Lay Brothers of Sempringham," *E.H.R.* 1 (1935), pp. 465-87; R. Foreville, *The Book of St Gilbert* (1986); B. Golding, *Gilbert of Sempringham and the Gilbertine Order* (1995). His canonization has been studied by R. Foreville, *Un procès de canonization à l'aube du XIIIme siècle. Le livre de saint Gilbert de Sempringham* (1943); *O.D.S.*, pp. 203-5; *O.D.C.C.*, p. 558. *N.C.E.*, 6, pp. 481-2, provides an article on the Gilbertines with a map showing the distribution of their foundations.

St Phileas, *Bishop and Martyr* (306)

An adult convert to Christianity, Phileas was chosen as bishop of Thmuis in the Thebaid in Egypt. He was, according to Eusebius, "a man esteemed for his patriotic activities and public services, and for his work as a philosopher," and one who "made his mark by his secular learning too." He was arrested and imprisoned in about 303 in the great persecution under Diocletian; from prison, shortly before his own death, he wrote an eloquent letter to the faithful of his diocese describing the appalling tortures to which the martyrs were being subjected by the governor, and their steadfastness: ". . . the Christ-bearing martyrs endured every kind of suffering and every outrage that iniquity could invent, not once but twice in some cases; and then their armed guards competed not only in making all sorts of threats against them, but also in carrying them out. They never wavered, because perfect love casts out fear."

He suffered with a number of other bishops of the Egyptian churches: Eusebius mentions Hesychius, Pachymius, and Theodore; besides these "there were countless other prominent persons who are commemorated by the churches in their area and locality." Fragments of the Greek Acts of his martyrdom, written some fifteen years after his death, survive. They describe the final interview between him and the prefect Culcianus, who seems to have been impressed by his standing and wealth—"You now possess such abundant resources that you can nourish and sustain not only yourself and your family, but also a whole city"—and also moved by the fate of his young wife and children, who were present at his trial. To this he seems to have replied, like Jesus when told that his mother and brothers were seeking him (cf. Luke 8:19-21), that his family were the apostles and martyrs. To the direct question "Was Christ God?" he replied that he was, not that he spoke of himself as such but that he showed the power of God: ". . . he performed the works of God in power and actuality. He cleansed lepers, made the blind see, the deaf hear, the lame walk, the dumb speak . . .; he drove demons from [God's] creatures at a command; he cured paralytics, raised the dead to life, and performed many other signs and wonders." Surely, asked the prefect, presumably aware of Phileas' reputation as a philosopher, Jesus was only a common man, not to be compared with such as Plato? To this Phileas replied that, "Indeed, he was superior to Plato."

His brother tried to save him by telling the prefect that "Phileas has asked for pardon," but Phileas firmly denied this, telling Culcianus not to "listen to this unhappy man. Far from desiring the reversal of my sentence, I am greatly obliged to the emperors, to you and to the court, for through you I become a co-heir with Christ, and shall enter today into possession of his kingdom." He was led out and beheaded together (according to another, Latin account) with a Roman official who was also a Christian, named Philomorus, who had been a witness to the trial and had told the prefect not to try to subvert Phileas' faith and determination.

Eusebius' references and extracts are in *H.E.*, bk. 8: 9-10 and 13. See also *A.C.M.*, pp. 319-53. The virtually contemporary Greek account is preserved in the Bodmer papyrus: see V. Martin, *Papyrus Bodmer XX: Apologie de Philéas évêque de Thmuis* (1964). See also *AA.SS.*, Feb., 1, pp. 464-70; P. Delehaye in *Anal.Boll.* 40 (1922), pp. 299-314; F. Halkin on the manuscript evidence of his Acts, *Anal Boll.* 81 (1963), pp. 1-27; *O.D.S.*, pp. 396-7, with further references.

St Isidore of Pelusium, *Abbot* (*c.* 450)

Isidore was born probably in Alexandria and became a monk at an early age, apparently renouncing great wealth in order to imitate the life of St John the Baptist in the desert. He may later have been ordained priest. He was appointed abbot of a monastery in the region of Pelusium in Egypt and was regarded by his contemporaries as a model of religious perfection. St Cyril of Alexandria (27 June), who was his patriarch, is said to have admired him greatly, though this does not ring very true to character. Isidore was a considerable diplomat and counselled Cyril carefully. He modelled himself on St John Chrysostom (13 Sept). He was a great letter writer, and over two thousand of his letters, written in such elegant Greek that it was suggested that study of them could profitably replace study of the classics, are still extant. They show the breadth of his theological learning and are full of excellent instruction on piety, prudence, and humility.

The whole volume of *P.G.*, 78, is devoted to his life, doctrine, and letters; see also *P.L.*, 67, 573-4; *AA.SS.*, Feb., 1, pp. 473-9; *N.C.E.*, 7, pp. 673-4; *Bibl.SS.*, 7, 968-71; C. H. Turner in *J.T.S.* 6 (1905), pp. 70-85; M. Smith in *Harvard Theological Review* 47 (1954), pp. 205-10.

St Modan, *Abbot* (? *c.* 550)

A legend in the much later Aberdeen Breviary makes him a monk given to great austerity of life, chosen against his will to be abbot, but actual information about his life, or even the century in which he lived, is vague. He is supposed to have preached in the area of Stirling and Falkirk by the Firth of Forth. Butler associated him with Dryburgh, but this is unlikely, since there was almost certainly no monastery there before the twelfth century. He is said to have spent long periods in the mountains rapt in contemplation and finally to have retired to a remote spot near the sea, where he died. According to Sabine Baring-Gould: "When old, he retired among the mountains of Dumbarton, and there died. His body was kept till the change of religion, with honour, in the church of Rosneath." The new draft Roman Martyrology also places his death at the monastery of Rosneath, in Dumbartonshire, but gives his dates as seventh/eighth century. He is the titular saint of the high church in Stirling.

AA.SS., Feb., 1; pp. 502-4; *K.S.S.*, pp. 400-2, denies any connection with Dryburgh; Aberdeen Breviary for 4 Feb.; *Bibl.SS.*, 9, 512-3.

St Rabanus Maurus, *Abbot and Bishop* (*c.* 784-856)

Rabanus (or Rhabanus) was born probably in Mainz, though it has been claimed that he was an Irishman or a Scot. He was educated first by his parents and then at the monastery of Fulda, which had been founded by St Boniface (5 June) and had a great reputation for learning under its abbot, Bangulf. An exceptionally eager and able student, he was then sent to Tours to study under Alcuin, the English biblical scholar and ecclesiastical adviser to Charlemagne's court. Alcuin took a great liking to him and was responsible for his nickname "Maurus," after St Benedict's favourite disciple (15 Jan.). Under his guidance, Rabanus became an integral and influential part of the great movement of both scholarship and spirituality known as the Carolingian renewal, of which the twin pillars were interest in the Bible and love of the liturgy.

He worked in the great library that Charlemagne had founded at the monastery of Fulda, learning Greek, Hebrew, and some Syriac in order to be able to comment on the scriptures. He expounded various books of the Bible for King Louis the Pious and King Lothair. He contributed to the developing spirituality of the laity, living now not in time of persecution but as part of an organized Christian order: prayer and austerity were to be their way of life, but austerity was not to be excessive. He set out a programme for "manner of doing penance," suitable to those occupying a high position in the world, in a letter to Queen Judith, the second wife of Louis the Pious.

He compiled treatises of counsels to the clergy, emphasizing an ordered life of prayer and preaching revolving around the divine office rather than inculcating any very deep inner piety. His treatise *On the Formation of Clerics* devotes considerable space to the rites for administering Communion. In his *Ecclesiastical Discipline,* however, he emphasizes uprightness of heart and purity of intention as being more important than outward manifestations such as over rigorous asceticism and the dangers of the *peregrinatio.* His *De modo poenitentiae* likewise sets out a theology of repentance and confidence in divine forgiveness rather than a list of severe penances, and he lays stress on "the joy that is to come." In two later books written for his friend Hatto Bonosus, with whom he had studied at Tours and who was to succeed him as abbot of Fulda, he develops a doctrine of contemplation linked with purity of heart, showing how desire for God in this life will bring us to the heights of contemplation.

His scripture commentaries, in common with others of the movement, laid no claim to originality but drew heavily on the Fathers and Origen: some were indeed taken bodily from Origen, in whom he admired the emphasis on the spiritual as opposed to the literal sense of scripture. He admitted openly that he had taken his commentary on Leviticus from that of Hesychius of Jerusalem. The purpose of his commentaries was to show the redemptive values of the scriptures themselves and to form a technique of meditating on them. He was also a contributor to the new hymns and poems, usually derived from the Psalms, being introduced into public prayer, and some of his compositions are still in use today. The best known of the hymns attributed to him is *Veni, creator spiritus,* "Come Holy Ghost, creator, come," or "Come Holy Ghost, our souls inspire." His treatises for the clergy define how these new devotions are to be used, as an "act" of contrition, adoration, and supplication. The main theme runing through his compositions and his instructions in treatises and letters is the glory of the victorious Redeemer, who is to be served by all. Christ's sceptre is the cross, and Rabanus composed a great treatise in praise of the Holy Cross illustrated with complicated figures on a background of letters which make up a poem: the first is the basis for the well-known hymn "King of Kings and Lord of Lords."

His writing was combined with a full and busy monastic life. In 805 he had to contend with a famine followed by an outbreak of pestilence. A few years later he was taken away from his books by the abbot and ordered to join in the physical labour of building works to extend the monastery. He was ordained priest in 815 and resumed his scholarly work, including teaching, becoming master of the monastic school. In 822 he was elected abbot, and during his term he oversaw the completion of building work on the monastery, as well as the building of one or two other monasteries and churches or oratories on all the estates belonging to Fulda. He was also in demand for a busy schedule of councils and synods held in various cities.

He was personally austere, abstaining from wine and meat and careful to follow all the observances laid down by his Order, despite the inroads these made on his time for study and writing. He was known for his great devotion and obedience to the Holy See, taking this so far that he was known as "the pope's slave." He also had a profound aversion to heresy in all forms, regarding all heretics as Antichrist, and was equally averse to new developments in dogma.

He resigned his abbacy to Hatto in around 840 and seems to have lived in retirement for some years. In 847, however, he was, at the age of seventy-one, elected archbishop of Mainz. Three months after his election he held a synod, which imposed tighter observance of the laws of the Church in a number of ways affecting his clergy. This was so unpopular that a number of them even plotted against his life, but the plot was discovered, and he forgave those responsible for it. At a second synod in 852 he condemned the teaching of a monk named Gottschalk, whose one-sided interpretation of Augustine's doctrines on grace and predestination had led him over the boundaries of orthodoxy. He visited his diocese with unflagging energy almost up to the time of his death, taking capable priests with him, preaching and reconciling. During another famine he fed three hundred people at his house every day. Eventually his health gave way, and after a short period spent bedridden he died in 856. He is especially venerated in Germany, and German martyrologies often describe him as a Doctor of the Church, though he does not have this as an official title and is not described as such by Baronius.

A Life by his disciple Rudolf is in *P.L.*, 107; *AA.SS.*, Feb, 1; and *M.G.H., Scriptores*: this Life is claimed by *N.C.E.*, 12, pp. 37-8, to be unreliable. The *N.C.E.* article reproduces a miniature of him being presented to St Martin, from the Vatican Library. His works occupy *P.L.*, 107 to 112, but there is no complete critical edition. See also *H.C.S.*, 2, ch. 4, with further refs.; *Bibl.SS.*, 10, 1339.

St Nicholas the Studite, *Abbot* (863)

He was born at Sydonia (the modern Canea) in Crete. His parents took him, aged nine, to the school attached to the monastery of Studius, of which his uncle Theophanes was abbot. He studied there until he reached the age of eighteen, when he entered the monastery. This was the time of the second outbreak of the Iconoclast conflict: supported by the Eastern emperor Leo the Armenian, the Icononclasts persecuted the orthodox in Constantinople and Greece, forcing Nicholas, along with the patriarch of Constantinople, Nicephorus (13 Mar.), and the great abbot of Studius, Theodore (11 Nov.), into exile. Leo was then murdered, and they were allowed to return. Theodore died in 826, and Nicholas became a great leader of the community. The next emperor, Theophilus, caried on the persecution until he died in 842, when his widow, Theodora, who took the orthodox view of images, restored them to churches and recalled the monks and others who had been banished.

Under Emperor Michael III there began a great dispute that was to have far-reaching consequences: in 858 Michael deposed Patriarch Ignatius of Constantinople (23 Oct.) and appointed his nominee Photius (venerated by the Greek Orthodox Church on 6 Feb.) in his place. Pope Nicholas I ("the Great," 858-

67; 13 Nov.) objected to this procedure, declaring Ignatius still patriarch. The dispute involved the major questions of the relative authority of Church and State, Rome and Constantinople. Nicholas the Studite took the side of Ignatius, refused to have any dealings with Photius, and went into voluntary exile. The emperor ordered him to return, but he refused, whereupon Michael appointed another abbot in his place. He spent several years wandering but was then arrested and held in his own monastery in strict confinement. Pope Nicholas wanted him to appear as a witness on behalf of Ignatius when he restored the latter to the patriarchate in 863, but his imprisonment rendered him unable to comply. Michael III was murdered in his turn in 867, and his successor, Basil, restored Ignatius and wanted to reinstate Nicholas as abbot. Nicholas refused the appointment, pleading his advanced age. He died surrounded by his monks and was buried beside his great predecessor, St Theodore.

P.G., 105, 863-925; *AA.SS.*, Feb., 1, pp. 544-57, has a Life by a contemporary monk of his monastery; see also *Anal.Boll.* 41 (1923), pp. 290-4, 306-10, for biographical material on Nicholas in the Life of St Evaristus the Faster printed there. *N.C.E.*, 10, p. 246, dates the Life to 916 and calls it "a most interesting document." See also F. Dvornik, *The Photian Schism*, p. 240; *Oxford Dictionary of Byzantium*, 2, pp. 14-71.

St Joan of France, *Foundress* (1464-1505)

Also known as Joan of Valois, Joan was the daughter of King Louis XI (reigned 1461-83) and his wife, Charlotte of Savoy. She was physically handicapped from birth, possibly hunchbacked or probably suffering from dwarfism (though both descriptions may not be technically accurate and may be no more than exaggerations of the fact that she was undersized and plain). Her father was unable to feel any affection for her because of her appearance and at one point even tried to kill her. She was betrothed at the age of eight days—a mere pawn in dynastic intrigues—and in 1476 was married to her father's cousin Louis, duke of Orleans, presumably not out of any great family feeling. Louis' treatment of her was no better than her father's. Her brother inherited the throne of France as Charles VIII (1483-98) on the death of their father and tried to have Louis executed for organizing a rebellion against him, but Joan pleaded on his behalf, and his life was spared. He then succeeded Charles on the throne, reigning from 1498 to 1515 as Louis XII and becoming known as "father of the people." His supposed benignancy did not, however, extend to his wife. He tried to have his marriage to Joan annulled, on the grounds that he had been forced into it against his will by his cousin, in order to be free to marry Anne, Charles VIII's widow. She would bring her inheritance of Brittany under the French crown. Commissaries sent at his request by Pope Alexander VI (pope from 1492 to 1503) to examine the case decided in his favour, and Joan's marriage was annulled in 1498, though the grounds given were consanguinity rather than defect of intention.

She had already sought comfort in religion against her husband's harsh treatment of her and made no objection to the annulment. Her husband rewarded her for her acquiescence with the duchy of Berry, the town of Pontoise, and other properties. She went to live in Bourges, devoting her life entirely to prayer and works of charity. Her confessor was a Franciscan friar later to be beatified as Gabriel Mary (27 Aug.), or "Gabriel ab Ave Maria," as Pope Leo X nicknamed him. He helped her to establish a foundation in the town, devoted to "the ten virtues of Our Lady," begun with eleven girls from a local school as postulants; some of these were not yet ten years old. He drew up a rule for them, which eventually received papal approval, and they became known as the Annonciades of Bourges. Joan was allowed to make a form of profession into the new Order on the feast of Pentecost 1504 without going through the usual novitiate. She did so in dramatic fashion: on this day the nobility traditionally gathered to pay her homage as duchess of Berry. She received them with a splendid banquet, put on the royal insignia, then went into the church and renounced her title and all her possessions. She died less than a year after her profession. The Order survived under the direction of the Franciscans into the twentieth century, and she was canonized by Pope Pius XII in the "Holy Year" of 1950.

Bibl.SS., 6, 560-5; *N.C.E.*, 7, p. 993; *AA.SS.*, Feb., 1, pp. 579-96; *A.A.S.* 16 (1949), pp. 151-2; *F.B.S.*, pp. 114-6. There are biographies in French by M. de la Clavière (1883); de Flavigny (1896; Eng. trans. *Daughter of France*, 1900); M. Cagnac (1930); A. Girard (1950). For the history of the Order see J. F. Bonnefoy, *Chronique de l'Annonciade* (1937); A. Redier, *Jeanne de France* (Eng. trans., 1946). In English, J. Gibbons, *Our Lady's Own Order* (1937), includes a biography. Two works were published for her canonization: de Levis-Mierpoix, *Princess and Saint* (1950); A. M. C. Forster, *The Good Duchess: St Joan of France* (1950).

Bd John Speed, *Martyr* (1594)

One of the group of four known as the "Durham martyrs of 1594," John Speed, also known as Spence, was a layman. Biographical details are scarce, probably because of his lay status: he was hanged in the city of Durham on 4 February 1594 for aiding and abetting priests, leading them from one safe house to another. Any form of assistance to priests had been made a capital offence under the Supremacy of the Realm Act of 1585. According to Challoner, he died "with constancy, despising the proffers that were made to him to bring him to conform."

The other Durham martyrs were John Boste, a priest, hanged, drawn, and quartered on 24 July; George Swallowell, a convert clergyman, executed at Darlington on 26 July; and John Ingram, a priest, also hanged, drawn, and quartered on 26 July, at Gateshead. All four were beatified among the eighty-five martyrs of England, Scotland, and Wales in 1929.

M.M.P., pp. 197, 202-8, 597-600; *Bibl.SS.*, 11, 1345; *N.C.E.*, 9, p. 328.

St Joseph of Leonessa (1556-1612)

Born at Leonessa near Spoleto in Umbria, then part of the Papal States, he was christened Eufranio, taking the name Joseph in religion when he made his profesion as a Capuchin friar at the age of eighteen. He developed great powers as a preacher, and in 1587 he was sent to a suburb of Constantinople as a missioner to Christians there, who included large numbers of galley-slaves. He became infected during an outbreak of plague but recovered. He was arrested for preaching Christianity to the Muslims, imprisoned twice, condemned to death, and tortured by being hung from a gibbet with a hook through one hand and one foot. When this failed to kill him, his sentence was commuted to banishment. Franciscan hagiography records this as a miraculous deliverance.

He returned to Leonessa, where he continued his preaching and missionary work, preaching at least "two or three and sometimes even seven or ten times a day. Neither bad roads nor rain or snow could stop him, so great was his desire to win souls for Jesus Christ" (*Auréole Séraphique*). He continued in this way, begging his bread, sleeping on boards, and wearing an old patched habit for twenty years, until he was afflicted by cancer. He retired to the monastery of Amatrice and underwent two operations, of course without any sort of anaesthetic; these were not succesful, and he died on 4 February 1612. He was beatified in 1737 and canonized in 1746.

Bibl.SS., 6, 1305-7; B.G., Feb., pp. 111-2, drawing on the Acts of beatification (1737) and canonization (1746); *Auréole Séraphique*, 1, pp. 157-9; *F.B.S.*, pp. 87-8; *N.C.E.*, 7, p. 1117. See also F. Brennan, *St Joseph of Leonessa* (1912). There is a Life in Italian: G. da Belmonte, *Vita di S. Giuseppe di Leonessa* (1896), and one in French: P. Ernest-Marie, *Le protégé des anges* (1936).

St John de Britto, *Martyr* (1647-93)

He was born in Portugal to a noble family connected with the court and as a child was the favourite companion of the *infante*, Don Pedro. His ambition, however, was to be a Jesuit missionary in the spirit of St Francis Xavier (3 Dec.), and at the age of fifteen he joined the Society of Jesus. He was a brilliant student who could have had a glittering academic career in Europe, but he insisted on his missionary vocation and in 1673 set sail for Goa with sixteen fellow Jesuits. He was to spend the rest of his life there, apart from one brief recall to Portugal.

He was appointed superior of the Madura mission and adopted the method pioneered by Fr de Nobili, dressing and eating like the indigenous population and abandoning any claim to superiority on the grounds of European origin. He followed the ascetic practice of a *sannyasi*, much respected by Hindus, including Brahmins. This had enabled the early Jesuit missionaries to achieve success with both high and low castes. They had made large numbers of converts and reconciled the Christians of the Syrian rite to Rome in 1599, though a serious schism in 1653 caused a fresh break with the West, largely resolved in 1662. John and his companions and their Indian catechists suffered constant persecution and occasional torture at the hands of Hindus, whipped up by the general state of insecurity in the country. In 1686 he was tortured so severely that he was given up for dead, and his recovery was regarded as miraculous.

He was summoned back to Lisbon, but despite the pleas of King Pedro II and the papal nuncio that he should remain there, he insisted on returning to India, where he laboured for three more years, until he was put to death at Oriur, near Ramuad, as a result of the machinations of a wife of the local Rajah, whom he had converted to Christianity and so from polygamy. After being held in prison for some time while the Rajah tried to find a way of avoiding the execution, ordered on the grounds that his teaching subverted the worship of the Hindu gods, he was beheaded before a large crown in the morning of 4 February 1693. King Pedro ordered a solemn service of thanksgiving in Lisbon, which John's mother attended, dressed for a celebration, not in mourning. He was canonized in 1947.

His brother, F. Pereira de Britto, wrote a Life: *Historia do Nascimento, Vida e Martirio do Beato João de Britto* (1852), which contains a long letter written by his companion Fr Francis Laynes a week after his martyrdom. Several of John's letters are in J. Bertrand, *La Mission du Maduré*, 3 (1850). In English there is an account written at the time of his canonization, mainly for young people: A. Saultière, *Red Sand* (1947). On the Malabar Christians see D. Attwater, *The Eastern Catholic Churches* (n.e. 1937). See also *N.C.E.*, 7, p. 1037; A. Bessières, *Le nouveau François Xavier* (1946).

R.M.

St Eutychius, martyr of Rome (? second century)

SS Papias, Diodorus, Claudian and Conon, martyrs in Pamphylia under Decius (third century)

St Laurence, bishop of Spoleto (fourth century)

St Aventinus of Troyes, hermit (fourth century)

St Aventinus, bishop of Chartres (*c.* 520)

ST AGATHA
Gold pincers on a red field.

51

5

ST AGATHA, *Martyr* (date unknown)

St Agatha has retained her place in the Universal Calendar following the reforms of 1969, even though nothing that can be called historical fact is known of her life. There is, however, good evidence of an early cult, with many versions of her legend recorded in both Greek and Latin, the Greek being the earlier, with the Latin dating from the early sixth century. This means that however fictitious the details of her Acts, she cannot be dismissed as a mere fiction altogether. Her Acts, though, are more of an indication of the type of woman held up for veneration as a saint in the early centuries than anything else. She is also the subject of an illustrated manuscript version of her passion, originating in Burgundy and dating from the late tenth century or early eleventh century, which illustrates the fact that only Lives of female saints show sexual mutilation: "Even among the early martyrs there are significant differences between men and women. Men are tortured, but they are not sexually mutilated as are women like Agatha, often virgins who refused marriage" (Barbara Abou-El-Haj).

She is described as a wealthy young woman who had dedicated her virginity to Christ. This, then, rather than her life, is the most precious thing she has to offer. Her birthplace is assigned to either Palermo or Catania in Sicily, and she is said to have died at Catania, which has the stronger historical claim to be her birthplace, that for Palermo dating only from the sixth century. Among those who try to prise the precious gift she had vowed to Christ from her is a consul named Quintianus (base-born, as opposed to her high rank, according to *The Golden Legend*, which makes his offences worse). He used the imperial edict against Christians to have her brought before him, then placed in a brothel run by a woman with the appropriate name (or possibly nickname) of "Aphrodisia" and her six (or possibly nine) assistants, referred to as her daughters. In this her story parallels that of St Agnes (21 Jan.). All tricks, assaults, and threats to make her yield her virginity fail, so she stands, with Agnes and many others whose stories may depend on theirs, as an example of "virginity as a symbol of sacred power, a concrete realization within this world of the divine spirit" (Eamon Duffy).

Quintianus then hands her over to be tortured, and her Acts dwell in a spirit of what has been described as "religious pornography" (Margaret Miles) on the tortures inflicted on her, culminating in the cutting off of her breasts, which were placed on a platter. The same details also occur in accounts of the martyrdom of St Eulalia of Mérida (10 Dec.), whose cult is evidenced in the martyrology of Jerome, the calendar of Carthage, and the songs of Venantius Fortunatus (14 Dec.), as is that of St Agatha, suggesting a common stock of images considered appropriate to such stories.

Perhaps because further details of her tortures involve her being rolled over live coals, she is invoked against fire in general. This may, though, be an extension of her protection against eruptions of Mount Etna, because she is associated with Sicily, and her legend states that after her death a flow of lava from Mount Etna was miraculously diverted by her silken veil held up on a staff. This is last recorded as happening in the 1840s, and her veil is still carried in solemn procession on her feast-day in Catania. By extension she protects against earthquakes everywhere. She is also patron saint of bell-founders. The association is ancient and certain, but the reason has not been determined: it may be that it derives from her protection against volcanic eruptions and fire, as bells were rung to warn of both. Another explanation given is that the molten metal involved in casting bells suggests the flow of molten lava. Her breasts also brought a more appropriate patronage, as she is invoked against diseases of the breast. Her breasts on a dish were often also mistaken for loaves in the Middle Ages, from which the custom arose of blessing bread brought on a dish to the altar on her feast-day.

Pope St Damasus I (366-84) composed a hymn in her honour. Two churches were dedicated to her in Rome in the sixth century, including one built by Pope Symmachus (498-514) on the Appian Way, now in ruins. Pope St Gregory the Great (590-604) had rich shrines made for some of her relics in Rome, then moved them to the monastery of San Stefano on the island of Capri. Other relics remained in Catania until 1840, when they were moved to Constantinople.

Whatever the facts behind her legend, Agatha remains one of the best-loved and most-invoked saints in Christian devotional life.

Agatha's Acts are in *AA.SS.*, Feb., 1, pp. 595-656 (1658 ed.); English Lives in C. Horstman, ed., *The Early South English Legendary* (E.E.T.S., 1887); and *ibid.*, *Early English Legendary* (1881); also in *The Golden Legend* (Princeton ed.) vol. 1, pp. 154-7. See also *Anal.Boll.* 68 (1950), pp. 58ff. for an encomium by Methodius of Constantinople. *O.D.S.*, pp. 6-7; *Bibl.SS.*, 1, 310-5; *N.C.E.*, 1, pp. 196-7; H. Musurillo, *Acts of the Christian Martyrs* (1972). There is a 2-volume Italian work on her by B. G. Consoli (1951) with further bibliography of works in Italian. For the representation of the female body in Christian art see M. R. Miles, *Carnal Knowing: Female Nakedness and Religious Meaning in the Christian West* (U.S. 1989; U.K. 1992), esp. pp. 53-77, with bibliography pp. 231-42. On the medieval cult of virginity see E. Duffy, *The Stripping of the Altars: Traditional Religion in England c. 1400-c. 1580* (1992), pp. 172-3. For further representations in art see *Saints in Italy*, pp. 4-5; on portrayals in England, *E.M.C.A.*, pp. 108-9. On the illustrated manuscript of her passion, see M. Carrasco, "An Early Illustrated Maunscript of the Passion of St Agatha (Paris, Bibl. Nat. MS lat. 5594)," *Gesta* 24 (1985), pp. 19-32 (cited in B. Abou-El-Haj, *The Medieval Cult of Saints: Formations and Transformations* [1997], p. 149; see also pp. 27, 137).

She features among the virgin martyrs in the mosaics in the basilica of Sant' Apollinare Nuovo in Ravenna. She also features in a splendid thirteenth-century mosaic in the Capella Palatina of the Palazzo Reale in Palermo, and there is a statue of her in the Duomo of Milan. In England there is a medieval wooden statue of her, with her breasts exposed and a broad knife thrust into the upper part of one, in the church of Wiggenhall St Mary in Norfolk; on painted panels at Heavitree and Ugborough in Devon she is shown with a sword thrust through both breasts; next to her in both St Lucy (13 Dec.) has a sword piercing her neck, which is a more accurate representation of the normal Roman *coup de grâce*; in stained glass in two Norfolk churches she is shown holding a flesh-hook, presumably a reference to more details of her tortures, when her flesh was torn with hooks. The element in her legend, found in *The Golden Legend*, that after her death her veil saved the people from an eruption of Mount Etna, is responsible for her depiction with a flowing veil, as in glass in Winchester Cathedral. The best-known later representation of her mutilation is probably Tiepolo's *Martyrdom of St Agatha* in the Gemäldergalerie, Berlin; there is a similar painting by Sebastiano del Piombo in the Pitti Gallery in Florence.

St Avitus of Vienne, *Bishop* (*c.* 525)

Avitus (Alcimius Ecdicius Avitus) is one of the many bishops of Merovingian Gaul to be canonized. This was particularly common of bishops associated with the royal families. Avitus was born in the Auvergne; his father, Isychius, was elected bishop of Vienne on the death of St Mamertus of Vienne (11 May), and his son succeeded him in the see in 490. This was before the Frankish king Clovis had been baptized and at a time when the king of Burgundy, which then embraced much of south-eastern France and south-western Switzerland, was an Arian of Vandal descent named Gundebald. Avitus was therefore not at this time a natural royal favourite but seems to have won the respect of pagan and Arian ruler alike. Living in a murderous time, he has been blamed for condoning Gundebald's murder of his brother.

The Burgundians crossed the Alps southward into Liguria in the early years of the sixth century and brought back a large number of captives. Avitus, according to Ennodius, who mentions him in the Life he wrote of St Epiphanius of Pavia (21 Jan.), who was on the same mission and who died as a result of a fever caught at the time, was responsible for ransoming a great number of these. He was then responsible for the conversion of Gundebald's son Sigismund to the Christian faith and later for bringing him to repentance for the murder of his son Sigeric as a result of a false charge being brought against him by his stepmother. So deep was his remorse that he rebuilt the abbey of Agaune (or Saint-Maurice) in Switzerland and after his death at the hands of three sons of Clovis was venerated as a saint (1 May).

Avitus was also known for his learning and for his writings, some of which survive: a collection of five poems with the general title *De spiritualis historiae gestis;* a separate one on virginity dedicated to his sister Fuscina and other nuns; seventy-eight letters; three complete homilies and fragments of some thirty others. His lost works have been described as "innumerable." One of the letters is addressed to Clovis on the occasion of his baptism by St Remigius of

Reims (13 Jan.) in 498 or 499. Ennodius and others praised him for his charity to the poor and other virtues as well as for his learning.

His works are in *P.L.*, 59, 191-398; they have been published in French: U. Chevalier, *Oeuvres complètes de S. Avit* (1890). The Bollandists published a short Latin Life in *B.H.L.*, 1, pp. 57-63 (1898; rp. 1949). See also *AA.SS.*, Feb., 1, pp. 666-74; G. Bardy, *L'Eglise et les derniers Romains* (1948); *Bibl.SS.*, 2, 658-62; *N.C.E.*, 1, p. 1138; Gregory of Tours, *History of the Franks* (1979), 2, pp. 73-4; *P.B.*, 2, pp. 301-10, with the comment that "ses écrits perdus sont innombrables." There are nineteenth-century Lives by Parizel (1850); V. Cucheval (1863); H. Denkinger (1890).

St Bertulf (*c.* 705)

More seems to be known—or at least related—about Bertulf's relics than about his life, which suggests that a competitive local cult is responsible for what information we have. Bertulf, or Bertoul, was born to a pagan family in Germany and migrated to Flanders while still young. Favourably impressed by the Christian society he found there, he received instruction and was baptized. Count Wambert made him his steward, an office he carried out wisely but making due provision for the poor. Such a position of power inevitably gave rise to murmurings against him, but Wambert and his wife Homburga continued to place their trust in him. They took him on pilgrimage to Rome with them, and Wambert eventually made him heir to his estates at Renty (or Renescure), a village on the present canal between Aire and Saint-Omer. After their death Bertulf organized their burial in one of the four churches the count had built and then retired to a monastery he founded at Renty, where he spent the remainder of his life.

His remains were enshrined in an iron casket in Ghent; "for many centuries it was believed that, at the approach of danger, the dead abbot knocked against the side of his own shrine" (S. Baring-Gould). His bones were scattered by the Huguenots in 1578. In art he is shown in monastic habit, distributing alms, with an eagle with its wings extended. This refers to a legend that he was protected in this way from rain in a heavy shower.

AA.SS., Feb., 1, 681-94; *Bibl.SS.*, 3, 116-7; *N.C.E.*, 2, p. 362. *Anal.Boll.* 17 (1898) contains a review of J. Ferrant, *Esquisse historique sur le culte et les reliques de S. Bertulphe de Renty en l'église d'Harlebeke* (1897), which it describes as a scholarly work. See also *B.G.*, Feb., p. 139, cited above.

St Adelaide of Vilich (960-*c.* 1015)

Adelheid (in German) was born in Germany, the daughter of Count Megengose of Guelder, who founded the convents of Vilich on the Rhine near Cologne and St Mary's in Cologne. Adelaide was abbess of both and died in the latter. She introduced the Rule of St Benedict to Vilich in about 1000. St Heribert, archbishop of Cologne (d. 1021; 16 Mar.), had a great respect for her and consulted her widely on both diocesan matters and the politics in which he was caught up as imperial chancellor. She ensured that her nuns should know Latin, in order to be able to follow the choir offices properly. She is recorded as having made great efforts on behalf of the poor during a famine. She was entombed in Vilich (now Pützchen bei Vilich), where she is still venerated and invoked against diseases of the eye, on account of a healing spring from where her tomb (now disappeared) once stood. She was portrayed in the Middle Ages with a book representing the *Rule of St Benedict,* in the seventeenth and eighteenth centuries as an abbess holding a model of a church from which issues the healing source. Her cult was confirmed on 27 January 1966.

There is a Life by a contemporary nun, Bertrada, in *AA.SS.*, Feb., 1, pp. 719-21. See also B.G., Feb., pp. 140-1; *N.C.E.*, 1, p. 126; *Bibl.SS.*, 1, 236-7.

R.M.

St Abraham, bishop of Arbela (Assyria), martyr under King Shapur II of Persia (345)

St Theodosius of Antioch, founder of monastery near Rhosus (Cilicia) (*c.* 430)

St Genuinus, bishop of Sabion (Tyrol) (605)

SS Indract and Companions, reputedly martyred on pilgrimage to Glastonbury (*c.* 710)

St Vodoaldus, Irish/Scottish recluse of Soissons (*c.* 720)

St Modestus, monk and missionary bishop in Carinthia (*c.* 772)

St Jerome, bishop of Nevers (Burgundy) (815)

St Polyeuctus, bishop of Constantinople (970)

St Sabas the Younger, abbot in Calabria (995)

St Albinus, bishop of Brixen (Tyrol) (1005)

St Agatha, wife of Count Paul of Carinthia (1024)

Bd Frances Mézière, martyr (1794)—see "Martyrs of the French Revolution," 2 Jan.

6

The Martyrs of Japan:
ST PAUL MIKI AND COMPANIONS

Worldwide missionary endeavour followed closely on the heels of the voyages of discovery and conquest made, first by the Spanish and Portuguese, from 1492 onward. Japan itself had become known to Europeans by accident when a Portuguese vessel bound for Thailand was driven off course by a typhoon and eventually made land in Japan. The Portuguese returned there in 1548-9 with mainly commercial missions, but Bishop John of Albuquerque accompanied them in 1548 and baptized the first Japanese Christians, and in 1549 St Francis Xavier (3 Dec.) accompanied them. He understood that missions to countries with their own highly developed civilizations could succeed only if missionaries learned to adapt so as to be able to communicate the Faith in intelligible terms, and in Japan—aiming in the Jesuit tradition for the centres of influence in a society—he set out to convert the people through winning the emperor to the Faith, believing that this would bring the state religious structure over to Christianity. But he found that the emperor's rule was effective in name only, with the country in a state of anarchy and power held largely by local lords, or *daimyos*. He also found that it was not possible for Christians simply to engage in dialogue with Buddhists as though different terms referred to similar concepts for each.

By 1551, when Francis returned to Goa, there were some one thousand converts, all from the lower classes. Francis' Jesuit companion Fr Cosmas de Torres was left in charge of these converts, who made up three Christian communities. The first *daimyo* to embrace the Christian faith was baptized in 1563, and others followed, as well as members of the samurai warrior caste and Buddhist monks, or *bonzes*. The people began to follow in increasing numbers, with several mass conversions taking place, until their numbers were in the tens of thousands. The missionaries respected Japanese culture and were prepared to work within it. This approach produced a large number of self-motivated indigenous leaders, priests, catechists, and other lay leaders. (One of these, the samurai Takayama Ukon, has been proposed for beatification, though he was not martyred.)

Internal political changes in Japan had already begun to affect the missionaries' fortunes. By the time they first arrived the emperor was a virtually powerless figurehead, and real power was passing to the commander-in-chief of the imperial army, who became known as the *shogun*. The "shogunate" is considered to have begun with Nobunaga in the 1560s; he succeeded in reducing the power of the *daimyos*. In the early 1580s the emperor appointed Hideyoshi as his regent, with almost unlimited authority; he did not take the title *shogun* but exercised effective power in the manner of a military dictator. He had originally been friendly to the missionaries but for various reasons turned against Christianity, and in 1587 he issued an edict expelling all the missionaries. The edict was not carried out, but the missionaries were forced to act with greater circumspection. Nevertheless, in the ten years from 1587 the Jesuits made a further sixty-five thousand converts. In 1588 Japan was finally elevated to a separate diocese, with the bishop's residence at Funai.

The Portuguese missionaries in Japan, unlike those in the colonies, received no support from the State and had to find means of supporting themselves. They engaged in the silk trade and also rented out houses which had been given to them. These procedures caused dissensions among themselves and also among their converts, though the numbers had grown to some 150,000 under Fr Torres' successor, Fr Francisco Cabral, despite his opposition to the type of accomodation specified by St Francis Xavier. The dissensions among the missionaries and their converts were largely removed by the skill of the apostolic visitor, Fr Alesandro Valignano, who reformed the mission and insisted on a return to the principles of Francis Xavier. He made the missionaries learn the language thoroughly and established two seminaries, which paved the way for an indigenous Japanese diocesan and regular clergy to come into existence. The union of the Spanish and Portuguese crowns in 1580 enabled Spanish missionaries to enter the area, which had previously been reserved to the Portuguese by the pope. The Jesuits had been granted an exclusive right by Pope Gregory XIII, but in 1585 Sixtus V established the province of San Gregorio, giving the Franciscans the right to set up missions in China and other Asian countries, which they took to include Japan, and in 1593 the Spanish governor in Manila sent a delegation of four Franciscans. They were followed by others; foundations were made in Mikayo (now Kyoto), Osaka, and Nagasaki, and within three years twenty thousand had been converted. The Franciscans in fact were already experienced in working with Japanese people: the Japanese travelled widely in Asia at the time, and many were living in the Philippines, where the Franciscans were established. Gonsalvo Garcia, one of the first martyrs, had previously lived in Japan and was fluent in the language; he became a Franciscan Brother in the Philippines and enabled the Franciscans to begin a mission to the ethnic Japanese there.

The Franciscans were at first more succesful at gaining Hideyoshi's approval than the Jesuits had been and achieved considerable success, but the missions were divided by dissensions between the two Orders and by even deeper rivalries between Spaniards and Portuguese. Hideyoshi, still fundamentally opposed to Christianity, exploited these divisions and was then presented with a pretext for more drastic action: the pilot of a Spanish vessel, the *San Felipe*, driven on to an unauthorized area of the coast of Japan by a storm when bound from Manila to Mexico, is supposed to have told him that the Spanish and Portuguese used missionaries only as preparation for conquest. The result of this was the first martyrdom of Nagasaki, in which six Franciscans, three Japanese Jesuits, and sixteen other Japanese (and one Korean) Christians were put to death. They had part of their left ears cut off and were led through various towns with blood streaming down their faces to warn others of the consequences of being Christian. They were tied to crosses with cords and chains on a hill outside Nagasaki, the crosses were raised in prepared holes, and they were run through with lances. This took place on 5 February 1597. Their garments were collected as relics, and miracles were ascribed to their intercession. They were canonized by Pope Pius IX on 8 June 1862.

The Franciscans were Frs Peter Baptist Blásquez, the commissary of the friars in Japan; Martin de Aguirre; Francis Blanco; Brs Francis de la Parilla; Philip de las Casas, who had been on board the *San Felipe* and was sailing to Mexico to be ordained; and Gonsalvo García. The priests were all Spaniards; Philip had been born in Mexico City and Gonsalvo in Bassein, near Bombay, of either Indian parentage (which would make him the first Indian to be canonized) or part Indian and part Portuguese. The most prominent of the Japanese Jesuits was Paul Miki, who came from a noble family and who had become a distinguished preacher. The other two were lay brothers (though, with Paul, given the title *presbyter* in the new draft Roman Martyrology): John Soan and James Kisai. The seventeen laymen were all Franciscan tertiaries; some were catechists and interpreters. They were Michael Cosaqui; his eleven-year-old son Thomas, one of the boys who served Mass for the friars; Thomas Danki, a pharmacist; Antony Doynan, another server, aged twelve; Leo Ibaraki, director of St Anne's hospital; his nine-year-old brother Louis, the third server; and his nephew Paul Ibaraki; Antony Doynan; Leo Karesuma; Matthias of Mikayo; Bonaventure of Mikayo; Joachim Saquior (or Saquijor or Seccakibara); Francis Kichi of Miyako, a native of Korea; Thomas Danki; John Quizia (or Quizuja or Kinoia); Gabriel Ize of Duisco; Paul Suzuki, director of St Joseph's hospital; Cosmas Raquisa (or Raquaja); Francis Danto; Peter Sequexein (or Sukejino). (The names vary in different lists; Mikayo is the contemporary name for Kyoto, where the victims were assembled: those with no known surname were designated "of Mikayo.") The last two named were not on the original list of twenty-four but refused to be parted from the rest of the company.

This first collective martyrdom failed to discourage the Franciscans, who resumed their work in Japan the following year. Indeed, it produced a fresh wave of conversions and a greater expansion of missionary activity. The Franciscans were joined by Spanish Dominicans and Augustinians from the Philippines, also taking advantage of the annulment of the exclusive rights previously enjoyed by the Jesuits. Despite the persecution the number of Christians in Japan reached some 300,000 by 1614. The first Japanese priests had been ordained in 1601.

Hideyoshi died in 1598, his death occasioning a renewed outbreak of wars among local lords. Tokugawa Ieyasu emerged as the victor of these and established a military dynasty that was to last until the Meiji restoration of 1865 opened the country officially to foreign trade and ushered in the modern Japan. At first Ieyasu appeared favourable to Christianity, which flourished in the early years of his rule. He changed his approach in around 1612, perhaps fearing that Christian *daimyos* might unite against the central government, possibly with outside help, and renewed persecution of the Christians. By this time the countries that had embraced the Reformation were becoming major players in world trade, and British and Dutch merchants were vying with the Spanish and Portuguese Catholic ones. At least according to Catholic accounts, it was the intrigues of Dutch Calvinist merchants that produced a fresh outbreak of persecution. Ieyasu isued an edict banning Christianity in 1603 followed with a decree banishing all foreign missionaries in 1614 and threatening all Japanese households with being burned alive should they have any dealings with Christians.

Eighteen Jesuits, seven Dominicans, six Franciscans, one Augustinian, and five diocesan priests defied the edict of banishment and remained in the country. The persecution grew in intensity, and every year there were many martyrdoms. In 1612 the Franciscan Luis Sotelo was condemned to death but won the support of the *daimyo* of Sendai, Date Mazamune, who sent him as his ambassador to the king of Spain and the pope, who appointed him bishop of eastern Japan. In 1617 one hundred died in the second mass martyrdom, including eighteen of the missionaries from the four Orders. Most prominent among the martyrs in this wave of persecution was Fr Alphonsus Navarete, a Spanish Dominican who had been sent to Japan from the Philippines. He was beheaded on 1 June 1617 together with the Augustinian Ferdinand Ayala and a Japanese catechist (see the separate entry for this date). In the same year John Baptist Machado, a Jesuit from Portugal, and Peter de Cuerva, a Spanish Franciscan, met their deaths, together with a Japanese catechist named Leo, who had been Fr John Baptist's server—the pattern of the first martyrdom being thus repeated. Fr John Baptist had worked unhindered for eight years in Nagasaki and was arrested only when he was sent to the Goto islands. Fr Peter was a linguist with an excellent command of Japanese. The two were imprisoned together and offered Mass daily up to the day of their execution. On the appointed day they heard each other's confession, said the litany of the saints together, and walked, crucifix in hand, to the place of execution, between Omura and Nagasaki. Here Fr Peter addressed the crowd, they embraced each other, and both died bravely.

The most common method of execution at first was by burning. Large crowds were usually assembled to watch the executions in the hope that this would stamp out Christianity through fear—though it sometimes had the opposite effect:

> This ordeal was witnessed by 150,000 people, according to some writers, or 30,000 according to other and in all probabililty more reliable chroniclers. When the faggots were kindled, the martyrs said *sayonara* (farewell) to the onlookers who then began to intone the *Magnificat*, followed by the psalms *Laudate pueri Dominum* and *Laudate Dominum omnes gentes*, while the Japanese judges sat on one side "in affected majesty and gravity, as in their favourite posture." Since it had rained heavily the night before, the faggots were wet and the wood burnt slowly; but as long as the martyrdom lasted, the spectators continued to sing hymns and canticles. When death put an end to the victims' suffering, the crowd intoned the *Te Deum*. (C. R. Boxer, *The Christian Century in Japan*, pp. 342-3, cited in translator's preface to *Silence* by Shusako Endo).

On 18 November 1619, twenty thousand people from the Nagasaki district were assembled to watch the burning to death of Br Leonard Kimura and four companions. Br Leonard was a Jesuit lay brother who had refused ordination because he felt himself unworthy. He was said to be a collateral descendant of another Kimura who had been among the first to befriend St Francis Xavier on his arrival in Japan. He had been an active catechist in the Nagasaki area, and even during the two and a half years he spent in prison had managed to baptize ninety-six people—fellow-prisoners or visitors. His four companions were two Japanese, a Korean, and a Portuguese; they had been accused of harbouring Fr Charles Spinola (10 Sept.) and other priests. Despite threats and promises all five remained steadfast in their witness to the last.

In 1622 twenty-two more martyrs were burned over a slow fire in Nagasaki, on 10 September. They included Dominicans, Franciscans, and Jesuits, who were still managing to enter the country despite the fate that fairly certainly awaited them, since the number of religious executed by now exceeded the number who remained after the edict of banishment. A further thirty, mostly Japanese converts, were beheaded. They included the catechist Augustine Ota, who was beheaded and thrown into the sea at Ichi. The executions were watched by a crowd of thirty thousand spectators. In 1624 the Franciscan bishop Luis Sotelo, who had entered his diocese two years earlier, was also burned over a slow fire. He sang the *Te Deum* as he died. From 1623 all Japanese had to declare their religious adherence publicly once a year. On 4 December that year, fifty Christians were taken out of the town of Yedo to be burned on a nearby hill. It is said that a Japanese nobleman riding by asked who these noble-looking criminals were, and on being told that they were Christians declared that he too was a Christian and ought to suffer with them. Among the crowd of onlookers at their execution were other Christians who fell to their knees and made their own profession of faith. Afraid that a riot might break out in support of the martyrs, the officials hurried the executions. Among those who died in 1627 was Luke Chiemon, a Japanese catechist beheaded at Nagasaki. These and other martyrs, to a total of 205, were beatified by Pope Pius IX in 1867.

From 1627 the form of public declaration of not being a Christian required was trampling on *fumie*, plaques imprinted with an image of the Virgin and Child. (A compelling description of this period can be found in Shusaku Endo's novel *Silence*.) Many thousands complied, making a mental reservation and not seeing this as apostasy. Many refused altogether, even if told that their hearts need not be in the trampling and all they were required to do was place a foot lightly on the image. Many of these *fumie* survive in museums, worn smooth by the—even light—pressure of tens of thousands of feet.

The authorities came to realize that making martyrs of missionaries would not achieve their ends. They had to force them to apostasize to have any effect on the mass of the faithful. This was achieved after more and more appalling means of torture were devised and applied. Eventually, in 1632, the Portuguese Jesuit provincial, Fr Christovão Ferreira, who had been a respected missionary and teacher in Japan for thirty-three years, gave the sign of apostasy after hours of torture by the method known as "the pit." This ingenious form of torture (*ana-tsurushi* in Japanese) was invented in the later stages of persecution specifically to get priests to apostasize. The victims were hung head downward from a gallows erected over a pit, tightly bound with ropes to restrict their circulation. It caused a slow and agonizing death from bleeding and suffocation, which could take up to three days. The third major group of canonized martyrs, St Laurence Ruiz and Fifteen Companions, were killed in this way between 1633 and 1637.

The final climax to persecution came with the the Shimbara Revolt of 1637-8. This was originally against excessive taxation by the magistrates of Nagasaki rather than against outright persecution of Christians, but it developed into a manifestation of Christian faith, with the insurgents carrying banners proclaiming devotion to the Blessed Sacrament and shouting the names of Jesus and Mary. The revolt was put down with extreme cruelty, some twenty-five thousand Christians being put to death. The Tokugawa Bafuku decided that no good could come of contact with foreigners; he cut all ties with Portugal and sealed Japan off from the rest of the world. Some missionaries still got through. Marcello Mastrilli came to make amends for Ferreira's apostasy; he died screaming in the pit but without apostasizing. A group of ten entered the country in 1643; they were all tortured into apostasy though most, if not all, later revoked their apostasy. One of them, who became the model for the hero of Shusako Endo's novel, died some forty years later, declaring himself still a Christian.

Young boys were executed with adults: the apparent barbarism of this has to be understood in the context of the Japanese doctrine that guilt apportioned to the head of a household extended to his whole family.

During the period 1614-40, between five and six thousand people are estimated to have died for the Christian faith in Japan. Christianity then went into hiding, but it was not entirely destroyed. When Japan was reopened to the outside world in 1865, thousands came out of hiding, asking the newly-arrived Westerners for statues of Jesus and Mary, speaking a smattering of Portuguese and Latin, clinging to some relics of the priests their ancestors had known and loved two centuries earlier. Old Christians in the Urukami valley and elsewhere still kept Franciscan names and named St Francis in their *Confiteor*. Today they are still numbered in thousands only, but the devout communities, mainly in Nagasaki and the islands of the Inland Sea, have perhaps more influence than their numbers would suggest.

AA.SS., Feb, 1, pp. 729-70; C. R. Boxer, *The Christian Century in Japan* (1951); Shusako Endo, trans. William Johnston, S.J., *Silence* (1969, 1976; King Penguin ed., 1988). Jedin-Holland, 2, pp. 710-2; L. Iriarte, O.F.M., *Franciscan History* (1979; Eng. trans. 1982), pp. 336-8. *N.C.E.*, 7, pp. 835-45, has a very full account detailing the different persecutions and giving the names of the martyrs; it also provides a full bibliography and illustrations. See also C. M. Cadeel, *Les Jésuites au Japon* (1583; rp., 1990); G. Boero, *Relazione della gloriosa Morte di 205 B. Martiri nel Giappone* (1867; French trans. *Les 205 martyrs du Japon*, 1968); L. C. Profillet, *Le martyrologe de l'Eglise au Japon*, 3 vols. (1897); *Anal.Boll.* 6 (1888), pp. 53-72; J. Laures, *Geschichte der katholischen Kirche in Japan* (1956); O. Carey, *Christianity in Japan* (1976).

Year-long celebrations were held from February 1997 to February 1998 in Bassein, India, to mark the fourth centenary of the martyrdom of St Gonsalvo Garcia (see p. 59, above), whom the Indians definitely honour as the first Indian saint as his mother was Indian, though his father was a Portuguese soldier. He is the second patron of the archdiocese of Bombay (after St Francis Xavier). At the closing ceremony Archbishop Ivan Dias of Bombay announced the setting-up of a new diocese of Bassein, the saint's birthplace. It has been claimed that he joined the Franciscans because the Jesuits were not willing to train and ordain "natives," but this refusal did not extend to the Japanese, for whom they had a high regard. They would not at the time, however, admit candidates form the Indian sub-continent even as Brothers. In the twentieth century, a large number of prominent Jesuits have been Indians.

St Vedast, *Bishop* (539)

Vedast (or Vaast) came either from western France or from the Périgord in the south-west but moved from there at a young age to the diocese of Toul in the Meuse region of eastern France, where he wanted to live as a hermit. The bishop, however, came to hear of him and ordained him priest in recognition of his qualities. At this time (496) King Clovis I had just won his victory over the Alemanni, which he attributed to his invocation of the Christian God worshipped by his wife, Clotilda, and was making his way to Reims to be baptized by his friend Remigius (13 Jan.). At Toul he asked for a priest to go with him and prepare him for baptism on the way. The bishop presented Vedast to him for that purpose, but it seems that Vedast had to exercise all his powers of persuasion and even to invoke supernatural powers.

On the way, we are told, Vedast prayed over a blind beggar sitting on a bridge over the River Aisne and restored his sight, which helped to confirm the king in his new faith. Vedast assisted Remigius in evangelizing the Franks until Remigius consecrated him bishop of Arras to the north-east. He entered the city in 499 to find it devastated after being sacked by the Vandals. His cathedral had been turned into a bear pit, and he found only the ruins of one church in which Christianity had been practised within living memory. Immense labours and perseverance over forty years, aided by another reported miracle of restoring sight, transformed the situation, and he left the church in Arras in a flourishing condition. According to Guérin he was "respectful toward the old, affable to the young, paternal with children. . . . What did he not do to win souls to Jesus Christ?" His name passed into English as "Foster," from which derives the dedication of a church to him in Foster Lane in London, which was rebuilt by Christopher Wren at the end of the seventeenth century. In French it became "Gaston."

In the tenth century there were widespread contacts between the district of Arras and England, which helped to develop his cult in England. There are churches dedicated to him in Norwich and Lincolnshire besides the one in London, and his feast features in several local calendars as well as in missals. His usual attribute in art is a wolf, with or without a goose in its mouth: he is said to have rescued a goose from a wolf and restored it alive to its poor owners. He is also shown with a child at his feet or a bear.

Two ancient Lives, one by Alcuin and the other by Jonas of Bobbio, are in *AA.SS.*, Feb., 1, pp. 790-823; also in *M.G.H., Scriptores merov.*, 3, pp. 399-427. There is another Life, by a monk of his monastery at Arras, in *P.L.*, 101, 663-82 (formerly erroneously attributed to Bede). See also *P.B.*, 2, pp. 329-36 (cited above); E. Guilbert, *S. Vaast, fondateur de l'église d'Arras* (1928); *N.C.E.*, 14, p. 585; *Bibl.SS.*, 12, 956-8; *O.D.S.*, p. 475. There is a privately printed *Life and Legend of St Vedast*, by W. and G. Sparrow (1896), in the British Library, and an edition of *Carmina Vedantina*, ed. W. Sparrow (1895). He features, with the wolf, in stained-glass windows at Long Melford and Blythburgh in Suffolk.

St Amandus, *Abbot and Bishop* (*c.* 584-*c.* 676)

Amandus (Amand) was a great missionary figure in Merovingian Gaul and the Low Countries and is known as the apostle of Flanders. Contemporary evidence of his life is scarce, but he is the subject of illustrated Lives dating from the eleventh and twelfth centuries, which ensured a major cult in the Middle Ages. He wrote a testament, which survives in a mainly authentic form, but the *Vita Amandi*, attributed to his disciple Baudemond of Elnone, was expanded and elaborated in the mid-ninth century by the monk-poet Milo, the head of the scriptorium at Elnone and one of a group of Carolingian writers engaged in expanding Lives and authenticating cults of great figures of the Frankish past. It was, however, Baudemond's version that served as the basis for the eleventh- and twelfth-century illustrated versions. These are the subjects of a new (1997) and extremely comprehensive study by Barbara Abou El-Haj.

He was born in the Lower Poitou district of Aquitaine in around 584 and at the age of twenty retired to a small monastery on the island of Yeu, in the Bay of Biscay north-west of La Rochelle. He then moved to Tours, after resisting his father's attempt to persuade him to return home, and he was ordained there. Moving east to Bourges, he spent some fifteen years living in a cell near the cathedral under the direction of the bishop, St Austregisilius (20 May). He made a pilgrimage to Rome and on his return to France was consecrated bishop with no fixed see but with a general brief to preach the faith to heathen peoples. These extended into the regions of present-day Flanders and northern France, and it was there that Amand directed his apostolic endeavours.

He had been supported in his mission by the Frankish king Dagobert I (d. 638) but was banished by him for reproving him fearlessly for his dissolute life. Dagobert, however, mended his ways on the birth of his son Sigebert, whom he wanted baptized by the holiest man in the kingdom. This was plainly Amandus, so Dagobert recalled him, and he baptized the boy with great pomp and ceremony in Orleans. Sigebert was to succeed his father as king and to be venerated as a saint (1 Feb., above).

Amandus persevered in his mission, founding monasteries at Elnone near Tournai (now Saint-Amand-les-Eaux), which he had been given by Dagobert and which became his headquarters, and in Ghent, where St Peter's is his foundation, though St Bavo's is probably not. At Elnone he built two churches within the monastic enclosure, one dedicated to St Peter and the other to St Andrew. He also, in association with Bd Itta, wife of Pepin of Landen, and their daughter St Gertrude of Nivelles (17 Mar.) founded the monastery of Nivelles for nuns. Three or four other foundations for nuns can also probably be attributed to him. He is thus the father of monasticism in Belgium as well the principal evangelizer of the country. It has been said that he was appointed bishop of Maastricht in 646, resigning the see many years later, but this seems uncertain and may be part of the tendency of medieval Lives to associate abbatial translations to episcopal ones; he spent most of his time on his missions working from monastic bases and was abbot of Elnone for about the last four years of his life. As such he was part of "a significant group . . . sponsored by kings like Dagobert to found the monasteries that they served as abbots, to extend and stabilize frontier zones, and to expand arable land as the Franks expanded the territory of their kingdom" (Abou El-Haj).

There are few details of his death in the early Life, but by the time Milo wrote, it was claimed that the church of St Peter's in the domain had become too small for the cult, so sixteen years after his death his body was translated into a new church dedicated in his honour. Milo also claimed that this ceremony was carried out by St Eligius (1 Dec.), the great metalsmith, who in fact died several years before Amandus. By the twelfth century he is recorded as having died before the altar of the Virgin in St Andrew's and being buried in St Peter's. The abbey was sacked by Norse raiders in 882 and 883, and Amandus' body was carried to safety at Saint-Germain-des-Prés in Paris. It was then retained in a Carolingian crypt at Elnone—the only part of the buildings to survive a great fire in 1066. After this it was processed through the countryside to raise funds for the rebuilding, with miracles reported along its route. By 1088 the abbey had been rebuilt, and the earliest illustrated account of Amandus' life dates from the period 1066-88.

His cult spread rapidly in Flanders and Picardy and reached England through visits by such as St Dunstan (19 May) to his monasteries at Elnone and Ghent. The Eyston family dedicated the chapel at East Hendred, in Oxfordshire, to him. The importance for Elnone of retaining his relics probably explains the insertion in his testament of a passage laying a curse on anyone who should remove them from there. He is generally accepted as one of the outstanding figures of the Merovingian period. *The Golden Legend* claims that "he set a powerful example of gentleness and holiness"; in the nineteenth century, Baring-Gould called him "the great apostle of Flanders," loving his people, opposing pagan cruelty, and reproving King Dagobert fearlessly. But we may know less about him than the extension of his cult suggests.

The *Vita Amandi* is in *AA.SS.*, Feb., 1, pp. 823-910; also in *M.G.H., Scriptores rerum merov.*, 5, 395-485. There is a considerable literature in French, including a biography by E. de Moreau, *Saint Amand* (1927); see also *idem*, "La *Vita Amandi Prima* et les fondations monastiques de S. Amand," *Anal.Boll.* 67 (1949), pp. 447-64, which proposes an end-seventh-century date for the Life. *O.D.S.*, p. 19, denies that he was ever bishop of Maastricht, against *P.B.*, 2, pp. 336-48, and *Bibl.SS.*, 1, 918-23. For the illustrated Lives see B. El-Haj, *The Medieval Cult of Saints: Formations and Transformations* (1997), principally Part II, and illustrations, pp. 378ff.

There is a copper-gilt and *champlevé* enamel reliquary figure of Amandus of thirteenth-century Flemish workmanship now in the Walters Art Gallery, Baltimore, Md. (illustrated in *N.C.E.*, 1, pp. 365-6).

St Guarinus of Palestrina, *Bishop* (1159)

Born in Bologna, Guarinus became a priest against the wishes of his family. Finding normal clerical life insufficiently austere, he joined the Holy Cross Congregation of Augustinian canons at Mortara (between Turin and Milan), in which he soon became generally venerated for the austerity and holiness of his life. He was elected to fill a vacancy among the local bishops but evaded consecration by climbing out of a window and hiding until a new election had been made. The pope, Lucius II (1144-5), was a native of Bologna and sent for Guarinus, who again tried to escape honour by pleading that after forty years in a monastery he was unfit for any sort of office. He was imprisoned for this refusal to give way to popular feeling but escaped. Lucius, however, insisted and consecrated him bishop of Palestrina, a post that carried the title of cardinal. Lucius showered gifts on him to suit him for this new dignity, but he gave them all to the poor of the city, thereby greatly increasing his reputation for holiness. He died at an advanced age surrounded by his clergy, to whom he gave his final spiritual instructions.

AA.SS., Feb., 1, pp. 923-5; *B.H.L.*, 2, p. 1272, *s.v.* "Warinus"; *Bibl.SS.*, 7, 435-6; *N.C.E.*, 6, pp. 827-8.

Bd Angelo of Furcio (1327)

He was born to parents long childless, who vowed they would dedicate any son granted them to God. Accordingly, when he was still young, his mother took him to the Augustinian monastery of Cornaclano, where her brother was ab- bot, to be educated. There he lived a life of prayer and study, and he was admitted to minor orders at the age of eighteen. He returned home on the death of an uncle, and attempts were made to arrange a marriage for him. His father did not wish to hinder Angelo's possible wishes by telling him of the vow but did so on his deathbed. Angelo, horrified that he might unwittingly have frustrated the course marked out for him, returned to the Augustinians at the monastery of Vasto d'Aimone.

He was a bright student, and he was sent to study in Paris, where he received his licenciate after five years study of philosophy and theology. He returned to Italy and offered his services to the prior general of the Order in Naples. He was appointed professor of theology at the Augustinian college in Naples, a post he occupied with great distinction for the rest of his life, refusing the offer of a bishopric. His cult was confirmed in 1888.

AA.SS., Feb., 1, pp. 935-9; *B.H.L.*, 1, p. 77; *Bibl.SS.*, 1, 1238-9. There are Lives in Italian by F. Lanza (189) and P. Paoluzzi (1946).

R.M.

St Antholian, martyr in Auvergne (third century)

St Silvanus, bishop of Emesa (Phoenicia), martyr, thrown to wild beasts (*c.* 235)

SS Dorothy and Theophilus, reputed martyrs, racked and put to death by the sword at Caesarea (? fourth century)

St Mel, reputed nephew of St Patrick and bishop (*c.* 490)

St Renilda, abbess in diocese of Lyons (eighth century)

St Aldric, O.Praem., monk in the Rhineland (1200)

St Brinolf Algotsson, bishop of Scara (Sweden) (1317)

7

St Moses, *Bishop* (*c.* 389)

Moses was an Arab by birth and spent many years as a hermit at Rhinoclura in the border region between Egypt and Syria, then on the fringes of the eastern Roman Empire. The Arab inhabitants of the region were mainly nomad tribes, animists who saw God in trees, rocks, flowers, and the stars, later given the name of Saracens. A warrior queen named Mavis from one of these tribes led bands of marauders to harass the imperial troops, who mounted an expedition against her; this took on a religious aspect and led to her agreeing to accept evangelization of her people provided they could have the holy hermit Moses as their bishop. Other accounts tell a rather different story: that Mavis was the widow of a Christian Saracen chief named Obadiah, that the empire waged war on her, and that she defeated its forces, dictating having Moses as bishop as her terms for peace—so that she was possibly already a Christian and that she won. The imperial soldiers would then have snatched Moses from the desert and commanded him to have himself ordained and consecrated, which he did. This element may account for confusion between him and Moses the Black (28 Aug.), one of the most remarkable of the Desert Fathers, whose death is generally put some sixty years later.

This was the age of the dominance of Arianism in the East, and Lucius, the archbishop occupying the patriarchal see of Alexandria, was an Arian. Moses refused to accept consecration from him and eventually travelled to be consecrated by orthodox bishops living in exile. He had no fixed see and spent his time journeying among his nomadic flock, converting many of them, and succeeding in keeping peace between the Romans and the nomad tribes.

He is mentioned by the historians Sozomen (*H.E.*, 6, 29 and 38) and Theodoret (*H.E.*, 4, 20), whose accounts form the basis for the entry in *AA.SS.*, Feb., 2, pp. 45-8. Rufinus, *H.E.*, 4, 36, is the origin of the Romans snatching him from the desert. B.G., Feb., confuses him with a fifth-century abbot martyred with six monks. *P.B.*, 2, p. 373, makes Mavis the widow of a Christian Saracen chief. See also *Bibl.SS.*, 9, 652-4.

St Richard, *"King"* (*c.* 720)

He was not a king, and his true name is unknown. The name and title derive from a legend developed at Eichstätt in Bavaria in the tenth century and at Lucca in Italy in the twelfth century on account of the fame of his holy sons Willibald (7 June) and Winnibald (18 Dec.) and daughter Walburga (25 Feb., below). The family came from Wessex, and father and two sons are known to have set out on pilgrimage to Rome in 720. They sailed from the River Hamble (by Southampton) across the Channel and up the Seine, landing at Rouen. After visiting several shrines in France they moved on to Italy, but the father died at Lucca in Tuscany before he could reach Rome.

Willibald joined St Boniface (5 June) in his work of evangelizing Germany, founded the double monastery of Heidenheim, and became first bishop of Eichstätt. Winnibald also became a missionary under Boniface and governed the monastery of Heidenheim with Walburga, who had likewise been sent out to help Boniface (who, like the brothers and sister, came from the West Country in England). When Willibald was interred at Eichstätt, it was proposed that the relics of Richard should be translated from Lucca and re-interred with those of his son. But the people of Lucca refused to part with them, and the inhabitants of Eichstätt were obliged to "content themselves with a little dust from his tomb" (Stanton).

It is from Heidenhein that the document known as the *Hodoeporicon* derives; this was written by a nun named Hugeburc, deals with the early life of Willibald, and tells us all we know about "St Richard." But in view of the eminent sanctity of his offspring and the fact that miracles had been reported at his tomb at San Frediano in Lucca, a suitable history of "St Richard, king of the English" was concocted. The title survived into the Roman Martyrology of 1956, but has been dropped in the new revision.

The *Hodoeporicon* is in *AA.SS.*, Feb., 2, pp. 69-81, as "De S. Richardo Rege, apud Anglo-Saxones in Britannia"; also in a better edition by Pertz in *M.G.H., Scriptores*, 15; there is also a modern English translation by C. H. Talbot in *Anglo-Saxon Missionaries in Germany* (1954), pp. 153-77. The nineteenth-century Life by T. Meyrick, *The Family of St Richard the Saxon* (1844), is corrected by M. Coens in "Légendes et miracles du roi S. Richard," *Anal.Boll.* 49 (1931), pp. 353-97. *O.D.S.*, pp. 415-6.

St Luke the Younger (955)

This Luke (or Loukas) came from a family of smallholders forced to move from the Greek island of Aegina by Saracen raiders, to settle in Thessaly. The third of seven children born to Stephen and Eusphrosyne, he worked in the fields as a child but after his father's death devoted himself to contemplation. His habit of giving away all he could to the poor brought him into conflict with his relatives, so he left home in search of a monastery. He settled as a hermit in the dangerous country on the borders with Hungary and Bulgaria, but he was captured by marauding wild tribesmen who took him for a runaway slave; they eventually released him, but on his return home he was accused of running away.

After some time he entered a monastery in Athens but was sent home by his superior, who told him that Euphrosyne had appeared to him in a vision, telling him that she needed her son. His mother greeted him with joy and surprise, but she was quite soon persuaded that Luke had a real calling to the religious life. He built himself a cell on Mount Joannitsa, near Corinth, and there led a hermit's life of great austerity combined with charity. His fame spread, and miracles were reported during his lifetime, so that he was given the title of *Thaumaturgus*, the Wonderworker. After his death his cell was converted into an oratory and named *Soterion*, the Place of Healing. The new draft Roman Martyrology dates his death to 955, as opposed to the previously accepted *c.* 946.

A Greek Life is printed complete in *Anal. Boll.* 13 (1895), pp. 82-121; there is an incomplete version in *P. G.*, 111, 442-80. See also *Oxford Dictionary of Byzantium*, 2, p. 1254; *Bibl.SS.*, 8, 222-31.

Bd Ricerius (1236)

On a date usually accepted as 15 August 1222 St Francis of Assisi (4 Oct.) preached a famous sermon in Bologna. This, as related in chapter 27 of the *Fioretti*, so impressed two aristocratic students at the university there that they came forward and offered to join the Friars Minor. One of these was Ricerius (Rizzerio, Riccerio, or Rizziero, named as Rinieri for some reason in the *Fioretti*), who came of a wealthy family from near Camerino. Francis is said to have prophesied that he would "serve his brethen," *i.e.,* become a minister (servant), and indeed Ricerius did receive Holy Orders and eventually became provincial minster of the Marches.

He is described as given to temptations to despair, which were clearly of an extreme nature. They were finally overcome by an assurance of Francis' special love for him, since he believed that if Francis loved him, then God would too. Francis is also supposed to have first confided to Ricerius his intentions with regard to the absolute poverty he ordained for his Order. Ricerius died in 1236, apparently at a young age (though his appointment as provincial minister of the Marches suggests at least a certain age and experience in the Order). It was a further six hundred years before his cult was confirmed, on 14 December 1838. In the Franciscan Order he is venerated on 28 March.

There are numerous editions of the *Little Flowers of St Francis* available. The early document reproduced in these is the *Actus beati Francisci*, chs. 36 and 37. See also the bibliography under St Francis of Assisi (4 Oct.) in the present work.

Bd Antony of Stroncone (1381-1461)

Born to a family in which the parents, Luigi and Isabella Vici, were both noble and who both became Franciscan tertiaries, Antony joined the Friars Minor at the early age of twelve. His religious training was supervised by his uncle, who was then commissary general of the Observant Franciscans in Italy. (The Observants were those who favoured a return to the strict practice of the original intentions of the Order but without the impossible idealism and resistance to any authority other than that of the Spirit preached by those who formed the

"Spirituals" of the thirteenth and fourteenth centuries. These eventually developed into sects condemned as heretical in Pope John XXII's Bull *Sancta Romana* of 30 December 1317).

Antony spent thirteen years as deputy novice-master at Fiesole and was then appointed by Bl Thomas of Florence (25 Oct.) to a mission aimed at suppressing the *Fraticelli*, the "brothers of the poor life," descendants of the Spirituals, who were then operating outside the control of either the Order or the hierarchy, though they were eventually to be reconciled in 1473. He spent ten years on this mission, mainly in the region around Siena but in Corsica for the last three. In 1431 he retired to the Friary of the Carceri outside Assisi, where he lived for a further thirty years practising penance and austerity to an extreme degree. In 1460 he was transferred to San Damiano in Assisi, and he died there on either 7 or 8 February 1461. He was beatified by Pope Innocent XI on 28 June 1687.

A short Latin version of the Lives by Mariano of Florence and Jacobilli of Foligno are printed in *AA.SS.*, Feb., 2, pp. 146-8. See also *Bibl.SS.*, 2, 197-8; *N.C.E.*, 1, p. 597; *Auréole Séraphique*, 1, pp. 224-34.

Bd Thomas Sherwood, *Martyr* (1551-78)

Thomas was the son of devout Catholic parents, and his mother also suffered for her faith: she was imprisoned for fourteen years after his execution and died in prison. He planned to study for the priesthood at Douai, but before he could go there he was arrested after being betrayed by the son of a Catholic woman whose house he had frequented, Lady Tregony. He was imprisoned in the Tower of London, where he was racked in order to get him to disclose the places where he heard Mass, this being by then an offence against "the Queen's Supremacy."

There is a relative wealth of contemporary information about him, unusual for one who was not a priest. His brother wrote an account of his sufferings, showing that he remained steadfast under constant torture; Thomas More's (22 June) son-in-law William Roper is known to have tried to help him; and a letter from the Privy Council to the lieutenant of the Tower is extant. Roper tried to send him money to alleviate his sufferings, but the only concession allowed was "six-pennyworth of clean straw" for him to lie on. The letter specifically directs the officers at the Tower to rack him "upon such articles as they shall think meet to minister unto him for the discovering either of the persons or of further matters . . ."—*i.e.*, to obtain information against other Catholics. He spent six months in the Tower before he was hanged at Tyburn. Information about his execution was conveyed to Douai, where the college Diary records: "On the first of march [1578] Mr Lowe returned to us from England bringing news that a youth, by name Thomas Sherwood, has suffered, for his confession of the Catholic faith, not only imprisonment, but death itself."

The new Roman Martyrology states that his cult was confirmed on 9 December 1896. This "confirmation" was actually recognition by Pope Leo XIII of the fact that Pope Gregory XIII (1572-85), by allowing portraits of the English martyrs who had suffered to be included in new frescoes in the English College in Rome, had "equipollently" beatified them, so in fact recognition of his martyrdom came very shortly after his death.

J. H. Pollen, *Acts of the English Martyrs* (1891), pp. 1-20; *M.M.P.*, pp. 11-12; *B.T.A.*, 1, pp. 273-4; *N.C.E.*, 9, p. 324; Stanton, pp. 57-8. See also "BB Martyrs of England and Wales," 4 May.

BB James Salès and William Saltemouche, *Martyrs* (1593)

France in the sixteenth century was riven by a series of wars, partly religious, partly political, between Catholics and Huguenots, with considerable brutality shown on both sides. The Huguenots were granted religious freedom by the Peace of Saint-Germain in 1570, but this was followed by the Massacre of St Bartholomew in 1572 in which between five and ten thousand Huguenots were killed at the instigation of Catherine de Médicis. A further peace, granting them almost full religious freedom, was followed by further restrictions, and when it seemed that the Huguenot Henry of Navarre would succeed to the throne, the Catholic League formed to prevent this tried once again to suppress Calvinism. The assassinations of the leaders of the League followed by that of King Henry III by a Dominican brought Henry to the throne as Henry IV. He was to return, at least nominally, to the Catholic faith in the year these two martyrs were put to death, in a region in which the Huguenots were still strong and religious tensions ran high.

James Salès was born in the Auvergne in 1556 and educated by the Jesuits, whose noviatiate he entered at the age of seventeen. He was then the first graduate of the newly-founded University of Pont à Mousson, from where he progressed to further studies in Paris. Apparently seeking martyrdom, he applied for permission to go on the missions in the Indies, but the Jesuit provincial, Fr Aquaviva, valued his talent for preaching and teaching too highly to spare him, telling him that he would find in France "all that the Indies have to give." William Saltemouche had been a college servant at the Jesuit college where James was educated and then became a Jesuit lay brother.

In the autumn of 1592 the mayor of Aubenas (in the Ardèche *département*, between Le Puy and Montélimar) asked the Jesuit provincial for a priest to preach the Advent course of sermons and to debate with local Calvinist ministers. James was chosen, and William sent as his companion. The Advent sermons were given, causing much controversy, and the mayor asked James to stay on till the following Easter, since Aubenas was without a resident priest. One night in February Huguenot raiders attacked the town. The most contentious point at issue between Catholics and Huguenots was the doctrine of the Eucharist, with the Sacred Species often being exposed to sacrilege when Huguenots raided Catholic churches. James and William withdrew to the church and consumed the hosts. The raiders found a way into the church and dragged them both off after demanding money and finding that they had virtually none.

They were brought before an unofficial tribunal of Calvinist ministers on 6 February 1593, and an acrimonious theological discussion took place. James' defence of the Catholic teaching on the Real Presence so enraged the Calvinists that the next day he was taken into the town square, shot with arrows, stabbed, and finally beaten to death. He had begged William to flee, but William would not leave him and was stabbed to death as he clung to the priest's body. They were both beatified on 6 June 1926.

There are two accounts of their lives and martyrdom in French: J. Blanc, *Martyrs D'Aubenas* (1906); H. Perroy, *Deux martyrs de l'Eucharistie* (1926). See also *Bibl.SS.*, 11, 598.

Bd Giles Mary (1729-1812)

He was born near Taranto in the Apulia region of Italy and learned the trade of rope-maker. When he was twenty-five he joined the Discalced Franciscans of St Peter of Alcántara (19 Oct.) in Naples. Naples had for long been known as a sink of depravity and crime and was then at one of the lowest points of its infamous history as the Bourbon régime gave way to the Napoleonic empire and this in turn tottered. There, like the more famous St Alphonsus Rodríguez (30 Oct.), he spent the remainder of his life as a porter. His duties included the distribution of alms to the poor, which he managed with such apparently miraculous dexterity that the more he gave away, the more there seemed to be available. To work consistently in this way for justice over such a long period in such social conditions would have required great courage and a remarkable purity of spirit. His charity also gained him a reputation for miracles of healing. He died on 7 February 1812 and was beatified on 5 February 1888.

C. Kempf, *The Holines of the Church in the Nineteenth Century* (1916); *F.B.S.*, pp. 98-101.

Bd Mary of Providence (Eugénie Smet), *Foundress* (1825-71)

Eugénie Smet was born on 25 March 1825, the third of six children of Henri Smet and Pauline Taverne de Mondhiver, a relatively prosperous couple living in Lille, in north-east France. She grew into a bright, lively child with nevertheless a deep piety and a firm sense of "duty" instilled by her mother. She received her religious instruction at the parish of Saint-Etienne and was confirmed—Confirmation being conferred before Communion at the time—at the age of nine. Testimonies to her childhood speak of her precocious feelings for the sufferings of the souls in purgatory. These were the days before the social teaching of the Church was developed, and she was kept at a distance by her class and education from the purgatorial sufferings of the poor of Lille, subject to every sort of exploitation at this early and savage stage of industrial revolution in France—an oversight, if such it can be called, that her later activities were to make up for on a heroic scale.

Her parents had built a small country house at Loos, a few miles outside Lille, and a reversal of fortune obliged them to move there. By this time, however, Eugénie was a boarder at the school of the Sacré-Coeur in the rue Royale in Lille. She threw herself with enthusiasm into the study and recreation of boarding-school life, showing herself a natural leader and organizer. But the thought of the suffering souls in purgatory still haunted her and she dreamed of a life of self-sacrifice offered up for them. These dreams were fortified by a retreat preached by a Jesuit in 1842, which she was to refer to as the year of her "conversion." But what that conversion was to entail was still, unsurprisingly, not clear, and the pupils at the Sacré-Coeur remained isolated from the sufferings around them. These were evidenced in poverty on a massive scale, child labour, a decade and a half when deaths in Lille exceeded births—conditions that were to lead to riots, strikes, and the revolution of 1848. It was in the school holidays that she discovered human suffering—though on a lesser scale—in Loos. She set out to remedy it by the sort of direct action that was to characterize her later religious life: she persuaded her father, who was settling into the life of a gentleman farmer, to let her take his windfall fruit to the poor, and he soon realized that it was not only the wind that was shaking his fruit trees.

This was a period when the Church in France was endeavouring to repair the ravages inflicted by the French Revolution on its influence and following by combining spiritual comfort with material assistance to an increasingly divided population. Inspired by a new bishop of Lille, Eugénie threw herself into a proliferation of charitable works, collecting so much money for missions in China that she received a personal letter of thanks from a bishop in Rome. She also, put up "No swearing here" placards in the cafés of Loos. Her inner spiritual life was also developing; she went to Mass every day and in 1850 dedicated herself to Christ with a vow of perpetual virginity. The focus of her faith was the Providence of God, in which she had a deep trust, reinforced throughout her life by "signs" she confidently expected and generally received.

In 1853 she became convinced of the need for a religious Order dedicated to relieving the suffering of souls in purgatory. She saw that there was an Order in the Church dedicated to every goal except this one, and she felt called to fill the vacuum. But in her usual manner of direct bargaining with God she told herself that she would need five "signs" if she was actually to found such an Order. These were: the success of her present efforts (an association in prayer), approval in writing from the pope, approval from the archbishop of Cambrai and several other bishops, five people to join her to form a new community, meeting a priest unknown to her who would share her aims. The five signs were to be granted within five years. In addition, she received encouragement from the Curé d'Ars (St John Vianney; 4 Aug.), whom she consulted by proxy. She heard that he "approved of your calling to the religious life, and of the new foundation, which, according to him, will spread rapidly in the Church." She then learned of the existence in Paris of a small community dedicated to the souls in purgatory, organized by a priest—unknown to her—of the parish of Saint-Merry. She saw this as final confirmation and took the train to Paris.

At first everything went badly. She could find only abominable lodgings, and her first meeting with the priest, Abbé Largentier, was a disaster. The situation was saved by a member of the community, Mlle Eugénie Lardin (who was later to succeed her namesake as superior general of the new Congregation). Largentier agreed to her demand that they obtain authorization from the archbishop of Paris, who had the grace to recognize something exceptional in Eugénie Smet and told her, when she admitted that she had absolutely no resources, that if faith could move mountains, it could build houses as well. She left the meeting with the archbishop's blessing, feeling "happier than she could tell." But she was no great planner, and there was still a long way to go. Largentier introduced her to a wealthy lady of charitable disposition, Madame Jurien, who promised to help. But Largentier held that only the education of children or care of the sick were avenues that could lead a new Order to success, which Eugénie saw as taking the means for the end, attaching far too much importance to material considerations without attending to spiritual aims.

She went back to Loos to think things over but returned to Paris on 25 March 1856 (her thirty-first birthday) accompanied by her youngest sister, Juliette, and determined to find better lodgings. If she was to succeed, she realized, she had to break free of Abbé Largentier, and this she did; he agreed to draw a veil over the past. She found a house "for sale or to let" at 16 rue de la Barouillère and knew it was meant for her. The rent was four thousand francs per year. With no resources, she persuaded the owner's notary to rent the building to her, inspired by a message from the Curé d'Ars: "This community cannot fail to succeed." Abbé Gabriel, the parish priest of Saint-Merry, took charge of the new community and in June 1856 declared that he was going to give them all their names in religion. Eugénie became Mary of Providence— a fitting name, given her unbounded faith in Divine Providence—and the new community took the name of The Helpers of the Holy Souls. She defined its aims as "through constant prayer and the practice of the works of mercy, to relieve and deliver the souls who are completing their expiation before being admitted to the bliss of heaven." A well-wisher sent five hundred francs in an envelope, asking only for prayers for his deceased relatives, and the rent was agreed.

Paris at the time was a huge building-site. Napoleon III had engaged Baron Haussmann as chief planner with the brief to turn Paris into "the most beautiful city in the world." He was to succeed but at immense social cost, as the old medieval streets with their close-knit communities and built-in crafts and trades were torn apart to make way for the long, straight boulevards. It was in this situation that Mary of Providence sought how to work out her aims in practice:

How to organize a truly religious life? What course to choose in order to respond truly to the will of God? The answer came, as usual, by chance, when someone knocked on the door asking if "one of the ladies would come and look after a poor woman of the neighbourhood, who refused to have a priest or a nun." Mary of Providence heard an inner voice saying, "This is how you will love me." Her Helpers from that time on went out to all who were alone or suffering in any way. They found a world they could not have imagined: alcoholism, destitution, expulsion, overcrowding. They went into it, cared for the sick and the suffering, and evangelized as they went.

Her spiritual vision took more definite shape, and she asked the pope to bless the new Institute, defining its aim as "to consecrate ourselves by a fourth vow to the relief of the Church suffering through the practice of works of zeal and charity recommended by the Church militant." Love for the souls in purgatory, in other words, was to be expressed by works of love carried out on earth. Still, on her own she felt unable to express her vision in defining form, but she was enabled to do so through her meeting with a young Jesuit priest, Père Basuiau, who became her spiritual mentor and persuaded the Institute to base its Constitution on that of the Society of Jesus. This was formally accepted on 25 March 1859. Postulants began to arrive in large numbers, and the house—which they had been able to buy through the charity of Madame Jurien in November 1857—was bursting at the seams. A wealthy young widow, Madame Simart, joined the Congregation, bringing much-needed furniture with her, and when she doubted her vocation decided that she had to stay or the Sisters would have nothing to sit on! In 1861 the postulants included Mary of Providence's sister Emma, some consolation for the fact that her only brother had died the year before. In 1863 a second house was opened in Nantes.

Her physical health began to deteriorate, adding another cross to those she bore as foundress and superior, which kept her away from direct involvement with the poor her Institute was dedicated to serving. In 1865 she hovered between death and life for a month with a sickness doctors failed to diagnose. It proved to be cancer, and in 1867 she saw herself "flung into eternity." But she still had four years left to live, marked by increasing pain.

In August 1867 Mgr Languillat, the Jesuit vicar general of Kiang Nang province in China, came to celebrate Mass at the Institute; he announced that he was "looking to the Helpers for helpers." Much against Mary of Providence's will initially, some thirty Sisters volunteered to go to China. These were eventually whittled down to six, the first of whom left in late 1867. They went into a situation where evangelization was just beginning to be possible after the persecution during the Opium War. From the start, they recruited Chinese Helpers. When foreign missionaries were forced out of the country by the Communists between 1945 and 1953, one hundred Chinese Helpers remained—and remained faithful to their mission during the thirty years during which no contact with the motherhouse was possible.

On 8 December 1869, the day the First Vatican Council opened, Mary received a note from Rome confirming her as superior general for life. A second "overseas" foundation was made, in Brussels. In January 1870 the Franco-Prussian War broke out, and she decided to send the novices to Nantes and Brussels to conserve future resources in the face of a worsening situation in Paris. Her last months were spent in beseiged Paris, short of food and fuel and with shells falling around the house. Forced to take refuge in the cellars, her cancer an open wound in her side, in intolerable pain but with her love for Christ and her faith in God's Providence undiminished, she died on 7 February 1871. She was beatified by Pope Pius XII in 1957.

The Constitutions of the Helpers declare: "We believe that there are no boundaries to love and that we are in solidarity with all those who follow Jesus Christ in his Paschal Mystery, whether they are on earth or have already passed through death. We support them through our prayer, action, and communion with them in their trials, knowing that God's transforming love is a gratuitous gift." Mary of Providence's vision, expressed inevitably in the language of her time, has since spread to four continents, with communities in twenty-five countries. The Helpers simply help the neediest wherever they are to be found. Unlike many nineteenth-century foundresses whose spirituality remained locked in the language and spirit of the age, Mary of Providence launched a movement that has shown lasting validity in time and space. A spiritualized original vision was earthed by experience: purgatory was, and is, to be found here on earth; many of those still on earth are living in death. It was in loving them that she found the true way to love Jesus. As a Chinese Helper wrote to her: "You love the fire of God and you light it in others."

The *Histoire des Origines* was written within twenty years of her death by a Helper, drawing largely on the History of the Institute written by Mary of Providence herself up to the year 1857; neither has been published, but both have been duplicated for internal use by the Institute. C. C. Morewood, *Eugénie Smet* (1927), takes some of the development of the Institute into account; see also I. G. Capaldi, S.J., *Mary of Providence* (1957); Marie René-Bazin, *She Who Lived by Her Name* (latest ed. 1963; also available in French). Thérèse Gardey de Soos, *Eugénie Smet: Bienheureuse Marie de la Providence* (1996), on which the above is based, provides a good modern account well aware of social and religious conditions. An English translation is in preparation.

R.M.
St Parthenius, bishop in the Hellespont (fourth century)
St Juliana of Bologna (*c.* 435)
St Laurence, bishop of Siponto (Apulia) (*c.* 545)
Bd Willmer of Leaval (seventh century)
St William, priest in Piedmont (thirteenth century)
St John of Triora, martyr (1816)—see "The Martyrs of China," 17 Feb., below.

8

ST JEROME EMILIANI, *Founder* (1481-1537)

Girolamo Emiliani (a surname popularly shortened to Miani) was born in Venice to Angelo Emiliani and his wife, Eleanor Mauroceni, in 1481. As a young man he served in the Venetian army at a time when Venice was an independent republic vying with other states for supremacy in trade. When the League of Cambrai was formed to resist Venetian expansion he was appointed commander of the fortress of Castelnuovo, near Treviso. The forces of the League took the town, however, and he was imprisoned in a dungeon, secured with chains. This reverse encouraged him to repent of his earlier life, which had not found much place for religion. He turned to prayer and vowed himself to Our Lady, which is said to have enabled him to make a miraculous escape. He made his way to Treviso, where he hung up his fetters in the church, and he was eventually appointed mayor of the town.

He did not remain in Treviso for long but returned to Venice to take charge of the education of his nephews and to study for the priesthood. He was ordained in 1518, at a time when famine and plague were causing widespread distress and suffering. Jerome devoted himself to relieving these wherever he could, concentrating particularly on abandoned orphans. He rented a house for them to live in, provided clothing and food for them out of his own resources, and instructed them in the doctrine and practice of the Faith. He did this by means of a catechism in question and answer form, which he composed himself, apparently the first to do so. The method was to feature in many catechisms, both Protestant and Catholic, in the decades immediately following. He himself caught the plague but recovered.

In 1531 he set out to found houses devoted totally to the care of unfortunates of various sorts. He founded orphanages in Brescia, Bergamo, and Como, as well a home for repentant prostitutes and a hospital in Verona. With two other priests he formed a new Congregation with a house in the village of Somasca, between Bergamo and Milan, in which postulants to the Congregation could make spiritual exercises. The Congregation took its name from the village, becoming known as the Clerks Regular of Somasca, or Somaschi for short. They looked after the spiritual and material welfare of the peasants living around the village, but their main work was the care of orphans.

Jerome caught an infectious disease from tending the sick, of which he died on 8 February 1537. St Charles Borromeo (4 Nov.) gave the Congregation his support after Jerome's death, and it was recognized by Pope Paul III in 1540.

Its numbers have declined, but those remaining continue to run schools and orphanages in Italy. Jerome was canonized on 12 October 1767, and in 1928, at the request of the superior general of the Congregation on the occasion of the fourth centenary of their foundation, Pope Pius XI declared him patron saint of orphans and abandoned children. In view of the importance of this patronage, he retained his place in the Universal Calendar of 1969, when his feast was moved from 20 July to the day of his death.

A Latin Life by A. Tortora written in 1620 is in *AA.SS.*, Feb., 1, pp. 217-74. There are two relatively recent biographies in Italian: G. Landini, *S. Girolamo Miani . . .* (1947); S. Raviolo, *San Girolamo Emiliani* (1947). See also *N.C.E.*, 5, 304-5. On the Somaschi see *L'Ordine dei Chierici Regolari Somaschi nel iv centenario della sua fondazione* (1928); G. B. Picata in *Enciclopedia Cattolica*, 11 (1953), 952-4.

St Quinta, *Martyr* (259)

Eusebius quotes St Dionysius, bishop of Alexandria from 247 to *c.* 265 (17 Nov.), writing to Bishop Fabius of Antioch with an account of martyrdoms in Alexandria under Decius, Roman emperor from 249 to 251: ". . . they took a female convert named Quinta to the idol's temple and tried to make her worship. When she turned her back in disgust they tied her feet and dragged her right through the city over the rough paved road, bumping her on the rough stones and beating her as they went, till they arrived at the [. . .] place, where they stoned her to death." Other accounts say that she was tied to the tail of a horse and died as a result of being dragged in this way. The new Roman Martyrology entry (in which she is named as Cointha) appears to be based on Eusebius.

Eusebius, *H.E.*, 6, 41; *Bibl.SS.*, 10, 1310-11.

St Nicetius of Besançon, *Bishop* (before 610)

The accounts we have of Nicetius (Nicet, or Nizier, in French) show the difficulty of being certain of the identity of bishops of the Merovingian period. The Life printed in the second February volume of the *Acta Sanctorum* makes him out to be a close friend and correspondent of Pope St Gregory the Great (590-604; 3 Sept.) and of St Columban (d. 615; 23 Nov.). The new Roman Martyrology follows a date for his death that would make this possible without giving any further details, but Duchesne maintains that while there was an early bishop of Besançon named Nicetius who was venerated there as a saint, this St Nicetius is the one who buried St Waldebert, abbot of Luxeuil (2 May) in 670, a date that would make it impossible for him to have known SS Gregory and Columban. If the earlier Life is correct he was a holy and learned man, a vigorous opponent of heresy, and he restored the episcopal see to Besançon from Nyon on Lake Geneva, where it had been moved after Besançon had been sacked by the Huns. Guérin, drawing on the *Vie des saints du Franche-Comté*, quotes the compilers of this work, the teachers at the Collège de Saint François-Xavier, as saying that Besançon was a heap of ruins after its devastation by Attila the Hun and that Nicetius had to rebuild the churches as well as the church community, an enormous task to which he was equal.

He is the titluar saint of the church at Mailley in the Haute Saône. In feudal times the Seigneur d'Augerans used to arrange a *jour de fête* for the children in honour of "Monsieur saint Nicet." His cult was confirmed only in 1900.

AA.SS., Feb., 2, pp. 167-8; *B.H.L.*, 2, p. 888.

St Paul of Verdun, *Bishop* (*c.* 649)

This Paul became a monk after being a courtier. He first retired as a hermit to Mount Voge (now named Paulsberg after him) near Trier, then entered the monastery of Tholey, where he was the monastic baker for a time and then became headmaster of the monastic school. Paulsberg had previously been known as Mount d'Apollon after a pagan custom in which the butchers of Trier used to throw a flaming wheel from the top of the mountain into the River Moselle below in order to ward off the devil. So the renaming was to replace a pagan tradition with a Christian one.

In about 630 King Dagobert I (reigned 629-39) appointed him bishop of Verdun, giving him land, the rents from which enabled him to appoint a staff of clergy. In this way he became part of the missionary movement helping the eastward expansion of the Frankish kingdom (see St Amandus; 6 Feb., above). Modelling himself on the apostle Paul, he was a notable bishop, a good pastor, and an able administrator. He restored the church community at Verdun, which had fallen on evil times, made the people observe a Christian Sunday, and did much to promote the dignity of the liturgy and canonical life. It has been claimed that he was a brother of St Germanus of Paris (d. 576; 28 May), but this is improbable, as there is a difference of sixty years in their ages. He was a friend of St Didier of Nevers (d. *c.* 679; 19 June), who also spent time as a solitary in the Vosges before becoming a bishop in 655.

In art Paul is shown with a taper in his hand or standing by an oven in memory of his time as baker at the monastery of Tholey.

AA.SS., Feb., 2, pp. 168-77; *Bibl.SS.*, 10, 280-1; *P.B.*, 2, pp. 376-81, refers to him as this "illustre prélat," citing Roussel, *L'histoire civile et ecclésiastique de Verdun* (1863). B.G., Feb., pp. 213-4, quotes "a very ancient anonymous Life" used by Restaurus, canon of Saint-Vito, writing around 887, in his *Hist. brevis episcoporum Virdunensium.*

St Elfleda, *Abbess* (653-714)

Elfleda (or Aelffled, as spelt by Bede, or Aelfflaed) was the daughter of King Oswy of Northumbria and St Enfleda (or Eanflaed; 24 Nov.). With a grand disdain for his daughter's possible wishes in the matter, Oswy vowed that if he were successful in battle against the heathen King Penda of Mercia he would dedicate her to the religious life and give lands for the foundation of religious houses. In 654 he won the battle of the river Winwaed against Penda and fulfilled his vow by giving Elfleda, "who was scarcely a year old," to Hilda (17 Nov.), then, as abbess of Hartlepool, reorganizing monastic life there in accordance with rules she had learned from Irish sources. In 657 Hilda moved to Whitby, to found (or re-found) the abbey there, and took Elfleda with her. Whitby was a double monastery; its influence spread far and wide, and it was famous for learning and as the site of the Synod of Whitby in 663/4.

Hilda died in 680, and Elfleda was eventually chosen to succeed her, following her widowed mother Enfleda, who had joined the abbey on Oswy's death in 670. During Elfleda's abbacy the earliest Life of St Gregory the Great (3 Sept.) was written at Whitby. Her influence as a conciliator was felt in the contentions between St Theodore of Canterbury (19 Sept.) and St Wilfrid (12 Oct.) over the creation of more dioceses in Northumbria, taking territory away from York and so from Wilfrid. She helped to resolve the matter at the Synod of the River Nidd in 705. She told the bishops that her brother King Alfrith's last testament was that he would obey the wishes of the papacy in the matter and charge his heir to do the same.

She was also a friend of St Cuthbert (20 Mar.), whom she met on Coquet Island: she is reported to have been cured of a crippling ailment by the touch of his girdle. He is also supposed to have prophesied to her that her brother King Egfrith would die within a year, to be succeeded by Alfrith, his half-brother, and that he himself would be forced to accept a bishopric—all of which came true. Elfleda died in either 713 or 714; in 1125 her relics were rediscovered at Whitby, despite the fact that the abbey had been thoroughly sacked by the Danes in around 800, and translated to a place of honour. She was famous enough for her death to be recorded in Irish annals, but there is no evidence of an early cult.

Bede, *H.E.*, 3, 24; 4, 26; *AA.SS.*, Feb., 2, pp. 177-86. See also B. Colgrave (ed.), *Eddius Stephanus' Life of Wilfrid* (1927), chs. 43, 59, 60; *Two Lives of St Cuthbert* (1940); *The Earliest Life of Gregory the Great* (1968). *O.D.S.*, pp. 154, 158 (Enfleda); 116-8 (Cuthbert); 492-4 (Wilfrid). *Bibl.SS.*, 4, 1018-9; *D.H.G.E.*, 15, 456-8; *N.L.A.*, 1, pp. 379-81.

St Cuthman (Eighth Century)

This Anglo-Saxon hermit was born in the south of England, probably around 681 at Chidham, near Bosham on the West Sussex coast. He is associated with nearby Steyning, where he lived and was buried and where a partly Saxon church survives, the successor of the wooden church which his Lives say he built with his own hands. He is described as a pious and dutiful son, and the best-known aspect of his legend is that after his father's death he built a wheel-barrow couch for his paralyzed mother in which, with the aid of ropes slung over his shoulders, he wheeled her wherever he went, travelling as a mendicant hermit. This became the basis for Christopher Fry's play *The Boy with a Cart* (1939).

He eventually settled at Steyning, where he first built a hut for himself and his mother and then embarked on the church, helped by the local people, who were inspired by his piety and zeal. In time Edward the Confessor gave the church to the monks of Fécamp in Normandy, who built cells for monks and later the stone church on the site of his wooden one, transferring his relics to Fécamp.

Two short Lives are in *AA.SS.*, Feb., 2, pp. 197-9, and his name appears in some early calendars, indicating a pre-Conquest cult. See also G. R. and W. D. Stephens, "Cuthman, a neglected saint," in *Speculum* 12 (1938), pp. 448-53; F. W. Cox, "St Cuthman; what is known of him," in *Sussex Notes and Queries* 4 (1933), pp. 204-7. The legend also appears in Gotha MS 1, 81, from which it was printed by P. Grosjean as "Codicis Gothani appendix," in *Anal.Boll.* 58 (1940), pp. 197-9. *O.D.S.*, p. 118.

Bd Peter Igneus, *Bishop* (1089)

The new Roman Martyrology preserves the reason for this Peter being nicknamed *Igneus*, "of the fire": "because he passed through fire unharmed." The story, which seems to be well attested in a contemporary letter, still extant, is that the citizens of Florence were incensed by the simoniacal appointment of Peter of Pavia to their see and demanded that right in the matter should be determined by the ordeal of fire. They appealed to the monks of Vallombrosa to carry out the test, and a monk named Peter Aldobrandini volunteered to face the ordeal. Two great piles of wood were prepared and lit with only a narrow lane two feet wide between them. Peter said Mass while the wood blazed fiercely, watched by a crowd of three thousand people. He then removed his chasuble and walked calmly between the two blazing piles of wood, each some ten feet long and nearly five feet high, "undaunted in mind and cheerful of aspect, having made the sign of the cross and carrying a crucifix in his hand . . . sustaining no injury either to his body or to any of the things which he carried." At the end he turned round and would have retraced his steps through the fire, but the crowd would not allow him to, convinced that God had clearly spoken. Whether Peter of Pavia was invited to take the same test, and what his reaction was, history apparently does not relate. But he was deposed from the see of Florence.

Fr Thurston, in a footnote to the previous edition of this work, points out that there are innumerable stories from all over the world of religious mystics performing this same feat (though more usual is the Eastern practice of walking over live coals, while Peter's story seems to be based on that of the "three children in the fiery furnace"). He also suggests that it was probably the example of Peter Igneus that caused Francis di Puglia to propose the same ordeal to the reforming preacher Savonarola some four hundred years later. He refused, and this brought about his downfall. Ordeal by fire was a common practice in medieval societies, a survival of pre-Christian practice into Christian times. Essentially, it asked God to witness to the innocence of the accused against accusations often made by the rich and powerful.

The rest of Peter's story is that Pope St Gregory VII (25 May) summoned him to Rome and appointed him bishop of Albano, a post that carried the rank of cardinal. He was sent as papal legate on missions to the Italian States, to France, and to Germany. He returned eventually to Vallombrosa, dying there on a date generally accepted as 8 February 1089. His name was introduced into the Roman Martyrology by Baronius in 1673.

I. M. Pieroni, *Vita e Gesta di S. Pietro Igneo* (1894); there is also a Life by A. Salvini (1928). The letter from the citizens of Florence is in *P.L.*, 146, 693-8; also in *AA.SS.*, July, 3, pp. 297-8, 330-1. Mann, *The Lives of the Popes*, 6, p. 302, points out that there is other contemporary corroborative evidence. See also *N.C.E.*, 11, pp. 218-9; *Bibl.SS.*, 1, 752-3.

St Stephen of Muret, *Abbot and Founder* (*c.* 1047-1124)

This Stephen is also called "of Grandmont," but this refers rather to the Grandmontine Order he founded, while his association with the monastery of Muret, in a valley near Limoges, is more direct. His Life, written by the seventh prior of Grandmont, makes him the son of a viscount (later identified as the vicomte de Thiers) from the Auvergne who went with his father to Rome and there decided to become a monk, obtaining authorization for the establishment of a separate Order directly from the pope. This has the ring of conventional stories of high birth set aside for the religious life, as well as of exalting the origins of the Order, but may be historically accurate in his case. After his visit to Rome he travelled in Calabria for a time and there came across eremitical communities of the kind that had been common in the Middle East; he decided to introduce this way of life into his own country.

In 1076 he renounced his inheritance in order to go and live as a hermit in the mountains near Ambazac, just north-east of Limoges, in west-central France. He remained there for forty-six years, living a life of great austerity. Disciples came to join him, and toward the end of his life the community was established as a monastery at Muret, which was dedicated to extreme poverty, resembling the Carthusians and the Camaldolese in its rule of life. This caused the monks to become popularly known as "Bons Hommes." Stephen himself declared that there was no need for a written Rule, since "there is no rule except Christ's gospel," and he regarded other Rules such as those of St Augustine (28 Aug.) or St Benedict (11 July) as merely secondary, but a Rule drawn up in 1143 by his disciple Hugh of Lacerta, the *Liber sententiarum seu rationum*, was attributed to him, though composed by the fourth prior, Stephen of Liciac. The Roman Martyrology praises him for encouraging conversion "not through domination but through charity," but the Rule is characterized by extreme severity, comparing the sort of monastic life he intended to a prison. "If you come here," he told aspiring recruits, "you will be fixed to the cross and you will lose your own power over your eyes, your mouth, and your other members . . . [but] if you go to a large monastery with fine buildings you will find animals and vast estates; here only poverty and the cross." His monks were to be "hermits" living in "deserts" and their model was St John the Baptist. They renounced absolutely everything, even begging and preaching or hearing sermons, and devoted their lives exclusively to liturgical and private prayer. Great stress was laid on material poverty, which may have been the reason for refusing to allow women, who would have brought dowries, to enter the Order. The aim was "interiority" in a direct relationship with God through the cultivation of humility and self-abandonment and a prayer of acquiescence and praise. In this, Stephen was wholly in tune with the spirituality of his age.

After Stephen's death his disciples moved to Grandmont in Normandy, from where the Order took its name. It initially grew rapidly in an age of enthusiasm for austerity but was never very widespread and began to decline after fifty years, with disputes arising between monks and lay brothers, who were made responsible for all the organization and relations with the outside world. This was deliberate policy so as to leave the monks as absolute recluses. The lay brothers were to follow the example of Martha and the monks that of Mary. The disputes were eventually resolved, but discipline gradually relaxed. A reform was brought about in 1643, with the formation of a Strict Observance banch, but this did not last long. The Order was finally extinguished in the French Revolution.

Three foundations were made in England from the thirteenth to fifteenth centuries, a typical site being that of Craswall Priory, under the north-eastern edge of the Black Mountains, mid-way between Hereford and Brecon (now in Wales). The Order was supported by King Heny II of England, at whose request Stephen was canonized by Pope Clement III in 1189.

The *Vita Sancti Stephani*, by the seventh prior of Grandmont, is in *AA.SS.*, Feb., 2, pp. 199-213; also in *P.L.*, 204, 1005-46, with the Rule of Hugh of Lacerta, 1085-136, and another *vita* by Hugh of Lacerta, 1181-222; the *Liber sententiarum seu rationum* is in *ibid.*, 1036-86. See also D. Knowles, *The Monastic Order in England* (1949), pp. 203-4; *N.C.E.*, 13, pp. 700-1; R. Graham and A. W. Clapham, "The Order of Grandmont and its Houses in England," in *Archaeologia* 75 (1926), pp. 159-210. J. Becquet, "Les institutions de l'ordre de Grandmont," in *Rev. Mabillon* 42 (1952), pp. 31-42; *idem*, "Les premiers écrivains de l'ordre de Grandmont," *ibid.* 43 (1953), pp. 121-37. *Dict. Sp.*, 4 (1961), "Etienne de Muret," pp. 1054-114. *O.D.C.C.*, p. 579; *O.D.S*, pp. 443-4, from which the above citation is taken; *H.C.S.*, 2, pp. 143-4.

Bd Josephine Bakhita (*c.* 1868-1947)

She was born in the Sud Darfur region of Sudan, some twenty-five miles north-east of the township of Nyala. At the age of about ten she was snatched by Arab slave-traders, who kept her in slavery for some years at El Obeid in Kardofan and then sold her to the Italian consul. He took her back to Italy and placed her with a family living in Mirano Veneto, in the region of Venice. She lived with the family for three years and then travelled back to Africa for a year with them before returning to settle permanently in Italy.

She was converted to Catholicism through contact with the Canossian Sisters in Venice and was baptized on 9 January 1890, receiving her First Communion and being confirmed at the same time by the cardinal patriarch of Venice, Domenico Agostino. On 7 December 1893 she entered the Institute of Canossian Daughters of Charity in Venice, where she was clothed two years later, making her solemn profession the following December. She spent the remaining fifty years of her life as a professed religious, gaining an ever-increasing reputation for outstanding piety and charity, so that a diocesan process of inquiry into her holiness was begun soon after her death, which took place on 8 February 1947. She was declared venerable in December 1978 and beatified by Pope John Paul II on 17 May 1995.

Bibl.SS., Suppl. 1, 114; *A.A.S.* (1993), p. 224.

R.M.
St Juventius, bishop of Pavia (397)
St Ciwa (Kigwe or Kewe), abbess in Gwent (fifth century)
St Theognius, bishop of Bethlehem (527)
St Jacut, abbot, brother of SS Gwenaloe and Guethenoc (sixth century)
St Honoratus, bishop of Milan (*c.* 570)

9

St Apollonia, *Martyr* (*c*. 249)

The story of Apollonia's martyrdom follows on from that of St Quinta (8 Feb., above) in Eusebius' *History*, still quoting St Dionysius of Alexandria writing to Bishop Fabius of Antioch: "Next they seized the wonderful old lady Apollonia, battered her till they knocked out all her teeth, built a pyre in front of the city, and threatened to burn her alive unless she repeated after them their heathen incantations. She asked for a breathing-space, and when they released her, jumped without hesitation into the fire and was burnt to ashes." She was a deaconess of the church in Alexandria.

St Augustine resolved the problem that in this account she effectively took her own life by saying that she must have received a special direction from the Holy Spirit. There are several altars and churches dedicated to her in the West, but no cult in the East, despite the fact that she suffered at Alexandria. In Rome she was confused with another Apollonia, martyred under Julian the Apostate, the confusion possibly aided by the proliferation of her relics in Roman churches: S. Apollonia, S. Maria Transtiberiana, S. Lorenzo fuori le Muri, S. Basilio. There are also relics in Naples, Antwerp, Brussels, Malines, Liège, Cologne, and elsewhere; most of these are a single tooth or fragment of jawbone—the total number of teeth to which they amount being uncounted. Later accounts ignored Dionysius' description of her as an old lady and made her into a beautiful young woman. Other legends, probably drawing on fairy-tale cycles, made her into a king's daughter who was tortured by her father and who promised just before she died to help all those suffering from toothache.

The fact that she had all her teeth knocked out (or pulled out, in other versions) made her the patron saint not only of dentists but also of all sufferers from toothache. Her attribute is a tooth held in a pair of pincers, or a tooth suspended from a necklace. In Boston, Massachusetts, there is a dentists' periodical named after her, *The Apollonian*.

Eusebius, *H.E.*, 6, 41. An account of her martyrdom was written by an Italian dental surgeon, G. B. Poletti, *Il martirio di S. Apollonia* (1934), and she has been the subject of an article in a French dental periodical, H. Nux, "Sainte Apollone, patronne de ceux qui souffrent des dents," in *Revue d'odontologie, de stomachologie* 3 (1947), pp. 113ff. See also M. Coens, "Une passio S. Apolloniae inédite," in *Anal.Boll.* 70 (1952), pp. 138-59. For representations in art in England see *E.M.C.A.*, p. 111; for those in Italy see *Saints in Italy*, p. 40. *O.D.S.*, p. 28.

She is depicted holding a tooth in a pair of pincers on several medieval painted wooden screens and in glass in Norfolk, Suffolk, and Devon. She is represented in frescoes by

Parmigiano in the church of S. Giovanni Evangelista in Parma; also in paintings by Carlo Dolci in the convent of Sant'Apollonia in Florence and in the Galleria Nazionale (formerly the Palazzo Corsini) in Rome.

St Attracta (? Fifth Century)

This Irish saint, associated with St Patrick (17 Mar.) in early accounts, is variously named Attracta, Athract, Araght, or Taraghata. There is a—not unusual—difficulty with her dating, as other associates mentioned belong to the sixth century rather than the fifth. Her legend makes her—again, not unusually—the daughter of a noble house whose father refused to allow her to dedicate herself to God. She fled to Coolavin, where St Patrick clothed her in the nun's habit. She founded a hospice for travellers by Lough Gara in Connaught (west of Boyle, in Co. Sligo). There she was credited with great powers of healing, largely through the use of herbal medicine. The hospice was renowned for its hospitality to travellers and survived to 1539. The name lived on after this: *The History of Sligo* records that in 1692 Lord Kingston was listed in the Quit and Crown Rents Book as "Tenant of the Hospital or Religious House called Termon Killeracht." The modern form of the place name is Killaraght (*Kill*, or *Cill*, meaning "church").

A local St Conall, who was supposed to be her half-brother, had a church at Drum, near Boyle; she wished to live in a cell near him, but he refused. Thereupon she cursed him in robust terms, wishing that his church might be reduced to insignificance, his good works come to nothing, and other things regarded as too extreme to be recorded. Another legend tells that she enabled a raiding party of men from Lugna to escape from the pursuing king of Connaught by parting the waters of Lough Gara: two natural weirs on the lake are named after her on this account. She is also reputed to have plaited her own hair to make harness for forest deer to enable them to drag timber for the construction of a fort by the king of Connaught, who had his revenge by forcing her to take part in the building work. Her feast was formerly celebrated in Ireland on 11 August, but the new draft Roman Martyrology follows the *Acta Sanctorum* in placing her commemoration on today's date.

AA.SS., Feb., 2, pp. 296-300, prints a Latin Life. There are references to her in Lives of St Patrick: see L. Bieler, *The Patrician Texts in the Book of Armagh* (1979); she is not mentioned in the martyrology of Oengus. See also *Bibl.SS.*, 2, 576-8; *Irish Saints*, p. 31, citing T. O'Rourke, *The History of Sligo*, 2, pp. 366-78.

St Teilo, *Bishop* (Sixth Century)

Teilo, monk and bishop, was a major figure in the church of sixth-century Wales, but no written Life of him survives from earlier than the eleventh century, so it is difficult to be certain of biographical details. In 1130 Geoffrey of Llandaff composed a sermon on his life; a longer version of this was then produced emphasizing the see of Llandaff, and this is contained in the *Liber*

Landavensis ("The Book of Llandaff"). It uses conventional legendary material to fill out Teilo's life but also gives some basic information that may be taken as trustworthy, especially where it is confirmed by earlier evidence of a cult.

It tells that Teilo was born near Penally, which is on the coast of Pembrokeshire in south Wales opposite Caldey Island, and that he was earlier known as Eliud. He studied first under St Dubricius (or Dyfrig; 14 Nov.) and then under St Paul Aurelian (12 Mar). During an outbreak of plague he went to Brittany, where he met St Samson (28 July), with whom he may have studied earlier at Llandaff. Samson may have been abbot of Caldey and was consecrated bishop by St Dubricius. His see was at Dol in Brittany, near the north coast, midway between Saint-Malo and Mont-Saint-Michel, and there he and Teilo are said to have planted an orchard "three miles long, reaching from Dol to Cai, which is still called after their names." Teilo returned to Wales after seven years, continuing his ministry from Llandeilo Fawr in Powys, where he was probably abbot of the monastery. He died there, and a dispute arose over whether Llandeilo, Penally, or Llandaff should claim his body—the Book of Llandaff claims that he was appointed bishop there in succession to Dubricius. The miraculous solution claimed is that it was multiplied into three during the night.

There is very little evidence on which to base an appreciation of his character. One remark attributed to him is a reply to a question put by St Cadoc (25 Sept.), founder of the great monastery of Llancarfan: "The greatest wisdom in a man is to refrain from injuring another when it is in his power to do so"— which at least indicates that he was on the side of mercy in an age characterized by local wars and dynastic disputes. But he is also described as praying for victory in one such—see below.

The manuscript book of *Gospels of St Chad* (*c.* 700) has marginal entries testifying to his cult and claiming that he founded a monastery named the *Familia Teliavi*. There are numerous churches dedicated to him in south Wales and some in Brittany, especially in the diocese of Quimper, where the name Landeleau is the equivalent of Llandaff (from the Gaelic root *âv*, meaning water—hence the common name river Avon). The Book of Llandaff mentions grants of houses to him at Llanarth, Llandeilo Pertholey, and Llandeilo Crossenny—the last by "King" Iddon ab Ynyr of Gwent in gratitude to Teilo for his prayers, which brought about a victory. His tomb is in Llandaff Cathedral; it was opened in 1850, when a record of an earlier opening, in 1736, was found. This stated that, "the parson buried appear'd to be a bishop by his Pastorall Staffe and Crotcher." The staff had decayed, but the pewter "crotcher" (crozier) still just held together; a large cup by his side had "almost perished." There was also a silver shrine in the Lady Chapel with a statue of Teilo on it. Penally, his birthplace, had a shrine of an unknown saint who was later identified as Teilo, but all trace of the shrine was lost when the monastic community there dispersed.

The *Liber Landavensis* was first published in 1840, then trans. and ed. J. G. Evans: *The Book of Llan Dâv* (1893). There is a critical edition of the Life of Teilo contained in it by J. Loth, in *Annales de Bretagne*, 9, pp. 81-5, 277-86, 438-46 (1893); 10, pp. 66-77 (1894). See G. H. Doble, *Lives of the Welsh Saints* (1971; rp., 1984), pp. 162-206; *idem, St Teilo* (1942). B.G., Feb., pp. 238-41, lists four Lives: by Galfredus of Llandaff; in the *Regesta Landavense*; in the *Liber Landavensis*; an anonymous one in Capgrave. *AA.SS.*, Feb., 2, pp. 303-10, contains the first and fourth of these and calls him *"Telliao, sive Eliud."* Information on the opening of the tomb from *O.D.S.*, pp. 449-50. The little town of Llandeilo Fawr lies just to the west of the Black Mountains in what is now Powys, but there are no traces of the monastery.

St Sabinus of Canosa, *Bishop* (*c.* 515-66)

His Canosa is Canosa di Puglia in southern Italy, some forty miles north-west of Bari, and not to be confused with the Canossa near Parma where Pope St Gregory VII (25 May) had the famous confrontation with the emperor Henry II. The other confusion to be avoided—if possible—is that of this St Sabinus with two others of the same name mentioned in the *Acta Sanctorum* for the same day. One of these lived earlier, but it is possible that details of all three lives have been mingled.

Sabinus was born at Canosa, of which he eventually became bishop. He is mentioned in the *Dialogues* of St Gregory as friendly with St Benedict (11 July). Gregory relates of him that an envious archdeacon who wanted to be bishop sent him a poisoned cup; Sabinus drank this but lived, and the archdeacon died from the poison of his own malice, to general satisfaction. Sabinus must have been a person of some intellectual eminence, as Pope St Agapitus I (535-6; 22 Apr.) sent him as emissary to Constantinople to support St Mennas, the newly-appointed patriarch (25 Aug.), in his disputes over the Three Chapters controversy. He attended the council over which Mennas presided in 536.

He became blind toward the end of his life but was reported to have compensated for this with the gifts of second sight and prophecy, though incidents illustrating this are of no great religious significance. He died at the age of fifty-one and was buried at Tripalta, from where his remains were translated to Bari, where they lay under a marble altar. In 1562 this was overlaid with silver, on which his chief actions were engraved. According to Baring-Gould, the confusion among the two or three SS Sabinus arose from the fact that his family was an eminent one, producing several saints and bishops, all probably related. The Sabinus who died in 537 was buried at Bari, where his remains were lost for many centuries, being rediscovered in 1901. A third Sabinus of Canosa was bishop of Lesina; his remains were discovered in a marble sarcophagus in 1597.

AA.SS., Feb., 2, pp. 310-36; St Gregory, *Dialogues*, 2, 15; 3, 5; B.G., Feb., pp. 241-5; *Saints in Italy*, pp. 302-3.

St Cronan of Roscrea, *Abbot* (*c.* 626)

Like so many Irish saints of the period, his fame came down through the centuries in oral tradition, more concerned with the traditions of a place than with biography, and the earliest written accounts draw on such some centuries after his death. These state that his father's name was Odran, a Munsterman from Eile; his mother was Coemri, from Clar and Connaught. He was born in the district of Eile O'Carroll, in Offaly (central Ireland). His mother's sister's sons were two local saints: Mobi and Mochoinne; Mobi was a close friend and probably his tutor in the monastic tradition.

Cronan was famous as a founder of monasteries, or at least cells: the first at Puayd was followed by some fifty others, which he relinquished successively to local anchorites as he built them. He apparently established larger communities at Lusmag in Co. Offaly and at Monahincha near Roscrea (which lies on the main road from Dublin to Limerick, in Co. Laois: it is said that he moved the community to the then main road because pilgrims had previously failed to find it, keeping Monahincha as a retreat). He lived to a great age, becoming blind toward the end of his life. It is told of him, as of St Brigid (1 Feb., above), that he worked an Irish miracle of Cana, providing guests with beer, but in his case it was in such quantity that they "all became inebriated" (Ryan); this probably contributed to his reputation for hospitality. He was formerly commemorated on 28 April, but the new Roman Martyrology, in which he is included for the first time, transfers him to today's date.

Plummer, *V.S.H.*, 2, pp. 22-31. See also J. Ryan, *Irish Monasticism* (1931); D. F. Gleeson, *Roscrea* (1947); *Irish Saints*, pp. 132-4. See also *N.C.E.*, 12, p. 673, *s.v.* Roscrea Abbey; *Bibl.SS.*, 4, 367-7.

St Ansbert of Rouen, *Bishop* (*c.* 695)

His Life claims to be the work of a contemporary, Aigradus, but this now seems doubtful, and it probably dates from at least one hundred years after his death, obviously calling into question the accuracy of the information it conveys. It tells that Ansbert of Chaussy was chancellor to King Clotaire III, so engaged in affairs of State as well as in those of the Church. At a dissolute court he managed to preserve his integrity and purity. He was at one point engaged to St Angradisma (14 Oct.), who went on to become abbess of Oröer-les-Vierges, near Beauvais, while he became a monk in 673, going on to be appointed abbot of the great monastery of Fontenelle (at Saint-Wandrille, on the Seine between Rouen and Le Havre) six years later as second in succession to its founder (St Wandregisilius; 22 July), following St Lambert (d. 688; 14 Apr.) when the latter was appointed bishop of Lyons. He built up the abbey library, in particular adding classical authors such as Cicero. He was confessor to King Theodoric III, who released him to become archbishop of Rouen on the death of St Ouen (Audoenus, d. 684; 24 Aug.). Despite the fact that he governed his archdiocese well and was widely renowned for his sanctity he incurred the displeasure of the effective ruler, Pepin of Herstal, who banished him on a false accusation to the monastery of Hautmont-sur-Sambre, in Hainault, where he died. His body was removed, to protect it from Norse raiders, to St Peter's church in Ghent; it was destroyed by Calvinists in 1578.

The best text of the Life is in *M.G.H., Scriptores rerum Merov.*, 5, pp. 613-43, supporting the later date for the Life, as does Duchesne, *Fastes*, 2, pp. 207-8. See also *N.C.E.*, 1, p. 580; B.G., Feb., pp. 246-7; *Bibl.SS.*, 1, 1366, which gives his date of death as 699.

St Alto, *Abbot (c. 760)*

Alto is another saint of Merovingian times of whom the only surviving account dates from centuries after his death, in his case from the eleventh century, written by Othlonus, an abbot of the monastery he founded, after it had been restored. He was probably one of the many Irish monks who went to the Continent as *peregrini*. In about 743 he settled as a hermit in a wood near Augsburg, from where the fame of his holiness came to the ears of Pepin "the Short" (714-68; son of Charles Martel and father of Charlemagne), who was then mayor of the palace and effective ruler of the Frankish kingdom. Pepin made him a grant of land, on which he founded a monastery. The place, in Bavaria, is now named Altomünster. St Boniface (5 June) dedicated the church there in about 750. He wanted to follow the strict Celtic custom of not allowing women anywhere within the abbey precincts, but Alto objected to this, conceding only that a well blessed by Boniface should be forbidden to them. The abbey decayed after Alto's death but was restored around 1000 and has survived as a house of Bridgettine nuns.

His Life by Abbot Athlonus is in *M.G.H., Scriptores*, 15, pp. 843-6; also in *AA.SS.*, Feb., 2, pp. 59-61. See also *N.C.E.*, 1, p. 354; *Bibl.SS.*, 1, 893.

Bd Marianus Scotus (*c. 1080*)

Muiredach Mac Robhartaigh (or, Anglicized, Murdoch McRoberts) was one of the many Irish *peregrini* who embarked on a "white martyrdom" by setting out from their native land to leave what they loved best for the sake of Christ. He had taken a monastic habit at an early age, though without joining any community, and in 1067 set out on pilgrimage to Rome—which he was never to reach. He and several companions got as far as Bamberg in southern Germany, where they were welcomed by Bishop Otto of Regensburg, living for a year as a secular community under his direction. They then joined the Benedictine monastery of Michelsburg, living apart from the rest of the community (it is said at their request, as they could not speak the language, though this difficulty is not recorded of other wandering Irish monks) in a cell at the foot of the mountain on which the monastery was built. He is known as Marianus

Scotus of Regensburg to distinguish him from a contemporary, Marianus Scotus of Mainz, who died in 1082.

They then continued on their way toward Rome but did not get very far, being persuaded by an Irish *inclusus* named Muirchetach to remain in Regensburg, where the Upper Monastery—for women—made them welcome. Marianus' particular talent was as a scribe, and he set himself to making several copies of the entire Bible for the abbess. He and his companions moved to a cell in the Lower Monastery—for men—where they prepared the vellum, and he wrote virtually unceasingly. His legend tells that one night the woman responsible forgot to prepare the lights he needed to work at night; remembering suddenly, she hurried to the cell, to find that he was holding up three fingers of his left hand, from which three jets of brilliant light issued. This was told to the abbess, and his fame began to spread.

Once more they tried to set out for Rome, but Marianus was apparently told in a dream to stay where he first saw the sun rise. Setting out early in the morning, he naturally saw the sun rise over Regensburg, so stayed there for the rest of his life, copying sacred texts and also composing his own works and poems. Several of his codices are still extant, including one of the Epistles of St Paul annotated by him and signed with his name in its Irish form. In 1076 the Benedictine nuns gave him the old church of Weih-Sankt-Peter outside the city walls with a plot of land, where he built a house for himself and those companions who wished to live with him. He worked there until he died some four years later. He seems to have had a modern sense of history before his time, making use of both ancient and medieval sources in compiling a chronicle of the world, in which he made many corrections to existing chronologies.

His fame reached his native country, and many new recruits joined the *Scotti* of Regensburg. With the help of a wealthy burgher of the city they built a new church and monastery, which were dedicated to St James in 1111. This flourished and became the motherhouse of eight Irish houses in the German-speaking part of Europe, which became known collectively as the *Schottenklöster* and constituted a separate branch of the Benedictine tradition, with the abbot of St James as their superior. This arrangement lasted till around the beginning of the fifteenth century, by which time the houses were in decline in both numbers and morals, and most were taken over by German Benedictine communities. In 1515 Scottish priests persuaded both the government and Rome that they were the genuine *Scotti* (the common Celtic roots of Scots and Irish being by then lost in the mists of time), and the last Irish monks were expelled from Regensburg. This brought to an end a thousand years of Irish monastic presence on the Continent, though some thirty "Irish Colleges" maintained an Irish religious presence. The former abbey of St James is now the major seminary for the diocese of Regensburg.

Marianus' copy of the Epistles of St Paul is in the State Library in Vienna; there is a volume of "Patristic Notes" by him in the library of Fort Augustus Monastery in

Scotland. The history of the Irish *peregrini* on the Continent has been the subject of much recent study: for a summary and bibliography see T. O'Fiaich, "Irish Monks on the Continent," in J. P. Mackey (ed.), *An Introduction to Celtic Christianity* (n.e. 1995), pp. 101-39 (bibliog. pp. 135-9). On Marianus and Regensburg in particular see P.A. Breatnach, "The Origins of the Irish Monastic Tradition at Ratisbon (Regensburg)," in *Celtica* 13 (1980); P. Mai, "Das Schottenklöster St Jakob zu Regensburg im Wandel der Zeiten," in *100 Jahre Priesterseminar in St Jakob zu Regensburg* (1972); for a general account see E. Duckett, *The Wandering Saints* (1959). See also *N.C.E.*, 9, p. 603; *AA.SS.*, Feb., 2, pp. 361-72; *Bibl.SS.*, 8, 1140-1.

St Sisebutus, *Abbot* (1086)

The monastery of San Pedro de Cardeña, outside Burgos in northern Spain, is for ever bound up with the figure of Spain's national hero, Rodrigo Diaz de Vivar, *El Cid Campeador*. He died in 1099, so it would appear that Sisebutus is the abbot referred to in the epic poem that tells his story. It has been claimed that this was composed at San Pedro de Cardeña, and it certainly contains episodes designed to enhance the monastery's position as a major stopping place for pilgrims on the route to Santiago de Compostela. The problem is that the abbot is referred to in the poem as Sancho, and scholars are now generally agreed that, at least under this name, he is one of the few fictitious characters in the poem. So it seems that the poem simply changes the name of a real figure, possibly in the interests of metre. Ramón Menéndez Pidal in his great *El Cantar de mío Cid* discounts the idea that that the poem was written by a monk of San Pedro: "A monk with access to the records of Cardeña would not have put in an invented abbot named Sancho, forgetting the historical abbot. This was no less than St Sisebutus, who ruled the monastery for twenty-five years, dying in 1085. . . . And it cannot be said that Sancho is a copyist's error, since the assonance requires this." So the author seems to have changed the name deliberately, and the relevant passages from the *Poema de mío Cid* may well contain at least germs of history that apply to Sisebutus.

The Cid had made grants to the monastery and afforded it his protection before he was exiled for a year as a consequence of a quarrel with the king. He left his wife, Doña Jimena, and his two daughters in the abbot's care, knowing that he could count on this in view of his own generosity:

The Cid made his way as fast as he could ride toward the monastery of San Pedro de Cardeña . . . and the first signs of day were appearing when the noble Campeador reached San Pedro. As dawn broke, that holy servant of God, abbot Sancho, was saying his morning prayers. . . .

The Cid's party knocked at the door, and the call was heard within. O Lord, what pleasure Abbot Don Sancho showed! . . . "Thanks be to God," cried Abbot Don Sancho, "for your arrival. The hospitality of this house is yours."

Replied the Cid, born in a blessed hour, "My thanks, worthy Abbot; I am pleased by your kindness. . . . I am leaving the country and I want to give you fifty marks. . . . I am giving you a hundred more marks to shelter Doña Jimena

and her daughters and their ladies during the year. In your trust, Abbot Sancho,
I leave my two little daughters; attend them and my wife with all heed." . . .
    The Abbot declared that he would gladly comply with the Cid's request.
(cantos 14-15)

"Abbot Sancho" is mentioned further in cantos 49 and 54; a later ballad tells
that when the Cid was at the point of death in Valencia, he ordered his body to
be carried "in full armour upon his horse Babieca to the church of San Pedro
de Cardeña outside Burgos," where he and Babieca were to be buried, thereby
exalting San Pedro to a position second only to Santiago itself on the road
there.

The *New Catholic Encyclopedia* is definite about the historicity, stating that
Sisebutus is also called Sancho, "as in the *Cantar*." The date given for Sisebutus
starting as abbot is generally given as 1056. Under his rule the abbey achieved
outstanding splendour, and as abbot he would have been involved in all the
religious and political affairs of the diocese. He was a close friend of the Cid
and of three noted contemporary abbots: St Dominic of Silos (20 Dec.), after
whom Dominic the founder was probably named, Ignatius of Oña, and García
of Alanza. He governed the abbey till 1081, then relinquished the rule to Sebastian, taking up the reins again when Sebastian was elected bishop of León and
governing it for the rest of his life.

His body was buried in a side chapel but was translated into the abbey church
in the fifteenth century, when the community began to sing an antiphon in his
honour. His remains were moved again, to the "chapel of the martys," in 1610,
but no cult was authorized till the time of Pius VI (1775-99). When the religious Orders were suppressed in Spain in 1835, his remains were moved into
Burgos Cathedral, where they still lie.

AA.SS., Feb., 2, p. 455, and *Bibl.SS.*, 11, 1244, support the identification between Sancho
and Sisebutus. See also R. Menéndez Pidal, *El Cantar de mío Cid*, 1 (1908; n.e.1944), p. 40;
idem, The Spaniards in Their History (1950), pp. 26-7; also, for a fuller account, *idem, The
Cid and His Spain* (1934). Citation above from J. G. Markley (ed. and trans.), *The Cid*
(1961), pp. 14-15; see p. 131, biographical index, entry on Sancho, which claims he is
fictitious. See also C. Smith, *The Making of the Poema de mío Cid* (1983).

St Miguel Febres Cordero (1854-1910)

He was born Francisco Febres Cordero Muñoz in the city of Cuenca, seven
thousand feet up in the Andes in Ecuador, on 7 November 1854. His grandfather had been a prominent figure in Ecuador's struggles leading to independence from Spanish rule in 1822. His father was also active in the troubled
politics of the country and at the time of Francisco's birth was professor of
English and French at the seminary college in Cuenca. His mother, Ana Muñoz,
was one of nineteen children born to another influential family in Cuenca:
always devout, she devoted herself increasingly to works of charity.

Known as Panchito in the family, Francisco was born with crippled legs, which caused his father to regard him as likely to be always a burden on the family. His mother, though, always trusted that he would in time grow strong. She took care of his education at home until he was nine years old, when he went to the new school opened in Cuenca by the Institute of the Brothers of the Christian Schools (known as the Christian Brothers in the U.S.A. and the De La Salle Brothers elsewhere). Founded in 1680 by St John Baptist de la Salle (7 Apr.), the Institute had been suppressed under the French Revolution but restored with the return of the monarchy in France. From 1837 it spread rapidly in the New World, first to Canada, then to the U.S.A., and making Cuenca its first foundation in South America in 1863, when six French Brothers arrived.

Francisco soon distinguished himself at school and was chosen to give a welcoming address on the occasion of a visit by President Gabriel García Moreno, who from then on kept in close contact with his family. He soon decided that his own future was to be with the Brothers: "From the moment I entered the school of the Brothers, God gave me a burning desire one day to be clothed in the holy habit of the Institute. I always enjoyed being among the Brothers." But the Brothers were poor, foreign, and unknown and carried none of the prestige of the older religious Orders, so there was fierce opposition in his family, especially from a formidable grandmother, Doña Mercedes Cárdenas. He was sent instead to board in the seminary of Cuenca, which he hated: "I remained at the seminary for only three months, but it seemed to me like three centuries. I suffered a great deal in my heart. . . . It was simply not the place where God wanted me to be and I was like a fish out of water." His health deteriorated with the stress, and he was allowed back in the Brothers' school, his father eventually giving his permission for his son to join the Institute. This he did on 24 March 1868, aged only fourteen—this being before the minimum age for joining a religious Order was set at sixteen—taking the religious name of Brother Miguel. After only a year of novitiate he was sent to teach in the capital, Quito. His father was enraged and wrote to the provincial demanding that he leave the Institute, but Miguel politely insisted that his salvation lay there and nowhere else: "I wish to assure you [the provincial] in the presence of God and without any human consideration that I believe that I have been called by God to the Institute . . . and that I could not be sure of my salvation or even be content in any other walk of life."

Reconciliation with his father eventually came about when the latter asked his son to intervene with the president to secure the release from prison of a friend of his, a Dr Arízaga, imprisoned for political reasons. Miguel went with the provincial to see the president, who granted his request. His father wrote to him expressing his gratitude and giving him his parental blessing; from then on relations between father and son remained cordial. Miguel's father died in July 1882.

The fifteen-year-old teacher arrived in Quito in 1869 and began a career that was to last with mounting distinction for the next thirty-eight years. He always prepared his lessons carefully and marked the individual potential of his pupils, while making no distinction between rich and poor. He was not yet twenty when he published the first of his many books, a Spanish grammar so good that within a year it was prescribed for all schools in Ecuador. Seven other textbooks followed within the space of a few years. He made his greatest impact, however, as a teacher of religion, especially in preparing the boys for their First Communion—then made in their early teens. But official recognition came for his mastery in teaching Spanish, and he was made a public examiner and inspector for the schools of Quito.

President García Moreno continued his support for the Brothers, and the school prospered, increasing in numbers from 250 in 1869 to 1,000 in 1875. But on 6 August that year, García Moreno was assassinated; his immediate successor continued supporting the Brothers, but he was replaced within a year by the more revolutionary General Veintimilla, whose anti-clerical policies threatened even to close the school, while at the same time he refused to let any of the Brothers leave the country. Things settled down again, though in a more hostile climate, and the school went on, with Brother Miguel so outstanding a teacher that his fame began to spread nationwide. In 1887 he was chosen to represent the Ecuadorian branch of the Institute at the beatification of its founder, the obvious choice even though he was not a superior, partly because he had translated St John Baptist's Life and a number of his writings into Spanish. He set out for Rome in November 1887, arriving there early in the following February in time for the ceremony on the 19th. "There I was," he wrote, "an unknown Brother from Ecuador who would never have dreamed of making a pilgrimage to Rome. Being there, I felt as if I had been carried up into the third heaven!" On his return to Quito he organized a triduum of celebration in thanksgiving for the beatification and in praise of the founder.

His studies of the Spanish language were now earning recognition in the highest academic circles. A new grammar he wrote was prescribed for all schools in Ecuador. The quality of his writing was summed up after his death by the then Ecuadorian ambassador to Spain, Dr Honorato Vásquez: "I do not know anyone writing in Spanish, whether in Spain or in South America, who can rival him in clarity, methodology, precision, ease of expression, and that special attentiveness that understands the workings of the young mind. . . . The work of Brother Miguel extends from the elementary courses all the way to the most advanced. His material is insightful, scholarly, and full of illustrations. It constitutes a sure guide for the study of the Spanish language. . . . Brother Miguel has steeped himself in the classics of Spanish literature and everything he writes bears the stamp of its noble origin." He corresponded at length with academicians and writers, and in 1892 he was elected to the Academy of Ecuador, an honour he accepted only under religious obedience. Once elected, though, he played a full and constructive part in its activities. Other honours followed: he automatically became a corresponding member of the Royal Academy of Spain; in 1900 he was awarded the diploma of the French Academy; in 1906 he was designated a corresponding member of the Academy of Venezuela.

In 1894 a separate De la Salle Institute was formed for adult education in the Celbollar district of Quito. Miguel was assigned to teach advanced classes in Spanish grammar and literature and to supervise the boarders. In the Holy Week of 1895 President Luis Cordero resigned, and General Eloy Alfaro took office at the head of another revolutionary government. The school in Quito depended on a monthly stipend from the government; after an incident in which the students had refused to sing the national anthem as a protest against Alfaro—many of them having lost relatives in his revolutionary uprising—the stipend was cancelled in January 1896. The Brothers closed the school and the De La Salle Institute, opening a free school for the poor with the support of the archdiocese. Miguel was offered important posts in goverment schools but refused to dissociate himself from the Institute. Once more he returned to elementary teaching and preparing children for First Communion. The French Brothers, it has to be said, seem to have acted with less than collective heroism in times of adversity, seeking to leave the country at the earliest opportunity and many actually doing so. Efforts were made to replace them with local recruits, and Miguel was made director of novices, a post he held—whenever there were any novices—from 1896 to 1905, with as much success as he achieved as a teacher. In 1902 he was appointed head of the free school, the Sagrada Familia, which had grown to over a thousand students, with a community of twenty-two Brothers. After only ten months, however, he was relieved of his post for reasons that have never been made clear. It may be that his talents were not best suited to a position of administrative responsibility.

At the same time, moves were afoot within the wider Institute to call him to Europe. The official request was made in March 1907, with a promise that he would be away only four or five years. He was to go to the motherhouse at Lembecq-lez-Hal in Belgium, where it had been moved after being expelled from Paris by an anti-clerical republican government. He travelled via Guayaquil (where he strangely made no attempt to visit his sister, who was living there, until ordered to do so), Panama, New York, where he embarked on the SS *Lorraine* for Le Havre, and Paris, where he immediately caught a chill that nearly killed him. Once again, he was a "fish out of water"; the Institute (operating a publishing house more or less clandestinely in Paris) failed to capitalize on his special abilities but set him to translating French textbooks into Spanish. He accepted this with good grace, but his letters back to Ecuador betray his homesickness: "Many times I have given full rein to sighs and tears, but only God has witnessed them. I say this only to assure you that I do not think that our separation and the distance between us have in any way erased from my memory the remembrance of all my friends."

97

In July 1907 he moved on to Lembecq, where the atmosphere was more international and more stimulating. By autumn the Belgian climate was taking a toll on his health, and the winter was spent in recurring bouts of fever. The following summer he was sent for the sake of his health to Premià de Mar, on the Mediterranean coast just north of Barcelona, where a junior novitiate had been opened. He taught and worked on more textbooks, both his own and translations. But here, too, anti-clericalism and revolution caught up with him, this time in what has become known as *la semana trágica*, "the tragic week," in Barcelona, which began with the declaration of a general strike on 26 July 1909. The Church was deeply implicated in the right-wing policies the strike was effectively against, and churches were soon set on fire. The Brothers and novices were advised to stay where they were to prevent the building being looted and burned, but with a knapsack for each packed in case they had to flee into the mountains. On the night of 28 July the nearby railway station was set on fire, but the novitiate was spared. The next day the Brothers sent emissaries to the government forces in Barcelona, who sent a tug and a gunboat to evacuate them the following day. They returned after about a week, to find the statue of Our Lady Miguel had placed in the window to protect the house still there and nothing disturbed.

The incident, however, caused a further setback to Miguel's health, and this time it was to prove terminal. For a time he continued writing and teaching as normal, and in October he even managed to visit the shrine of the Virgin of the Pillar in Zaragoza, to his great joy. But toward the end of January 1910 he caught a bad cold, which quickly developed into pneumonia. He was given the Last Sacraments on 7 February, and two days later he died, whispering, "Jesus, Mary and Joseph, I give you my heart and my soul."

When the news of his death reached Ecuador, the whole country felt a sense of loss, which soon developed into a conviction that in him Ecuador should have its first recognized saint. The informative process was begun in 1922, and his cause was formally introduced in 1935. His remains were translated to a sealed casket in the chapel wall at Premià in 1925. The chapel was pillaged by left-wing forces in the civil war in 1936, but his remains survived, and the Ecuadorian consul in Barcleona, alerted to the danger by a young ex-Brother, was given permission for them to be returned to his native country. They were received at Guayaquil with rejoicing on 5 February 1937 and processed in triumph to Quito, with cures recorded on the way. The apostolic process was opened in Rome in 1938. In 1950 great celebrations in Ecuador marked the centenary of his birth, and a huge marble and bronze memorial was dedicated to him in Quito in 1955. He was finally beatified by Pope Paul VI, with his fellow De La Salle Brother Mutien-Marie Wiaux (Mucianus; 30 Jan.), on 30 October 1977, and he was canonized by Pope John Paul II on Mission Sunday, 21 October 1984. Among those present at the latter ceremony was the newly-elected president of Ecuador, León Febres Cordero, whose great-grandfather was the brother of Miguel's grandfather.

It was, of course, not for his scholarship, or even for his devotion to his pupils and to the religious life he embraced so consistently at such an early age, that he was eventually canonized, and when one looks for the underlying qualities in his personality, it is, as one biographer says "not easy to present this aspect of the man in such a way as to make it understandable and attractive to people today" (Luke Salm, F.S.C.). His spirituality was very much of his time, and very much a Latin spirituality of his time. He himself kept a spiritual diary, including all the resolutions made during annual retreats, for forty years. This shows a remarkable consistency in his spiritual life, built round meticulous examination of conscience and observance of the rule of the Brothers. Yet there is something beyond these that made those who knew him recognize outstanding holiness in him from an early age: it has to be the love of God that inspired all he did and wrote. The expressions of this may sound cloying today, and even theatrical—he once wrote a declaration of love of God in his own blood—but it was nevertheless the mainspring of his life. His particular devotions were to the person of Jesus as symbolized in his infancy and in his Sacred Heart, to St Joseph, and above all to Mary, devoting each day to a special aspect of her. But his devotion issued in apostolic mission, in care for his colleagues and his students. His whole life radiated service to others.

N.C.E., 17 (Suppl. 2), p. 35, citing *Osservatore Romano* 45 (1977), 3, 9, for his beatification; *N.C.E.*, 18 (Suppl. 3), p. 34, citing *Osservatore Romano* 46 (1984), 6, 7, for his canonization. The above account is based on L. Salm, F.S.C., *Brother Miguel Febres Cordero, F.S.C.: Teacher, Scholar, Saint* (1984), from which extracts are taken.

R.M.
St Romanus, hermit near Antioch (fifth century)
St Raynald, O.S.B., bishop of Nocera in Umbria (1222)

ST SCHOLASTICA (over page)
White dove on blue field.

10

ST SCHOLASTICA (547)

All the information available concerning the sister of St Benedict (11 July) comes, as indeed does the information about Benedict himself, from the *Dialogues* of St Gregory the Great (3 Sept.). These were written in Rome in 593-4, some forty years after Benedict died, and Gregory claimed to have derived his information from abbots of Monte Cassino after Benedict's death and from other abbots who had known him. But just as Benedict's name makes him "the blessed man," so hers makes her "the learned woman," and the question has to be asked how far his "biography" was devised to fit his foundation and hers to fill out his.

Her story is that she dedicated herself to God from an early age, settling at Plombariola near Monte Cassino when Benedict moved there, probably founding and supervising a monastery of nuns about five miles to the south of Monte Cassino under Benedict's direction (though the structure of this is not definite enough to earn her the title "abbess" in the Roman Martyrology). She used to visit her brother once a year, meeting in a house outside his monastery, which she, as a woman, was not allowed to enter. These visits were spent in colloquies on spiritual matters and praise of God.

Book 2, chapters 33 and 34, of the *Dialogues* gives a famous and delightful account of their last meeting. Scholastica, with a foreboding that she was shortly to die, begged her brother to stay the night so that they might prolong their spiritual dialogue. He refused, saying that his Rule obliged him to return to the monastery. Scholastica bowed her head in prayer, whereupon such a violent thunderstorm broke out that Benedict and his companions were prevented from leaving the house. He accused her of provoking this, to which she replied: "I asked a favour of you and you refused it. I asked it of God, and he has granted it." They spent the night discoursing on the joys of heaven, to which she was called three days later. Benedict, praying in his cell, saw her soul rising to heaven in the form of a dove and sent some monks to fetch her body, which he had placed in a tomb he had prepared for himself. He died some four years later and was buried with her. The tomb survives at Monte Cassino, despite the allied bombardment in 1944, but some accounts say that her relics were taken to France and deposited at Le Mans, while her brother's were taken to Fleury.

She is the patron saint of Benedictine nuns. The date of her death is usually given as 543, but the new draft Roman Martyrology assigns it to 547.

The *Dialogues* of Gregory the Great are ed. A. de Vogüé in *S.C.* (1978). See also *AA.SS.*, Feb., 2, pp. 392-412; *Bibl.SS.*, 11, 742; *B.H.L.*, 2, pp. 1089-90. The translation of the relics is discussed in W. Goffart, "Le Mans, St Scholastica and the literary tradition of the translation of St Benedict," in *Rev.Bén.* 77 (1967), pp. 107-41. *O.D.S.*, pp. 428-9. See also C. Cary-Elwes, O.S.B., and C. Wybourne, O.S.B., *Work and Prayer* (1992), pp. 166-8.

St Austreberta (704)

Austreberta (or Eustreberta) was the daughter of the count palatine Badefrid, one of the foremost courtiers of King Dagobert, and of St Framechildis (no longer commemorated). Her story tells that as a child she saw her reflection in a pool with a veil over her head. When her father planned a marriage for her, she ran away and went in search of St Omer (d. 670; 9 Sept.), bishop of Thérouanne, near where she was born, who clothed her in the religious veil. The new Roman Martyrology, however, states that she received the veil from St Philibert (d. *c.* 685; 20 Aug.), abbot of the great monastery of Jumièges, near Rouen, founded by St Audoenus, or Ouen (d. 684; 24 Aug.), and that she remained there as a nun.

According to the older Life, though, her father eventually consented to her entering the monastery of Port (now Abbeville) on the river Somme, where her piety and cheerful disposition won all hearts and soon produced stories of miracles. She eventually became abbess of Port and was then persuaded by St Philibert to take over the monastery of Pavilly. This had been founded by a man named Amalbert, who had placed his daughter Aurea in it. Austreberta found the nuns undisciplined and set about imposing a stricter rule; this caused offence, and some of the nuns denounced her to Amalbert on various trumped-up charges. He threatened her with his sword; she calmly bent her neck to receive the blow, but he came to his senses in time and left her to govern the nuns in the way she thought fit.

Her Life was written probably in the early eighth century not long after her death: in *AA.SS.*, Feb., 2, pp. 417-29. According to *D.H.G.E.*, 5, 790-2, this contains some errors, corrected in the Life in *AA.SS.Belgii* (ed. Ghesquière, 1780), though what these are is not mentioned. *Anal.Boll.* 54 (1936), pp. 155-66, says that her life needs further clarification and research. The account in *Bibl.SS.*, 2, 629-30, probably provides the best modern account. A Life of her mother reinforces some points, in *Anal.Boll.* 38 (1920), pp. 155-66.

St William of Malavalla (1157)

Details of his early life are lacking: he seems to have been a Frenchman and a soldier who, repenting of his dissolute life, made a pilgrimage to Rome and asked Pope Bd Eugenius III (1145-52; 8 July) to impose a penance on him. But it appears that his early life was later deliberately erased from records, so there is no way of knowing if it really had been dissolute or whether he was simply tired of the military way of life and what it entailed. Eugenius enjoined a pilgrimage to Jerusalem; not content with fulfilling this, William spent the next eight years in making other pilgrimages. He then settled in Tuscany in 1153, trying to lead a hermit's life, but by this time he must have established a reputation for holiness, as he was constantly sought out by would-be religious and disciples, and he was eventually persuaded to govern a monastery near Pisa. He found the laxity of the monks' way of life intolerable and withdrew to nearby Monte Pruno. Disciples joined him there, but they proved little better than the monks, so he withdrew once more, this time to a wilderness near Siena, a remote and daunting valley, called in Latin *Stabulum Rhodis* but in the vernacular *Malavalla*, "bad valley."

He established himself there, at first in a cave or a hole in the ground in 1155. The local lord of Buriano then built him a cell. He lived alone on roots and herbs for a year and was then joined by a disciple named Alberto, who was to write an account of the last thirteen months of his life. His penances and austerities were outstanding—beyond the reach of imitation by his disciple, who left an account of his hair shirts, prayer, contemplation, and mortification. A doctor named Rinaldo also joined them shortly before William died. He and Alberto buried his body in the garden; others came to join them, and in time a chapel was built over the grave. A hermitage was added to this, and the community grew, taking the name of Gulielmites, or Hermits of St William. They later spread to other parts of Italy and into France, Flanders, and Germany. Later many of their members joined the Augustinian hermit friars; Pope Gregory IX (1227-41) moderated their Rule and made the remainder join the Benedictines. William was one of the first saints to be formally canonized under the papal reserve, by Pope Innocent III in 1202. His relics were later dispersed in wars between what were then the city-states of Siena and Grosseto.

Life by Alberto in *AA.SS.*, Feb., 2, pp. 435-93, together with a Life attributed, but doubtfully, to Theobald, archbishop of Canterbury. S. de la Haye, *De veritate vitae et ordinis S. Giullelmi* (1857); *Bibl. SS.*, 7, 471-3, refers to him as "Giulelmo il grande"; *N.C.E.*, 14, p. 927.

Bd Hugh of Fosses, *Abbot* (c. 1093-1164)

Hugh was born at Fosses-la-ville, between Charleroi and Namur, south-east of Brussels in present-day Belgium. He was orphaned at an early age, brought up by a nearby Benedictine community, and then entered the service of Bishop Burchard of Cambrai. Burchard was a friend of St Norbert (6 June), the future founder of the Premonstratensian Order, then a wandering preacher, going about barefoot and dressed as a penitent. Hugh was accompanying the bishop when one day they unexpectedly met Norbert, who made such an impression on Hugh that he asked to become his first disciple and was accepted.

In 1119, by which time Hugh had been ordained priest, the two embarked on an apostolic mission in the provinces of Hainault and Brabant. Norbert was asked by the bishop of Laon to undertake the reform of a community of canons regular, and this was to lead to the establishment of a monastery at Prémontré, then a wild place in the diocese, followed by the founding of further houses and the drawing up of a religious Rule, which was largely Hugh's work. Norbert was frequently called away on various apostolic tasks, and the adminstration of the motherhouse devolved more and more on Hugh. In 1126 Norbert was elected archbishop of Magdeburg, which took him away even more often, on missions now political as well as apostolic. Hugh was unanimously elected abbot and superior general two years later. He was to govern the Order for the next thirty-five years and can with justice be regarded as its second founder. By the end of his adminstation more than one hundred foundations of "white canons," as the Premonstratensians came to be known, had been made. The steady success of his tenure seems to have been despite a certain hastiness and intolerance of character: he once complained to St Bernard of Clairvaux (20 Aug.) in terms that made Bernard—hardly the most patient or tolerant of men himself—reply in vehement tones in a letter that has survived, though Hugh's reply to this—if he made one—has not.

He died on 10 February 1164 and was buried in front of the altar of St Andrew in the church at Prémontré. In 1279 his remains were translated to near the high altar. The church was set alight during fighting in the First World War, but the relics survived. He was never formally beatified, but his cult in the Order grew, and it was confirmed by the Holy See in 1927.

A.A.S. for 1927, pp. 316-9, summarizes his career in the decree confirming his cult. St Bernard's letter is trans. B. Scott James, *The Letters of St Bernard of Clairvaux,* (1953, rp. 1998), no. 328. *AA.SS.*, Feb., 2, p. 378; *Bibl.SS.*, 12, 756-8, states that the date of his death is disputed. *N.C.E.*, 7, p. 191, suggests that he may have been the "Hugh Farsitus" who wrote the *De miraculis d. Mariae Suessionis* (*P.L.*, 79, 1777-80), but this is not certain. See also under St Norbert, 6 June, for the *Vita Sti Norberti*, one version of which it is claimed was written by Hugh.

Bd Clare of Rimini (1346)

Chiara Agolanti represents, it has to be said, the excessive practice of penitence that characterized developments of the *devotio moderna* of the later Middle Ages with its obsessive concern for physical details of the imitation of Christ. Her cult was confirmed in 1784, so veneration of her must have been considerable when Alban Butler was composing his original Lives, but she earns one of the most guarded comments, not to say outright strictures, in the previous edition of this work: "It is important to remember that the authority and approval of the Church are by no means involved in such extravagances as we read of in [his] acount of Bd Clare of Rimini. It is extremely improbable that if such a cause were now introduced for beatification it would succesfully pass the tests required by the Congregation of Rites. She is styled Blessed because from her death onwards she seems to have been venerated locally at Rimini. . . . We must also bear in mind that . . . standards of taste in such matters as manifesting contempt of the world's opinion have altered very much since the fourteenth century."

Standards have again changed since those words were written, and it is possible to view her story in a different light: as that of a woman being condemned for youthful excess in a way that would never happen to a man. She is described as a wealthy young woman, twice married, leading a worldy life from which she was converted by a vision of the Virgin Mary. She joined the Third Order of St Francis, was allowed by her second husband to live virtually as a nun, and after his death gave herself over to severe mortifications. In Lent she lived in a hollow in the city wall; on Good Friday she had herself dragged through the streets with a rope round her neck in imitation of Jesus on the road to Calvary. She nearly died from trying for too long to experience Our Lord's thirst on the cross. She went blind in the last years of her life and spent the last few months of her life in a coma, from which she emerged unable to speak.

But her works show that she learned not only to punish herself but to help others. She nursed her banished brother and many others; she helped some Poor Clares who had been forced to flee from Regno to establish themselves in Rimini, carrying wood for them like a servant—they locked her up to prevent her from going back to her hollow in the wall. She sold herself as a slave to ransom a man who was about to have his hand chopped off: the magistrate, moved to pity by her action, pardoned the man. She had a convent built for her disciples.

Her relics are preserved in the church of her convent in Rimini.

Her Life by Mazzara is in *Leggendario Francescano* (under 2 Feb.); see also *Auréole Séraphique*, 1, pp. 235-8. *N.C.E.*, 3, p. 914, says that her feast is not in the Franciscan calendar, but it is in Franciscan records, such as the above and Wadding, 7, pp. 394-400; *F.B.S.*, pp. 104-5. The extract above is from *B.T.A.*, 1, pp. 297-8.

R.M.

SS Zoticus and Amantius, martyrs in Rome (second/third century)

SS Charalampius, Porphyry, Dauctus, and three women companions, martyrs in Asia Minor under Septimus Severus (third century)

St Zeno, hermit of Antioch (*c.* 416)

St Trojan (Troyen), bishop of Saintes (Aquitaine) (*c.* 550)

St Protadius, bishop of Besançon (*c.* 624)

St Sigo, bishop of Clairmont (Aquitaine) (*c.* 873)

Bd Arnold of Padua, O.S.B., abbot of S. Justina in Padua, died in prison (1254)

Bd Peter Fremond and five companions: his sister Katherine; Mary Louise Du Verdier de la Sorinière; Louise Margaret Bessay de la Voute; Mary Anne Hacher du Bois; Louise Poirier, martyrs (1794)—see "Martyrs of the French Revolution," 2 Jan.

11

OUR LADY OF LOURDES (1858)

This second entry in the calendar year dealing with the Virgin Mary examines the phenomenon of apparitions as exemplified in the history of the shrine of Lourdes and reflects briefly on the practice of pilgrimage to such shrines. This requires an outline of the course of the visions, but the life of St Bernadette will be found treated at greater length under her feast-day, 16 April, while the doctrine of the Immaculate Conception is considered in the entry for 8 December.

Between 11 February and 16 July 1858, a fourteen-year-old girl named Marie Bernarde Soubirous insisted that she had experienced and reported a series of visions of a "Lady" in a cave beside the river Gave de Pau near her home town of Lourdes on the northern slopes of the Pyrenees (in the Hautes-Pyrénées *département* of France). The cave was a natural cavity in the rock-face known as Massabielle on the south bank of the river, across from the town. The vision was seen every time by her alone, though she told others, and gradually increasing crowds accompanied her to the spot.

She described what she saw the first time as a beautiful young woman, no taller than herself, dressed in white, with a blue girdle and carrying a rosary—which Bernadette also carried in a pocket. She had been sent with two slightly younger companions to collect firewood, and was about to cross a stream when she became conscious of a rustling sound in the trees near her, and, looking up, saw the figure, which seemed to invite her to pray. She knelt down and took out her rosary, and the "Lady" accompanied her over five decades, after which she vanished. That evening Bernadette told her mother, who said she had seen a soul from purgatory and forbade her to go back to the cave. After a few days, and after consultation with the local priest, who was not impressed, she received her father's permission to go back, and the figure reappeared to her, but not to the companions she had taken with her, as she was saying her rosary. She went into a trance and had to be dragged away from the spot. No one believed her story, but some people nevertheless took her back there four days later, when the vision, speaking in the local dialect, apparently asked her to come back every day for a fortnight. Her words as reported by Bernadette were, "Please do me the favour of coming here for a fortnight. I do not promise to make you happy in this world, but in the other."

On the following Sunday she was accompanied by a sceptical doctor, who took her pulse as she went into a trance. She was closely questioned by various local officials, who concluded that, though deluded, she was sincere. Over the next few days the crowds who went with her grew to several hundred strong. On Wednesday 24 February there came the next verbal message: "Penance! Penance! Penance! You will pray for sinners. Go and kiss the ground for the conversion of sinners. Go and drink at the spring and wash yourself in it. You will eat a herb that grows there." There was no spring in the cave, but the next day Bernadette scratched at the soil where the apparition had indicated, and muddy water began to ooze out, soon turning clear so that she was able to wash her hands in the stream and drink from it. The water was very soon tumbling down into the Gave, and it has flowed ever since, now at rate of thirty-two thousand gallons a week. The following day, however, there was no apparition, and Bernadette disappointed a crowd of four thousand. But the crowds grew, and on Tuesday 2 March there came the next message: "Go and tell the priests that people should come here in procession and build a chapel here." The Thursday of that week was the last day of the fortnight.

On Thursday 25 March Bernadette asked the "Lady" who she was, and the reply, again in dialect, came: *"Que soy era Immaculada Conceptiou,"* "I am the Immaculate Conception." This had been proclaimed a dogma binding on all the faithful four years earlier, a fact that has given rise to attempts to dismiss the whole sequence of events as a clerical effort to popularize the dogma. If the history as related by Bernadette is accepted, however, the clergy had been almost entirely sceptical up to this point, with only one priest—not the parish priest—going with the crowds to the site, which seems an improbably remote one to choose if there was to be a conspiracy to influence the masses. There was another apparition on 7 April, which was the Wednesday of Easter week, and a final one, the eighteenth, on 16 July, the feast of Our Lady of Mount Carmel. By this time the local authorities had fenced off the area of the grotto, and Bernadette saw the Lady, "as beautiful as ever," from the far bank of the Gave.

Despite the scepticism of church and local authorities for a few years, the shrine very quickly established itself as a major pilgrimage site, "not only the most visited place of pilgrimage in a country already rich in historical holy places, but the world centre of prayer and active charity" (A. Latreille). There was initially a period of secular opposition, when the mayor of Lourdes barricaded the grotto and spring for what he called "hygienic reasons." The shrine became the property of the diocese of Tarbes in 1861; ecclesiastical approval for pilgrimages there was given in 1862, and a chapel was built into the grotto of Massabielle. The bishop of Tarbes, in whose diocese Lourdes lies, first encouraged his faithful to come in procession. After the Franco-Prussian war they were soon being followed by pilgrimages from other French dioceses, using the new technology of the railways, with carriages modified to take stretchers. The annual French national pilgrimage, led by the Assumptionists, and Rosary pilgrimage, led by the Dominicans, date from the 1870s. By the quarter-centenary of the apparitions in 1883 national pilgrimages from other countries were being organized; by the half-centenary in 1908 they were coming from virtually all countries in Europe. A gothic church to replace the chapel was begun in 1862, and the first Mass in it was said in 1871. It was made a minor basilica and consecrated in 1876, before a crowd of 100,000 pilgrims. During the ceremony a marble statue of "the Lady" was crowned by the papal nuncio. Further increases in numbers of pilgrims necessitated the building of another church, known as the Rosary Basilica, built between 1893 and 1901, with a huge open space, the "place of the rosary," cleared in front of its west end for pilgrims to assemble, with two great curved ramps leading up to it and walks laid out for processions as well as a *via crucis* winding up the mountain-side. An office and Mass of Lourdes were approved for the province of Auch by Pope Leo XIII in 1891, and in 1907 Pope Pius X (26 Aug.) extended the feast for the whole Church. By the 1950s the facilities were quite inadequate for the crowds and a huge underground church was built, known as the Church of Pope St Pius X, while the assembly and processional spaces were further enlarged. In the 1990s some three million people visited the shrine each year. Their needs have also given rise to huge associated building works: the *acceuil* ("welcome") hospitals, hospices, hotels, and boarding houses; their presence has produced the notorious rash of souvenir shops, stigmatized by J. K. Huysmans as early as around 1890 as "the devil's revenge" on Our Lady.

How did a humble girl in a remote spot persuade the Church and the world in this way? One reason has to be Bernadette's steadfast attitude in the face of official disbelief. People simply found her more credible, and her story was soon being confirmed in people's minds by a number of remarkable cures reported by people who had visited the shrine and drunk or bathed in the waters from the spring. The first of these was reported in 1858; by 1861 the first commission had pronounced fifteen cures miraculous. The cures continued over the years, though they appear to have virtually ceased since the 1960s, many completely defying medical explanation. By 1960 fifty-eight of some five thousand reported cures had been declared miraculous. Acceptance of a "cure" as such has long been subject to the strictest medical analysis, with its lasting nature having to be established over several years. All are carefully logged, and the number accepted as authentic runs into several hundred—which is, of course, a tiny fraction of the number of sick who have visited Lourdes over the years.

One of the most carefully documented cures, witnessed, recorded, and monitored over the years by an outstanding medical practitioner, was that of Marie-Louise Bailly in 1902. She was a young woman of twenty-three, from a family with a disastrous history of tuberculosis, on the point of dying from tubercular peritonis. The astonishing story of her cure in a matter of hours is told by Alexis Carrel, who in 1912 was to win the Nobel prize for medicine and who, having lost his childhood faith, was the opposite of credulous in such matters. He had, by chance, accompanied her on an excruciating train journey from Lyons, where she was a patient of his. She had insisted on making the journey, even though she had been warned it might well kill her, and was convinced she would be cured, so there was an element of faith healing in her cure. Carrel was quite prepared to accept that such cures could happen, though not of organic diseases, and this was an organic disease, whose diagnosis he was convinced he could not have mistaken, in its terminal stages. He made notes as he saw her condition change before his astonished gaze: water from the baths was applied to her abdomen, which was hugely distended with solid tumours and fluid, at 2.20 p.m.; by 4.15, "the protrusion of the abdomen has completely disappeared. She tells me that she feels very well. . . . Her appearance has changed so much that everybody notices. . . "; by 7.15, "The abdomen's wall is supple, elastic, and with a slight depression which is normal with a twenty-two-year-old woman who is very slim." Marie got up the next day, recovered weight steadily, accepted her cure with no evidence of hysteria, joined the Sisters of Charity, and died in 1937 after a life of exceedingly hard physical work caring for the sick, during which she was never ill again.

Carrel was eventually reconciled to the Catholic Church, but not immediately by what he had seen and had no science to explain. His reaction was rather to suppose that science would one day be able to explain such an event and to work toward making this possible—in the event he was to develop a technique for keeping tissue living outside the body and a heart pump and so become a precursor of modern heart surgery, as well as developing mystical theories about humanity that led to his best-known work, *Man the Unknown*. He wrote a dramatized version of his experience at Lourdes, which was not published until after his death, using the name Lerrac (Carrel spelt backwards) for himself. In correspondence with the medical director of the clinic at Lourdes the year following the cure he made the perceptive comment: "It seems to me that twenty out of a hundred patients do improve. In truth, these are hysterics. But hysteria is a very disagreeable thing to treat, and a remedy that cures hysterics deserves the right to be recognized by doctors. If pilgrimages did not exist, they should be invented." The sick and their helpers still flock from all over the world, some in the hope of a physical cure, perhaps, but with many more deriving comfort from the special community and mutual healing experience that such a pilgrimage, usually organized on a parish or diocesan basis, can provide as no other experience seems to be able to do.

Recent analysis of this experience distinguishes three main features: separation from the *status quo*; passage through a threshold; regeneration and return to social responsibility leading to social and spiritual renewal. "The widespread data of pilgrimages show that almost all of them conform in some way to three related stages of (1) separation from a spatial, social, and psychological *status quo* and the passage into (2) a marginal or liminal space and set of social relations within which a theophany takes place resulting in a profound sense of community, which usually leads the pilgrim (3) to re-enter society as a changed, renewed human being" (D. Carrasco). Lourdes is a prime example of the personal change and renewal hoped for and experienced, but it also conforms to the other two aspects. To go there requires separation from normal life; it is—or was originally, before the huge development needed to accomodate such numbers—a marginal space, outside a centre of population. This marginality usually reflects the status of the person who receives the message: Bernadette was young and poor, but she and not the church dignitaries received the communication. In time the official Church comes to accept the genuineness of the experience, classifies it as a new private revelation, and takes over—as it did in the case of Lourdes, further marginalizing Bernadette herself in the process.

In some ways, then, Lourdes conforms to a pattern: it echoes the paradigmatic apparition at Guadalupe in Mexico in the humility of the messenger—though its message lacks the tone of racial, social, and then national liberation that made and continues to make Guadalupe so influential. Its geographical setting is also fairly typical, its remoteness embodying the durability of popular religion far removed from the centres where official pronouncements are made, and its rock and spring giving it echoes of pagan tutelary divinities. In other ways it is distinct from other reported apparitions: Bernadette alone saw the visions, so there was no aspect of collective hysteria, no thousands claiming to see the sun spin in the sky, for example. Lourdes also lacks the political and nationalistic overtones of the popular twentieth-century shrines of Fatima and Medjugorje, the former helping to usher in the Salazar régime in Portugal, asking prayers for the conversion of Russia (and leaving somewhat banal or sinister "secrets" for later revelation), the latter with its implication in the Croat-Serb ethnic conflict (and now forbidden to official diocesan pilgrimages). The messages "received" by Bernadette were the basic gospel injunction to a change of heart—*pénitence* being the equivalent to *metanoia* rather than simply "doing penance." Even official church approval, it should be remembered, leaves the "experience" with the one who experiences it: *Receptum est in recipiente secundum modum recipientis*, "It is received by the recipient according to the manner of the recipient," in the words of St Thomas Aquinas.

In the latter part of the the twentieth century the practice of pilgrimage is increasing while that of regular church attendance is declining, at least in the secularized West. One explanation for this might be that "pilgrimage is not theory (orthodoxy) but action (orthopraxis)" (R. Panikkar). Another might be that the location of a church is decided by human agencies; that of a shrine by "the sacred person or force that manifests itself there . . . a place that the community or its hierarchy would never have thought of choosing" (Jaime R. Vidal). As such, a shrine offers a closer connection between heaven and earth. This leads to a feeling—while reason tells us that God hears our prayers equally everywhere—that God will listen to prayers at a shrine more easily than in a parish church: "A place thus becomes a shrine by the experience within it of the presence of the sacred to an extraordinary degree" (Vidal). This can happen through historical association (Jerusalem, Rome) or through a perceived miracle (Guadalupe, Lourdes), and it is the latter type that seems to speak more powerfully to the modern world or at least to that part of it seeking reassurance in a world-view not dominated by rationalism and science. The Virgin Mary is central to this process, offering healing, love, and forgiveness, nowhere more so than at Lourdes.

The question of the "genuineness" or otherwise of apparitions of heavenly beings is a matter of debate between two world-views, one admitting the supernatural, the other not, which is never likely to be resolved by "evidence" one way or the other, or by rational debate. The Church is, as in case of Lourdes, slow to accept them; in most other cases, it eventually rejects them. Apparitions of the Virgin Mary tend to increase as the natural world becomes perceived as a more threatening place; hence also, her reported pleas to "recipients" for penance, prayer, and peace. In modern times the "recipients" have usually—and here Lourdes fits the pattern—been adolescent girls, thereby encouraging psychological speculation that their visions are hysterical in origin or related to typical traumas of adolescence: Bernadette herself was small for her age and subject to asthmatic attacks. The vision itself—and again Lourdes is no exception—tends to fit a contemporary popular image corresponding, not unnaturally, to the religious education of the recipient. So the image of the "Lady" at Lourdes derives from baroque piety as exemplified by the well-known painting by Murillo. Such images were multiplied into popular prints in large numbers following the definition of the dogma of the Immaculate Conception.

Recipients of visions have recently also generally "condemned the Council's opening to the modern world, or served as a rallying-point for pre-conciliar attitudes, even while their messages do not overtly reject the Council." And their messages tend to appeal to a certain type: "In the pilgrims who flock to such places one often detects a thirst for certainty and for clear directions in life, as well as for emotionally convincing evidence of the supernatural" (Vidal). Lourdes, with its emphasis on healing, has by and large remained free of this sort of bias. Pilgrimages made in specific quest of healing have, though, been criticized for offering a hope most likely to be disappointed, with resulting bitterness, rather than encouraging people with disabilities to come to terms with them and take control of their lives. But the overwhelming experience of Lourdes among the sick, their helpers from *brancardiers* (stretcher-bearers, or now those who pull and push wheeled stretchers) to *popotiers* (dish-washers in the kitchens), and the healthy who go for their own reasons, is a reaffirmation of faith and hope through an exercise of communal charity that would be hard to find paralleled anywhere else.

Citations above from D. Carrasco, "Those who go on a Sacred Journey: The Shapes and Diversities of Pilgrimages"; J. R. Vidal, "Pilgrimage in the Christian Tradition"; R. Panikkar, " A Pilgrimage to Kailâsa and Mânasasaras"; all in *Pilgrimage* (*Concilium* 1996/4), pp. 13-24, 35-47, 48-54. On expectation and disappointment see L. Evely, *Our Prayer* (Eng. trans., 1969), p. 112. The literature on Lourdes is vast: the principal collection of primary documents is R. Laurentin, B. Billet, O.S.B., and P. Galland (eds.), *Lourdes:*

Histoire authentique des apparitions de Lourdes (7 vols., 1957-66), containing documents to 1866; also R. Laurentin and M.T. Bourgeade, *Logia de Bernadette: Etude critique de ses paroles de 1866 à 1879* (3 vols., 1971). A basic work is L. J. M. Cros, *Histoire de Notre-Dame de Lourdes d'après les documents et les témoins* (3 vols., 1925-7); see also F. Trochu, *Sainte Bernadette Soubirous* (1957); in English, H. Petitot, *The True Story of St Bernadette* (1949; trans. of *Histoire éxacte des apparitions de N.D. de Lourdes à Bernadette*, 1935); D. C. Starkey, *After Bernadette* (1965); J. K. Huysmans, trans. W. H. Mitchell, *The Crowds of Lourdes* (1925). Recent popular accounts include C. H. Odell, *Those who saw Her* (1986; n.e. 1995), pp. 89-104; J. M. Miller, *Marian Apparitions and the Church* (1993), pp. 3-15. For an account of the cures see R. Cranston, *The Miracle of Lourdes* (1988, revised ed., with updated records from the Medical Bureau of Lourdes); *N.C.E.*, 8, pp. 1031-3; see also the entries for the Immaculate Conception, 8 Dec., and Our Lady of Guadalupe, 12 Dec., in the present work. Citations above from Alexis Carrel, *The Voyage to Lourdes*, Eng. trans. of *Le Voyage de Lourdes* . . . (1950, rp. with introduction by S. L. Jaki, 1994). Carrel's handwritten notes are preserved in Dossier 54 of the Archives of the Grotto at Lourdes.

A collection of imposing banners, left behind by national pilgrimages during the period 1858-1908, has recently (1996) been discovered in the belfry of the basilica. They include a magnificent double-sided banner from China, showing Our Lady talking with mandarins; another, from the first Egyptian pilgrimage, in 1885, depicts the Flight into Egypt. St George and the Dragon feature from England, as does St Andrew from Scotland. The oldest is dated 1872, fourteen years after the apparitions (information from Dom Alberic Stacpoole).

St Soteris, *Martyr* (304)

Knowledge of this martyr derives from two passages in the works of St Ambrose (7 Dec.), who claimed her as an honour to his own family; these are *De virginibus* 3, 7, and the *Exhortatio virginis*, 12. He claimed her as a near relative and regarded her with great pride. The martyrology of Jerome also tells us that she was originally buried on the Via Appia, her body being later translated by Pope Sergius II to the church of San Martino di Monti.

She is said to have been wealthy and beautiful and to have consecrated herself to God. Brought before the magistrates after the edicts of Diocletian and Maximian against Christians, she was insulted, tortured, and eventually beheaded. It is possible, however, that the examination and torture may belong to an earlier period, under Decius, with the execution alone taking place under Diocletian.

AA.SS., Feb., 2, pp. 386-9; *Saints in Italy*, p. 411. Ambrose's treatises are in N.P.N.F., 10, with Eng. trans.

St Evagrius Ponticus (345-99)

Evagrius Ponticus makes a first appearance as a saint in the West in the new Roman Martyrology. He had featured earlier in the synaxaries of Constantinople and Alexandria, but he is not recognized as a saint in the Orthodox East on account of the condemnation of some of his writings. He is now recognized as a major spiritual writer, above all on the monastic life, following on from St

Gregory of Nyssa (10 Jan.), whose thought he systematized and spread throughout the monastic circles of Egypt. Until the early twentieth century his main works had been attributed to St Nilus the Elder (12 Nov.), but since then studies have confirmed his authorship and made the original Greek texts available in the West, and he is now seen to have marked a real turning-point in the development of spirituality, as has always been recognized in the Syrian tradition. While there is now no doubt about what he wrote, there is still debate about whether his influence was altogether beneficial.

He was born in Pontus and ordained lector by St Basil the Great (2 Jan.), then ordained deacon either by Basil or by St Gregory Nazianzen (also 2 Jan.), whose close companion he became in Constantinople, where he had been present at the council in 381 and was famous as a preacher. He stayed for some months in Constantinople collaborating as a theologian with Patriarch Nectarius to combat the Eunomian heresy (the teaching that there is a single supreme Substance rather than a triune God). He then retired to the desert of Skete in Egypt to cultivate his soul in greater seclusion. This marked a definite change in his development, the reasons for which are not quite clear. Palladius tells that his retreat from Constantinople was owing to his falling in love with a great lady there; he would have settled into married life with her, but he was warned against her in a dream and in 382 fled to Jerusalem, where Melania, an ascetic from Rome who had been part of St Jerome's (30 Sept.) circle there and had then founded a Latin monastery in Jerusalem, influenced him to choose the monastic life. He spent the rest of his life as a monk in the Egyptian desert, where he became a disciple and friend of St Macarius the Elder (19 Jan.), whom he is recorded as consulting in the "sayings" of the Desert Fathers: "The abbot Evagrius said: Tormented by the thoughts and the passions of the body, I went to find the abbot Macarius. I said to him: 'My father, give me a word that I may live by it.' Then Macarius said to me: 'Attach the rope of the anchor to the rock and, by God's grace, the ship will cross the diabolic waves of this deceptive sea and the tempest of the darkness of this vain world.'" Evagrius spent the rest of his life working out this renunciation of the world into an elaborate doctrine. He died in 399, nine years after both his former companion Gregory Nazianzen and Macarius and about four years after Gregory of Nyssa.

His work was, in esssence, to bring to the monasticism of the Egyptian deserts the erudite spirituality, delving into abstract thought, that had characterized the Cappadocians. The main influence on him was Origen, whose complete works he had read and whom he accepted without the reserves expressed by the Cappadocians. This led to his condemnation as a heretic after 553, but in fact he constructed his own system of spirituality out of Origen. His works were generally very brief in form but dense in content, which has led the collection of the "sayings" of the Desert Fathers to be attributed to him, though this is now considered unlikely.

He evolved a view of the universe, embracing cosmology, anthropology, asceticism, and mysticism, in which the origin of the universe is wholly spiritual and matter the consequence of evil, to be spiritualized to the maximum by reparation for sin. Temptations come from evil spirits working on the *pathe*, the disordered affections—was he thinking back to his experience in Constantinople?—which the flesh, the body, awakens in the soul and thereby paralyzes the free play of the spirit. The spirit (*nous*) is bound to the body through the soul (*psyche*), and it is the task of the ascetic, the monk not only in practice but also in spirit, to free himself of the body and return to the will of God in the spirit. Evagrius backed this up by positing a development in the spiritual life from "practice" to "gnosis," thereby opening up the whole current of abstract thought that was to be pursued by Pseudo-Dionysius and influence the Middle Ages in ways that can be seen as being at least as dangerous to Christian spirituality as beneficial to it.

He categorized the virtues and vices into hierarchies, and in the process produced a famous description of the "midday demon" or "noonday devil" of Psalm 91, describing *acedia*, disgust with spiritual things: "the most oppressive of all the demons [who] attacks the monk toward the fourth hour and beseiges the soul until the eighth hour. He begins by giving the monk the impression that the sun is hardly moving or not moving at all, and that the day has at least forty hours. . . ." He included *acedia* in a list of eight principal vices, the others being the familiar seven capital sins. The virtues start from faith and lead to detachment from worldly appetites, *apatheia*, which in turn forms the basis of charity, *agape*. St Jerome, anxious to distance himself from any taint of Origenism, caricatured Evagrius' concept of *apatheia* as making us "a stone or else God," but Evagrius saw it essentially as a purification, not a denial or suppression, of human reason. Where he treads new ground is in passing from detachment *through* charity into "gnosis," rather than seeing charity as the desired outcome in itself, and here he ushers in a whole new phase of Christian spirituality.

He defines stages in "gnosis," the final one being "contemplation of the holy Trinity," which involves the stripping away of all definite thoughts—so initiating a current that runs on to *The Cloud of Unknowing* and beyond. This gnosis is "pure prayer," described as "the state of the soul that destroys all the reasonings of earth." This contemplation cannot be achieved by the exercise of the human spirit; it requires "a superabundant grace from God," but this does not exclude conscious effort on our part. The spirit—*nous*—becomes like what it knows, so when it knows God, it becomes God-like. Evagrius even calls it God: "When the *nous* is admitted to the gnosis of the holy Trinity, then, by grace, it is called God, as having arrived at the full image of its creator." He has been accused of failing to embody any Christian theology of the Trinity in this "gnosis," which aims simply at a supreme divinity, but Louis Bouyer has defended his teaching as leading to an experience of the divine life that could include the relationships within the Trinity without conceptualizing them.

113

Whatever meaning his own mysticism may have had for him, Evagrius' expressions "introduced a lasting threat into the Christian mystical tradition: the fatal attraction of pure abstraction" (Bouyer). Contemplation in his understanding tends to become detached from scripture and doctrine and from the stages in the spiritual life leading up to it, "pure prayer" being set apart from all other sorts of prayer and inevitably reserved to a tiny minority. His influence has been great on Eastern and Western traditions—to an extent all the more remarkable in that it has only recently been recognized as being his. The Syrians, Nestorians, and Monophysites regard him as their great doctor of mystical theology; among the Greeks he influenced St John Climacus (30 Mar.), St Maximus the Confessor (13 Aug), and the Hesychasts, while in the Latin tradition his main follower was St John Cassian (23 July), who adopted his ascetic tradition and passed it into Western monasticism. His admittance to the new Roman Martyrology perhaps reflects an awareness of the current popularity of currents of Eastern spirituality that he so closely approaches.

Several of his treatises have been preserved in Greek, and his writings have also survived in Syriac and Armenian translations. One collection of ascetical maxims is divided into one hundred chapters for uneducated monks, the *Praktikos*, and fifty for more cultured ascetics, the *Gnostikos*. His *Gnostic Centuries* exists in two versions, one apparently faithful to the original, while the other has been corrected to excise Origenist tendencies. His *Mystic Sentences*, or "Mirror for Monks and Nuns," was translated into Latin by Rufinus of Aquileia (d. 410; who might himself have featured among the saints but for his quarrels with Jerome). Sixty-seven of his letters have survived in Syriac and Armenian, including a doctrinally important early one to Melania the Elder, orthodox in tone, following the Cappadocians.

The above is based largely on *H.C.S.*, 1, pp. 380-94, with further bibliographical references. His works are in *P.L.*, 40, 1213-86; the *De Oratione*, attributed to Nilus, is in 79, 1165-1200. His importance was first noted by W. Bousset, *Evagrios Studien* (1923); I. Hausherr firmly attributed the *De Oratione* to him and brought out the coherence of his teaching: "Le Traité de l'Oraison d'Evagre le Pontique," *Revue d'Ascétique et de Mystique"* 65 (1934), pp. 34-93, 113-70, rp. as *Evagre le Pontique: Traité de l'Oraison* (1960). English translations of his works include *The Praktikos* and *Chapters on Prayer* (both 1981) and *Ad Monarchos—The Mind's Long Journey to the Holy Trinity* (1993). Information on his works in *N.C.E.*, 5, p. 644-5, which also has an illustration of part of his letter to Melania, from Add. MS 17192, fol. 63a, in the British Museum. See also *Bibl.SS.*, 5, 356-63; *Dict.Sp.*, 4, pt. 2, 1731-44; Owen Chadwick, *John Cassian* (1950).

St Caedmon (680)

All that we know of Caedmon is found in book 4, chapter 24, of Bede's *Ecclesiastical History*, and his account is quoted in full in the previous edition of this work as being "too precious to be abbreviated." Readers of this edition are referred to the good modern translations now available. Bede accepts the attributions to him of a series of poems (now known to be of a later date) that for many centuries earned him the reputation of "the father of English sacred poetry" despite the lack of any real evidence that he could have been the first to write religious verse in the period. This rested partly on the attribution to him of poems found in the unique Bodleian MS Junius II, of *c.* 1000, published by François Dujon (Franciscus Junius) in Amsterdam in 1655. Entitled *Genesis, Exodus, Daniel,* and *Christ and Satan,* they have now been shown to date from the eighth century and to be the work of different hands. They were attributed to Caedmon because they used the formulaic device of "kennings," also found in Old English versions of the one fragment known to be his.

They were attributed to him because the essence of his story is that he was a herdsman on lands belonging to the monastery of Streanaeshalch, usually identified as Whitby, who at an already advanced age was told in a vision, or otherwise discovered, that he had a gift for composing religious verse. He was convinced he had no gift for verse, and used to "get up from table and go home" when it was his turn to sing at a feast. One night he did this and went out to the stables, it being his turn to look after the animals there, when

suddenly in a dream he saw a man standing beside him who called him by name. "Caedmon," he said, "sing me a song." "I don't know how to sing," he replied. "It is because I cannot sing that I left the feast and came here." The man who adressed him then said: "But you shall sing to me." "What should I sing about?" he replied. "Sing about the creation of all things," the other answered. And Caedmon immediately began to sing verses in praise of God the Creator that he had never heard before."

Bede then quotes a Latin paraphrase of a few lines, which are all that can be attributed to him with any certainty. The following is a modern English version of Bede's Latin:

Now we must praise the ruler of heaven,
The might of the Lord and his purpose of mind,
The work of the glorious father.
For he, God eternal, established each wonder,
He, holy creator, first fashioned the heavens
As a roof for the children of earth,
And then our guardian, the everlasting God,
adorned this middle earth for men.
Praise the almighty king of heaven!

A Northumbrian version, preserved in an eighth-century manuscript in Cambridge, may represent his original words.

He told his dream to "his superior the reeve," who took him to the abbess of Whitby, Hilda (13 Jan.), who told him a passage from scripture and asked him to render it into verse. He returned the following morning with "excellent verses." Hilda persuaded him to enter the monastery, learn the scriptures, and put his gift to the use of the Church. That he had this gift and did put it to wide

use is evidenced not only by the above lines, recorded in several early manuscripts of Bede in various dialects, but also by the obvious importance Bede
attaches to him and his verse, listing the many books of the Bible and the
Christian mysteries on which he composed poems. Such poems would have
been easy to memorize and a great aid to devotion in a society used to listening
to verse. As D. H. Farmer has commented: "The special importance Bede
attached to this topic is shown by the elaborate biblical structure of the account.
Both the skill and the wide range of Caedmon's poems made them a powerful
aid to preaching; their impact could be continuous through learning by heart,
while their appeal to a race familiar with poetry and music transcended all
classes. Caedmon adapted ancient themes and formulas to the revolutionary
new idea of Christianity. The disappointment for us is that none of Caedmon's
poems has survived, but from the age of Bede we have the unique poem *The
Dream of the Rood.* . . ." There is no question that *The Dream of the Rood* is a
splendid poem, but unfortunately its existence provides no clue to the quality of
the verse Caemon might have produced in his biblical paraphrases. The existence of such Christian poetry of the period complements the message of its
contemporary Christian art.

Caedmon is said to have foretold the hour of his death and to have awaited it
calmly, dying fortified with the Eucharist, which he had requested some hours
earlier. It was brought to him, although as he had been talking and joking some
hours earlier no one believed that he was on the point of death. He asked all
those present if they had any grudges against him, was assured that they felt
nothing but charity, as he assured them he felt for them, received the Eucharist, asked how long it was until the monks began to sing the night office and
on being told that it was "Not long," replied, "Good, let us wait until then,"
lay back on his pillow, and died peacefully in his sleep.

Bede, *H.E.*, 4, 24 (pp. 248-51 in Penguin Classics ed.); D. H. Farmer citation above from
p. 372 (note to p. 250). See E. V. K. Dobbie, *The Manuscript of Caedmon's Hymn and Bede's
Death Song* (1937), which gives a long account of the Creation Hymn; G. P. Krapp (ed.),
The Junius Manuscript (1931); C. L. Wrenn, *The Poetry of Caedmon* (1947), for the
significance of the Creation Hymn in the tradition of early English poetry; R. T. Gaskin,
Caedmon, The First English Poet (3d ed., 1902); F. P. Magoun, "Bede's Story of Caedmon,"
Speculum 30 (1955); C. W. Kennedy, *The Caedmon Poems* (1916); see also *idem, Early
Christian Poetry* (1960), with preface and good translations. The Hymn is printed in its
Northumbrian and West Saxon versions in A. H. Smith (ed.), *Three Northumbrian Poems*
(1968), pp. 38-41. *The Dream of the Rood* is ed. M. Swanton (1970). See also *AA.SS.*, Feb.,
2, pp. 552-3; *Bibl.SS.*, 3, 636; *N.C.E.*, 2, p. 1042.

St Gregory II, *Pope* (*c.* 669-731)

He was born in Rome, his father's name being Marcellus, and was ordained
subdeacon by Pope St Sergius I (687-701; 1 July). He held the posts of treasurer and librarian of the Church of Rome under the next four popes (John VI,
John VII, Sisinnius, and Constantine). He studied scripture and the Fathers

assiduously and became an expert theologian. For this reason Pope Constantine chose him to accompany him to Constantinople to help resolve certain doctrinal and disciplinary problems arising from the Council *in Trullo* (or Quinisext Council) of 692. In their debates he proved both wise and strong-minded. At this time he was a deacon, but he was elected pope to succeed Constantine on the latter's death, being consecrated bishop on 19 May 715.

His pontificate coincided with the reigns of the Lombard king Luitprand (712-44) and the Eastern emperor Leo III, founder of the Syrian dynasty (717-41), and his dealings with both were to prove decisive for both the Church of Rome and for orthodoxy. His relationship with the emperor was tense from the beginning, as Leo imposed onerous new taxes on his subjects in Rome and Ravenna. These were nominally levied to pay for imperial protection from the Lombards, but this was not forthcoming. Gregory, as custodian of the Church's patrimony, was responsible for the largest contribution from Italy, and he made himself leader of the protest against the payment of these unfair taxes. Leo even ordered Gregory's arrest, but the Roman militia remained loyal to him and prevented this. The hostility became deeper with the outbreak of the Iconoclast controversy. This originated in the East, where its roots went deep. The movement spread to Asia Minor, largely through the influence of certain bishops despite the opposition of the patriarch of Constantinople, St Germanus (12 May), and was supported by Leo III, who took a decisive step by destroying the much-venerated icon of Christ at the Chalke Gate of the imperial palace. This caused a revolt, which was put down with much bloodshed. Gregory had remonstrated with Leo by letter, and their correspondence lasted two years without producing any agreement. In the course of it Gregory enunciated the principle that "the dogmas of the Church are the concern not of emperors but of the bishops, and they need to be defined with exactitude." "No pope," Eamon Duffy writes, "had ever addressed an emperor in tones as defiant as those used by Gregory II during the height of the Iconoclastic disputes, and no pope had ever shown so clear a sense of the real source of the papacy's strength: 'The whole West has its eyes on us, unworthy though we are. It relies on us and on St Peter, the Prince of the Apostles, whose image you wish to destroy, but whom the kingdoms of the West honour as if he were God himself on earth. . . . You have no right to issue dogmatic constitutions, you have not the right mind for dogmas; your mind is too coarse and martial.'" In 730 Iconoclasm became official imperial policy.

King Liutprand took advantage of the quarrels between pope and emperor to attempt to unite the whole of Italy under Lombard rule. In 728 he invaded the exarchate of Ravenna and pushed on toward Rome, which he beseiged the following year. But Gregory, who had rebuilt large parts of the city walls, stood firmly against him, and instead of occupying the city, Liutprand, who was by now at least nominally Catholic, gave "Peter and Paul" the land of Sutri in recognition of the wishes of its inhabitants, thereby effectively by this "donation of Sutri" initiating the role of the papacy as temporal ruler that was to play such a major part in the affairs of the Western Church for over a thousand years. Luitprand was "brought to such remorse" that he left his armour and weapons as offerings at the tomb of St Peter.

Gregory was also a great missionary pope, his main achievement in this area being to commission St Boniface (5 June) as apostle to the Germanic peoples, as his predecessor Pope St Gregory the Great (3 Sept.) had commissioned Augustine as "apostle to the Angles." Boniface, then known by his native English name of Winfrid, had come to Rome in May 719 seeking the papal blessing on his missionary work. Gregory gave him every help, giving him the name Boniface, and on a second visit consecrated him bishop for the purpose. He continued to send him advice, which was largely responsible for the Roman character of the church Boniface established in Germany—eventually to become the model for the Carolingian reform of the Frankish Church.

In Rome, besides restoring the city walls Gregory rebuilt and restored many churches as well as the great monastery near St Paul's Outside the Walls. He built a hospital for old men and converted the house in which his mother lived into the monastery of St Agatha after she died in 718. He also assisted St Petronax (6 May) in rebuilding the abbey of Monte Cassino, which had been laid waste by the Lombards, and in restoring Benedictine life there, appointing Petronax abbot. He carried out measures of liturgical reform and instituted the "station" Masses on Thursdays in Lent. He summoned local synods to enforce church discipline and extirpate superstition. As a former treasurer, he kept a firm eye on the mounting funds of the church of Rome, ensuring that they were used for constructive and charitable purposes. He welcomed growing numbers of English pilgrims to Rome, and his pontificate saw the establisment of a church, a school, and a cemetery for them in Rome. He helped St Nothelm (later archbishop of Canterbury; 17 Oct.) with his researches in the papal archives, which were to make a major contribution to Bede's *Ecclesiastical History*. He also received King Ine of Wessex, who became a monk in Rome.

In his dealings with those in power Gregory was always firm, but in personal relationships he could be gentle. He became pope at a critical time at the height of his intellectual powers, and his decisions left the papacy and the Church the benefits of his clear-sightedness, which were to last for many decades. He died on 11 February 731 and was buried in the basilica of St Peter.

The main sources for his Life are collected in *AA.SS.*, Feb., 2, pp. 692-705. See also *Lib. Pont.*, 1, pp. 396-414; *Geschichte des Papstums*, 2, pp. 643-64; *O.D.P.*, pp. 86-7. Citation above from E. Duffy, *Saints and Sinners: A History of the Popes* (1997), p. 64, citing W. Ullmann, *A Short History of the Papacy in the Middle Ages* (1974). The history of the Iconoclast conflict is in Jedin-Dolan, 3, 1, pp. 5-7, 26-36; further bibliog. on the papacy of the period, p. 477. B. Mondin, *Dizzionario Enciclopedico die Papi* (1995), with further bibliog. See also *Bibl.SS.*, 7, 287-90; *O.D.S.*, p. 213; *N.C.E.*, 6, p. 770; *Saints in Italy*, p. 206; G. Ferrari, *Early Roman Monasteries* (1957); G. M. Grasselli and P. Tarallo, *Guia ai Monasteri d'Italia* (1994), pp. 300-1, 318-9.

St Paschal I, *Pope* (824)

Paschal was a Roman by birth, his father's name being Bonoso. He was educated in the school of the Lateran *patriarchium*, received Holy Orders including the presbyterate, and became abbot of the monastery of San Stefano Maggiore near the Vatican. There is frankly not a great deal known of him that would seem to entitle him to a place in the Roman Martyrology, though the *Liber Pontificalis* extols his holiness, piety, chastity, and theological learning.

He was elected pope on the very day (24 February) his predecessor, Stephen IV (816-7) died. In this hasty election the electors were exercising the new privilege of freedom in papal elections granted to the church of Rome by the emperor Louis the Pious only a month earlier and formally issued as the *Pactum Ludovicianum* on the very day that Stephen died. Paschal was consecrated bishop and enthroned the following day, and only then was the emperor notified, in accordance with the letter of the privilege. Louis returned a "pact of confirmation" of the election—the earliest of which a text is known.

Paschal invited Louis to come to Rome formally to ratify the various pacts and agreements made between the Frankish kings and the Holy See—the earlier *Promissio* made by Charlemagne to Adrian I and St Leo III (12 June) as well as the new *Ludovicianum*. These recognized papal dominions outside the duchy of Rome—the Pentapolis, Tuscany, Lazio, and Corsica—with a promise that the emperors would not interfere in these. Louis did not come in person but in 822 sent his son Lothar, together with his eminent counsellor Wala, the most conversant with the Italian situation, to reside south of the Alps for three years, thereby incorporating this region into the Holy Roman Empire. The following Easter Paschal crowned Lothar co-emperor in Rome, following the pattern set by Stephen IV in crowning and anointing Louis and his empress in Reims in 816.

The meeting in Rome had unfortunate consequences, however. Lothar and Wala interfered in the internal affairs of the Papal State when they exempted the abbey of Farfa from the annual tax due to the Holy See. After they had departed some of Paschal's men killed two high papal functionaries on the grounds that "in every respect they showed themselves to be loyal to the young emperor Lothar." Louis the Pious appointed an examining committee to look into the affair, but nothing came of it: Paschal in effect stymied it by swearing his innocence in the affair and declaring that those responsible had been executed as traitors. No one believed this, and when Paschal died suddenly early the following year, the Romans would not allow his body to be carried into St Peter's. There are conflicting opinions over the responsibility for this: one view is that it was a popular reaction because his "self-willed and harsh government" had made him "many enemies and [he] was widely detested in Rome" (*Oxford Dictionary of Popes*). Another is that it was the Roman *nobility* only who delayed the burial to ensure the election of their nominee and that Paschal, "troubled in his lifetime, insulted when he died . . . is accounted a saint" (*The Popes*). The tumult caused by the affair delayed the election of a successor, but Wala eventually secured the election of the "imperial candidate" as Eugenius II. He calmed the people and Paschal's body was allowed into the basilica a few months later.

Paschal oversaw the further expansion of missionary activity in northern Europe, sending a group of monks to evangelize Denmark in 822, with Louis' agreement, and another group into Sweden the following year. Toward the end of his pontificate the Iconoclast controversy broke out again. Theodore the Studite (11 Nov.) refers to a letter written by Paschal to the emperor Leo V (assassinated in 820) in defence of the cult of images, but it seems doubtful that he had time to devote much of his attention to the quarrel. The building of churches in Rome occupied more of his time; he was responsible for moving the bodies of many early saints from the catacombs and enshrining them under altars in churches; he also oversaw, among others, the rebuilding and embellishment of Santa Prassede, Santa Maria *in Domnica*, and Santa Cecilia in Trastevere. All these are still basically in the form he left them and have mosaics commissioned by him. A story, which survives in Latin in letters of stone in Santa Cecilia, tells that he could not find the body of St Cecilia (22 Nov.), but one day he fell asleep during the office in St Peter's and dreamed that a renewed attempt would be rewarded with success—as it was. He brought her intact and incorrupt body into Rome and buried it in the new church he had built on the site of her former home.

B. Mondin, *Dizzionario Enciclopedico dei Papi* (1996), pp. 100-1; *O.D.P.*, pp. 99-101; E. John, *The Popes*, p. 146. Jedin-Dolan, 3, 1, pp. 107-12. E. Duffy, *op. cit.* (previous entry), p. 78, picture of Leo III's mosaic on p. 74. On the Roman churches, see S. G. A. Luff, *The Christian's Guide to Rome* (n.e. 1990), pp. 106-7, 212-4, 254-6, 287.

The statue of St Cecilia in her church in Trastevere, on Stefano Maderno the sculptor's oath, shows her body just as it was when it was exhumed in 1599. Paschal is depicted in the apse mosaics of S. Maria *in Domnica* (or della Navicella) with a square halo, indicating that he was still alive at the time: he is kneeling at the feet of an enthroned Madonna—one of the earliest instances of her depiction in the place where Christ would traditionally be. He is also depicted in the mosaic in the apse of Santa Prassede.

R.M.

St Desiderius, bishop and martyr, reputedly by the sword at Langres (304)

St Castrensis, martyr under the Vandals (*c.* 450—but possibly Priscus, formerly bishop of Castra in N. Africa)

St Macedonius *Kritophagos* ("barley-eater"), hermit near Antioch (*c.* 430)

St Secundinus, bishop in Apulia (fifth/sixth century)

St Severinus, abbot of Agaune (Switzerland) (sixth century)

St Theodora, empress, retired to a monastery (867)

St Ardanus, abbot of Tournus (Burgundy) (1006)

12

SS Saturninus, Dativus, and Companions, *Martyrs* (304)

The first imperial edict against Christians issued by the emperor Diocletian, marking the beginning of the persecution that led to so many martyrs, ordered all copies of the scriptures to be destroyed by fire. Many Christians obeyed, but more held out. One of the latter was Saturninus, a priest in Abitina, in proconsular North Africa. He and his congregation were seized one Sunday by the local magistrates with a troop of soldiers. Saturninus, his four children, and a senator named Dativus led the party to be questioned by the magistrates. They all replied so bravely that even their interrogators praised them, but they were sent, shackled, to Carthage, to be examined by the proconsul.

The examination has been preserved in *acta* that are undoubtedly basically genuine, though in the form in which they have survived they may have been edited to support the strict Donatist position as it emerged in the controversy a century after their deaths. This would have emphasized the point that all attended worship on the Lord's Day, and the inclusion of the child Hilarion is a rare instance of a child being allowed to attend Mass at the time. Dativus was questioned first and professed himself a Christian who worshipped with Christians. He was taken away to be racked even before he had told where assemblies for worship took place. One of the women from the congregation, Thelica, said that "the holy priest Saturninus and all of us with him" were the leaders of the Christians. The women proved as brave as the men: a young woman named Victoria, who had escaped from an arranged betrothal by jumping out of a window and taking refuge in a church, refused the offer of being returned to the care of her pagan brother, saying that no one who did not acknowledge the law of God could be a brother of hers. The child Hilarion even laughed at the judge's threats to cut off his ears and nose if he did not recant. Saturninus and his companions were not executed, it seems, but died in prison either from long exposure to harsh conditions or a result of the tortures inflicted on them.

The text of the Acts is in *AA.SS.*, Feb., 2; also in *P.L.*, 8, 705-15. On its possible editing in favour of the Donatists see P. Monceaux, "Les martyrs Donatistes," in *Revue de l'histoire des religions* 48 (1913), pp. 146-92. See also *Bibl.SS.*, 11, 682-4; B.G., Feb., p. 259, giving the numbers as thirty men, nine women, and the boy Hilarion (following Augustine).

St Meletius of Antioch, *Bishop* (381)

Meletius played an important part in the tangled affairs of the Church in the East during the long-drawn-out Arian controversies and power struggles. He was born in Melitene and came from a distinguished family of Lesser Armenia. Virtually nothing is recorded of his early life, but by the time he became a prominent churchman he was known for his conciliatory ways, and he managed to gain the trust of both orthodox Catholics, upholding the Creed of the Council of Nicaea (325), and Arians.

He was appointed bishop of Sebaste in Armenia, but here he ran into the first of many quarrels that there were to cause him to lead an exceedingly unstable life as bishop. Forced to flee by an opposing faction, he retired first to the desert, from where he was transferred to the town of Beroea in Syria. The church historian Socrates claims that he was bishop there.

The church of Antioch had been prey to Arianism, usually supported by the emperors, for many decades. Its bishop, Eustathius, a great theologian and staunch enemy of Arianism, had been forced into exile in Thrace in 331 by a party led by Eusebius of Nicomedia, which brought influence to bear on Constantine. He was succeeded by a run of bishops who upheld the Arian position. Then quarrels broke out among different factions within Arianism, and these were responsible for the banishment of the last of the pro-Arian bishops of Antioch, Eudoxius. Some Catholics and some Arians agreed on Meletius as their choice to be his successor. This was in 361, which was also the last year of the reign of Constantius II, Constantine's son and a firm upholder of Arianism, as emperor in the East. Other Catholics opposed his appointment, believing him to be too much beholden to the Arians who had helped to elect him, who in turn hoped he would favour them.

Meletius undeceived them when Constantius visited Antioch. The emperor ordered him and several other prelates to expound the text from the Book of Proverbs: "The Lord created me at the beginning of his work" (8:22). The "me" referred to is "wisdom," but Meletius interpreted the text in an uncompromisingly anti-Arian way, making the words refer to the Incarnation. This angered the Arians, who persuaded Constantius to banish Meletius to Lesser Armenia and gave the see to Euzoïus, thereby giving rise to what is known as the schism of Antioch, though a *de facto* state of schism had really existed from the time Eustathius was banished in 331. Socrates does not record that the exposition was made in the presence of the emperor (though Theodoret and Epiphanius do) but that "the emperor being informed of this, ordered that he [Meletius] should be sent into exile; and caused Euzoïus, who had before been deposed together with Arius, to be installed bishop of Antioch in his stead. Such, however, as were attached to Meletius, separated themselves from the Arian congregation, and held their assemblies apart. Nevertheless, those who originally embraced the homoousian opinion would not communicate with them, because Meletius had been ordained by the Arians, and his adherents had been baptized by them. Thus was the Antiochian Church divided, even in regard to those whose views on matters of faith exactly corresponded" (*H.E.*, 2, 44).

On the death of Constantius his cousin Julian succeeded as emperor. His and the subsequent reigns were to see Meletius banished and recalled several times, as first Julian attempted to restore paganism, and then after he was killed in 363, Jovian, who died in February the following year, restored Christianity to its position under Constantius and held Meletius in high esteem. His successor Valens sympathized with the Arians, and the consequent jockeyings for power ebbed and flowed. Valens died in 378, and Meletius was reinstated as bishop, only to find another orthodox contender for the see, Paulinus, in possession of it and recognized by Rome and by the leading orthodox champion, Athanasius (2 May), while Meletius had the support of most of the Christians of Antioch itself.

Jerome (30 Sept.) appealed to Pope Damasus to impose a solution from Rome: "I know nothing of Vitalis; I reject Meletius; I have nothing to do with Paulinus. 'He that gathers not with you scatters.'" Basil of Caesarea (the Great; 2 Jan.), however, saw that only recognition of Meletius could end the schism and tried to reconcile Meletius with Rome. Writing to Count Terentius, he says, "I shall never be able to persuade myself . . . to ignore Meletius, or to forget the church which is under him, or to treat as small, and of little importance to the true religion the questions which originated the division." Basil died in 379, and Meletius was left as champion of the orthodox party. He summoned a synod at Antioch in the autumn of that year at which 152 bishops declared the unity of their faith with that of Rome. This was now also imperial policy, and Gratian, emperor in the West, promulgated an edict endorsing the Catholic version of the faith in 380, with the Nicene Creed held to contain the true definition of this faith. The idea of a second ecumenical council had been growing since the death of Valens, and Theodosius I, emperor in the East, finally summoned this to meet in Constantinople in 381. Meletius led the bishops from the East and presided at the first session, but he died unexpectedly only a few days after the opening. All the fathers of the council and the faithful of Constantinople attended his funeral. He had endeared himself to all by his evangelical meekness in extremely stressful and contentious circumstances. St Gregory of Nyssa (10 Jan.) preached the funeral oration, in which he refered to Meletius' "sweet calm look and radiant smile, the kind hand seconding the kind voice." A further panegyric was preached on the anniversary of his death five years later by St John Chrysostom (13 Sept.). The texts of both these orations are still extant, and the new Roman Martyrology mentions a further one by St Gregory Nazianzen (2 Jan.).

AA.SS., Feb, 2, pp. 584–602; *B.H.G.*, pp. 109-10; *D.C.B.*, 3, pp. 891-3. *Bibl.SS.*, 9, 296–300; *N.C.E.*, 9, p. 631, on the "Meletian Schism." Sozomen, *H.E.*, 7, 10; Socrates, *H.E.*, 2, 45; 3,9; 4, 26; Theodoret, *H.E.*, 3, 2; 5, 7; *P.G.*, 52, 630, has a letter from St John Chrysostom to Meletius. See also *Anal.Boll.* 67 (1949), pp. 187-202; W. A. Jurgens, "A Letter of Meletius of Antioch," *Harvard Theological Review* 53 (1960), pp. 251-60.

St Ethilwald of Lindisfarne, *Bishop* (740)

Ethilwald (also Ethelwald, Æthelweald) was a Northumbrian who became a disciple of St Cuthbert (20 March) and a monk of Cuthbert's abbey at Melrose on the east coast of Scotland, where he became prior and eventually abbot. His ability and piety led to his being chosen to succeed Edfrith (d. 721; 4 June) as bishop of Lindisfarne (Holy Island). Edfrith, besides being a bishop, was a most distinguished calligrapher, responsible for the Lindisfarne Gospels, described by Plummer as "the fairest manuscript that has ever come under my notice" and still preserved in the British Library. Ethilwald showed his respect fo his predecessor's work by commissioning a binding for it from the hermit Billfrith (also venerated as a saint in the diocese of Durham on 6 March), who used gold, silver, and precious stones. This binding has unfortunately disappeared, perhaps a victim of its monetary value. Ethilwald also compiled a work known as the *Ymnarius Edilwaldi*, which is a partial source for the *Book of Cerne*.

Ethilwald ruled his diocese for many years, dying with a reputation for sanctity proved by the fact that his relics were moved with those of St Cuthbert. He was buried in his cathedral, but to save the relics from the ravages of Viking marauders who destroyed Lindisfarne in 875 they were embarked by members of the community on a lengthy peregrination around northern England and south-west Scotland, reaching a permanent home in Durham only in 995. A stone cross bearing his name was also eventually moved from Lindisfarne to Durham. Ethilwald's relics were translated to Westminster by King Edgar.

The source for information about Ethilwald is Bede, *H.E.*, 5, 1, 12. On the Lindisfarne Gospels, see T. D. Kendrick *et al.*, *Codex Lindisfarnensis* (1960); F. Henry, "Codex Lindisfarnensis," in *Antiquity* 37 (1963), pp. 100-10. *AA.SS.*, Feb., 2, pp. 605-7, 897; *O.D.S.*, p. 168, *s.v.*; pp. 116-8 (Cuthbert); pp. 145-6 (Edfrith). See also the recent study by Michelle P. Brown, *The Book of Cerne* (1996).

St Benedict of Aniane, *Abbot* (751-821)

Benedict, whose feast is moved in the new Roman Martyrology from the previous day (his date of death is generally agreed as 11 February, but his funeral on the following day was generally celebrated as his feast-day), was perhaps the most influential reformer of the observance of the Benedictine Rule in the West. He lived at a time when varieties of observances and many abuses had crept into Western monasticism and in a place, the Frankish empire, where any effective action had to carried out in close consultation with the emperor. Perhaps for these reasons, despite his personal holiness and austerity of life, he has remained a structural rather than a spiritual influence.

He came from a noble Visigothic family, his father being Count Aigulf of Languedoc, and his original name was Witiza. As a young man he served both King Pepin and his son Charlemagne at court as a page and in the office of cup-bearer of Queen Bertrada. At the age of twenty he underwent a religious conversion but still served in the Lombardy campaign as a soldier, distinguishing himself at the siege of Pavia in 774. He then decided to withdraw from the world, influenced by an episode in which he tried to save his brother from drowning and was nearly drowned himself. Advised by a hermit named Widmar, he became a monk at Saint-Seine, near Dijon, in 780. Because of his court connections this was not easy: to do so he had to invent the pretext of going to visit the court at Aix-la-Chapelle. He adopted an extremely austere rule of life, which owed more to the earlier Rules of Pachomius (14 May) and Basil (2 Jan.), of which he made a special study, than to that of St Benedict (11 July) himself. He refused the abbacy when the then abbot died, knowing that the monks would not be able or willing to follow the strict style of life he had adopted. Instead he retired to a piece of ancestral property by the shore of the brook Aniane, in Languedoc, and lived alone for some years as a hermit. He was joined by others who came to live under his direction, all leading a simple life of manual labour, manuscript copying, and severe fasting. He would use only the simplest materials, even for celebrating Mass, but later modified his stance on this question somewhat.

The numbers increased to a point where the community had to leave the banks of the Aniane for more spacious surroundings in which they could build a monastery. Here he built a church and allowed that rich vessels and ornaments could properly be used in the liturgy. His influence grew, and he was appointed overseer first of all the monasteries of Provence, Languedoc, and Gascony. His new style of monasticism came to the attention of Margrave William of Toulouse, whom he helped to found the monastery of Gellone in 804. His friendship with the chancellor of the royal court of Aquitaine, Helisachar, helped to spread his influence more widely. Charlemagne had been crowned emperor by the pope in 800, and Benedict's reforms earned his approval. The Frankish "Holy Roman" empire assumed a far greater role in the affairs of the Church than had the kingdom it superseded. Charlemagne died in 814 and was succeeded by Louis the Pious, whose main interests were theology and church reform and with whom Benedict developed even closer relations. Charlemagne had built the first imperial capital at Aachen, strategically situated near the eastern border of the empire, and Louis wanted Benedict close to the capital. He summoned him to the imperial court and installed him first in the abbey of Maurmünster in Alsace, then moved him closer still, to a monastery he built for him on the little river Inde, later known as Kornelimünster, a mere five miles south-east of Aachen. This was consecrated in 817 as an imperial foundation, together with a nearby palace school. From there, Benedict directed the course of monastic reform throughout the empire. He also became one of Louis' most trusted counsellors in secular affairs, presiding at assemblies summoned to consider particular questions.

Louis summoned a church council to consider reforms at Aachen in August 816, at which Benedict presided. He drew up the canons directed at the reform of monastic observance. These imposed the Benedictine Rule on all monasteries, supplanting earlier varied observances such as the Roman, the *laus perennis* (unceasing celebration of the divine office, stemming from the Burgundian royal abbey of Saint-Maurice in the sixth century), and the *cursus Scotorum*, or Irish observance. Monks were to live apart from the world with the laity removed from monastic enclosures, to include manual work in their daily routine, not run schools except for the oblates, and to observe the prescribed liturgical Hours. Their measures of food and drink were also to be standardized. Supervisory commissions, over which Benedict presided, were to be sent to the monasteries, starting on 1 September 817, to see that the reforms were carried out. His measures were codified in the *Capitula* of Aachen, which were appended to the *Rule of St Benedict*, to apply to all monks throughout the empire. The extra liturgical practices he enjoined together with his insistence on the importance of *lectio divina* and the pursuit of knowledge, with study of the scriptures, Origen, St Augustine, St Jerome, and above all St Gregory, would have made the day an impossibly long one if strictly observed. Manual labour was partly abolished and teaching substituted as more suitable work for a largely clerical Order. The aim of his reforms was that through prayer, study, meditation, and reading the monk would pass "from faith to sight," that understanding would blossom into contemplative love of God.

Needless to say, this grand and detailed design was hardly observed in every respect. Benedict had to abandon many details of observance for the sake of getting major reforms accepted by all the abbots. His decrees nevertheless marked the greatest turning-point in the history of Benedictine monasticism since its foundation. He remained its major intellectual influence, at least down to the tenth century, and substantially influenced the reforms of Cluny, Gorze, and those of St Dunstan (19 May) and St Ethelwold (1 Aug.) in England. But the unity he sought to impose depended on the unity of the empire, and this began to disintegrate around the time of his own death. His mortifications and endless work had taken their toll, and his later years were plagued with sickness, but he died peacefully in his monastery at the age of seventy-one.

Besides his measures codified in the *Capitula* of Aachen he compiled the *Codex Regularum*, which is a collection of monastic Rules from East and West, beginning with that of St Basil, and the *Concordia Regularum*, which coordinates the text of the *Rule of St Benedict* with texts from Rules composed by other monastic Fathers. His concern was with regulations and practice rather than directly with spirituality, but Cluny was to follow his concerns for elements of the monastic life such as stricter observance of silence, the lengthening of the choral office, and the dominance of liturgy over manual work, with the elaboration of ritual and splendour of the church setting that these concerns brought in their train.

His Life by his disciple Ardo Smaragdus is in *M.G.H., Scriptores*, 15, 1, pp. 198-220. The decrees of the Council of Aachen were newly edited by K. Hallinger, *Corpus Consuetudinum*

Monasticarum, 1 (1963), pp. 451-81. See also J. Naberhaus, *Benedikt von Aniane* (1930); P. Schmitz, "L'influence de saint Benoît d'Aniane dans l'histoire de l'ordre de saint Benoît," *Il monachesimo nell'alto medioevo e la formazione della civiltà occidentale* (1957), pp. 401-15; W. Williams, "St Benedict of Aniane," *Downside Review* 54 (1936), pp. 357-74. *O.D.S.*, pp. 47-8; further bibliog. in Jedin-Dolan, 4, p. 509; *H.C.S.*, 2, pp. 77-8. *N.C.E.*, 2, pp. 280-1, includes an illustration of an early MS of Benedict's "Epitome," the original of which is in the British Museum.

St Antony Kauleas, *Patriarch* (*c.* 901)

Antony, whose last name is also spelt Cauleas, was born near Constantinople at a place to which his parents had retired for fear of persecution by the Iconoclasts. When his mother died, he entered a monastery in Constaninople at the age of twelve, rising eventually to become abbot. As such, he is properly "Antony II Kauleas," as he was preceded by Antony I Kassymatas (821-37). His father entered the monastery and was clothed by his son.

The Byzantine Church at the period was in a state of considerable confusion. The patriarch Photius, who had been intruded into the see when Ignatius of Constantinople (23 Oct.) was expelled by the emperor in 867, had been forced to abdicate for the second time in 886, apparently simply because the new emperor, Leo VI, wished to have his own younger brother, Stephen, as patriarch. Photius retired to a monastery and died around 891. The followers of Ignatius refused to recognize Stephen, as he had received the diaconate from Photius. Stephen died in 893, and Antony was chosen to succeed him. He was energetic in his peacemaking efforts between the two factions and eventually succeeded in persuading the leader of the Ignatians, Metropolitan Stylian Mapas, to cease his opposition. As his own ordination had taken place under either Methodius (d. 847; 14 June) or Ignatius, he was not vulnerable to the same attack on the validity of his orders as Stephen had been. Whether or not the intervention of the papacy helped resolved the dispute or merely sanctioned a resolution effected by Antony is not clear, but Rome and Constantinople both recognized "Ignatius, Photius, Stephen and Antony" as forming an authentic succession of patriachs. This peace was made in 899, and Antony died not long after. Apart from his place in general church history as outlined above, not much is known of Antony, though contemporaries wrote of his spirit of mortification, prayer, and penance. He had founded and then restored a splendid monastery, in which he was buried, subsequently renamed in his honour the *tou koulea*, or *tou kyr antoniou*.

AA.SS., Feb., 2; *P.L.*, 106, 181-200, gives a *vita* from the fourteenth century by Nikephorus Gregoras. On the background see F. Dvornik, *The Photian Schism: History and Legend* (1948), with references scattered throughout; *idem*, *The Patriarch in the Light of Recent Research* (1958). Jedin-Dolan, 3, p. 404; *Oxford Dictionary of Byzantium*, 1, p. 125.

Bd Humbeline, *Abbess* (*c.* 1092-*c.* 1136)

She was the sister of St Bernard of Clairvaux (20 Aug.) and is known from accounts of his relations with her, dealt with in all Lives of Bernard. Relations between the siblings were close and affectionate, as evidenced by Bernard's grief on the death of his brother Gerard (13 June: see the entry in the present work), and indeed on Humbeline's own death, but Bernard's harsh streak could be applied to them as well. A year younger than her great brother, Humbeline was said to resemble him in physical beauty. She married Guy de Marcy, a nobleman of the house of Lorraine, and in due course went to visit Bernard at Clairvaux, dressed in a manner suited to her station and accompanied by a great retinue. Bernard refused to see her until she promised to do exactly as he told her—which was basically to amend her life and do away with all this finery. She burst into tears but had the wit to reply: "I may indeed be a sinful woman, but it was for such as me that Christ died, and because I am so sinful that I need the help of godly men." Whether or not his rebuke was still stinging some years later, she obtained permission from her husband to enter a convent, joining the nuns at Jully-les-Nonnains near Troyes, where she eventually became abbess. Her mortifications became her way of making up for years of vanity and fine living, and she died in the presence of three of her brothers, Bernard (who held her in his arms), Andrew, and Nivard. Her cult was confirmed in 1703. She was formerly commemorated on 21 August, but the new Roman Martyrology places her on today's date.

See, on Humbeline specifically, *N.C.E.*, 7, pp. 230-1; *Bibl.SS.*, 9, 1172-3, *s.v.* Ombelina; *D.H.G.E.*, 24, 926-7.

BB Thomas Hemerford, James Fenn, John Munden, John Nutter, and George Haydock, *Martyrs* (1584)

The name of Thomas Hemerford heads this list, as his was the name that identified the process of the group of English martyrs beatified in 1929; George Haydock appears last, as he was not beatified till 1987.

Thomas Hemerford was born in Dorset in 1554, the son of Edward and Olive Hemerford. He was educated at Hart Hall and St John's College, Oxford, from where he graduated in 1575. He went to Reims to study for the priesthood in July 1580 and the following month was sent on to the English College in Rome. He was ordained priest there in March 1583 and left Rome for England in April, stopping in Reims on the way and arriving in England in June. Before the end of the year he had been captured and imprisoned in the Marshalsea. He was indicted for being a Catholic priest in the court of the King's Bench, with thirteen others, on 5 February 1584, and committed to the Tower of London. For reasons that remain unclear, only five of the fourteen indicted were condemned to death and executed; these were hanged, drawn, and quartered at Tyburn on 12 February. He is described as "a short man with a dark beard, severe of look but of a sweet disposition and very pleasant and exemplary in conversation."

James Fenn, born in about 1540, came from Montacute in Somerset and had two brothers, John and Robert, who also became priests but escaped execution, though Robert was arrested on the very day James was executed; he was subsequently banished. James was a chorister at New College in Oxford, from where he went on to Corpus Christi College in 1554 but was expelled from there in 1560 for refusing the Oath of Supremacy; he went on to become a tutor at Gloucester Hall and a schoolmaster in Somerset. He was married and had two children, Frances and John, but his wife died, and he went to Reims to study for the priesthood in 1579. He was ordained at Châlons the following year and sent to England in May. He was soon captured, at Brimpton in Somerset, and imprisoned first at Ilchester nearby and then in the Marshalsea. He spent two years there during which he ministered to his fellow prisoners, both Catholics and others, bringing at least one criminal into the Church. He was put in the dock with George Haydock and accused of conspiring with him in Rome (where he had never been) to kill the queen, though the two had never met before. Both were condemned on this charge, but the attorney general came to Fenn in prison after the trial and offered him a reprieve if he would acknowledge the queen as head of the Church. This he refused to do, and he was accordingly dragged on a hurdle to Tyburn for execution. His daughter Frances witnessed his death and asked for his last blessing before he was killed.

John Munden (also Mundyn, or Mondayne) was born in 1543 at Mapperton in Dorset and educated at Winchester School and New College, Oxford, of which he became a Fellow in 1562. He, too, was expelled, presumably also on religious grounds, from his college in 1566, and according to evidence given by another priest, John Chapman, in 1582, was also a schoolmaster, "of Dorchester and divers other places in that county [Dorset], and sayeth that he was accounted a papist and was in trouble for religion during the time of his being there." He went to Reims in October 1580, received minor orders there, and was sent to Rome the following year, returning to Reims in July 1582, where he must have been ordained, although there is no record of this. He left for England on 6 August 1582 and was arrested as he stepped off the boat at Dover. A £15 bribe secured his temporary freedom, but he was re-arrested travelling from Winchester to London in February 1583, having been betrayed to the authorities by a lawyer named Hammond; he was committed to the Tower. He too was accused at the trial of plotting abroad to kill the queen, an arbitrary charge brought against all the defendants with an apparently equally arbitrary sentence of either death or banishment. Munden looked so cheerful when the verdict was given that bystanders thought he must have been acquitted. He was the last of the five to die.

John Nutter was born in Clitheroe, near Burnley in Lancashire. He had a younger brother, Robert, who was to go to Reims with him and eventually also to suffer a martyr's death, in 1600 (26 July). John was educated at St John's College,

Cambridge, graduating in about 1576. The brothers arrived in Reims on 23 August 1579; after two years there John was sent to teach the juniors in Verdun, which delayed his ordination for a year. He was ordained in September 1582 and sent to England two months later. He landed at Dunwich in Suffolk and was confined there with a high fever until he was arrested on 15 January 1583. His efforts to pass himself off as a merchant from York were frustrated by the fact that his luggage contained five hundred catechisms and fifteen copies of the recently-printed Reims New Testament. He was sent to London and committed to the Marshalsea. After the trial and sentence, John was committed to the Tower, heavily manacled, and plunged into the Pit. There he found his brother Robert, who had been arrested in Oxford five days earlier.

George Haydock was a member of a remarkable Lancashire family. His brother Richard also became a priest, together with their widowed father Ewan (or Vivian), though these both survived to die a natural death, in 1605 and 1581 respectively. An uncle was William Allen (1532-94), founder of the English Colleges at Douai, Rome, and Valladolid, instigator of the Douai translation of the Bible and later cardinal. George went to Douai in 1574 and moved with the college to its new site at Reims in April 1578, being sent to Rome about three months later. There he was ordained deacon, but he was then sent back to Reims owing to ill health and was ordained there together with Robert Nutter on 23 December 1581. He was sent to England the following month and in London learned of his father's death from Lancashire friends whom he visited. He was arrested there early the following month and imprisoned in the Gatehouse, having been robbed of most of the meagre sum of money he carried by those who arrested him, the notorious priest-hunters Norris and Sledd. He spent two years in prison before being tried and condemned. He was only twenty-seven years old when he died, and the year before had been described as "having no beard, [looking] even younger." He was the first to die and was supposed to be treated with even more than the usual barbarity so as to frighten the others, but the execution was bungled so that he was dead before he could be disembowelled, whereas the other four were cut down while still alive.

Anstruther, 1, pp. 161-2, 113-4, 239-40, 258-9, 158-9, is the main source for the above entry. *M.M.P.*, 1, pp. 87ff., 94, 588; J. H. Pollen, *Acts of the English Martyrs* (1891), pp. 252, 253, 304; Stanton, pp. 65-6. For the general literature on the English martyrs see under 4 May and 25 October in the present work.

R.M.

St Eulalia of Barcelona, martyr (early fourth century)—see St Eulalia of Mérida, 10 Dec., of whom she is generally held to be a "double"

St Benedict Revelli, bishop of Albenga (Liguria) (900)

St Felix, abbot of Rhuys (Brittany) (1038)

St Ludan, Scottish pilgrim (1202)

13

St Polyeuctus, *Martyr* (Third Century)

His name is famous from the tragedy *Polyeucte* by Corneille (1606-84), who used fictitious elements from his Acts to build a moving drama of religious conviction conflicting with family love. But there is early evidence of his cult in the shape of a church dedicated to him in Melitene in Armenia, where he suffered, before 377; and his historic existence, however fanciful the story assigned to him, cannot be doubted.

He came from a Greek family and was an officer in the Roman army. His Christian friend Nearchus converted him to Christianity, and the two were arrested, tortured, and condemned to death in the persecution initiated by Decius, emperor from 249 to 251. Decius required all Roman citizens to produce a certificate of the fact that they had sacrificed to the pagan gods, and his efforts to secure compliance ensured that the majority of Christians did so. Many accounts of martyrdoms assign the victims to this outburst of persecution, and the new Roman Martyrology says that Polyeuctus suffered under Decius, but the accounts may be using Decius simply as a type of persecutor. The date generally accepted for Polyeuctus' death is around 259, by which time several years of tolerance had been followed by a renewed outbreak of persecution under Decius' next-but-one succesor, Valerian (253-9), which came to an end with his capture by the Persians and death.

The dramatic element in his Acts and in Corneille's tragedy is provided by the entreaties and arguments of his wife, Paulina, his children, and his father-in-law, opposed by his growing conviction and acceptance of martyrdom. Melitene claims a large number of martyrs, though accounts of these persecutions concentrate more on North Africa, but all that can be known with some certainty is that Polyeuctus and others were beheaded there sometime in the middle of the third century. His feast is celebrated in the Armenian and Greek Orthodox Churches.

There are two ancient editions of the Acts, one in Greek and one in Latin: see *AA.SS.*, Feb., 2, pp. 650-6. The Greek text of the Acts was published by B. Aubé, *Polyeucte dans l'histoire* (1882). On the Decian and Valerian persecutions see bibliog. in Jedin-Dolan, 1, p. 483. See also *Bibl.SS.*, 10, 994-5.

St Ermengild, *Abbess* (c. 700)

Ermengild (or Ermenilda) belongs to a royal line boasting a plenitude of saints. Her father was King Earconbert of Kent; her mother was St Sexburga (who also died in 700; 6 July), who besides having two sons who became kings also had another daughter venerated as a saint, Earcongota, commemorated variously on 21 or 26 February or 7 July. Sexburga was in addition the sister of St Etheldreda, foundress and abbess of Ely (23 June), and eventually retired to live under her sister's rule there, succeeding her as abbess in 679. Ermengild's daughter Werburga, also commemorated as a saint (3 Feb.), became a nun at Ely as well and possibly succeeded her mother as abbess there.

Ermengild, described by John of Brompton as sweet-tempered, humble, chaste, and just, married Wulfhere, king of Mercia from 657 to 674. She converted him to Christianity, and under her influence he did much to spread Christianity in his kingdom. The other of their two children was a son, named Coenred, who was king of Mercia from 704 to 709 and then retired to become a monk in Rome. On Wulfhere's death Ermengild joined her mother, who was building an abbey at Minster on the Isle of Sheppey, off the north coast of Kent. She became a nun there and lived under her mother's rule until Sexburga retired to Ely to live under the rule of her sister. Ermengild followed in her mother's footsteps, succeeding her as abbess of Minster and then also retiring to Ely, so placing herself under her mother's rule once again. Sexburga died some twenty years later, and Ermengild again succeeded her as abbess, becoming the third abbess of royal blood in succession: Etheldreda, Sexburga, Ermengild. Sources differ as to whether Werburga succeeded her mother as abbess.

Apart from her complicated history, virtually nothing is known about Ermengild, though her early cult was extensive and she features in several pre-Norman Conquest calendars, some of which wrongly describe her as a virgin. The actual day of her death is also unknown.

Bede, *H.E.*, 3, 8 (for Earconbert); William of Malmesbury, *Gestis Regum* (R.S. 90), 1, pp. 77-8; *Gesta Pontificum* (R.S. 52), p. 323; Thomas of Ely, *Liber Eliensis* (ed. E. Blake, 1962). An Anglo-Saxon fragment is reprinted in R. Cockayne (ed.) *Leechdoms, etc.* (R.S. 35), 3, pp. 430-3, providing some details. See also F. Wormald, "The English Saints in the Litany in Arundel MS 60," in *Anal. Boll.* 64 (1946), p. 82. *O.D.S.*, p. 161. The church at Minster still stands as the Church of St Mary and St Sexburga, with surviving Saxon stonework.

Bd Jordan of Saxony (c. 1177-1237)

The successor to St Dominic (8 Aug.) as master general of the Dominicans was elected unanimously by the general chapter of 1222, only two years and a few months after he had taken the habit. He held the degree of master of arts from the university of Paris and had aready been provincial of the Lombardy province for a year. His energies as master general were to be devoted mainly to recruiting for the Order, largely from the ranks of university students, and to making new foundations. He was also a writer of distinction, providing much significant material on Dominic himself, and he has left us an unusually detailed insight into his personality through the series of letters he wrote to Bd Diana d'Andalo (9 June).

He came from somewhere in Saxony and was named Gordanus, or Giordanus, but neither the date nor the place of his birth is known with any precision. Despite the relative wealth of biographical material his age at his death is never mentioned, though he is described as "an old man," which suggests at least sixty and would put the date of his birth at no later than 1177. The Bollandists, based on chronicles of the Order, identify his place of birth as "Borcberg" Castle, Borgentreich near Paderborn; others suggest Padberg near Westphalia.

He is first heard of studying in Paris, where, as he came from a wealthy family, he would have lived in relative comfort in the national "school" with masters and other students from Germany. He followed the *Trivium*—grammar, rhetoric, and logic—followed by the *Quadrivium*—arithmetic, music, geometry, and astronomy—before at some stage becoming a student lecturer in the school of theology; he had become a "bachelor" of theology by 1219. Though students were "clerics" there was no necessary correlation between academic advancement and progress in major orders, and he was still only a subdeacon when Dominic visited Paris in 1219 and advised him to proceed to ordination as deacon, setting him to study under one of his first scholar-disciples, Reginald of Orleans (1 Feb., above). He was ordained deacon and then priest before deciding to enter the Order of Preachers.

Jordan was clothed with the Dominican habit at the priory of Saint-Jacques in Paris on Ash Wednesday of 1220, and he very soon rose to prominence in the Order. While still a deacon he was summoned to the first general chapter of the Order in Bologna. This drafted the Constitution of the Order, which was to take definitive form under Jordan's successor, St Raymund of Peñafort (master general 1238-40; 7 Jan.). From then on, his rise was meteoric; in his absence he was elected prior provincial of Lombardy at the general chapter of 1221. By the following year Dominic was dead, and Jordan was elected master general. By this time he must have been over forty years old, and the questions arise of what he had been doing in the intervening years and why his rise in the Order was so swift. Some historians have claimed that he was the Jordanus Nemorarius, or Jordan de Nemore, whose brilliant mathematical treatises were to last three hundred years and be praised and used by Leonardo da Vinci. The identification is still debated, but both his possible places of birth would have been in forest regions, so the appelation "Nemorarius," "of the forest," is quite possible. Once he had become a Dominican and left the field of mathematics, a more easily identifiable name would have been needed, and "of Saxony," was the simplest. Writing in the early fourteenth century, some eighty years after Jordan's death, the English Dominican chronicler Nicolas Trivet claimed that the preacher was also a famed geometrician who had later transferred to the study of theology: "Brother Jordan, by nationality a Teuton of the diocese of Mayence, was made successor to Blessed Dominic in the mastership of the Order of Friars Preachers; who, being held to be great in the secular sciences and particularly in mathematics, is said to have been the author of two very useful books, one *De Ponderibus* and the other *Lineis Datis*. Afterwards he transferred to the study of theology." Even if the identification is not certain, without it we are left with an improbably unrecorded period of ten to fifteen years, after which a relatively obscure person was suddenly elevated within the space of two years to the master generalship of the Order. If he was a famed recruit, this makes his progress far more understandable. The number of university students that he attracted to the Order also suggests academic renown. He also professed his preference for arts students over theological ones, comparing them to peasants used to drinking water who are quickly inebriated by the heady wine of the gospel truth.

He was himself the first historian of the Order and so records his own course within it. He had seen the first Dominican students arrive at Paris and been impressed by their asceticism and apostolic zeal. He knew of Dominic's foundations in Rome and Bologna, then the leading centre of juridical studies in Europe. Dominic spent several weeks in Paris in the spring of 1219, held long conversations with Jordan, and advised him to proceed to ordination as deacon but did not attempt to persuade him to join the Order. Reginald of Orleans had previously been prior of the Dominican house at Bologna, where he had achieved dramatic results; Dominic had sent him to Paris, despite the protests of the students of Bologna, the year before. He was to live only a few months after his transfer to Paris, but Jordan made his profession to him in January 1220. He records a dream in which he saw a fountain drying up and being replaced by two clear streams, which—he writes—he had the temerity to interpret as the death of Reginald and the adhesion of himself and his lifelong friend and university companion, Henry of Marbourg, to the Order. The date was 12 February 1220, Ash Wednesday.

Only two months later he was chosen as one of four "definitors" from Paris to attend the general chapter summoned to prepare a Constitution for the Order. He travelled to Bologna by way of Provence and Genoa. What emerged was a document framed in highly juridical terms, as was to be expected from Bologna: the ethical and apostolic aims of the Order had already been established. It recognized that the Order's specific contribution to the saving of souls (including the conversion of the Albigensians) was—besides the witness of poverty—knowledge and teaching of doctrine, so study replaced the manual labour of the traditional monasteries. Jordan saw that therefore the recruiting ground had to be the universities.

He was sent back to Paris to lecture on the Gospel of St Luke for the academic year (14 September to 29 June) 1220-1, but the number of recruits entering the Order from the arts faculties indicates that his activities spread beyond the school of theology. The second general chapter, held in Bologna at the end of May 1221, elected Jordan, in his absence, provincial of the Lombardy province. This, the major province of the Order at the time, comprised ten houses and included the university of Bologna. He left Paris for Bologna soon after the end of the academic year, on foot, with one of his recent and most distinguished converts to the Order, Everard of Langres (venerated in the diocese on 5 Aug.). They followed the old Roman roads through Burgundy and across the Alps, preaching as they went. But Everard fell ill and died at Lausanne at virtually the same time as Dominic himself was dying, and Jordan proceeded alone to Bologna.

He was later to describe Bologna as "a very special city, and the dearest inheritance of my heart." In the Middle Ages, law meant both civil and canon law, and in the twelfth century Gratian had made the Benedictine Abbey of San Felice in Bologna the greatest centre of canon law teaching in Europe; there was no school of theology there until the mid-fourteenth century. Law students came from far and wide, and the faculty was divided into thirteen "nations." The Dominicans established themselves near the law schools, at St Nicholas of the Vineyards, in the highest quarter of the city. The house was soon attracting students of the highest calibre, some destined for sainthood. Some, however, were led into strange personal enthusiasms, perhaps by the heady success of the Order, and Jordan had to exercise wise leadership to restore order. Part of his remedy was through liturgy: he instituted the singing of the *Salve Regina* in candle-lit procession at the end of Compline, which had a calming effect. The custom was followed in the other Lombard houses and after the general chapter of 1228 was spread to all Dominican houses, being taken later by Jordan's successor Raymund of Peñafort to the churches of Rome. The success of the priory of St Nicholas necessitated expansion, and Jordan embarked on a course of building work, completed in 1233.

Dominic had determined to establish a convent for women in Bologna, but his death left Jordan responsible for the project, which had suffered a number of reverses. This brought him into contact with Diana d'Andalo (9 June), then probably around twenty years of age, the lively daughter of a great family of the city. Converted from her worldly ways by the preaching of Reginald, she had decided, encouraged by Dominic himself, to enter the religious life and make the convent in Bologna, modelled on those of Prouille and St Sixtus, her life's work. Her father was opposed to the project but eventually, persuaded by Dominic, relented and made a donation to the Friars Preachers, enabling them to buy a suitable plot of land. The first humble foundation, named St Agnes, was made by Diana and four others Sisters, who, like her, had been biding their time as religious in a nearby convent. Jordan oversaw the purchase and became Diana's spiritual director. He wrote to her regularly; the letters were copied devoutly by the nuns of St Agnes, which has helped to ensure the preservation of some fifty of them. The relationship developed into a great spiritual friendship reminiscent of that between Francis and Clare of Assisi (4

Oct. and 11 Aug.) and foreshadowing that between Francis de Sales and Jane Frances de Chantal (24 Jan. and 12 Dec.). His overall theme was "God is sweet to those who seek him." In the first letter preserved he writes:

Bees collect from earthly flowers an earthly honey, carrying it into their hives and keeping it there for the future. If your spirit is not refreshed by spiritual honey, it will die; for I know it is very delicate and disdains to use the grosser foods. Send your spirit then, my dear, toward the flowers of the celestial meadows which never fade, so that it may there gather honey on which to live. This honey is not destined to be consumed at only one meal; we keep a part of it in the hive of the heart, so that when we come to a failing of desire, we can find in ourselves and in this storehouse which we carry in our hearts something to delight in. My dear one, when this good to which all your great desires tend shall be yours, do not forget your needy correspondent.

As master general, one of his first major projects was to establish a Dominican house in Padua, another great university city, where discontented masters from Bologna often went, taking their students with them. This was achieved in 1223. In Paris, rapidly growing numbers of students, from thirty in 1219 to 120 in 1223, required expansion at Saint-Jacques; this was carried out, but too hastily, as the new buildings fell down. Eventually a building was secured on the site of the present Boulevard Saint-Michel through a donation from the queen, Blanche of Castile (who was also to encourage her husband, Louis VIII, to undertake the Crusade against the Cathars). She was in addition a contributor to the rebuilding of Chartres Cathedral, to replace an earlier structure destroyed by fire, and later gave another house to the Dominicans in the town, which had a university to which discontented masters from Paris tended to migrate. The bishops and canons objected to a foundation outside their control but were quelled by a peremptory Bull from Pope Gregory IX, which enabled the Dominicans to found a priory, church, and school there.

Jordan was back in Bologna for the general chapter held in June 1223 and was able to see Diana d'Andalo and the four other Sisters installed in the beginnings of St Agnes Convent: they took their solemn vows on the feast of SS Peter and Paul. From Bologna he travelled to Ravenna and thence by sea to Venice to oversee the foundation of a new priory there. He returned via Padua, where he spent some weeks preaching to gain new recruits in the university— without much initial success: "The students are terribly cold," he wrote to Diana, "so far only one has allowed himself to be won over." In the end they warmed to his preaching, however, and by the end of August thirty-three had been added to the Domincans' numbers. He summoned Brother Ventura from Bologna to oversee the founding of a priory there. His next call was to Brescia to oversee the solemn translation of the relics of the patrons of the city. There he succumbed to "marsh-fever," probably malaria, which was to recur for the rest of his life.

Instead of returning to Bologna first, as he had planned, he had to journey to

Paris via Milan and Besançon, where the bishop, Gerard de Rougemont, had established a Dominican priory. There Jordan had a relapse of his fever and had to submit to convalescing in considerable comfort in the bishop's palace. Meanwhile the convent at St Agnes was growing in numbers and had "outside friends" associated with it—the nucleus of the Third Order. He wrote to Diana that nuns from Prouille would soon be sent to give them guidance and support but later changed his mind over this transfer. In Paris, where he was committed to preach the Advent course of sermons, forty more novices entered the Order, including Hugh of St Cher and Humbert of Romans, who was to become the fifth master general, from 1245 to 1263; Hugh went on to become a cardinal and to write the first complete commentary on the Bible.

In the following year Jordan journeyed on to Lille, Brussels, and Trier. He became acquainted with, and devoted to, the mystic Lutgardis (16 June); he became her spiritual director and embarked on another long correspondence. His tour then took him south through Provence and finally back to Bologna in the spring of 1225. Pope Honorius III eventually sent some nuns from St Sixtus in Rome to St Agnes. After the general chapter of 1225 Jordan travelled to Germany, writing on the way to console Diana for the death of her brother Brancaleone, mayor of Genoa. By late September he was in Magdeburg, having crossed the Brenner Pass despite a recurrence of his fever, which kept him in Verona for a time. Magdeburg had a flourishing priory, founded the year before along with Trier and Strasbourg (that at Cologne had been founded in 1221). His beloved companion Henry of Cologne died in his arms in Magdeburg in October; Diana's sister Otha had also died, and he wrote to her that "It is good for us to be saddened at the same time, to go sowing our seed in tears." Before Christmas he was back in Paris and able to communicate the good news of twenty-one more recruits to the Order, all from university circles.

He continued travelling tirelessly for the next year, taking in Germany and Venice, opening new priories, scouring the universities for suitable masters to instruct the novices in them, sending suitable young women to St Agnes—with instructions that they should have companions able to speak their native language. But tensions and defections were surfacing at St Agnes, and in order to bring these under control Jordan engineered a Bull to be addressed to him by Pope Honorius III ordering him to bring the convent under direct Dominican authority. In the winter and spring of 1226-7 he travelled round Italy, endlessly recruiting. He was in Rome in late 1226 and there nearly lost his life: a friar considered mad had been tied up; Jordan judged him calm enough to be untied, but the friar slashed his throat with a razor as he was taking his siesta; fortunately the wound was not deep, and within a few days Jordan was preaching again as usual. From Rome he sent Diana the pope's confirmation of the Rule for St Agnes. This delighted Diana so much that she profesed herself eager to die, but Jordan urged patience; "I do not wish you, by an excessive compunction or immoderate mortifications, to hasten toward your end. . . ."

In March 1227 Pope Honorius III died and was succeeded by Cardinal Ugolino, who had been a close friend of St Dominic and proved himself the great patron and protector of the Order. He took the auspiciously reforming name Gregory IX. He saw the Order of Friars Preachers (rather than the largely illiterate Franciscans) as his chief weapon in stamping out heresy and establishing peace and true doctrine everywhere. He had studied at Paris and probably also at Bologna and was in spirit very close to Jordan. As papal legate in Lombardy he had overseen and protected the rapid growth of the Order there. On 29 March 1227 he granted the Dominicans Bulls giving them the right to preach everywhere, independent of episcopal jurisdiction (the Bull referred to above as resented by the bishop of Chartres). Jordan went to Rome to receive this privilege; there he discussed with the pope the agenda for the vital general chapter of 1228, to be held in Paris. This provided for the expansion of the Order by opening four new missionary provinces, in the Holy Land, Greece, Dacia (north-central Europe), and Poland. That in the Holy Land corresponded to Gregory's call for a Crusade made only four days after his election: the presence of the friars there was to provide a sure support to—and a measure of control over—the crusading knights. There had already been scattered foundations made in the other new provinces, but now their presence was to be made secure and effective.

Amidst all the expansion and his own travels Jordan's main preoccupation was with houses of study. The Domincans' teaching was public, aimed at the education of the entire clergy, not just their own members: a Dominican priory in a diocese was effectively a school of theology, and on these grounds they were generally welcomed by the bishops despite their independence. In September 1228 the Dominicans were conceded a chair of theology at the university of Paris. Its first occupant was Roland of Cremona, author of the most important *Summa* of the period. The tireless Jordan was back in Milan to preach before Lent 1229, then went on to Bologna to preach the Lent sermons there, remaining there for that year's general chapter. There was further trouble at St Agnes, apparently over the ease with which "outside friends" (who may have included rather superficially repentant prostitutes) were being admitted to profession, but Jordan seems to have smoothed this over without recourse to the harsh measures advocated by some of his companions.

Further travels followed in Italy and Germany with ever more novices joining from university ranks. Jordan was nicknamed "the Siren of the Schools" for his ability to attract academics to the Order—some despite their own best endeavours, as Walter of Strasbourg, a great "catch," recorded of himself. In 1229 he was in Genoa, from where he set out for Montpellier on his way to the formal opening of the university of Toulouse, one of the principal fruits of (at least political) peace in the Languedoc. Pope Gregory had entrusted the Domincans with the teaching of history there, and Jordan had arranged for Roland of Cremona to be moved from Paris to occupy the first chair. Roland spoke the *langue d'oc* and was notably belligerent in his arguments with heretics and other opponents: Jordan made the appointment deliberately as a contribution to the continued crusade against any resurgence of Catharism.

At the pre-Lenten carnival in Paris in 1229 rioting and fighting broke out between "town and gown"; this became endemic, and over the next two years there was a considerable exodus of masters and pupils to calmer provincial universities and to as far afield as Oxford. Calm was not restored for two years, and in 1230 Jordan went to preach the Lent sermons in Oxford. He arrived in England, whither his reputation had preceded him, in January, and after making some visits in London moved on to Oxford. His sojourn there is recorded in a letter to him from Robert Grosseteste, then bishop of Lincoln, written in 1235. His visit resulted in the opening of priories at Arundel, Chichester, and Salisbury in England, and in Edinburgh, Perth, and Ayr in Scotland over the next few years. He was back in Paris in May, staying there till September. He clothed John of St Giles, English by birth, already famous for his learning in the arts and medicine, which he never ceased to practise, in the Dominican habit; he was to be installed in the second chair of theology conceded to the Order in 1233. Major foundations were made in Bordeaux and then in Naples, whose university rivalled that of Bologna, despite opposition from the emperor, Frederick II.

Jordan preached the Lent sermons of 1231 in Padua, where thirty more novices were professed. In May he finally returned to Bologna for the general chapter, to the great joy of Diana and the other nuns of St Agnes, who nevertheless complained about the short duration of his visit and expressed anxieties about his health. But he set off on his preaching tours once more; he planned to go to Germany by way of the recently-opened Gotthard Pass, but his fever recurred and he was forced to stay in Milan for the winter. Even he admitted that he was exhausted, but he still found the energy to mediate in the complicated struggles taking place between the citizens of Genoa and those of Alessandria (between Genoa and Milan), which involved passing harsh judgment on at least one of his brethren compromised in the various intrigues. He was due to go to Paris for the general chapter held at Pentecost in 1232, but his sickness prevented him. After that, there is a gap in our knowledge of his movements, though he seems to have been in Lausanne in the autumn, preached the Advent sermons in Padua, and moved on to Reggio before returning to Bologna for the general chapter the following year. This was to see the solemn translation of the relics of St Dominic, which Jordan described in a circular letter to all the priories, which has been preserved. It seems that he finally made the jouney to Germany over the Gotthard Pass in the summer of 1233; the journey is documented, with attendant miracles, in the *Vitae Fratrum* but not dated. Having stayed for some time in Zurich, he visited the provinces of the Rhineland in 1234. He received the news of St Dominic's canonization at Strasbourg in August. He spent the winter in Paris, where seventy-two more novices

were professed; the continued accession of students was to give him progressively more joy as he grew older. His health was now declining, and at some
point he lost an eye, giving rise to the unkind sobriquet "One-eye." He preached
the Lent sermons of 1235 in Naples and was in Paris for the "Most General
Chapter" of 1236, which decided that he should undertake a visitation of the
priories he had established in the Holy Land. He preached to the Knights
Templar in Jerusalem, as we know from an anecdote in the *Vitae Fratrum* in
which he excuses himself for his mediocre French. It was probably from Palestine that he wrote his last letter, to Diana: "O Diana, how miserable is the
present state which we must endure since we cannot love another without
sorrow or think of one another without anxiety." The sorrow and anxiety were
soon to end: Diana may well have died befoe receiving the letter; the ship in
which he sailed back was caught in a storm and lost with all hands on 13
February 1237. His body was washed up on the shore at Acre and buried in the
priory church there. Soon after, the Turks sacked the town, and all trace of his
remains disappeared for ever.

He has been overshadowed both by the dynamic figure of St Dominic and to
an extent by the achievements of his successor Raymund, and although he was
hailed as a saint immediately after his death, he was not beatified till 1827 and
has never been canonized. In fact, though, the advance and vitality of the early
Dominican Order, and above all its insertion into the forefront of the intellectual life of the thirteenth century, were due in very large measure to his multi-
ple talents and ceaseless activity. It was he who centralized authority in the
general chapters and established communication between them and the ever-
growing number of priories. He also established the Second Order, of nuns,
and through them the tertiaries. His example, preaching, and teaching showed
a large number of brilliant young men how the religious life of prayer and
penance could be combined with the intellectual life—a new departure. Great
adminstrator and great spiritual director, he could seem a somewhat cold and
remote figure were it not for the warmth and tenderness—never straying beyond the appropriate level—of his letters to Diana d'Andalo. All of hers to him
have unfortunately been lost. Physically separated by their vows, Jordan expressed their union together in God: "In him, who is our bond, my heart is
always united to thine . . . thou who dost stay corporeally in the cloister, I take
with me in spirit." Unable to live together on earth, they strove to "live in
heaven."

The chief sources for his Life are his own letters and early Dominican chronicles and *Acta*,
including his own *De Initiis Ordinis*. See also Mortier, 1, pp. 137-274, for a systematic
study. There is a biography in German by H. C. Schebeen (1937); Marguerite Aron, *Un
animateur de la jeunesse au XIIIme siècle* (1931), was trans. into English as *Saint Dominic's
Successor* (1955), which is the main source for the above entry. Jordan's letters to Diana
d'Andalo are trans. M. Aron (1924), and also in G. Vann, O.P., *To Heaven with Diana*
(1960); also ed. B. Altaner, *Die Briefe Jordan von Sachsen* (1925). See also N. Georges, *Bd
Diana and Bd Jordan* (1933); W. A. Hinnebusch, *The Early Friars Preachers* (1951); the

early years of the Dominican Order are summarized in Jedin-Dolan, 4, pp. 173-7; see also the entries in the present work for St Dominic, 8 Aug.; St Raymund of Peñafort, 7 Jan.; BB Diana, Cecilia, and Amata, 9 June.

There is a portait of Jordan in Fra Angelico's *The Crucifixion* in the chapel of San Marco, Florence, of which a copy is reproduced in the Eng. trans. of M. Aron's biography. The Latin caption added to the copy reads, "Beatus Jordanus de Alemania, II Magister Ordi" (Bl. Jordan of Germany, second master of the Order).

Bd James of Naples, *Bishop* (1308)

Jacobo Capoccio was born in Viterbo, some fifty miles north-north-west of Rome. He entered the Augustinian Order at an early age and in view of his intellectual ability was sent to study in Paris, which attracted the brightest students from many Orders at the time. There he attended lectures by Aegidius Romanus, a distinguished Augustinian scholar who had been a pupil of St Thomas Aquinas (28 Jan.). He returned to Italy to lecture in theology to members of his Order there, then went back to Paris to take a doctorate in theology, lecturing there for a time and then in Naples.

His work *De regimine christiano* ("On Christian Government") shows his approach to questions much discussed in his day.

Pope Boniface VIII (1294-1303) appointed him archbishop of Benevento, in the Neopolitan Apennine mountains some thirty miles north-east of Naples, in 1302 but after only a few months transferred him to the archiepiscopal see of Naples itself. He earned the veneration of the people by his manifest virtue and learning, and a cult developed soon after his death in 1308, though this was not confirmed until 1911.

A.A.S. 3 (1911), p. 319, gives the rescript for the confirmation of his cult. The *De regimine christiano* is ed. H. X. Arquillière (1926).

Bd Christina of Spoleto (1458)

She was born Augustina Camozzi, the daughter of a physician who lived near Lake Lugano (between Lakes Maggiore and Como on the Italian-Swiss border). She lived a somewhat wild life in her youth, was married and widowed at a very young age, and continued to lead a dissolute life after being widowed. She then turned to the other extreme, joined the Third Order of St Augustine, and embraced penance of a most severe kind, which undoubtedly contributed to her death at the age of twenty-three.

A more colourful account, repeated in the *Acta Sanctorum* in the seventeenth century, made her a runaway daughter of the illustrious Visconti family, but this was later shown to be a fabrication and is not repeated here. The confusion has also disappeared from the new draft Roman Martyrology. Christina died in Spoleto, south of Assisi in Umbria, on 13 February 1458. Her body rests in the church of S. Gregorio Maggiore in Spoleto. Her cult was confirmed on 19 September 1834.

Her true identity was established by M. E. Motta in *Bolletino storico della Svizzera italiana* 15 (1873), pp. 85-93. See also *Anal.Boll.*13 (1894), p. 114, and 37 (1920), pp. 434-5; *AA.SS.*, Feb., 2, pp. 799-802; *N.C.E.*, 3, p. 655; *Bibl.SS.*, 4, 340-1; N. Concetti, "De beata Christina a Spoleto," *Analecta Augustiniana* 5 (1913-14), pp. 457-65.

Bd Eustochium of Padua (1433-59)

The extraordinary—and, we would have to say today, tragic—story of Eustochium is well attested by contemporary evidence, so the basic facts are not in doubt: it is rather the interpretation of them by her companions and other contemporaries that seems incredible.

She had, one might say, little chance from the start. Her mother was a nun who strayed from the path of chastity and gave birth to her in the very convent in which she was professed. She was christened Lucrezia and might perhaps have grown up in at least a protective environment had not the scandal come to the ears of the bishop, who dispersed the community, presumably removing her mother from her. Yet she was sent to school in the same convent. By this time she was subject to strange manifestations, which were attributed to Satanic possession. Nevertheless, she managed to behave in an exemplary fashion in school and in due course applied to join the community. The circumstances of her birth were still held against her, and most of the nuns opposed her admission, which was, however, sanctioned by the bishop.

She took the name Eustochium in religion, after the disciple of St Jerome (28 Sept.). No sooner had she begun her novitiate than she began to manifest what now appear to have been symptoms of serious mental illness, oscillating wildly betwen periods of gentleness and outbreaks of dangerous temper. She also inflicted injuries on herself with knives—now commonly recognized as a cry for help. These symptoms, too, were, not unnaturally, attributed to diabolical possession, though being labelled the daughter of a seduced nun and suspected of devil-possession were probably cause enough. The treatment she was given is something that at least belongs to the past. She was tied to a pillar for days and deprived of food and drink. Despite this, she seems to have recovered, but then the abbess became ill, and Eustochium was accused of having poisoned her by diabolical means. Rumours of what was happening in the convent reached the townspeople, who tried to storm the convent and have her burned as a witch. The bishop appeared to believe the accusation and had her kept prisoner in a cell for three months, with nothing but a little bread and water every other day. The abbess recovered, and perhaps more surprisingly, Eustochium survived, in full possession of her senses. The nuns tried to persuade her to leave the convent and marry, but she held firm to her vocation and stayed. Through her patience and devotion she gained the respect of her companions in the convent.

The violent symptoms and self-mutilation returned at intervals but with decreasing frequency, and after four years she was allowed to take her vows. All she had been through, however, had taken its inevitable toll on her health; she became bedridden, suffered great pain, and died on 13 February 1459. The name Jesus was found carved on her chest. She was just twenty-six years old. Apparitions and miracles were soon reported at her tomb, and her body (found to be incorrupt) was translated three and a half years later to a place of greater honour—on the orders of the bishop who had been responsible for so much of her suffering. A short sketch of her life was compiled by Pietro Barozzi, who in turn became bishop of Padua, eighteen years after her death. A strong local cult developed, but this has never been officially confirmed by the Holy See. Nevertheless, her case for inclusion here seems at least as good as that of many who have inflicted suffering on themselves with far less cause.

The most reliable account of her life is by the Jesuit historian Giulio Cordara, first published in 1765, based on a manuscript drawn up by Fr Jeronimo Salicario, the confessor to the community during Eustochium's time there and indeed a leading player in the drama. There are other early Lives by G. M. Giberti (1672) and G. Salio (1734). See also H. Thurston, S.J., "A Cinderella of the Cloister," in *The Month*, Feb. 1926; *N.C.E.*, 5, p. 638; *F.B.S.*, pp. 107-10; *Bibl.SS.*, 5, 305-6.

R.M.
St Martinian, hermit of Caesarea (*c.* 398)
St Castor, hermit in Moselle (fourth century)
St Benignus of Todi, martyr (fourth century)
St Stephen, bishop of Lyons (*c.* 515)
St Stephen of Rieti, abbot (*c.* 560)
St Gosbert, monk, bishop of Osnabruck and missionary to the Suevi (874)
St Guimera, bishop of Carcassonne (*c.* 931)
St Fulcran, bishop of Lodève (Languedoc) (1006)
St Gilbert, bishop of Meaux (1009)
Bd Wulfrid, monk in Wales (*c.* 1200)
Bd Paul Lieou-Han-Tso, martyr (1818)—see "The Martyrs of China," 17 Feb.
St Paul Le-Van-Loc, martyr (1859)—see "The Martyrs of Vietnam," 2 Feb.

14

SS CYRIL (827-69), and METHODIUS, *Bishop* (815-84)

These brothers (of whom Cyril was the younger but is placed first because he died earlier) have long been venerated as apostles of the southern Slavs and fathers of Slavonic literary culture and are now honoured as apostles of Europe. Their principal missions embraced territories now occupied by the provinces of Bohemia and Moravia, which make up the Czech Republic; Croatia; Slovenia; and Serbia. They were venerated by the Orthodox long before their feast was universalized in the Roman Calendar and must be seen as vital figures in ecumenical relations between the Churches and of great significance for the troubled regions of former Yugoslavia.

The background to their mission is a complex chequer-board of ecclesiastical, imperial, and national politics. The missions to the Slavs were traditionally the domain of the great German centres such as Regensburg, Passau, and Salzburg, which implied Frankish suzerainty and allegiance to Rome rather than to Constantinople. In the 830s Duke Movimir united the Moravian tribes against the Franks; they, however, under Louis the German, overthrew him and installed his Christian nephew Ratislav in his place. But Ratislav also fought for Moravian independence, until he was captured by Louis the German, blinded, and sent to a monastery. He saw that acceptance of Christianity, with the consequent incorporation of Moravia into the orbit of Western Christendom, would consolidate it as a State. At the same time he sought to shake off the influence of the ecclesiastical province of Salzburg with its overtones of German political dominance. So in 862 he invited the emperor at Constantinople to send missionaries to evangelize his domains from there—which goes to show that the seeds of twentieth-century conflicts in the area were sown a long time ago. He made the request that missionaries should be able to teach in Slavonic. The emperor, Michael III, chose a delegation and appointed the brothers Cyril and Methodius its leaders. Ratislav's nephew, Svatopluk, then took over the dukedom, negotiated the independence of Moravia, and extended its control over Bohemia to the west and as far as Galicia and Silesia to the east.

Cyril had been born in 827 and christened Constantine, adopting the name Cyril in religion only toward the end of his life. He was sent to study at Constantinople under Leo the Grammarian and Photius in 842. He studied the secular sciences rather than theology, but in spite of this he was ordained deacon (and perhaps priest) and took over the professorship from Photius when the latter was summoned to court. He gained a geat reputation, earning for himself the epithet "the philosopher." He retired to a religious house for a time, after which, in 860, he was sent by the emperor on a mission of a joint religious and political nature to the Chazars in what is now Ukraine. It was on his return from this that he was commissioned to lead the mission to the Moravians.

Methodius was born twelve years before his brother. Less seems to be known about his early years, but his career combined imperial and ecclesiastical appointments. In 840 he was *strategos*, or governor, of one of the Slav colonies in the Opsikion province, on the river Styrmon. He then withdrew to a monastery, of which he was made abbot. He and Cyril both spoke Slavonic from childhood, as it was spoken in their native Thessalonika; at this time its variants had not developed into separate dialects or languages, so they were able to make themselves understood in Moravia.

The Western Church recognized only the three languages of the inscription placed on Jesus' cross—Hebrew, Greek, and Latin—as sacred languages and therefore suitable for the liturgy. This understanding was not current in the Eastern Church, however, and so Cyril and Methodius had no hesitation in translating the Bible, Greek liturgical texts, and the Roman Mass, known as the "liturgy of St Peter," into Slavonic. Slavonic, however, was a popular spoken vernacular but not yet a literary written language, so in order to produce these translations they had to create a script. The result was the Glagolitic script, based on the Greek alphabet—some authorities say the lower-case characters, others the capitals—with the addition of specially devised characters to represent specifically Slavonic sounds. This was later developed into the Cyrillic script (named after Cyril) in which the Slav languages are written today, and the southern Slavonic language of Cyril and Methodius has, as Old or Church Slavonic, remained the liturgical language of the Bulgarian, Byelorussian, Hungarian, Romanian, Russian, Ruthenian, Serbian, Slovak, and Ukrainian churches, both Orthodox and Catholic.

The two brothers evangelized in Moravia with such success, largely because they spoke the language of the people, that the Bavarian mission was pushed into the background. But they were not bishops and so could not ordain priests. The German bishop of Passau, leader of the Bavarian mission, refused to do so, and the brothers set out for Constantinople in 867 to seek help. They did so in an atmosphere of heightened rivalry between the Churches of East and West: Patriarch Photius had been excommunicated by Rome, and the use of Slavonic in the liturgy was being strongly criticized in Rome. They reached Venice and there received an invitation from Pope Nicholas I (858-67) to come to Rome. They accepted this and changed course, but by the time they reached Rome Nicholas was dead.

His succesor, Hadrian II (867-72), organized a triumphal reception for them, largely because they were carrying the supposed relics of St Clement (d. *c.* 100; 23 Nov.), which Cyril claimed to have miraculously recovered, even though

Clement had been thrown into the sea with an anchor round his neck (fortunately, angels are said to have built a tomb, which was uncovered once a year at low tide, so the location was known) on his mission to the Chazars some years earlier. The relics were buried in the church of San Clemente on the Coelian Hill, built on the site of the third-century pastoral centre known as the *titulus Clementis*. But in Rome Cyril and Methodius also met opposition to their use of the vernacular in the liturgy. Pope Hadrian, however, supported them and even had their Slavonic liturgy celebrated in Roman churches. He ordained Methodius to the priesthood, together with some of his companions who had travelled to Rome with him, while others were ordained deacons. Some sources claim that both brothers were consecrated bishops, but this does not seem certain.

Cyril died in Rome on 14 February 869. Methodius wanted to take his body back for burial in the lands in which he had laboured, but the pope argued that so distinguished a man should be buried in the most distinguished city of Christendom; he was entombed in the church of San Clemente, in which the relics he had brought back had been enshrined. Methodius returned to his mission fields with papal recommendation, subject only to the condition that the Epistle and Gospel of the Mass should be read first in Latin. Kocel, prince of Slovenia, petitioned the pope for the revival of the ancient archbishopric of Sirmium (now Mitrovitsa, near Belgrade), and Methodius was the obvious candidate. He returned to Rome, where Pope Hadrian consecrated him in 870. His province embraced all the Serbo-Croatian, Slovene, and Moravian mission territories. Politically, Rome was making the statement that it controlled the ancient Roman province of Illyrium, of which Sirmium had once been the capital. To the east, Bulgaria had reverted to its allegiance to Constantinople, so Sirmium was in effect the eastern outpost of the Western Church.

Methodius still had to contend with the opposition of the Bavarian mission and soon found himself on a collision course with the metropolitan of Bavaria; he was actually arrested in Moravia by Carloman, son of Louis the German, and brought before a Bavarian synod in Regensburg in November 870. Despite an appeal to the pope, he was imprisoned in Swabia. Hadrian II protested in vain and was to die without securing his release, which was eventually achieved by his successor, John VIII (872-82). John, however, reversed earlier papal approval of the use of Slavonic in the liturgy and forbade Methodius and his followers to use it. He gave Methodius the title "Apostle to the Moravians," but at the same time declared him subject in ecclesiastical matters to Duke Montemir of Slavonia, a Serbian.

Ratislav had been succeeded as prince of Moravia by his nephew Svatopluk, whom Methodius criticized for his lax morals. Svatopluk and his henchman Bishop Wiching of Neitra delated him to Rome for continuing to use Slavonic in the liturgy, even accusing him of heresy for omitting *filioque* from the creed, though this was not in general use in the West at this time, even in Rome.

Methodius, however, succeeded in persuading the pope of his orthodoxy and to restore the use of Slavonic in the liturgy. This was in 880. During the last four years of his life he completed a translation of virtually the whole Bible into Slavonic and also compiled a manual of Byzantine ecclesiastical and civil law, known as the *Nomokanon*. The fact that he found time to do so may suggest that the Bavarian faction was preventing him from carrying out a full-time mission in his territory. In 882 he went to Constantinople, where he was cordially received by both emperor and patriarch. He died on 6 April 884, probably at Stare Mesto (now Velehrad in the Czech Republic).

His success in establishing the Moravian province places him in the first rank of missionary apostles, on a par with such as Boniface (5 June), but his success was not to be as lasting, and his death brought about a crisis. Pope Stephen VI (885-91) favoured the German mission; he forbade the use of Slavonic in the liturgy once again and named Methodius' opponent Wiching administrator of the metropolitan see of Sirmium. Methodius' remaining disciples fled to Bulgaria, where they reverted to the Byzantine rite but using Slavonic. Moravia collapsed under successive Magyar incursions; Bohemia reverted to East Frankish suzeranty; Croatia remained loyal to the Slavonic Roman liturgy. With due allowance for the dangers of hindsight, one might be forgiven for seeing the seeds of so many conflicts in the area, lasting to the present day with the same combination of religious and national elements, set eleven hundred years earlier. The introduction of the vernacular in the liturgy of the Roman Catholic Church in the 1960s has also heightened interest in Cyril and Methodius as pioneers in this respect, and the recent debates on that subject are not unreminiscent of the trials they went through.

The feast of SS Cyril and Methodius has always been observed in the lands they evangelized but was extended to the whole Western Church only in 1880 by Pope Leo XIII. It was celebrated on 9 March or 7 July until the Calendar Reform of 1969 moved it to the date of Cyril's death. In the East it is observed on 11 May. Pope John Paul II has nominated them patrons of Europe, together with Benedict (11 July), and because they are venerated by both East and West they are regarded as patrons of ecumenism.

There is a Greek Life in *P.G.*, 136, 1194-1240. See also F. Dvornik, *The Slavs. Their Early History and Civilization* (1956); P. Duthilleul, *L'évangelisation des Slaves. Cyrille et Méthode* (1963); A. F. N. Tachiaos, *Cyril and Methodius of Thessalonika* (1989). There are articles on their legends and their sources in *Anal.Boll.* 73 (1955), pp. 375-461; 74 (1956), pp. 189-240 (the "Italian Legend") and 441-69 (the "Moravian Legend"). Further refs. in *O.D.S.*, p. 123; see also *N.C.E.*, 4, pp. 379-81, with an illustration of their representation in a fresco in San Clemente, Rome; *P.B.*, 3, pp. 303-10, has a long account compiled from Slav sources. Fuller biblio. in Jedin-Dolan, 3, p.512; for background see *ibid.*, pp. 149-51. The Czech composer, Leoš Janácek used old Church Slavonic in his *Glagolitic Mass*, of which various recordings are available.

St Valentine, *Martyr* (? Third Century)

St Valentine presents the interesting case of being a name familiar to a large part of the world's population through the appropriation of his feast-day by lovers, while being a historical figure about whom it is very difficult to disentangle any facts, let alone determine how St Valentine's day came to be the day of valentines. An additional complication has been that earlier editions of the Roman Martyrology, including the last complete one available (1956), recorded first, "At Rome, on the Via Flaminia, the birthday of St Valentine, Priest and martyr, who after many wondrous works of healing and teaching, was scourged with rods and beheaded under Claudius Caesar"; followed by, "At Terni [some sixty miles north of Rome], St Valentine, Bishop and Martyr, who, after lengthy ill-treatment was imprisoned; and since he could not be overcome, he was brought out of his prison in the silence of midnight and beheaded, at the command of Placidus, prefect of the city." There are also three other martyrs recorded on the same day as having been beheaded while keeping watch over Valentine's body at Terni. With such differing traditions, the theory that there were two was long accepted, but it is now generally agreed that if two saints of the same name are commemorated on the same day, the likelihood is that they are in fact one and the same person. This is the conclusion reached by Delehaye: his tomb is "situated at the first milepost of the Flaminian Way. In the Martyrology, Valentine is associated with Interamna [Terni], at the sixty-fourth mile along the same road, where a basilica had been built in his honour. This circumstance led to the *doubling of the personage*, and to Valentine the Roman martyr being distinguished from a Valentine, bishop of Interamna, who never existed." The new draft Roman Martyrology, perhaps accepting the researches of the Bollandists, has followed this and records simply: *Romae via Flaminia millario II, sancti Valentini martyris, quem etiam Interamna sibi vindicat*, "At Rome, two miles out on the Flaminian Way, [the birthday] of St Valentine, martyr, whom Interamna also claims for itself."

The evidence for an early cult in Rome is strong, with a basilica erected on the Flaminian Way where his martyrdom is supposed to have taken place as early as 350. A catacomb was formed on the spot with the remains in a known place within this, and Valentine's relics were translated by Pope St Paschal I (817-24; 14 May) to the chapel he built on to the church of St Praxedes (21 July) as a shrine for Valentine and the martyr Zeno (23 June). There is also evidence, though later, for a Bishop Valentine of Terni. He is recorded in the *Hieronymianum* and elsewhere. There was also a Furius Placidus, who not surprisingly became "Furiosus Placidus," who was consul in Terni in 273. So one possibility is that Valentine was a priest from Rome who was appointed bishop of Terni, martyred in Rome, but whose relics were taken back to Terni. This however, has to remain conjecture, though it would explain the special cult in Rome and the fact that Terni also claimed him "for itself." Details of a Roman

Valentine are in fact less secure than the early cult there might suggest, as the story told in his Acts is taken bodily from those of the legendary SS Marius and Martha, whose cult was suppressed in 1969. Butler, following the best sources available to him, described Valentine as "a holy priest in Rome, who, with St Marius and his family, assisted the martyrs in the persecution under Claudius II," and goes on to say, "He was apprehended, and sent by the emperor to the prefect of Rome, who, on finding all his promises to make him renounce his faith ineffectual, commanded him to be beaten with clubs, and afterwards to be beheaded, which was executed on February 14, about the year 270." This obviously relies on the same sources as inspired the summary in the 1956 Roman Martyrology, but the most that can now be said about the details is that they are uncertain.

The origins of his connection with lovers are also uncertain. It is usually traced back to Chaucer, who suggested that birds chose their mates on this day. Another theory is that it was a means of Christianizing the Roman feast of Lupercalia, and Butler refers to this: "To abolish the heathen's lewd superstitious custom of boys drawing the names of girls, in honour of their goddess Februata Juno, on the 15th of this month, several zealous pastors substituted the names of saints in billets given on this day." Such a praiseworthy endeavour is associated with St Francis de Sales (d. 1622; 24 Jan.) but cannot be traced back much earlier. Michael Walsh has pointed out that "it has recently been argued that Chaucer's poetic association of the saint with lovers refers not to the Valentine of 14 February but to another Valentine, bishop of Genoa, whose feast-day was 2 May. On 3 May 1381 Richard II was betrothed to Anne of Bohemia: Chaucer's remarks in his poems may stem from this. According to this theory, the identification of the patron saint of lovers with the Roman Valentine occurred by accident sometime after Chaucer's death" (*Butler's Lives of Patron Saints*, p. 425).

It had certainly occurred by February 1477, when *The Paston Letters*, a collection of letters preserved by a well-to-do Norfolk family, written between about 1420 and 1504, record Elizabeth Drew writing to John Paston, the prospective bridegroom of her daughter: "And, Cousin, upon Friday is St Valentine's Day, and every bird chooseth him a mate, and if it like you to come on Thursday at night, and so purvey you that you may abide there till Monday, I trust to God that you shall speak to my husband, and I shall pray that we shall bring the matter to a conclusion." And Margery, the daughter, wrote boldly to John: "Unto my right well beloved Valentine John Paston, Squyer, be this bill delivered . . . my right well beloved Valentine, I recommend me unto you, full heartily desiring to hear of your welfare . . ." (no. 783). In her next letter to him she promises to be "a good true and loving Valentine . . . as I may be your true lover and bedewoman during my life." The custom did not retain its popularity consistently before the recent large-scale (and usually less delicately expressed) revival. Parson James Woodforde in his eighteenth-century Diaries refers to a different custom associated with the day, which seems to have at least one element of the "trick or treat" now practised on Hallowe'en: his entry for 14 February 1777 has, "To 36 Children being Valentines Day and what is customary for them to go about for in these Parts [Norfolk] this Day gave 0. 3. 0. being one penny apiece to each of them"; and again in 1786 he records, "To 53 Valentines to Day gave 0. 4. 5." The previous (1950s) edition of the present work could refer to it as "at the present time . . . hardly more than a memory."

The Acts of the supposed two Valentines are both in *AA.SS.*, Feb., 2, pp. 752-63. H. Delehaye argues that there was only one Valentine in *Propylaeum*, "14 Februarii"; see also Delehaye, *Les origines du culte des martyrs* (1933), pp. 270, 315-6; *C.M.H.*, pp. 92-3. *The Paston Letters* are most recently ed. Norman Davis (3 vols., 1971, 1976, and forthcoming); M. Drabble (ed.), *The Oxford Companion to English Literature* (1995). James Woodforde, *The Diary of a Country Parson* (Folio Soc. ed., 1992), pp. 152, 251. On the church of St Praxedes see O. Marucchi, *Il cimitero a la basilica di S. Valentino* (1890; arguing for two Valentines); S. G. A. Luff, *The Christian's Guide to Rome* (new ed. 1990), pp. 212-4. M. Walsh (ed.), *Butler's Lives of Patron Saints* (1987). See also *Bibl.SS.*, 12, 896-7; *N.C.E.*, 14, p. 517.

St Maro (*c.* 423 or 433)

Much admired by St John Chrysostom (13 Sept.), Maro was a hermit near the city of Cyrrhus (modern Cyr) in Syria. He had a hut covered with goatskins but is said to have made little use of it and to have lived mainly in the open air. He was a pupil of St Zebinus, who gave advice as succinctly as possible so as to be able to spend the maximum possible time in converse with God.

Maro found the ruins of a pagan temple, dedicated it to the one true God, and made it his place of prayer. Visitors who came to consult him were received with courtesy but encouraged to pray with him, which often involved standing all night. He gained a reputation for both physical and psychical healing powers, and his fame as a spiritual adviser was widespread. Of the crowds who flocked to him many became hermits or monks, so that Bishop Theodoret of Cyrrhus could say that virtually all the monks in his diocese had been instructed by Maro. He died after a short illness, decimated by the rigours of his life, and possession of his remains was disputed by neighbouring provinces. They were eventually enshrined in the monastery that became known as Beit-Marum, in the Apamée region of Syria, close to the source of the river Orontes. This is claimed by the Maronite Christians as their origin; they venerate St Maro as their founder and include his name in the Canon of their rite of Mass. It has been disputed, however, whether their origins in fact go back beyond the seventh century, when they became separated from the orthodox Church through their adoption of Monothelitism, which was condemned at the Council of Chalcedon in 680. In this case, their name is more properly associated with that of John Maro, who—provided that he existed, which is regarded as problematic, at least by some Western scholars—was a monk of

Beit-Marum, was nominated bishop of Botyrs in 676 at the insistence of Patri-arch Macarius, but deposed because of his Monothelite tendencies, dying in 707.

The monastery was destroyed by Arab invaders in the tenth century; another was founded at Kefr-Nay in the Botyrs district of Syria, and Maro's head was taken there. In 1182 forty thousand Maronites were converted to Catholicism as a result of the Crusades, and the Maronites have remained in union with Rome ever since as a Uniat Church, with its own liturgy, which is basically an Antiochene rite using the Syriac language, with a separate Calendar for the Church year, which begins in October. The Maronites then enjoyed a period of prosperity under the patronage of Rome. Pope Gregory founded a Maronite college in Rome in 1584, and this attracted a considerable number of scholars. In the nineteenth century they suffered dreadfully at the hands of the Turks: many were massacred in 1860, when the abbot of Deir al-Khamar was horribly tortured and sixteen thousand faithful were driven from their homes. Several victims of this massacre were beatified by Pope Pius XI in 1926. There were fresh massacres during the First World War, forcing many Maronites to flee to the New World; those who remained in Lebanon were involved in the factional conflicts of the 1980s.

Knowledge of St Maro himself is derived from the *Philotheus* of Theodoret, chs. 18, 22, 24, 30, and from St John Chrysostom, Epistle 36. On the Maronites see D. Attwater, *The Catholic Eastern Churches* (1935). *O.D.C.C.*, p. 861, with *D.T.C.*, 10, pt. 1, 1-2 (quoting M. Moosa, *The Maronites in History*, 1986); and *Oxford Dictionary of Byzantium*, 2, p. 1304, insist there is no connection with this St Maro. *N.C.E.*, 9, pp. 244-5, takes the opposite view: "The whole development of monasticism at Cyr derives from Maro. Whatever position Maronite authors held in the dispute over Monothelitism, Maro, a friend of St John Chrysostom, had always supported orthodoxy." P. Day, *The Liturgical Dictionary of Eastern Christianity* (1993), has entries on Maronite Liturgy, Maronites, and their Liturgical Calendar, pp. 181-2.

St Abraham, *Bishop (c. 422)*

This Abraham (one of many), or Abraames, came from Cyrrhus in Syria and became a solitary in the desert. Theodoret, a near contemporary, relates that at one point he went to preach in a pagan village on Mount Lebanon. The Chris-tians went into a hut to say the divine office; this made the villagers suspicious, thinking they were casting spells. They climbed on to the flat roof and poured in large quantities of sand, with the intention of burying the Christians, but some of the elders stopped them. Abraham and his friends not only forgave the villagers but paid their taxes when the Roman tax-gatherers came round. This made them very popular, and the inhabitants listened to his sermons with respect thereafter. He instructed them for three years and then left them in the care of a priest and returned to his desert. He was appointed bishop of Carrhae in Mesopotamia. This was the Harran or Haran of Genesis 29-45, where Jacob, fleeing from Esau, served his father-in-law for seven years without wages for the prize of Rachel's hand. Abraham died in Constantinople after having established the Faith and peace in Carrhae. The emperor Theodosius II (see next entry) was, according to Theodoret, at first disconcerted when he met Abraham, an old man in a country smock, unable to speak Greek, but came greatly to admire him. He summoned him to Constantinople, and after his death he kept a piece of his hair shirt, which he even wore on certain days out of veneration for him.

Theodoret provides the main source of information in *H.E.*, 4, 25, and *Philotheus*, both cited in *AA.SS.*, Feb., 2, pp. 768-9. See also *D.C.B.*, 1, p. 8; *Bibl.SS.*, 1, 115.

St Auxentius (473)

Apparently the son of a Persian named Addas, Auxentius spent the greater part of his life as hermit in Bithynia, the region on the side of the Hellespont opposite Constantinople. He had been one of the equestrian guards of the eastern Roman emperor Theodosius II, who ruled from the age of seven in 408 to his death in 450 and espoused the Monophysite cause. Auxentius, after coming to know many hermits during his militay service, decided to embrace their way of life completely and established himself on the desert mountain of Oxia, some eight miles from Constantinople. He gained a reputation for holiness, and many people came to consult him on spiritual matters, but he also seems to have been suspected of Monophysitism, the doctrine, originating with Eutyches (*c.* 378-454), that after the Incarnation there was only one—divine—nature in Christ. This appears to be the reason why he was summoned to the fourth ecumenical council, at Chalcedon (just opposite Constaninople) in 451. This condemned and deposed Eutyches, but Auxentius cleared himself of the imputation and went free.

Sozomen writes of him that "he was noted for his very faithful piety, his zeal for his friends, the moderation of his life, his love of letters, and the greatness of his attainments in pagan and ecclesiastical literature. He was modest and retiring in deportment, although admitting to familiarity with the emperor and the courtiers. . . . His memory is still revered by the monks and zealous men, who were all acquainted with him." He built a new hermitage on the slopes of Mount Skopa, near Chalcedon, and devoted the remainder of his life to the practice of mortification and the instruction of ever-increasing numbers of disciples. Like many hermits, he loved solitude but was unable to turn away those who came to him for counsel. Toward the end of his life these disciples included a number of women, who lived together in community at the foot of Mount Skopa and were known as the *trichinaraeae*, "the wearers of hair," from the rough clothes they wore. When Auxentius died, probably on 14 February 473, they gained possession of his remains, which they interred in their convent church.

The sources of the Life of Auxentius were studied by J. Pargoire in *Revue de l'Orient Chrétien* 8 (1903), who concluded that all versions stemmed from one primitive source. Quotation above from Sozomen, *H.E.*, 7, 21. See also *P.B.*, 2, pp. 512-15; *AA.SS.*, Feb., 2, pp. 769-82. On Chalcedon, Eutyches, Theodosius, see *O.D.C.C.*, *s.v.*, and general Histories of the Church.

St Antoninus of Sorrento, *Abbot* (830)

He was born probably at Picenum in what is now the Campania region in southern Italy and became a monk in a monastery under the rule of Monte Cassino, though not, it seems, at Monte Cassino itself. Duke Sico of Benevento was ravaging the countryside, and Antoninus was forced to move to Castellammare, at the southern end of the Bay of Naples, near Sorrento. The bishop, (St) Catellus, received him cordially, and they formed a close friendship. Catellus withdrew to a mountain-top to live a hermit's life, entrusting Antoninus with the care of his diocese; he, however, preferred to follow his friend to the mountain-top, which became known as Monte Angelo as a result of a reported appearance of the archangel Michael to the two. Catellus was summoned to Rome on a charge of neglecting his diocese and imprisoned there. The inhabitants of Sorrento begged Antoninus to come down and live among them, since their bishop was in prison. He entered the monastery of St Agrippinus in Sorrento, eventually becoming its abbot.

Tradition has it that as he lay dying he asked to be buried niether inside nor outside the city walls, and was accordingly entombed in the thickness of the wall itself. From there he became the protector of the city against the attacks of Sicard of Benevento (the son of Sico), who was unable to break down that portion of the wall with battering rams. Not only that, but Antoninus appeared to him in a dream and beat him black and blue with a stick, and his daughter also became mad at the time he was trying to batter down the wall. Sico was therefore convinced he was offending God by his attack and appealed to Antoninus, through whose intercession his daughter was cured. He was again reputed to have saved the city from attacks by the Saracens in 1354 and 1358 and is accordingly venerated as the chief patron of Sorrento.

His Life, written not long after his death, was first printed in 1626 by A. Carraciolo in *Antonini coenobii Agrippinensis abbatis vita*; rp. in *AA.SS.*, Feb., 2, pp. 784-96. See *Bibl.SS.*, 2, 87-8.

The ancient shrine of Monte Sant'Angelo is in fact on the other side of the Italian peninsula overlooking the Gulf of Manfredonia. It dates from 493, when the archangel Michael is reputed to have appeared three times to the bishop of Siponto in a cave, so it would appear that either Catellus and Antoninus made a very long trek and adopted the legend of the appearance of St Michael as their own or decided that the diocese of Sorrento should have an equally prestigious shrine.

St John Baptist of the Conception, *Founder* (1561-1613)

The reformer of the Trinitarian Order in Spain was born Juan García Gijón at Almodóvar del Campo, in south-central Spain, on 10 July 1561. He studied at Baeza and Toledo, concentrating on scripture and theology and engrossed in Lives of the saints as embodied in the *Flos sanctorum*, and took the Trinitarian habit at the age of nineteen. The Trinitarians had been founded in France in 1198 by St John of Matha (d. 1213; 17 Dec.) and St Felix of Valois (d. 212;

local cult only since 1969) and devoted themselves especially to the ransoming of captives held by the Moors. Like other Orders in Spain, they had degenerated in practice and were then caught up in the great sixteenth-century movement of reform typified by the Discalced Carmelites led by St Teresa of Avila (15 Oct.), who knew John Baptist personally, and St John of the Cross (14 Dec.). John Baptist was to be their equivalent for the Trinitarians, though his efforts were to prove even more divisive within the Order.

In 1594 a general chapter of the Order decreed that in every province two or three houses should be set aside for observance of the Rule in its primitive strictness. In this it was following the Dominicans in Italy, who had adopted the practice, with varying levels of success, in the hope of preventing the sort of split that had divided the Franciscans into Conventuals and Observants. Little was done to implement this immediately, however, and the decree may have been drafted simply to satisfy the increasingly austere religious views of King Philip II. John Baptist of the Conception, as he was in religion, was scandalized at this lack of will or action and in 1597 was able to found a monastery for reformed Trinitarians in Valdepeñas (some 130 miles south of Madrid). He was encouraged in this by a benefaction from the marquess of Santa Cruz. Two years later he travelled to Rome to secure the approval for the "Barefoot Reformed" Congregation from Pope Clement VIII. But the pope entrusted oversight of the reform of the Order to Discalced Carmelites and Franciscan Observants, and this effectively split the Order into two factions, which were never to be reconciled.

Opposition was intensified by the fact that the reformed branch was soon attracting larger sums destined for the ransom of captives. In an incident reminiscent of the treatment meted out to St John of the Cross by the unreformed Carmelites, a band of unreformed Trinitarians came to the convent at Valdepeñas one night, tied up John Baptist and threw him into a ditch, making off with a large sum of money. He recovered, and the Barefoot reform advanced steadily, so that by the time of his death, which took place in Córdoba on 14 February 1613, there were thirty-four reformed convents in Spain. This is now the only Trinitarian Order in existence, with headquarters in Rome, and so St John Baptist deserves the title of founder. A year before his death, a Second Order for nuns was also founded. The principal work of the monks is in the fields of education and nursing, and they took a prominent part in ransoming black slaves during the era of the slave trade, while the nuns devote themselves to general works of mercy. John Baptist was beatified on 26 September 1819 and canonized by Pope Paul VI on 25 May 1975.

Primary documents of the Order are reproduced in *Acta Ordinis S. Trinitatis* (1919-23), vol. 1. For his Life see P. Deslandres, *L'Ordre des Trinitaires pour le rachat des captifs*, 1, pp. 227-8. See *A.A.S.* 68 (1976), pp. 97-106, and *Osservatore Romano* 23 (1975), pp. 6, 12, for the decree of canonization. See also *N.S.B.* 1, pp. 48-9; *N.C.E.*, 7, p. 1030. *P.B.*, 2, pp. 515-24, has a long notice drawn from a French biography by F. De Saint-Louis (n.d.) and the History of the Order by Deslandres.

R.M.

St Felicula, reputed martyr (? second century)

St Eleuchadius, bishop of Ravenna (? second century)

St Zeno, martyr in Rome (? third century)

St Proculus, martyr of Terni (Umbria) (third century—but probably bishop of Terni, fourth century)

SS Bassian, Tonion, Protus, Luke, Cyrion, Agatho, Moseus, Dionysius, Ammonius, and others, martyrs, some by the sword, some by drowning, some by burning, at Alexandria (? third century)

St Peter, second bishop of Alexandria (380)

St Nostrianus, bishop of Naples (fifth century)

15

St Berach, *Abbot* (Sixth Century)

Two Lives of this disciple of St Kevin, patron of Killardy, exist, but both are late in date, collected from oral traditions, and full of fables. He appears to have been born around 615 and was the son of Nemnald, a descendant of Brian, prince of Connaught, and his wife, Finmaith. He was brought up by his uncle, St Froch, went to Glendalough, and studied under St Kevin (3 June). He went on to become abbot of Cill Beraigh, or Kilberry. Many legends were told of him, mostly relating to nature and the elements as is common in Irish traditions concerning the saints: he made a willow tree bear apples and sorrel to help a sick child recover; he was shut out of his monastery by an enemy, but a blazing fire appeared to warm him.

AA.SS., Feb., 2, pp. 832-9; Plummer, *V.S.H.*, 2, pp. xxxiii, 75-86; *Bibl.SS.*, 2, 1266-8.

St Walfrid, *Abbot* (*c.* 765)

Galfrido della Gherardesca was born in Pisa and became a distinguished citizen of that city. He and his wife Thesia had five sons and at least one daughter before they both felt called to the religious life. With two friends who felt the same inclination, a relative named Gunduald, and Fortis, who came from Corsica, they discussed how to plan this new way of life and chose a site at Palazzuolo on Monte Verde, between Volterra and Piombino (some forty miles south of Pisa), on which to found a monastery for the men, which was to follow the Benedictine Rule of Monte Cassino. They dedicated the monastery to St Peter and founded a separate establishment at some distance for the women; there Walfrid's wife and daughter both took the veil.

Many novices came to join the monks, including Walfrid's favourite son, Gimfrid, and Gunduald's only son, Andrew, who was to become the third abbot and to write Walfrid's Life. Soon the community numbered sixty. Some time after he had been ordained priest, Gimfrid fled from the monastery, taking a quantity of men and valuables with him. Walfrid sent a search-party after him but also prayed that he might be given a sign to remind him for the rest of his life of his moment of weakness. Gimfrid was brought back on the third day, with the middle finger of his right hand so mutilated that he could never use it again. He repented and became abbot after the death of his father, who had ruled the monastery wisely for ten years after the incident. Walfrid's cult was confirmed by Pope Pius IX on 12 September 1861.

156

The Life by Andrew is in *AA.SS.*, Feb., 2, pp. 843-7; see also *N.C.E.*, 14, p. 775. B.G., Feb., p. 309, is perhaps a bit harsh in judging that "there is nothing of remarkable interest in his life."

St Sigfrid, *Bishop* (*c.* 1045)

The apostle of Sweden was probably an Englishman and a monk of Glastonbury, though York has also been claimed as his monastery. He was reputedly sent originally, in 995, as a missionary bishop to King Olaf Tryggvason of Norway by King Ethelbert of England and then moved from Norway to Sweden. The history of the evangelization of the Scandinavian countries is complex and further complicated by conflicting accounts, with plainly legendary elements, designed largely to enhance the reputation of the archbishops of Bremen, under whose jurisdiction the territories fell.

Norway had become a kingdom in the ninth century under Harold Fairhair, but dynastic struggles forced many of his descendants to live elsewhere. These included Olaf Tryggvason, king from 995 to his death in battle in 1000, who was converted in England and baptized at Andover. He was the first king to establish a lasting mission, which he did ruthlessly; his campaign was continued by St Olaf (d., also in battle, 1030; 29 July), venerated as the apostle of Norway. Sweden had been partially evangelized, also in the ninth century, by St Anskar (3 Feb., above) but then relapsed into paganism. The king of Sweden at the end of the tenth century was also named Olaf, known as "the Tax King." He ruled from 995 to around 1022 and was converted and baptized by Sigfrid in 1008. With two fellow-missionaries from England, John and Grimkel, Sigfrid built a church at Växjö and established bishoprics for East and West Gothland.

He had taken with him, so tradition tells, three nephews of his, named Unaman, Sunaman, and Vinaman, and he left these in charge of his diocese while he set out to evangelize more distant provinces. They were murdered in his absence by a gang of marauders, who cut off their heads, threw them into a pond in a box, and buried their bodies in the forest. The heads were recovered and placed in a shrine. The king caught the murderers and would have put them to death had not Sigfrid intervened on their behalf; their sentence was commuted to a heavy fine, but Sigfrid refused to accept the money even though he was in dire need of funds.

Sigfrid died after many more years of missionary labour in Sweden and Denmark. Miracles had been recorded even during his lifetime: the spring at Husaby in which he had baptized Olaf of Sweden was credited with miraculous powers—but miracles were used to frighten pagans into belief. He is reputed to have been canonized in 1158 by Adrian IV, the only English pope, who himself had been a missionary in Scandinavia, but this is doubtful, though the date is still recorded in the new draft Roman Martyrology. His cult was established by the thirteenth century in Norway, Sweden, Denmark, and Finland. In old Swedish calendars 15 February was marked by a cross and a hatchet—the cross for Sigfrid and the hatchet for his three nephews. He was held in great veneration by the people of Sweden until the Reformation. There are relics in Copenhagen and Roskilde.

The earliest history of the evangelization of Scandinavia is Adam of Bremen, *Gesta Hammaburgensis ecclesiae pontificum*, in *M.G.H. Scriptores*, ed. B. Schneider (3d ed., 1917); this is to be read with caution on account of its stance in favour of the archbishops of Hamburg-Bremen and consequent minimizing of the efforts of English missionaries. Latin Lives of St Sigfrid, dating only from the thirteenth century, are in *Scriptores Rerum Suecicarum*, vol. 2, 1, pp. 345-70. There are accounts in Swedish by T. Schmid (1931) and M. Rydbeck (1957). See also C. J. A. Opperman, *The English Missionaries in Sweden and Finland* (1937), reviewed in *Anal. Boll.* 57 (1939), pp. 162-4, where it is claimed that he is cavalier with his sources; "Trois légendes de St Sigfrid," in *Anal. Boll.* 60 (1942), pp. 82-90, reproducing three MSS, from the British Museum, Lund, and Copenhagen, ed. and annotated T. Schmid. See also *AA.SS.*, Feb., 2, pp. 848-52; *Bibl.SS.*, 11, 1038; *P.B.*, 2, p. 645. On the background see Jedin-Dolan, 3, pp. 230-4, with further bibliog. on pp. 521-2. *O.D.S.*, p. 436.

He is variously portrayed in art, usually as a bishop, with the three heads of his nephews in his hands, though these are sometimes, and rather gruesomely, transmuted into three loaves of bread. Other representations show him in a ship with a devil.

Bd Angelo of Borgo San Sepolcro (1300)

Relatively little is known of this Augustinian friar, born in Borgo San Sepolcro in Tuscany to the Scarpetti family. He is remembered mainly through his association with St Nicholas of Tolentino (10 Sept.), who was clothed in the Augustinian habit at about the same time. He was a humble and patient friar and worked in the disease-ridden slums of several Italian cities as well as founding Augustinian houses. The decree confirming his cult in 1921 states that he spent part of his life as a religious in England and founded several Augustinian houses there. But the early Life reputedly written by John of St William has disappeared, and all that remain of his time in England are legends of not very convincing miracles, such as that when an offender whom he had rebuked raised his arm to strike him, the arm was suddenly paralysed, and its use was restored only when Angelo prayed for this. (Interestingly, the same story is repeated in essentials of Fr Dominic Barberi—Bd Dominic of the Mother of God; 27 Aug.—some seven hundred years later: a shoemaker mocked him and blasphemed against the cross, whereupon his arm was suddenly withered and paralysed; he did not recover its use. Perhaps it is an English "urban myth.")

Angelo's body was interred at Borgo San Sepolcro and was reported to have remained incorrupt at least till 1583, exhaling a sweet fragrance. He was venerated as a saint from the time of his death.

The decree of confirmation of his cult is in *A.A.S.* 13 (1921), pp. 443-6. For the episode involving St Dominic Barberi see M. Heimann, *Catholic Devotion in Victorian Britain* (1995), p. 161.

St Claude La Colombière (1641-82)

Claude was born into a relatively wealthy, pious family at Saint-Symphorien d'Ozon, near Lyons, in 1641. He was sent to study at the Jesuit college in Lyons and applied to join the Society of Jesus. He made his two-year novitiate at Avignon, followed by the standard course of philosophy study at the Jesuit college there. From 1661 to 1666 he taught grammar and then the humanities at the college. This was carried out against the background of civil unrest: Avignon was still papal territory, and an affray involving the papal guard and the suite of the French ambassador had resulted in Louis XIV's troops occupying the town in 1659. Peace was restored, and in April 1665 Avignon, where St Francis de Sales (24 Jan.) had spent part of the last months of his life, celebrated his canonization.

There were two convents of the Visitation nuns founded by St Francis in Avignon, and Claude was invited to preach at the older of these, where the celebrations were concentrated. He was not yet ordained but proved himself a natural preacher, with obvious intellectual and oratorical gifts. He was then sent to complete his years of theology in Paris, where he was singled out to be appointed tutor to the two sons of Louis XIV's financial minister Jean-Baptiste Colbert (1619-83). This post was, however, abruptly terminated when Claude wrote a satirical article which came into Colbert's hands. He was recalled to his own province in 1670.

Appointed festival preacher at the Jesuit college church in Avignon, Claude prepared a series of sermons, distinguished in both doctrine and language, of which he was later to make use in England. This was the period when the Jesuits were locked in theological combat with the tenets of Jansenism. Claude adopted St Bernard's (20 Aug.) views when questions arose about attitudes to predestination and the views being expressed at the Jansenist abbey of Port-Royal. So, for example, in his *De l'Amour de Dieu*, he wrote: "'Why have you given me liberty, if you do not wish to leave me the full use of it?' . . . 'But why should I have given my life and blood for you, if you were bound to perish for ever?'" (*Oeuvres,* vol. 4, p. 306). Claude ended his sermon with the conclusion: "He loved us before we existed and even when we resisted" (citing St Bernard's "*Dilexit autem non existentes, sed et resistentes"*). The debate began to acquire political and social overtones. It was temporarily calmed by the "Peace of the Church" imposed in 1668-9. For the Jesuits, Jansenism was the infiltration of the doctrines of Luther and Calvin into the Catholic Church, with evil consequences for both doctrine and practice. One weapon they used to combat it was the growing devotion to the Sacred Heart of Jesus, and this became a central teaching in Claude's sermons, especially after his devotion had been fostered by the retreat he made before his final profession during which he consecrated himself to the Sacred Heart. This was to prove fortuitous in his next appointment.

Two months after his solemn profession he was appointed superior of the Jesuit house at Paray-le-Monial, in Burgundy, some seventy-five miles north-west of Lyons. Four years earlier, Margaret Mary Alacoque (16 Oct.) had entered the convent of Visitation nuns in the town. She, like Sister Anne-Marguerite Clément in 1661, Sister Claude Garnier and Mother Anne-Marie Rosset in 1667, and Mother Marie-Constance de Bresson in 1668, became the recipient of an extraordinary series of visions and private revelations telling her of the love of Jesus' heart for humanity, but was more specific that it was the divine will that an annual feast be kept in honour of the Sacred Heart of Jesus. Her superior and confessor had failed to understand or appreciate these revelations, and Claude came to her as if heaven-sent: "I heard in my soul," she wrote, "the words 'He it is I send you.'" He became her confessor, and she immediately felt she could unburden herself to him: "He consoled me greatly and told me not to fear God's leading as long as I was obedient. . . . He taught me to cherish the gifts of God and to receive his communications with faith and humility." For Claude, Margaret Mary provided direct confirmation, straight from God, as it were, of the value of his own special devotion to the Sacred Heart, and he became one of the great proponents of public devotion to it.

After a short stay at Paray he was recommended by Louis XIV's confessor, Père La Chaise, as preacher to the duchess of York, Maria of Modena (wife of the future James II of England), at the Queen's Chapel at St James' Palace in London. His predecessor, Père St Germain, had been arrested for embracing the feigned conversion of the apostate Frenchman Luzancy and forced to leave England in 1675. Claude arrived in London on 13 October 1676, wearing lay dress. Despite his *incognito*, his reputation as a preacher had preceded him, and the chapel was filled to overflowing to hear him, at least some of those present being Protestant visitors. At the Queen's Chapel he preached again the sermons he had devised in Avignon (with the result that the duchess of York's name is generally attached to them in printed editions). Sister Margaret Mary had in 1675 talked to him of Christ exposing his heart to her: "'The Heart so deeply in love with men . . . all I get back is ingratitude—witness their irreverence, their sacrilege. . . .'" This equation of ingratitude with heresy was central to Claude's devotion to the Sacred Heart. He clearly saw the Protestant Church as constituting this irreverence and sacrilege. Margaret Mary had demanded a "solemn act of reparation" in her Third Revelation, and he discharged this by instituting the Feast of the Sacred Heart, inaugurating the devotion to the Sacred Heart in 1677 as the climax to his great sermon on England delivered at the Queen's Chapel: "Dear God, when will you cause so great a scourge to cease? How can we at length appease you, and oblige you to unite us all in one and the same fold, as we had been throughout the space of thirteen or fourteen centuries?" Claude consoled the duchess of York upon the death of her third child in 1677 by reference to the continuation of English Protestantism, James concurring with, "Look, until we are able to bring up our children in the true religion, not one will live." The Franciscan Fr Wall, who visited him on the feast of All Saints 1678, made mention of the "Mass at the little Altar of the Sacred Heart, which Father de la Colombière had erected in his oratory."

His early biographers seem to have made a point of painting his ministry in London, and his personality, in such a way as to make him seem as retiring and colourless as possible, even saying that he never looked out of the windows of St James' Palace for fear of being contaminated by the wicked city. Their motive was presumably to allay any possible suspicion of guilt of the acts of which he was to be accused, but the truth would seem to be rather different: that his acts were those of an extraordinarily brave man in the face of anti-Catholic politics. He visited the secret Catholic community of Francis Bedingfield in St Martin's Lane and preached against the Test Act on the feast of All Saints, asking, "How many subterfuges daily bring men to yield God's interest to those of the State?" According to the allegations of Du Fiquet, he sent potential converts to Cardinal du Bouillon, to Clermont College, and to Paris and was "on the look out for priests, so as to send them to Virginia," succeeding in at least one instance.

Claude was caught up in the "Popish Plot" of Titus Oates and fell victim to the parallel allegations of Du Fiquet. At 2 a.m. on the morning of 24 November 1678 armed guards broke into his apartments in St James' Palace, arrested him, and dragged him off to prison. He was brought before the bar of the House of Commons in May 1679 for trial, where he calmly read his breviary as the proceedings progressed. Louis XIV intervened to save him from execution, and he was banished back to France, after serving three weeks in prison after his trial and being allowed a further ten days' grace on the grounds of ill health, returning to France in June. The imprisonment proved to have permanently destroyed his health, and his remaining three years of life were largely those of an invalid. He was sent to Lyons and to Paray again in the hope that the climate farther south might be beneficial to his health, and St Margaret Mary persuaded him to stay at Paray to die there. He died peacefully in the evening of 15 February 1682. Margaret Mary claimed to have direct knowledge that his soul went directly to heaven, but it took until 1929 for the Church officially to sanction this view.

His legacy is to have instituted a devotion that spread worldwide as a religious rite—to Poland in 1765 and to the universal Church in 1856—with global political repercussions as well: the president of Ecuador, for example, publicly dedicated his country to the Sacred Heart in 1873. He was beatified by Pope Pius XI on 16 June 1929 and canonized by Pope John Paul II on 31 May 1992.

Surviving works include ninety sermons and "*Réflections Chrétiennes.*" All 138 of Colombière's letters were republished in Italian by Luigi Filosomi, S.J., as *Lettere spirituali*, under the auspicies of the Segretario Nazionale dell'Apostolato della Preghiera (1990, Ital. trans. of *Lettres spirituelles*, vol. 6 of *Oeuvres complètes du vénérable P. Claude de la Colombière*, 1901). A selection of his works in Eng. trans. (1934) is re-issued as *The Spiritual Direction of Saint Claude de la Colombière* (1998). Earlier studies culminated in the large French biography by G. Guitton, S.J., *Le B. Claude La Colombière, son milieu et son temps* (1943, Eng. trans. by W. Young, *Perfect Friend—The Blessed Claude La Colombière,* 1956). Since 1943 works have included "B. Claudio de la Colombière," in *Principi di vita cristiana dagli scritta del Beato a cura di Don Giovanni Barra* (1961); A. Ravier, *Bienheureux Claude La Colombière* (1982); M. Monier-Vinard, "Claude de la Colombière," in *Dict.Sp.,* 2, 939-43; A. Lijuma, "Claudio de la Colombière," in *Diz. Encic. di Spiritualità* (1990), pp. 553-5. Earlier studies in English include: Sr M. Philip, *A Jesuit at the English Court* (1922); M. Yeo, *The Three Hearts* (1940). The reassessment of his ministry at St James' Palace owes much to D. Baldwin, *Regular and Secular Orders and Confraternities Attached to The Queen's Chapel* (1997) and *The Queen's Chapel, 1623-1688* (forthcoming). See also F. Edwards, S.J., *The Jesuits in England: from 1850 to the present day* (1985), pp. 81-2, 87.

R.M.

SS Faustinus and Jovita, martyrs of Liguria (? second century—cult dropped from universal Calendar in 1969)

St Majorus, martyr of Gaza (fourth century)

St Dochow (Dochau, Dogwyn), abbot, possibly bishop, from Wales (473)

St Georgia, hermit in the Auvergne (*c.* 500)

St Quinidius, bishop of Vaison (Provence) (578)

St Severus, from the Abruzzi (sixth century)

St Decorosus, bishop of Capua (Campania) (*c.* 695)

Bd Druthmar, abbot of Corvey (Saxony) (1046)

16

St Elias of Caesarea and Companions, *Martyrs* (310)

Elias and his companions were Egyptian converts who went to visit and comfort other converts who had been condemned to work in the mines in Cilicia (southern Turkey). They are named as Jeremias, Isaias, Samuel, and Daniel, Old Testament names they had taken on their conversion. The new draft Roman Martyrology goes on to mention Pamphilus and his companions, martyred, according to Eusebius, after this group on the same day, but in view of the importance of Pamphilus, in the present work they are accorded a separate entry on the traditional date of 1 June.

Persecution in the Eastern Empire was fierce under Emperor Galerius Maximian (305-11), who carried on and intensified the general persecution initiated by Diocletian (284-305). On their return from Cilicia Elias and his companions were arrested by imperial guards in Caesarea in Palestine. The church historian Eusebius was in Caesarea at the time, witnessed their fate, and wrote an account of it in his *Martyrs of Palestine*. They were taken before the governor, Firmilian, racked and otherwise horribly tortured, and then asked their names and country of origin. Elias gave their convert names and their country as Jerusalem, meaning their destination, the heavenly Jerusalem. After further tortures they were beheaded.

Eusebius gives the date of the martyrdom of both groups as 16 February 310. His account is in bk. 11 of his *Martyrs of Palestine*, trans. and ed. H. J. Lawlor and J. E. L. Oulton (1929); see also *AA.SS.*, Feb., 2, pp. 866-8.

St Maruthas, *Bishop* (*c.* 415)

Maruthas was bishop of Maiferkhat in Syria, between the river Tigris and Lake Van. This was near to the border of the kingdom of Persia, where Christians were subject to frequent attacks. Yezdigerd I became king of Persia in 399, and Maruthas went to Constantinople to request Emperor Arcadius to use his influence with the new king on behalf of the suffering Christians. The imperial court, however, was too preoccupied with the affair surrounding the banishing of St John Chrysostom (13 Sept.) to pay much attention to this appeal. Maruthas was left isolated, but his troubles came to the ears of Chrysostom, who wrote from exile to his close friend St Olympias (17 Dec.) saying that he had twice written to Maruthas without receiving an answer and asking her to visit him: "I need him badly for Persian affairs. Try and find out what success he has had in his mission. If he is afraid to write it himself, let him tell me the result through you. Do not delay in trying to see him about this."

Maruthas went to the Persian court and tried to secure the good will of King Yezdigerd toward his Christian subjects. His mission was helped, so the historian Socrates tells, by his knowledge of medicine, which enabled him to cure Yezdigerd of violent headaches. The Zoroastrian priests, afraid that this gift might lead to the king embracing Christianity, devised a stratagem to discredit Maruthas. They hid a man under the floor of the temple, and when the king came to worship, he emerged apparently from nowhere, crying, "Drive from this holy place him who impiously believes a priest of the Christians." Yezdigerd was impressed by this apparition and was on the point of dismissing Maruthas, but Maruthas persuaded him to go back to the temple and showed him the concealed trapdoor through which the "spirit" had emerged.

Whatever the truth of this story, Yezdigerd certainly tolerated the Christians, though he never converted to Christianity himself and never became the "Constantine of Persia" as the Christians had hoped he would. While there was peace in Persia, Maruthas was able to rebuild churches destroyed in the earlier persecution under King Sapor. He also compiled the Acts of the martyrs of this persecution and brought so many of their relics to his episcopal city that it was named Martyropolis, under which name it is still an episcopal see today. He wrote several hymns in honour of the martyrs, which are still in use in the Syriac rite. Persecution broke out again, inspired by the violence of Bishop Abdas of Susa, probably in the year of Maruthas' death. The exact date of this uncertain, but he is known to have predeceased Yezdigerd, who died in 420. He is honoured as the chief of the Syrian Doctors on account of the writings attributed to him.

Maruthas is mentioned by the historian Socrates, by Bar Hebraus, and in the *Liber Turris* of Mari ibn Sulaiman. A later biography in Armenian was printed with a Latin translation by the Mekhitarists at Venice in 1874. This is translated into English with a valuable commentary in *Harvard Theological Review* (1932), pp. 47-71. See also *B.H.O.* (1910), pp. 157-8; O. Bardenhewer, *Geschichte der altkirchen Lieratur* (1913-32), 4, pp. 381-2; W. Wright, *Syriac Literature* (1894); Hefele-Leclerq, 2, pp. 159-66; *Bibl.SS.*, 8, 1305-9.

Bd Philippa Mareri (1236)

She was born toward the end of the twelfth century at Cicoli in the diocese of Rieti, some thirty-five miles north-east of Rome, in the Abruzzi, where her devout family were the largest landowners in the district, her father being lord of Mareria. St Francis of Assisi (4 Oct.) is said to have been received in their house when preaching in the district, and he inspired Philippa to devote her life to poverty and union with the sufferings of Christ. Her parents, though, had destined her to marriage; to avoid this, she cut her hair short, wore the most unattractive clothes, and locked herself away in a corner of the house. Her brother Thomas did everything he could to change her mind, but she left home and seems to have collected some like-minded companions and established a hermitage on Mount Marerio. Evidence for this period of her life is, however, sketchy and overlaid with appropriate legend.

Thomas is supposed to have repented of his earlier harsh behaviour toward her to the extent of helping her to rebuild a deserted religious house on an estate belonging to him, at Borgo San Pietro near Rieti, where she collected a community of nuns. St Francis appointed one of his disciples, Bd Roger of Todi (14 Jan.), spiritual director, and the convent adopted a Rule similar to that of St Clare (11 Aug.), with Philippa as its first abbess. She was not to occupy this post for long, however, as she quite soon developed a painful illness and died surrounded by her Sisters in the convent. Roger of Todi preached her funeral oration, claiming that her soul was already in heaven. The actual date of her death seems to be in some doubt: the new draft Roman Martyrology gives it as 16 February 1256; earlier sources say 1236, but 13 February. The new day has been adopted here, but the earlier year preferred. Her cult was confirmed by Pope Pius VII on 30 April 1806.

Leggendario Francescano (1676), 1, pp. 233-5; *Auréole Séraphique*, 1, pp. 257-60; Constantini, *Vita e miracoli della b. Philippa Mareri* (n.d.); A. Chiappini, "S. Filippa Mareri," in *Miscellanea francescana* 22 (1922), pp. 65-119; L. Ziliani, *La baronessa santa* (1935). See also *Bibl.SS.*, 8, 754-6; *N.C.E.*, 11, pp. 276-7.

Bd Nicholas Paglia (1256)

An early recruit to the Friars Preachers, he was a student at Bologna University (on which see under Bd Jordan of Saxony; 13 Feb., above) when he heard St Dominic (8 Aug.) preach there and was so inspired that he asked to join the Order. He is said to have come from a noble family that possessed estates at Giovenazzo in Paulia, and it may have been his inherited wealth that enabled him to found the Dominican priory at Perugia in 1233 and that at Trani some twenty years later. He may also have been responsible for the foundation at Todi. He was appointed prior provincial of the Roman province as early as 1230 and again in 1255, shortly before his death. The *Vitae Fratrum* describes him as "a holy and prudent man, well versed in sacred lore," and adds anecdotes suggesting that he received heavenly visions.

He was present at the translation of the body of St Dominic in 1233. He died in Perugia in 1255 or 1256 (the latter date is preferred by the new draft Roman Martyrology, which also moves his commemoration from 14 Feb.) and was venerated there as a saint from the time of his death. His cult was confirmed by Pope Leo XII on 26 March 1828, some five years before that of Jordan of Saxony, who might be thought to have had a prior claim.

Gerard de Frachet, *Vitae Fratrum*, provides a contemporary account. See also S. Razzi, *Historia degli huomini illustri . . .* (1596), 1, pp. 237ff.; Mortier, 3, 611; *N.C.E.*, 10, p. 455, where he is described as "prudent, charitable and compassionate [preaching] fraternal charity and joy"; Taurisano, *Catalogus Hagiographicus O.P.*, p. 14; *Bibl.SS.*, 10, 41-3.

Bd Joseph Allamano, *Founder* (1851-1926)

Giuseppe was born in Castelnuovo d'Asti in Italy on 21 January 1851. He was a nephew of St Joseph Cafasso (1811-60; 23 June), the moral theologian and preacher who was a major influence on St John Bosco (30 Jan.). He was spiritually guided by Don Bosco during his secondary education at the Salesian Oratory in Valdocco. He then studied for the priesthood at the diocesan seminary in Turin, where he was ordained on 20 September 1873.

In 1880 he was appointed rector of the Santuario della Consolata, a Marian shrine in Turin that had a residence for priests attached to it. He developed this into a major centre of Marian piety. He was made a canon of Turin Cathedral in 1893 and became widely known and popular as a preacher and confessor, as well as promoting many charitable works. In 1901 he founded the Institute of the Consolata for Foreign Missions, for men, and followed this in 1910 with a companion Institute for women, the Missionary Sisters of the Consolata. He himself found and trained the first candidates for both, wrote a Constitution for them, and directed both Institutes till his death. Their missionary endeavours were directed mainly to Africa, where houses were founded in Kenya in 1902, Mozambique in 1905, Ethiopia in 1913, and the then Tanganyika in 1922. Missionaries were also sent to South America.

He acted as the promoter of the cause for the beatification of his uncle Joseph, who was beatified on 3 May in the Jubilee Year of 1925 and canonized in 1947. Joseph felt that in achieving the beatification he had set a seal on his life's work. He died in Turin on 16 February 1926. The *decretum super scripta* in his own cause of beatification was introduced in 1960, and the decree of beatification was pronounced by Pope John Paul II on 7 October 1990.

N.C.E., 1, pp. 319-20; L. Sales, *Il servo di Dio Giuseppe Allamano* (3d ed., 1944); Anon., *La dottrina spirituale del servo di Dio Ca. G. Allamano* (1949); F. Hölbock, *Die neuen Heiligen der katholischen Kirche*, 3 (1994), pp. 222-5, with two photos.

R.M.

St Juliana, martyr in Campania (? *c*. 305)

St Tanco, monk, abbot of Neustadt and missionary bishop to the Saxons (808)

Bd John Menard, martyr at Angers (1794)—see "Martyrs of the French Revolution," 2 Jan.

17

THE SEVEN FOUNDERS OF THE SERVITE ORDER

(Thirteenth Century)

The Order of Servants of the Blessed Virgin Mary, or Servites, grew out of a lay brotherhood in Florence in 1233. Its founders were seven young men from the patrician and merchant classes who led a life devoted to spirituality amidst the general feuding and moral laxity that characterized the life of the city, while its religious life was affected by Catharism. It is not known whether the seven were friends already when, between 1225 and 1227, they all joined the Confraternity of the Blessed Virgin, known as *Laudesi*, or "Praisers." The chaplain to the *Laudesi* was a man of considerable spiritual insight named James of Poggibonsi; he encouraged the seven to a life of service to the Blessed Virgin and increasing renunciation of "the world."

The seven were Buonfiglio Monaldi, the eldest and their leader; Alexis Falconieri; Benedict dell'Antela; Bartholomew degli Amidei; Ricovero Uguccione; Geraldino Sostegni; and John Buonagiunta. (The forms of the names vary in different accounts.) Four of them were married, though two of these were widowers; three were celibate. Inspired by a vision of the Virgin Mary on the feast of the Assumption (15 Aug.), they all determined to withdraw into solitude; those who had dependents made arrangements for them, the bishop gave his consent, and they gathered in a house outside Florence called La Carmazia. It was not far enough away; they were constantly beseiged with visitors from Florence coming to admire their prayer and penances. So in 1233 they went farther afield, to the wilderness of Monte Sennario, where they built a simple church and hermitage and lived lives of great austerity.

Visitors found their way here, too, and several wished to join them, but they refused to accept recruits. The fame of their holiness reached the ears of Cardinal Castiglione, who came to visit them with the bishop of Florence. He told them that they were living like wild animals and should moderate their austerities and take more care of their bodies, since "the enemy of souls often hides himself under the appearance of an angel of light." They accordingly asked the bishop to give them a Rule by which to live. He retired to ponder this, asking them in the meantime to accept recruits. The seven prayed for guidance and received a vision of Our Lady carrying a black habit, with an angel bearing a scroll inscribed "Servants of Mary." They ascribed to her a message that this should be their name and that they should follow the Rule of St Augustine. They adopted both in April 1240, and their former chaplain

167

from the *Laudesi* came to join them. They were clothed in their new habits by the bishop of Florence, who rejoiced to see them leading a less extreme life. In due course all except Alexis went on to become priests; Alexis humbly asked to be excused major orders on the grounds of his unworthiness. All took names in religion based on the meaning of their original names.

The new Order attracted postulants in large numbers and grew rapidly, resembling the new mendicant Orders (see St Domini, 8 Aug.; St Francis, 4 Oct; Bd Jordan of Saxony, 13 Feb.) rather than the older monastic Orders, though it was not to rank officially as a mendicant Order till 1424. New foundations were made in Siena, Pistoia, and Arezzo initially, followed by Carfaggio, Florence, and Lucca. There was, however, alarm in the Vatican at the number of new Orders springing up, and official recognition by the papacy was withheld, not being forthcoming till 1259, with formal approbation following in 1304 from Pope Benedict XI (7 July).

Buonfiglio had been elected the first superior, and he remained superior general to 1256, when he begged to be relieved of his post owing to advancing age. He died peacefully during a conference of his brethren in 1261. He was followed in office by (John) Buonagiunta, the youngest of the original seven, but he died in chapel not long after his election during the reading of the day's Gospel. Amadeus (Bartholomew degli Amidei) had been appointed prior of the house at Carfaggio, but as fourth superior general he returned in old age to Monte Sennario, where he died. Manettus (Benedict del'Antella) became the fourth superior general; under him, missionaries of the Order went as far afield as Asia. He retired in favour of Philip Benizi (d. 1285), the greatest promoter of the Order, who preached tirelessly throughout Italy and Germany and worked to restore peace in the endless feuding between Guelphs and Ghibellines. Of the surviving three founders, Hugh (Ricovero Ugiccione) and Sostenes (Gerardino Sostegni) founded convents in Germany and France respectively, were recalled in 1276, and both fell ill and died in the same night. Alexis alone lived on into the following century, dying in 1310 at the reputed age of 110. Philip Benizi had founded a Second Order for women, and a Third Order was started by St Juliana Falconieri (d. 1341; 19 June), Alexis' niece, who lived at home as a tertiary with a community whose members devoted themselves to the care of the sick. They became known as *Mantellate*.

The Order was largely responsible for spreading the devotion to Our Lady known as the Seven Sorrows of the Blessed Virgin Mary, a development of late medieval devotion to Our Lady of Pity, with a Confraternity of the Seven Sorrows claiming its foundation in the Servite church of the Annunziata in Florence in 1266. The Servites were given permission to celebrate a feast of the Seven Sorrows in 1688; this was extended to the whole Church in 1814 by Pope Pius VII as a thanksgiving for his return to Rome from captivity in France under Napoleon. The seven founders were jointly canonized by Pope Leo XIII in 1888. The Order today has houses all over Europe and also in

South Africa, Australia, and North and South America. Its best-known house is at the Annunziata in Florence, where the church is still served by the Order. Their first houses in England were opened in the nineteenth century, and several survive today.

Early information is scarce, confined to a short chronicle by Peter of Todi and reminiscences by Fr Nicholas Mati: see *Propylaeum*, pp. 59-60. See also F. A. dal Pino, *I prati servi di S. Maria dalle origine all'approvazzione*, 3 vols. (1972); *O.D.S.*, p. 433; M. Walsh, *A Dictionary of Devotions* (1993), pp. 241, 247. The feast of Our Lady of Sorrows (distinct from that of the Seven Sorrows) is now celebrated on 15 September with the rank of Memorial.

St Theodore Tiro (*c.* 306)

He is the subject of an early panegyric attributed to St Gregory of Nyssa (10 Jan.), which implores his patronage, asking him "as a soldier [to] defend us." On the basis of this he came to be venerated with SS George (23 Apr.) and Demetrius (8 Oct.) as one of the three great "warrior-saints" of the East, adopted by the Crusaders as their patrons in battle. He is known as *tiro* (meaning "recruit," whence "tyro"), but it is not certain that he was ever a soldier.

What is certain is that a cult of a young martyr developed around his shrine at Euchaïta, later renamed Theodoropolis in his honour. The earliest account of his *passio* tells that his legion was sent into winter quarters in Pontus, and he refused to join his co-recruits in worshipping the Roman gods. After one examination he was dismissed, but he called attention to his Christianity by burning down a pagan temple. After a second examination he was tortured but stood firm in his confession of Christian faith. Examined once again, he was condemned to death and burned. His ashes were requested by a woman named Eusebia, who had them interred in Euchaïta.

These Acts, unreliable in themselves, were later further embellished with miracles and legend until he became one of the three great warrior-saints. By the tenth century the legend had become so complex that a second St Theodore, a general in the imperial army, had been devised as more fitting to some of the details. Relics were translated to Venice and Chartres, accounting for his cult in the West, evidenced by the choir windows of Chartres Cathedral, which depict scenes from his legend, as do mosaics in St Mark's in Venice; the church of San Teodoro at the foot of the Palatine Hill in Rome is also named after him. In the East, Emperor John Zimiskes attributed his victory over the Russians at Dorystolon on 17 February 971 to his intercession, and it was he who renamed Euchaïta in his honour. He is still much venerated in the East and is mentioned in the "preparation" of the Byzantine liturgy together with SS George and Demetrius. His feast-day in the West was formerly 9 November but has been moved to that observed in the East, the anniversary of the battle of Dorystolon.

Theodore has been extensively studied. The panegyric attributed to Gregory of Nyssa is in *P.G.*, 64, 736-48. P. Delehaye, *Les légendes grecques des saints militaires* (1909), edits five different texts of the *passio* and miracles. In *AA.SS.*, Nov., 4, pp. 11-29, Delehaye also examines at length the story of Theodore Tiro and the fictitious general Theodore (Stratelates; formerly 7 Feb., in *AA.SS.*, Feb., 2, pp. 32-7), devised to take up some of the inconsistencies in the legends. See also *Anal.Boll.* 42 (1925), pp. 41-5, 389; *O.D.S.*, p. 451.

St Mesrop, *Bishop* (362-441)

There is a tradition that the gospel was first taken to Armenia by the apostles Bartholomew (24 Aug.) and Jude (28 Oct.). Whatever the truth of this, Armenia had been evangelized by Gregory the Enlightener (d. *c.* 330; 30 Sept.), and a state Church was established by him and King Tiridates in the year 310, eleven years before Constantine made Christianity the state religion of the Roman Empire. This Church was organized on Greek lines by Nerses (or Narses) the Great (d. *c.* 373; 19 Nov.). His son, Isaac the Great (d. 439; 9 Sept.), confirmed the autonomy of the Church from that of Cappadocia, built monasteries, did away with the custom of married bishops, and laid the foundations of Armenian vernacular literature. In this last endeavour, his principal helper was Mesrop.

He had been a "civil servant," and then, when Armenia was partitioned between Persia and the eastern Empire in the 420s, he retired to live a solitary life, was ordained priest, and carried on his studies of the Greek, Syriac, and Persian languages. He found himself handicapped in his missionary work among the people of Armenia by the fact that there was no vernacular version of the Bible and the liturgy; the versions he had to use were in Syriac, and there was no current vernacular alphabet in which to write down a translation. So, in conjunction with St Isaac and a Greek calligrapher named Rufinus, he adapted the lower-case Greek alphabet together with elements from other sources and so produced a usable alphabet. This had thirty-six letters, and its introduction produced a considerable growth in national literature. Some years later, a complete translation of the Bible was prepared, Mesrop supposedly being responsible for the translation of the New Testament and Proverbs. He can thus justly be called the founder of Armenian ecclesiastical literature.

The Bible was followed by a translation of the liturgy and patristic writings, after which Mesrop extended his preaching into Georgia, where he performed the same service for the Georgian alphabet. He established schools in Georgia, returned to Armenia, and, with Isaac's encouragement, established a school of his own there. In this school, further translations from Greek and Syriac into Armenian were made.

Mesrop died at the age of over eighty in February 441. The Armenian Church celebrated the sixteenth centenary of his birth in 1962.

His Life was written in Armenian by his disciple Goriun (or Koriun); this survives in at least two versions, one of which was trans. into German: S. Weber, *Ausgewälte Schriften der Armenischen Kirchenwäter*, 1 (1927). See also *idem, Die katholische Kirche in Armenien* (1903); Tournebize, *Histoire politique et religieuse de l'Arménie* (1910), esp. pp. 503-13, 633-

6. P. Peeters upholds the validity of Goriun's biography in *Anal.Boll.* 53 (1935), pp. 148-50, 298, but queries it in *Anal.Boll.* 54 (1936), pp. 339-41. See also *Bibl.SS.*, 9, 374-9; *N.C.E.*, 9, p. 713; *B.H.O.*, pp. 45-6, with a detailed list of references; *Oxford Dictionary of Byzantium*, 2, p. 1239. On liturgical aspects of the Armenian Church see P. Day, *The Liturgical Dictionary of Eastern Christianity* (1993), pp. 23-4.

St Fintan of Clonenagh, *Abbot* (603)

This Fintan, not to be confused with Fintan Munnu (d. 635; 21 Oct.), was born in Leinster and educated by St Columba of Tir da Glas. An early litany describes him as a descendant of Eochaid. All sources, including the *Félire* of Oengus, emphasize the exceptional austerity of his life: he is said to have lived on nothing but barley bread and a few herbs and to have drunk muddy water. Some regard his asceticism as excessive—and say so. He settled as a hermit at Clonenagh (Clúain Édnech) in Leix, where disciples gathered round him in ever-increasing numbers, so that the settlement grew into a great monastery with so many monks that "there is not room to enumerate them by reason of their multitude."

His Lives recount numerous miracles, in the more traditional Irish manner, as well as dwelling on his austerities, which belong more to an Eastern tradition. As with St Brigid (1 Feb.) and others, however, the miracles are not recounted as marvels for their own sake but show his gentleness and kindness. These qualities also emerge from episodes related in the Lives, such as his lenience in mitigating his strict rule of life for monks who complained that they could not live up his standards—local hermits had complained that the diet he prescribed, combined with manual labour, were more than flesh and blood could bear—and his forgiveness of several who left as *peregrini* without asking his permission. When raiders brought the heads of members of a rival clan whom they had killed, he had these buried near the monastery so that the close proximity of the most important part of their bodies to a place of prayer might stand them in good stead on the Day of Judgment. He is said to have been haloed in dazzling light when he prayed. St Columba (9 June), according to the version of Fintan's Life probably compiled about 1225, is said to have to told "a young man called Colmán," who wanted to return to Ireland, to "'go to that holy man whom I see every Saturday night standing among the angels before Christ's tribunal.' The blessed youth said: 'Who is that saint, and what manner of man is he?' St Columba answered: 'He is a holy and beautiful man of your race, ruddy of face with bright eyes, little hair and that white.' The youth said: 'I know of no such man in my province save St Fintan.' . . . Then St Colmán received the licence and blessing of St Columba and returned cheerfully to Ireland."

Plummer, *V.S.H.*, 2, pp. 96-106; J. Ryan, *Irish Monasticism* (1931), pp. 127-8. The story of St Columba is taken from R. Sharpe (trans.), *Adomnán of Iona: Life of St Columba* (1995), p. 365. See also *Bibl.SS.*, 5, 838; *AA.SS.*, Feb., 3, pp. 16-21.

St Finan of Lindisfarne, *Abbot and Bishop* (661)

Finan was born in Ireland and became a monk at Iona, from where he was sent to succeed St Aidan (31 Aug.) at Lindisfarne on the latter's death in 651. As bishop, his see extended over the modern counties of Durham, Northumberland, and York, and he ruled this wide area with a firm hand for ten years. In 653 the Mercian sub-king, or prince, Peada, came to Northumbria to ask for the hand of King Oswy's daughter Achfled in marriage. Peada was the son of the pagan Penda; Oswy was Christian and insisted that Peada be baptized before he could marry his daughter. Finan baptized Peada at Oswy's estate on Hadrian's Wall (known as At-Wall) and then sent St Cedd (26 Oct.) and three other priests, Adda, Betti, and Diuma, to evangelize Mercia, where their efforts reaped a plentiful harvest of converts. Diuma was to be consecrated first bishop of the Middle Angles and Mercians by Finan two years later. King Sigebert of the East Saxons also asked Finan for missionaries, asking in particular for Cedd, whom Finan eventually consecrated bishop of the East Saxons.

At this time the argument about the date of Easter had broken out in Northumbria. King Oswy, who had earlier been exiled to Ireland, had encouraged northern Irish monks to come to the kingdom, and they generally held to the Iona usage, as did Finan. One, however, named Ronan, had been schooled in Gaul and Italy "in the authentic practice of the Church," and disputed the matter with Finan. Finan, whom Bede (who strongly supported the Roman cause against the Celtic) describes as "a hot-tempered man whom reproof made more obstinate and openly hostile to the truth" (3, 25), remained unmoved by the arguments, but he did agree to Wilfrid going to Rome from Lindisfarne, and Wilfrid was to make the Roman observance prevail at the Synod of Whitby in 663/4.

Finan built a wooden church on Lindisfarne "suitable for an episcopal see, constructing it, however, not of stone, but of hewn oak, thatched with reeds after the Irish manner" (3, 25). It was to this church, later dedicated to St Peter, that the bones of St Aidan were transferred "and buried at the right side of the altar in accordance with the honour due to so great a prelate" (3, 17). A later bishop, Eadbert, replaced the thatch with lead and covered the walls also in lead.

Finan died after ruling the see wisely and helping to preserve peace throughout the kingdom of Northumbria and was succeeded by Colman, another Irishman, who was to lead the defenders of the Celtic custom at the Synod of Whitby.

Bede, *H.E.*, bk. 3, chs. 17, 21-2, 25. See also R. Sharpe (trans.), *Adomnán of Iona: Life of St Columba* (1995), pp. 40-2; *N.C.E*, 5, p. 520; J. O'Hanlon, *Lives of the Irish Saints* (1891), 2, p. 610; *B.G.*, Feb., pp. 325-7.

St Silvin, *Bishop* (*c.* 720)

Nothing is known about Silvin's origins, though it has been claimed (by Duchesne) that he was probably a "Scot" (or wandering Irishman) who made his way to France to the court of Childeric II, king of Austrasia and then of all the Franks (662-75). He was about to be married when he felt called to poverty and celibacy and abandoned his bride-to-be and the court. He went to Rome, where he was ordained. He later became a bishop, most likely a "regionary" bishop with no fixed see, though his name has been associated with Toulouse and Thérouanne. He devoted the whole of the rest of his life and his personal wealth to works of charity, evangelizing, and building churches in the north-eastern region of France, then largely pagan. He lived as humbly and austerely as possible, living on vegetables and fruit and eventually owning nothing but a horse, which he needed when he became too weak to walk around his territory. He was much loved for his holiness and charity and revered during his lifetime for the gift of healing. He seems to have died near Arras and was buried in the monastery of Auchy-les-Moines.

AA.SS., Feb., 2, pp. 24-32, contains a Latin Life amplified and revised from an account written by his contemporary Bishop Antenor. See also Duchesne, *Fastes*, 3, p. 134.

St Evermod, *Bishop* (1178)

Evermod was one of the first converts made by St Norbert, founder of the Premonstratensian canons (6 June.). He heard Norbert preaching in Cambrai in 1120 and was so impressed by his eloquence that he joined the Order. He went with Norbert to Antwerp, where he helped his master undo the damage done by a heretical teacher named Tanchelm. In 1134 he succeeded Norbert as superior of the monastery of Gottesgnaden, but four years later he was trans-ferred to the Abbey of the Blessed Virgin at Magdeburg. He spent the next sixteen years as superior there and was then consecrated as first bishop of Ratzeburg (now in Germany, between Hamburg and Lübeck), which was in Wendish territory and administered from Magdeburg, where he remained un-til he died. He was much admired for the energy with which he administered his diocese and is venerated as one of the apostles of the Wends.

AA.SS., Feb., 3, pp. 47-51, contains an account made up from various sources. There is no formal biography. See also *Bibl.SS.*, 5, 391-2; *P.B.*, 2, pp. 566-7 (written when Ratzeburg was in Denmark).

Bd Luke Belludi (1200-*c.* 1285)

Little is known of the life of Luke Belludi, who seems to an extent to have had holiness thrust upon him through his association with St Francis of Assisi (4 Oct.) and especially with St Antony of Padua (13 June). He came from a wealthy family in Padua but embraced the Franciscan life of poverty when St

Francis preached in the city in 1220, receiving the habit from him in person. He became a companion and close friend of Antony, who is recorded as miraculously restoring a dying child to health at his request. He looked after Antony as he lay dying at the house of Aracoeli in Padua.

His lasting monument is the basilica of St Antony in Padua. Antony was canonized in 1232, within eleven months of his death, and the province immediately set about constructing what they considered a more fitting resting-place than the little church of Santa Maria Mater Domini, which Antony had loved and in which his body was initially buried. The first nave of the resulting vast basilica (built over the existing church), now the central nave, was built first; between 1256 and 1263, by which time Luke was provincial general, two lateral naves were added, and the apse was enlarged. The remains of St Antony were solemnly translated to the basilica in 1263. In 1265 work on five domes and two campanile was begun. Luke himself was buried in the empty marble tomb which had originally held the body of St Antony; the tomb is now in the chapel that bears Luke's name. The honour in which he has always been held in Padua led to the confirmation of his cult in 1927.

A.A.S. 19 (1927), pp. 213-6, contains the decree of confirmation. A study was published two years later: B. Mariangeli, *Cenni sulla vita del b. Luca Belludi* (1929). See also *F.B.S.*, pp. 112-4; *Bibl.SS.*, 2, 1085-6; *N.C.E.*, 8, p. 1067. For the basilica see G. Farnedi, O.S.B., *Guida ai Santuari d'Italia* (1996), pp. 125-7.

Bd William Richardson, *Martyr* (1572-1603)

The last English martyr to suffer under Queen Elizabeth I was born in the village of Wales, near Sheffield. In 1591 he was in some capacity attending to priests imprisoned in Wisbech. They sent him over the Channel to Reims to study for the priesthood, but when he arrived there in July 1592 he was sent on to the English College in Valladolid, which he reached on 23 December of the same year. He studied there and at Seville but was given the *viaticum,* or permission to go on the English mission, only in 1600. He travelled to England under the *alias* of Henderson; nothing is known of his ministry there, but he was betrayed and captured in Clement's Inn in London on 12 February 1603. He was kept in Newgate jail for a week with no visitors allowed and then brought to trial before the lord chief justice, Sir John Popham.

There are several anonymous accounts of his trial. One states that "the L[ord] C[hief] J[ustice] came on purpose, and interrupting other trials called for him to be indicted of high treason for being a priest coming to England, all of which he confessed; and there being no evidence against him the chief justice gave his confession in writing to the jury, who found him guilty. He thanked God and told the chief justice that he was a bloody man and sought the blood of catholics. He denied that he was a Jesuit or knew Garnet; the chief justice left the bench, willing the recorder to pass sentence. He was executed next morning and died most cheerfully, to the edification of all beholders and the great honour of the common cause, the very adversaries being confounded at his constancy and little fear of death." Other accounts also remark on the fact that Popham interrupted his normal circuit to try Richardson and then brutally gave him no respite between sentence and execution to prepare for death, "as common thieves have." Popham was evidently in a fury against Catholic priests and seems to have been determined to put as many to death as possible in what he knew were the closing days of the reign: "When on his circuit he would have put four more to death at Bury but the queen forbade it." The queen herself died the following month. According to the Gregorian Calendar, adopted then on the Continent but not in England, the actual date of his death was 28 February (and would be the 18th by "Julian Calendar" reckoning), but the new draft Roman Martyrology commemorates him on today's date.

See Anstruther 1, with refs. to original sources; *M.M.P.*, p. 269; Gillow, 5, p. 414.

The Martyrs of China (from 1748 to 1900)

The first form of Christianity to reach China, in the seventh century, was Nestorianism, of which some traces were still extant in the sixteenth century. A Franciscan mission was briefly established by John of Monte Corvino in 1294, and this survived until about the middle of the fourteenth century. After a long lapse, brought about by the Black Death and political factors, the opening-up of new trade routes encouraged Catholic missionaries from Europe to penetrate the country in the sixteenth and seventeenth centuries. Europeans were permitted to trade in Canton but not to spread throughout the country. The first to arrive were the Jesuits in 1583, followed by the Dominicans, Franciscans, Augustinians, Paris Foreign Missions, and the Lazarists in 1784. Numbers remained small: there were some 120 at the beginning of the eighteenth century, reduced to around forty by the end of the century as a result of the suppression of the Jesuits and other factors. By then much of the work was being done by Chinese priests and catechists—the first recorded ordination of a Chinese, Gregory Luo Wenzao, dates from 1658.

In the 1640s the Ming dynasty collapsed, and the Manchus (otherwise known as Manchu Tartars) invaded China in 1644. They claimed to be "avenging" the Ming but instead installed their own dynasty, the Ch'ing. Sporadic local wars continued, and it was in the context of one of them that the first beatified martyr of China, the Dominican Francis de Capillas (15 Jan.), was executed on suspicion of being a spy in 1648.

The problem the Europeans faced was that now known as "inculturation"— how to preach and apply the gospel in a civilization with its own ancient religious tradition, all too often written off as "paganism." The Jesuits had made a serious effort in the seventeenth century. Matteo Ricci, who had studied the Chinese classics, eventually moved to Beijing and concentrated his efforts on court officials. He used his scientific prowess to impress the court, as did his fellow Jesuits Adam Schall and Ferdinand Verbiest; their ultimate aim was the conversion of the emperor himself. Adam Schall became a personal favourite of the first Ch'ing emperor, Shun-chih, who called him "Grandpa." By 1692, after the Jesuits had been first deposed from favour and then rein-stated, their successors had succeeded in having an imperial edict of toleration for Christianity promulgated, which led them to believe they were on the eve of the mass conversion of the entire Chinese people. Their methods, however, were attacked not only by factions at court but by other Western missionaries, notably Franciscans and Dominicans, who saw their attempts at devising an "inculturated" liturgy incorporating the Chinese concept of "filial piety" as making concessions to heathenism. The result was the "Chinese Rites Contro-versy," decided when in 1704 Pope Clement XI denounced the practice of the rites of filial piety and forbade Catholics to take any part in them or adapt them in any way. The emperor, K'ang-Hsi, seeing this as a major affront to Chinese culture and morality, demanded that all missionaries sign a document accept-ing his position under pain of expulsion. Most of the Jesuits signed; other missionaries refused, but not all of them were in fact expelled. In 1723 some Jesuits were accused of plotting over the imperial succession: all missionaries except those needed in Beijing were restricted to Canton and Macao; some three hundred churches were destroyed, and Christianity was branded as a heterodox sect. The new emperor, Yung-cheng, eventually relented, saying, "The distant barbarians come here attracted by our culture. We must show them generosity and virtue." But from then on Christianity was always under a cloud, and missionaries needed to be circumspect in their activities. Some proved to be so, others not.

The martyrs of the eighteenth and early nineteenth century, however, can-not have the later general charge of being "agents of imperialism" levelled against them; their stories are more individual. The first to die as a result of persecution were Peter Sanz, Francis Serrano, Joachim Royo, John Alcober, and Francis Diaz (26 May). They were all Spanish Dominicans and were executed at Foochow in Fukien province in 1748.

Louis Gabriel Taurin Dufresse (1752-1815), of the Paris Society of Foreign Missions, suffered at Chengtu, the capital of Szechwan province, which in 1802 boasted forty thousand Catholics and sixteen Chinese priests. He had worked in China for seven years before being denounced in a wave of persecu-tion in 1785. Rather than compromise fellow missionaries he gave himself up, was imprisoned for a time in Beijing, then deported to Manila. He returned to Szechwan four years later and was consecrated titular bishop of Tabradca as auxiliary to the vicar apostolic. From 1800 to 1811 there was relative freedom from persecution, and he was able to establish a considerable organizational structure in the province. Then a new search for foreign preachers was or-dered; this eventually extended to the provinces, and Bishop Dufresse was betrayed and taken to the capital. The local mandarins treated him, aged sixty-four, with courtesy: he was allowed to keep his books and even to preach at the provincial court. He was interrogated but listened to with respect. The governor, however, responsible for carrying out imperial decrees, sentenced him to death by beheading. This sentence should, by law, have been confirmed by the emperor in person, but the governor ordered it to be carried out on the spot, in front of other Christians who had been summoned to witness it in order to frighten them. But the bishop's bearing and last words rather inspired them to declare that they too were ready to die for the Faith. Dufresse's head was exposed on a pole and his trunk was also put on public display for a week before the local Christians were allowed to give him a proper burial.

A year later, the Italian Franciscan John Lantrua (1760-1816) was strangled in Changsha, capital of Hunan province. He was born in Liguria and had taught theology for a time before being allowed to join the overseas mission. He reached the interior of China, via Macao, in 1799. After many years of lonely struggle in the provinces of Hupeh and Hunan during which he made many converts, he was delated to the authorities and taken to Changsha, where he was kept with fetters on his neck, feet, and hands for six months. He was dragged over a crucifix so that he might be said to have trampled on it (see the practice of making Christian prisoners trample on images, *fumie*, in Japan; 6 Feb., above) but was heard by those present to bear witness that he was being forced to do so against his will. He was sentenced to death and executed on 7 February 1816. Also executed in this early period were two laymen, Paul Lieu in 1818 and Peter Lieu in 1834.

An outstanding figure was Francis-Régis Clet (1748-1820). He was born in Grenoble and joined the Lazarists at the age of twenty-one. He was for a time professor of theology at Annecy, then was appointed novice-master at Saint-Lazare in Paris in 1788. His aim was always to be a missionary in the Far East, and he secured a passage to Macao in 1791, making his slow and difficult way from there into the interior of the empire. There he spent thirty years of almost unimaginable hardship. His mission was hampered by the fact that he found it very difficult to learn the language. The climate was harsh in the extreme, communications with his superiors in Beijing were virtually impossible, and he was prey to endless local rivalries and brutalities. Neverthless, he made converts, by whom he was much loved. In 1818 a general wave of persecution broke out when the emperor was persuaded that an unusual darkness in the capital was caused by the deities being offended by the presence of foreign religions. The arrest of all foreign misionaries was decreed. Fr Clet evaded capture for a number of years but was eventually betrayed, taken before the local court, and treated with extreme brutality, particularly in view of his venerable seventy-two years, which might have been expected to secure him more respectful treatment in China. After imprisonment and horrific tortures he was slowly strangled at Wuchang in the province of Hupeh on 17 February

1820. It is his martyrdom that determines the date of commemoration of the martyrs of China as a group, though outstanding figures, such as the five Spanish Dominicans, also have their own commemorations on the date of their death.

In 1840 John (Jean-Gabriel) Perboyre was strangled after being denounced during a new wave of persecution and suffering horrific tortures. He was a Lazarist (Congregation of the Mission) priest who had held important posts in Rome before being sent to China in 1835. He was beatified in 1889, the first missionary to China to be so honoured, and is separately commemorated on 11 September. (His canonization in 1996 caused a furor as there was an understanding that none of the European martyrs in China would be canonized before a Chinese candidate).

A later victim was Augustus Chapdelaine (1814-56). He was born to a large peasant family near Coutances, and when the family had to abandon farming through the death of two sons, leaving an insufficient number to work the land, he studied for the priesthood and was ordained in 1843. He was trained at the Foreign Mission Society and left for China in 1852. Two years later he was denounced to the local mandarin, who proved friendly and released him. He made converts, despite his struggles with the language. When a new mandarin was appointed, Augustus was again denounced, by a young pagan woman who had quarrelled with her convert husband. The charges were ludicrous, but he was arrested with many Chinese Christians of his flock and this time was horribly tortured, being hung in a *cang* by the neck with his feet unable to reach the ground. He was placed opposite Agnes Sao Kuy (see below), so that they could see each other but were unable to speak from the pressure of the cage. Brought to court, he refused to answer the mandarin's questions and received a hundred blows in the face with a leather strap, which broke his jaw and knocked out many teeth, and then three hundred blows on the back with a rattan cane. After further dreadful tortures he was offered his release on payment of a bribe, but he refused to consider asking his Christians for the money and was beheaded on 29 February 1856. He was beatified in 1900. Laurence Pe Man was a faithful convert of Chapdelaine's who hurried to join him on hearing of his arrest. He brought several women to the court to reclaim their arrested husbands; they were sent away, but the mandarin vented his fury on him. He was beaten, had a *cang* placed round his neck for the night of 25-6 February, was brought to court the next day and, as he refused to apostasize, beaten with canes and then beheaded. Agnes Sao Kuy, the daughter of a physician, orphaned at fifteen and taken in and educated by the mission orphanage, had married a Christian who died three or four years later. Left without support, she was invited by Chapdelaine to come and teach his young women converts. She was arrested on 24 February, put in chains, brutally questioned and finally hung from her neck in a *cang* facing Fr Chapdelaine. After four days of this torture she died. Others from the same period beatified in 1900 or 1909 include a lay catechist, Jerome Lu; a school teacher, Agatha Lin, who was beheaded (both 1858); a seminarist, Peter Shang (1861); a priest of the Paris Foreign Missions, John Peter Néel, executed in Kay-Tcheu, together with Martin, his catechist (1862).

A major expansion of Western missionary endeavour took place in the mid- and late nineteenth century. This inevitably became bound up with Western colonial expansion, as weak Chinese administrations were forced by military power to make trade and territorial concessions. The First Opium War, between Britain and China from 1839 to 1842, imposed a series of treaties on the Chinese government; these opened five ports to foreign residents and brought easier times for European missionaries. The French used the death of Chapdelaine as an excuse to join England in the next Opium War, from 1856 to 1860. The resulting treaties of 1858 and 1860 gave the missionaries unprecented rights: they were allowed not only to preach and practise their religion throughout China but also to purchase land on which to build churches, and they were given government protection. These rights were often opposed by local leaders, which in turn led some missionaries to call in the military power of their own nations to protect them, with the inevitable result that they were branded as agents of imperialism. The missionaries could separate the rightness of their religious cause from an imperialist cause in their own minds, but this was a distinction the Chinese were—unsurprisingly, given the situation into which they were forced—unable to make. A huge influx followed, and a vast programme of "assistance" in the form of hospitals, leprosaria, orphanages, dispensaries, and schools was undertaken. The European missionaries were appalled at the poverty they found in China and worked heroically to relieve it, but some at least were quick to attribute it to "paganism" and liable to welcome those who came for material help as candidates for instruction. Converts in their hundreds of thousands were made, but they proved a divisive element in Chinese society: missionaries were accused of encouraging "rice Christians"—converts for the sake of the material benefits brought by the missions. There is no doubt that at least some missionaries, Catholic and Protestant, the French most prominent among them, used their new privileges to interfere in local politics and to secure favours for their converts. By 1863 the new French plenipotentiary, Jules Berthémy, was obliged to make repeated efforts to curb missionary intrusions into domestic politics, and Bishop Faurie wrote in 1864 that "the trouble . . . is that we allow too many persons to worship who were saddled with lawsuits. This results in the alienation of the 'good people.'" This theme recurs constantly from the 1860s to the Boxer Rebellion of 1900, which brought the next major wave of persecution, though again it should be stressed that individually the missionaries came in a heroic spirit of self-sacrifice and obedience to the gospel command to "go out and make disciples of all nations."

By the end of the nineteenth century four-fifths of China's external trade was in British hands, and elements in Chinese society began to see the country going the way of India. A sense of national humiliation was inevitably widespread, with China's crushing defeat by Japan in 1894-5 proving the final blow. A nationalist secret society, originally as hostile to the ruling Manchu Ch'ing dynasty as to foreigners, had been in existence throughout most of the nineteenth century. This emerged in 1898 with a popular uprising in Shangtu province. The society was called *Yi Ho Chuan*, meaning "Righteous Harmony Boxers," so referred to in English as "the Boxers." Some higher officials decided to make use of the uprising and at the same time channel the violence away from the government by encouraging massacres of Europeans and of Chinese converts to Christianity. The dowager empress, Tzu-hsi, shameslessly supported them while it looked as though they might be victorious but quickly dissociated herself when they lost. These massacres began in the winter of 1899-1900. Inevitably, the names of many who might be described as martyrs are not known, and there are more detailed records of European than of Chinese victims, and of clerical than of lay among the Europeans. Of the Catholic European victims, five were bishops, twenty-nine priests, and nine nuns. The total number of European missionaries killed was about 250; the bulk of them were therefore Protestants, including women and children. The estimates for numbers of Chinese is twenty-five thousand Catholics and two thousand Protestants—Catholic communities being still much larger than Protestant ones. Several thousand individual names of the Catholics have been forwarded to the Vatican, and their causes are under consideration.

The first Catholic missionary to suffer under the Boxer Rebellion was an Italian Franciscan priest, Cesidio Giacomantonio. Born in 1873, he had been in China only seven months. He was caught by the Boxers on 4 July 1900 as he was trying to consume the Blessed Sacrament to prevent its desecration; he was beaten, then wrapped in cloth soaked in oil, which was set alight, slowly burning him to death. He suffered at Hengchow in Hunan province and was not yet twenty-seven years old. The news of his death led to two more martyrdoms. Bishop Antony Fantosati, vicar apostolic of southern Hunan, had been born in Umbria in 1842 and professed in the Franciscan province of Assisi. When Garibaldi's troops occupied Umbria in 1860, he continued his studies in the Papal States and was ordained in Rome, assisted by his godfather, Pope Leo XIII's brother. He left for China in 1867 and served in upper Hupeh, founding a whole network of centres and building two cathedrals. In 1892 he was elected vicar apostolic of southern Hunan. He was on a pastoral visit when news of an impending Boxer attack on Hengchow reached him, and he hurried by river to Hengchow to try to defend his flock. His companion was another Italian Franciscan, Fr Joseph Gambaro. Born in Novara in 1869, he had joined the Franciscan novitiate in their Turin province in 1886. He had arrived in China in March 1896; after directing seminary studies he supervised the Christian community in Yenchow. Boxers surrounded their boat, pushed them ashore and stoned them; Joseph died from this, but the bishop had to be finished off with a spear some two hours later.

The leader of the largest group of martyrs who suffered was Gregory Grassi (1833-1900). He was a Franciscan from Piedmont, was ordained in 1856, and had been a missionary in China for forty years, becoming mission promoter, director of the orphanage, and seminary choirmaster in Tai Yuan. In 1876 he was appointed coadjutor to the vicar apostolic of Shansi, taking charge of the vicariate in 1891. In May 1900 a notoriously anti-Christian governor, Yu Hsien, had been appointed to Tai Yuan, in Shansi province, where the vicariate seminary was situated. On 27 June the Boxers raided the Protestant missions in the town; Bishop Grassi ordered the seminary to be closed, having rejected the proposal by a friendly local mandarin, supported by some of the Franciscans, that they should mount armed resistance to the Boxers. Most of the students managed to escape to their homes, but five were caught, arrested, and taken before the sub-prefect, who called on them to renounce their faith; they refused and were imprisoned in a building known as "The Inn of Heavenly Peace." They were John Chiang, a Franciscan tertiary, who had entered a minor seminary at the age of eleven and was now aged twenty-three; Patrick Tung, a seminarian since the age of twelve, a brilliant student of philosophy and theology who had been taken to the 1898 International Exhibition of Turin and travelled around Europe as a reward for his studies: he died at the age of sixteen; Philip Chiang, of whom little other than his good nature is recorded; John Chiang junior, another Franciscan tertiary, aged twenty-two; and John Wang, the youngest of the group, aged sixteen, who had also been taken to Turin.

Also in the town was an orphanage run by Franciscan Missionaries of Mary (founded in 1877 by Mother Mary Helen de Chappotin de Neuville), who had first come to China in 1886. Bishop Grassi urged the nuns to dress in Chinese clothes and escape, but they preferred to risk death with their bishop. They tried to get the orphans to safety but were turned back and, after being almost trapped by flames from burning houses, were taken to the Inn. Their superior was Hermina Grivot: born in Burgundy in 1866, she possessed a teaching diploma, was consecrated in 1896, and had only recently arrived in China. The other nuns were Mary Giuliani, from Italy, the mother superior's assistant and the youngest of the group; Clare Manetti, also from Italy, professed in 1898, the first to be beheaded; Mary de St Juste Moreau, born in 1866 in Rouen, where she was well known for her charitable works, and clothed in 1890; Natalia Kerguin, from Brittany, born in 1864, who had also been a missionary in Africa; Amandine Jeuris, born in 1872 into a remarkable family from Belgium: she had three sisters also nuns and four cousins missionaries in China and was in charge of the dispensary; and Adolphine Dierkx, from Holland, born in 1866 and professed in 1892.

Also taken to the Inn was Francis Fogolla (1839-1900), Bishop Grassi's coadjutor, an Italian Franciscan from Tuscany. Born in 1839 and professed in 1859, he read philosophy at Bologna and theology at Parma, was ordained in 1859, and joined the China mission in 1866. Fluent in Chinese, he preached at the China synods held in 1880 and 1885. He took the seminarians to the Turin Exhibition and round Europe, appealing on behalf of the mission. Another Franciscan priest taken there was Elias Facchini, born near Bologna in 1839, professed at the age of twenty, and ordained in 1864, who had been training young clergy in Shansi for thirty years. The third Franciscan priest was Theodoric Balat, born in 1858 near Albi in southern France; he spoke good Chinese, had been in charge of a remote mission station in the mountains for ten years, and was chaplain to the Sisters at the time of their and his arrest. Andrew Bauer was a Franciscan lay brother from Alsace, a man of great physical strength, who had been exiled to England as an oblate, then returned to France for military service as a *Cuirassier*. After this he returned to his friary and joined the China mission in 1899. He was at first in favour of armed resistance.

On 9 July the Boxers broke into a neighbouring Protestant mission, whose thirty-four inhabitants were all killed. The Catholics were taken to court and condemned to immediate death. Bishop Grassi gave the Catholic group absolution. Yu Tsien himself killed him and his coadjutor with a sword. The nuns knelt and sang the *Te Deum*; they all had their throats cut. The other three Franciscans were killed by the sword, as were a further nine Chinese, catechists, servants of the mission, and others who refused to save themselves. These were Thomas Sen, a Franciscan tertiary who had been Bishop Grassi's servant for ten years; Simon Tseng, another tertiary who had had to abandon his ambition to become a priest due to ill health; he had been Bishop Fogilla's servant for thirty years and had accompanied him to Turin; Peter Wu, who had also aspired to be a priest but was instead educated to become an intermediary between the missionaries and the civil authorities; he was a poet and had written a small handbook of prayers; Francis Chang, a farmer from a family with a long Christian tradition who became doorkeeper at the mission orphanage; Matthias Fun Te, the guard at the bishop's house, aged forty-five; James Yen, from the poorest class of hired farm labourer, who prepared vegetables for the mission and rose to be undercook; Peter Chang, who was not attached to the mission but came in to do odd jobs; he came deliberately when he saw others running away in fear; Peter Wang, an orphan who worked in the mission kitchen; James Chao, a temporary servant who had not been imprisoned in "The Inn of Heavenly Peace" but had come to visit his fellow-Catholics there every day and refused to be separated from them in death. All these, twenty-nine in all, were beatified on 24 November 1946. At the ceremony were two Missionaries of Mary who had witnessed some of the martyrdoms and another who was a grand-daughter of one of the martyrs.

An Italian missionary, Alberic Crescitelli (1863-1900), was beatified separately. Born near Naples, he had gone to China in 1888 and had spent his years there in the territories bordering the Han River preaching and establishing schools. He was seized by the Boxers in Shansi, tortured for twenty-four hours, and hacked to death on 22 July. In 1955 four French Jesuits and over fifty Chinese lay men, women, and children, also martyrs under the Boxers, were beatified as Leo Ignatius Mangin, Anne Wang, and Companions.

The Catholic martyrs were beatified only after careful scrutiny that they had been killed for religious and not political reasons. A key document was a proclamation by the governor Yu Hsien: "The European religion is wicked and cruel; it despises the spirit and oppresses peoples. All [Chinese] Christians who do not sincerely repudiate it will be executed. . . . Christians, hear and tremble! Give up this perverse religion! Let all Christians hear and obey: the Boxers will not hurt persons—it is this religion they hate."

The carnage of the Boxer Rebellion by no means put an end to missionary endeavours in China: quite the reverse, in fact, but lessons had been learned. While numbers of European and later American missionaries increased, numbers of Chinese priests, nuns, and lay helpers grew more rapidly, so that a real indigenization of the Christian Churches in China took place in the first half of the twentieth century. General Chiang-Kai-Shek became a Methodist in the 1920s. Missionaries of all denominations continued their practical works of charity on an ever-increasing scale during the chaotic period of the 1920s and the even worse times of the Japanese invasion. By the time of the Communist victory in 1948 there were some five million Christians in China—still less than one per cent of the population and with the suspicion that a large number of these were still "rice Christians." The Communists, taking over an age-old nationalist and anti-foreign tradition, imprisoned and then expelled all foreign missionaries. Forty years later, when the régime brought about another opening to the outside world, the official estimate of the number of Christians had risen to some seven million, with unofficial estimates far higher. Protestant numbers increased even faster in the last decade of the twentieth century, with one 1997 estimate putting them at fourteen million as against ten million Catholics ("patriotic" and other). The foreign missionary presence may never have lost its taint of cultural imperialism, but the missionaries developed indigenous Churches with their own leaders, which can now look to the future with considerable hope.

The primary sources for the literature on the China missions are scattered among hundreds of unrelated archives; they include Chinese trial and local government records that are only now being made available. Among general studies see R. Hart, *These from the Land of Sinim. Essays on the Chinese Question* (1901): Robert Hart, who had spent fifty years in the Imperial Chinese Customs Service, wrote that the tacit alliance between the missionaries and imperialism would lead to "future upheavals and disasters never even dreamt of. In fifty years' time there will be millions of Boxers in serried ranks and wars' panoply at the call of the Chinese government." Also, D. M. Paton, *Christian Missions and the Judgement of God* (1953); C. Cary-Elwes, O.S.B., *China and the Cross: Studies in Missionary History* (1957); J. C. Gibson, *Mission Methods and Mission Problems in South China* (1902); J. Gernet, *China and the Christian Impact: A Conflict of Cultures* (Eng. trans. J. Lloyd, 1985); J. K. Fairbank (ed.), *The Missionary Enterprise* (1974); P. A. Cohen, *China and Christianity* (1967); E. S. Wehrle, *Britain, China and the Antimissionary Riots, 1891–1900* (1966); C. F. Moule, *Christians in China before the Year 1550* (1930); K. S. Latourette, *The Expansion of Christianity: Vol. III (1500-1800)* (1944). For a Chinese view, Hu Sheng, *Imperialism and Chinese Politics* (1955). For most of these references and many more see A. J. O'Grady, *The Dragon and the Cross* (thesis: Politics Dept., Caulfield Campus, Monash University, Australia, 1993), on which general comments above depend. There is a life of Fr Clet in English by A. S. Foley (1941). On the seven nuns, see *Vie de la Mère Marie-Hermine de Jésus et de ses compagnes* (Rome, 1902, abr. by M. T. de Blarer, Paris, 1946); on the group martyred under the Boxers and beatified in 1900/1909, *Les vingt-neuf martyrs de Chine . . .* (1946); also *Osservatore Romano* (Eng. weekly ed., 28 Aug. 1996), pp. 3-7. A letter from Mgr Guillemin describing the martyrdom of Fr Chapdelaine and his two converts in gory detail appears in *New Glories of the Catholic Church* (1870), p. 130-51. A list of European missionaries killed in China between 1815 and 1923 appears in *Missions de Scheut* (1924). See also Ann Ball, *Modern Saints*, 1 (1983), pp. 155-62, for Bd Gregory Grassi and Companions.

N.C.E., 3, pp. 602-3, reproduces a Chinese-style *Last Supper* by the twentieth-century artist Wang Su Ta, in the Lateran Museum; also, p. 596, a Chinese *Virgin and Child* from the Ming Dynasty.

R.M.

St Bonosus, bishop of Trèves and disciple of St Hilary of Poitiers (*c.* 373)

St Donatus and eighty-nine companions, martyrs of Porto Gruaro (Venice) (fourth century)

St Auxibius, bishop of Soli (Cyprus) (*after* sixth century—formerly claimed to have been ordained by St Paul)

St Constabilis, abbot of Cava, patron of Castelabate (Campania) (1124)

St Peter Ryou Tjeng Rioul, martyr (1866)—see "The Martyrs of Korea," 21 Sept.

18

St Sadoth, *Bishop*, and Companions, *Martyrs* (342)

In the year 341 King Sapor II of Persia unleashed a violent persecution against Christians in his kingdom. Bishop Simeon Barsabae and his companions (21 Apr.) are honoured in the Roman Martyrology with one of its longest entries, as principal victims of this wave of persecution. Sadoth and his companions were to suffer similarly the following year.

Sadoth had been deacon to Simeon, bishop of Seleucia-Ctesiphon (twin cities on the river Tigris), had represented him at the Council of Nicaea in 325, and was chosen as his successor when he was martyred. He and some of his clergy were driven into hiding, from where they still managed to minister to their flock. In a dream, Saboth saw a ladder reaching up to heaven, with Simeon standing in glory at its top. Simeon called to him to come up, saying, "I mounted yesterday and it is your turn today." Saboth took this as meaning that "as he was slain last year, I am to follow him this year."

King Sapor came to Seleucia and arrested Sadoth together with a number of priests, lesser clergy, and dedicated virgins, numbering 128 in all. They were thrown into dungeons, where for five months they were horribly tortured and told that their sufferings would cease if they would obey the king and worship the sun. Sadoth replied for them all that the sun was only a creature, made by God for humankind, and that only the Creator was worthy of worship. The whole company of martys declared: "We shall not die but live and reign eternally with God and his Son, Jesus Christ." They were led out of the city chained in pairs and were put to death. Sadoth was separated from his flock and taken to Bait-Lapat, where he was beheaded. He had been bishop for less than a year.

Assemani, *Bibliotheca Orientalis*, 1, p. 188; 3, pp, 399, 613; Gregory Barhebraeus, *Chronicon*, 2, 38.

St Helladius, *Bishop* (633)

Helladius is known from an account of him left by St Ildephonsus of Toledo (d. 667; 23 Jan.), whom he was to ordain deacon. He is first heard of as an official at the court of the Visigothic kings. Learned and able, he had represented the court at the Council of Toledo in 589. Even then, according to Ildephonsus, he was drawn to the religious life and used to help the brethren at the monastery of Agalai, on the banks of the River Tagus, in their manual labour. He entered this monastery and in 605 was elected its abbot. As abbot, according to Baronius, he carried out all manner of tasks in the monastery, down to carrying wood for the stove. He was so generous to the poor that "it was as if his own warmth and vitality flowed into their limbs and entrails." In 615 the metropolitan see of Toledo fell vacant on the death of Archbishop Aurasius; despite his reluctance to be separated from his monastery he accepted election as the new archbishop. Little is known of his eighteen-year episcopate other than his great generosity to the poor. It has been conjectured that he was responsible for encouraging King Sisebut to expel the Jews from the kingdom, but there is no firm evidence of this.

A.A.SS., Feb., 3, pp. 81-4; *P.B.*, 2, p. 584, quoting Baronius.

St Colman of Lindisfarne, *Bishop* (676)

Colman was the third bishop of Lindisfarne, following St Aidan (31 Aug.) and St Finan (17 Feb., above), and like them came from Ireland and had been a monk at Iona. He was bishop for three years only, from 661 to 664, and is remembered chiefly for the part he played in the Synod of Whitby (663/4), at which he was the main spokesman for the Irish (also Scottish, Pictish, British, Northumbrian, or "Celtic") side in the debates on the dating of Easter, the style of tonsure, and ultimately the role of bishops and the relationship between local Churches and Rome. Colman was defending an ancient but insular tradition but finally had to give way to arguments produced by Agilbert (11 Oct.), who asked Wilfrid (12 Oct.) to speak for him, as his knowledge of Old English was imperfect, based on the practice of the wider Church, against which only the two westermost islands held out, and they only partly. The argument (given fully by Bede, Book 3, chapter 25) turned on the authority given by Christ to Peter as opposed to that attached to local traditions and saints such as Columba (9 June), however great.

Colman, however, though forced to accept the conclusion, did not change his own beliefs or way of life. He collected a band of followers who also remained loyal to the "Irish" traditions and returned with them to Iona. He took with him a portion of the relics of St Aidan but left others, directing that they be enshrined in the sanctuary at Lindisfarne. Bede, though fully supportive of the "Roman" side at Whitby, can find no quarrel with Colman's way of life: "So frugal and austere were Colman and his predecessors that when they left the seat of their authority there were very few buildings except the church; indeed, no more than met the bare requirements of a seemly way of life. They had no property except cattle, and whenever they received any money from rich folk, they immediately gave it to the poor . . ." (3, 26).

From Iona Colman moved back to Ireland, where he founded a monastery on the island of Inishbofin off the coast of Galway (there is another off Donegal: the name means "Isle of the White Heifer"). Rome wisely left them to follow the traditional practices, trusting in time to resolve a dispute which, in effect, involved no point of doctrine. Colman had taken both Irish and English monks from Lindisfarne, and a dispute arose between the two groups (on lines that might be called racially stereotypical), the English complaining that the Irish spent the summer visiting friends and relations instead of helping to bring in the harvest, which they then returned to consume equally with the English monks (see Bede, 4, 4). So Colman found a site on the mainland in Co. Mayo to which he moved the English monks, leaving the Irish alone on Inishbofin. The mainland monastery, known as "Mayo of the Saxons," flourished, developing strong ties with York and living under a Rule imposed by canonically elected (as opposed to the Irish hereditary) abbots. For this and for the frugality of their life, supplying all their own needs by the work of their hands, they were praised by Bede and subsequently by Alcuin (see under St Angilbert, below).

Colman remained abbot of the two communities to his death, recorded variously by chroniclers as taking place in 672, 674, 675, or 676. His cult was confirmed on 11 July 1898 on the basis of his entry in the *Aberdeen Breviary*, based in turn on his entry in the *Félire* of Oengus. His feast-day was included in 1961 in the calendar of Argyll and the Isles, which has not subsequently been revised, for today's date, but in some parts of Ireland it is observed on 8 August.

The chief source for his life is Bede, *H.E.*, 3, 25-6 and 4, 4. On the controversy over the date of Easter see P. Grosjean, "Débuts de la controverse pascale chez les Celtes," in *Anal.Boll.* 64 (1946), pp. 200-46. On the date of the Synod of Whitby (given by Bede as 664 but possibly held in the autumn of 663) see P. Grosjean, "La date du colloque de Whitby," in *Anal.Boll.* 78 (1960), pp. 233-55. See also *N.C.E.*, 3, p. 1031a; 14, p. 861c, on his participation in the synod; H. Mayr-Harting, *The Coming of Christianity to Anglo-Saxon England* (1972), pp. 94-116; *O.D.S.*, p. 106. Colman is a heroic figure in Melvyn Bragg's novel *Credo* (1996).

St Tarasius, *Patriarch (c. 730-806)*

Tarasius was pitched from a lay position as chief secretary to the eastern empress Irene to the patriarchate of Constantinople in 784. The ecclesiastical background to this was the Iconoclast controversy, which surfaces in several entries in the present work. Some summary of its course leading up to Tarasius' appointment is, however, necessary here for an understanding of his actions as patriarch.

Iconoclasm—the movement against the production and veneration of images in the name of doctrinal purity—had been a growing movement amongst the bishops of Asia Minor in the early eighth century. It gained the support of Emperor Leo III (the Isaurian), who published an edict against the cult of images in 730 and forced Patriarch St Germanus (12 May) to abdicate. Icons were strongly defended by St John Damascene (4 Dec.), who argued in their favour from the theological doctrines of the creation and Incarnation. Leo's son, emperor as Constantine V from 741 to 755, decided to summon a council to resolve the dispute. This met at Hiereia, on the Asiatic side of the Bosphorus, in 754, with neither the pope nor the patriarchs of the Oriental churches represented, though 338 bishops did take part under the presidency of Theodore of Ephesus. It eventually produced a decree stating that Christ is not capable of being represented, condemning both the making and the honouring of icons. Iconoclasm thus became a dogma of the Eastern Church. This could have resulted in indifference, had not Constantine V forced the issue by confiscating monasteries where icons were still displayed, converting them into barracks and forcing the monks into the imperial army. The monasteries of Bithynia, then the most important centre of monasticism in Europe, were depopulated and largely destroyed. Although the people were mainly on the side of the monks, the army remained resolutely loyal to the emperor, and resistance was ineffective.

Constantine died in 775, and his son Leo IV (775-80) abandoned his father's persecution. On his death his widow, Irene, became regent for their son, Constantine VI. Though she was a scheming and violent woman, the cult of images was close to her heart and she worked to restore it, which led to a reopening of the monasteries. Full restoration of the cult of images, however, would require a council to overturn the decree of Hiereia, which had regarded itself as having ecumenical authority; this would require a new patriarch who would uphold the cause. In one of the shrewder moves of her career, Irene chose her chief secretary, Tarasius. The current incumbent, Paul IV, had supported Hiereia; he was asked to resign and retire to a monastery. As a layman, Tarasius was uncompromised by membership of the monastic faction and was a suitable person to make peace. He accepted the appointment on condition that a new council be summoned, and was consecrated bishop of Constantinople *per saltum* (leaping over the intervening orders) on 25 December 784.

Early the following year Tarasius contacted the Holy See by letter to notify Pope Adrian I (772-95) of his elevation direct from the lay state, to profess his orthodoxy including his support for the veneration of images, and to make his request for a new ecumenical council. His letter was backed up by one from Irene, also requesting a council. Pope Adrian, despite his reservations about Tarasius' strictly uncanonical elevation and his objections to the use of the term "ecumenical patriarchate" for the bishopric of Constantinople, nevertheless welcomed the proposal for a council to undo the work of Hiereia and sent two representatives, stressing his right to confirm its decrees.

The council met first in a church in Constantinople, but it was disrupted by imperial soldiers acting on behalf of the iconoclast bishops against Irene. She ordered them to be removed to counter an (invented) Arab threat and moved the council to Nicaea, calmer and redolent of the authority of the first ecu-

menical council, held there in 325. It was finally able to convene at the end of
September 787. Tarasius was asked to direct the discussions, even though the
papal representatives theoretically held the presidency. Supported by the papal
representatives, he used his diplomatic skills to tone down the demands of the
monastic faction, which wanted all ordinations carried out by iconoclast bishops declared invalid. Tarasius ruled that only those who had actively taken part
in persecutions—apparently not many—should be deposed. The debates were
characterized by an almost total lack of serious theological discussion on the
issue: it was Tarasius' distinction to shake his fellow bishops out of complacent
acceptance of legends and to insist on the precise distinction between *latreia*
(adoration) and *proskonesis* (veneration). Veneration of icons was declared orthodox doctrine, justified in that it was offered to the person represented by
the image, not to the image itself.

Tarasius also guided the council to consider other matters, notably simony
and the need for austerity and high moral standards in the lives of clerics and
monks, in which he himself set an outstanding example. He sent Pope Adrian a
report of the council, whose final document included twenty-two disciplinary
canons, receiving in return the official *acta* through the papal legates. Tarasius
had steered the council wisely and humanely, but resentment still smouldered
among the monks who had called for stronger action against iconoclast bishops.

He was then drawn into the imperial machinations of Irene, who insisted on
being co-ruler even though Constantine VI had reached an age at which he was
able to rule on his own. She forced her son to break off an engagement to
Rotrudis, daughter of Charlemagne, and forced him to marry Mary the
Paphlagonian, whom she then proceeed to calumny and may even have tried to
poison. Constantine declared his resolve to divorce Mary, a resolve strength-
ened by his attachment to Theodota, one of her ladies-in-waiting. He attempted
to persuade Tarasius that Mary was preparing to poison him, a ruse Tarasius
saw as an attempt to hoodwink him. He was faced with three canonical questions: that of grounds for divorce; that of remarriage after divorce; and that of
successive bigamy. There was also the question of the application of canons to
the person of the emperor. At first he took a strong line, refusing to countenance the divorce and threatening Constantine with excommunication. But the
marriage was solemnized by a priest named Joseph: with or without Tarasius'
tacit approval cannot be determined; in any event, he censured Joseph but took
no canonical steps against the emperor.

Partly on grounds of principle—that Church law, so recently re-established,
was being sacrificed to practical considerations—and partly for political reasons—because Constantine was advised and supported by formerly iconclast
bishops—the monastic faction, led by Abbot Plato of Sakkudion (4 Apr.) and
his nephew Theodore the Studite (11 Nov.), accused Tarasius of laxity and
withdrew from communion with him, branding the emperor's marriage as
adultery. Constantine retaliated by having Plato and Theodore imprisoned and

then banished, thereby alienating the church reform movement. In 797, sensing that her son was without support in either Church or army, Irene had him imprisoned and blinded and assumed the position of sole ruler. Tarasius was obliged to excommunicate Joseph, brand Theodota an adulteress, and disinherit her child. Five years later, Irene was deposed by Nicephorus and banished to the island of Lesbos. This left Tarasius in relative peace for the remaining four years of his patriarchate.

He was personally humble, with a dislike of pomp and circumstance. He made his clergy wear simple vestments, with cinctures made of goats' hair, and would not let servants wait on him. He walked openly among his people and talked to them. He was perhaps temperamentally unsuited to deal with the likes of Irene and her machinations. Shortly before his death—so his biographer Ignatius the Deacon, who was keeper of the sacred vessels and later became bishop of Nicaea, relates—he fell into a trance in which he appeared to debate the events of his life with a series of accusers. But serenity supervened and he died peacefully after a patriarchate that had lasted twenty-one years, most of them troubled. He had steered a prudent course throughout, unlike virtually all the others, saints and otherwise, involved in the theological, ecclesiastical, and political debates shaking Byzantium at the time. But he left the Iconoclast controversy ultimately unresolved. It broke out again in 814, when Emperor Leo V (the Armenian) began removing icons from churches once more and banished Tarasius' successor, Patriarch Nicephorus I (13 Mar.), like him a layman elevated directly to the patriarchate. In the West, a faulty translation of the decrees of the Second Council of Nicaea led to a manifesto against it, published by the Frankish bishops in the *Libri Carolini* (Caroline Books) in 790, and to subsequent condemnation by bishops meeting in Paris in 828. Papal authority combined with theological explanation eventually rectified the mistranslation, but the Iconclast controversy underlay the general mistrust leading to the Great Schism between East and West in 1054.

Jedin-Dolan, 3, chs. 6-7, pp. 32-9. Tarasius' personal qualities are related by Ignatius the Deacon: Latin trans. in *AA.SS.*, Feb., 3, pp. 577-94; also in *P.G.*, 98, 1271-99; I. A. Heikel (ed.), *Acta Soc. Sc. Fennicae* (Helsingfors Academy) (1891), pp. 395-423. General works on the Iconoclast controversy include E. J. Martin, *A History of the Iconoclastic Controversy* (1930); see also *Bibl.SS.*, 12, 987-91; *N.C.E.*, 12, p. 938; *P.B.*, 3, pp. 22-5; *O.D.C.C.*, *s.v.* for further bibliography.

St Angilbert, *Abbot* (814)

Angilbert belongs to the "Carolingian Renaissance," which reached its full flowering when Alcuin, formerly director of the cathedral school at York, joined a distinguished group of teachers at Charlemagne's court school in 782. This school prepared both clerics to occupy important posts (see, *e.g.*, Paulinus of Aquileia; 11 Jan.) and laymen for a career in the secular administration of the empire. Modelled on classical lines following the *trivium* and *quadrivium* that made up the seven liberal arts and presided over by the king himself, it developed into a sort of academy, with regular meetings at which the members discussed learned topics, read their poetry, and even solved riddles. The apparently somewhat precious atmosphere was completed by aliases used by its members. Angilbert was one of those with a reputation for the quality of his verses and was accordingly known as "Homer." Others took the names of Old Testament prophets, others figures from classical literature. This was more than a learned game: it was designed to express the aim of re-creating classical civilization in a Christian setting and for the purpose of advancing Christian learning.

Angilbert was one of Charlemagne's particular favourites, was present at his coronation, and is said to have either married his daughter Bertha or to have had two children by her out of wedlock. A monk named Nithard claimed that he and his brother Harnid were the sons of Angilbert and Bertha. This has been taken as an indication of moral laxity among the higher clergy, but it is not certain that he had received any degree of orders at the time—or, indeed, that the marriage or liaison is a fact, though it has been said that he married Bertha, with Charlemagne's consent, after he had been ordained priest. Lives of him date from the late Middle Ages, and there is considerable doubt as to their reliability. He is said to have turned to the religious life after a dangerous experience when the Danes sailed up the river Somme. Bertha took the veil at the same time. Angilbert, who held the office of *missus*, or royal emissary to the northern coastal provinces of France, prayed at the tomb of St Riquier (Richarius; 26 Apr.), vowing that he would become a monk if the danger were averted; his prayers were answerd by a violent storm that completely disrupted the Danish fleet.

Whether he became a monk at this stage or not, he continued to enjoy Charlemagne's favour. He was invested with the revenues of St Riquier's abbey of Centula, near Amiens, with grants that enabled him to rebuild it in magnificent style. At the end of 795 Pope Adrian I, who had been a close friend of Charlemagne, died and was succeeded by Leo III. By this time Lombardy had been incorporated into the Frankish kingdom, and Charlemagne's role was changing from that of king to that of emperor of what was soon to be called the "Holy Roman Empire," extending over the ancient geographical areas of Gaul, Germany, and Italy. Leo III was elected and consecrated without consultation with Charlemagne, thereby declaring Roman sovereignty over Italy. Charlemagne had set out his own responsibility for ecclesiastical order and education in the *Libri Carolini* and elsewhere; he had also apparently heard less than flattering reports of Leo's personal life. He sent Angilbert as *missus* to Rome with an admonition in which he told him to "admonish the pope to lead an honourable life, to observe the canons zealously, and to rule Holy Church in piety. . . ."

Angilbert became abbot of St Riquier, built a fine library there, and instituted the *laus perennis*, the continuous choir service lasting day and night. Since this meant that the monks no longer had time for manual labour, others had to do what was needed. The monastery grew to become the centre of a "holy city" of some three thousand people, with three hundred monks, one hundred children in the monastery school, and its own soldiers. It had three main churches and five smaller chapels, between all of which the monks processed chanting litanies.

Charlemagne made him one of his executors, and he travelled to Aaachen to append his signature to the emperor's will. By this time he was an old man, and he died only twenty-two days after his great patron.

The late medieval Lives by Hariulf and Anscher are in *AA.SS.*, Feb., 3, pp. 88-105. See also *P.B.*, 2, pp. 578-84; *Bibl.SS.*, 1, 1249-50; *N.C.E.*, 1, p. 524, which supports his two sons being born out of wedlock. For the Carolingian Renaissance and the development of the empire see Jedin-Dolan, 3, chs. 12-14, pp. 70-95. On the liturgy at St Riquier see J. Hubert, "St Riquier et le monachisme bénédictin en Gaulle à l'époque carolingienne," in *Il monachesimo nell'alto medioevo e la formazione della civiltà occidentale* (1957), pp. 293-309; E. Bishop, "Angilbert's Ritual Order for St Riquier," in *Liturgica Historica* (1918), p. 330.

St Theotonius, *Abbot* (1086-1166)

Theotonius is the subject of a contemporary biography that, in the words of the previous edition of this work, has "no extravagant miracles, but . . . breathes in every line a true and reverent affection for the saint which it commemorates." He was born in Portugal, where he is held in great honour. A nephew of Cresconius, bishop of Coïmbra, he was destined for the priesthood from an early age. After ordination he was priest and then archpriest in the town of Viseu, where his holiness and austerity coupled with his prowess as a preacher attracted the whole town and notables from further afield, including the queen and her husband, Henry, count of Portugal. They repeatedly urged him to accept a bishopric, but he always refused.

Every Friday he sang a solemn Mass for the souls in purgatory followed by a procession to the cemetery in which the whole population of the town joined, giving large sums in alms, which were then distributed to the poor. He was no respecter of rank: when the queen, widowed and openly living with Count Ferdinand, attended his Mass, he preached a sermon against vice that obliged them to leave; on another occasion the queen had the temerity to ask him to make his Mass shorter, to which he replied that the Mass was in honour of a greater sovereign and that she was free to stay or go. Penitent, she stayed, and she asked his forgiveness at the end.

He had interrupted his ministry to make a pilgrimage to the Holy Land, and he later made a second one. At this time, a new monastery was being built at Coïmbra for the Canons Regular of St Augustine. Theotonius decided to join them and was one of the original members of the community, of which he soon became prior. He was notable in office for his insistence on strict and reverent recitation of the daily offices. In 1139 Count Alphonsus Henriques ended Portuguese vassalage to the kings of Castile, assumed the title of king of Portugal, and in 1143 declared the country a fiefdom of the papacy. This attracted Crusaders, who by 1147 had helped him reconquer most of the country from the Moors. Known as "The Conqueror," he held Theotonius in high regard and heaped gifts on the monastery, attributing his victories to Theotonius' prayers; in return, Theotonius persuaded him to set free his Mozarabic Christian captives. He spent the last thirty years of his life in this Monastery of the Holy Cross, of which he became abbot, and died at the age of eighty. When King Alphonsus heard of his death, he is recorded as exclaiming, "His soul will have gone up to heaven before his body is lowered into the tomb."

The contemporary Life, by a fellow-monk of Holy Cross, is in *AA.SS.*, Feb., 3, pp. 108-22. See also *España Sagrada* 23, pp. 105ff.; *Bibl.SS.*, 12, 366-8; *N.C.E.*, 14, pp. 75-6; E. A. O'Malley, *Tello and Theotonius: The Twelfth-Century Founders of the Monastery of Santa Cruz in Coimbra* (1954); Carvalho da Silva, *Vida do admiravel Padre S. Theotonio* (1764). On Portugal and the papacy see Rui de Azevedo, *Documentos Medievais Portugueses* (1958); summary in Jedin-Dolan, 4, p. 27. The Monastery of the Holy Cross, extended throughout the Middle Ages and Renaissance, is one of the great architectural monuments of Portugal.

Bd John of Fiesole (Fra Angelico) (*c.*1400-55)

The Florentine painter known to the world as Fra Angelico was beatified by Pope John Paul II on 3 October 1982 and declared the patron of Christian artists. He was born Guido di Piero in Vicchio di Mugello, a village near Fiesole on the hills overlooking Florence. The traditional date given is 1387, but recent sources suggest around 1400 as more probable. He entered the studio of a Florentine painting master and was active as a painter by 1417 while still a layman, when his name is found among the members of the Company of San Nichola, a painting fraternity, so he was a painter before he became a friar. He was paid for his part in decorating the church of San Stefano al Ponte in 1418, his earliest known professional commission. If he painted secular subjects at this time, none from the period has survived, and all his surviving works are purely religious in subject matter.

He joined the Dominican Order around 1420, entering the Convento di San Domenico in Fiesole, a Dominican reformed house, and taking the name Fra Giovanni in religion. There he first became friends with Antoninus, the future archbishop of Florence and saint, canonized in 1523 (2 May). He also met a Camaldolese monk named Piero de Giovanni, a painter known as Lorenzo Monaco, whose disciple he became. Lorenzo painted in the tradition of Andrea Orcagna, with broad brush strokes and generous forms, but also taking a colour sense and lyrical line from the school of Siena, which influenced Fra Angelico's sense of colour and technique.

Fra Angelico took major orders in 1427-9, by which time the community from Fiesole had moved into the Convento di San Marco in Florence, which was then rebuilt in 1437-52 through the patronage of the Medicis, the rulers of the city-state. Cosmo de Medici the Elder deposited his rich collection of Greek and Byzantine manuscripts there, and Fra Angelico learned iconography from these, bringing Eastern themes into Western art. There he embarked on the decoration of the walls, on which he was to work for the remainder of his life, producing a unique body of religious art. Michelozzo, the architect employed by Cosmo de Medici and his brother Lorenzo to undertake the rebuilding, features on the ladder in the fresco of the *Descent from the Cross*.

Enough of his work has survived to enable us to appreciate both his quality as a painter and his personality. He represents the transition between the Middle Ages and the Renaissance, combining the religious fervour of the former with the love of beauty for its own sake of the latter: "The sources of his feeling are in the Middle Ages, but he *enjoys* his feelings in a way which is almost modern; and almost modern also are his means of expression." His work shows "Perfect certainty of purpose, utter devotion to his task, a sacramental eagerness in performing it" (Bernard Berenson). Two major works from the period 1430-3 survive. The *Last Judgment* was painted for the Camaldolese Convent of Santa Maria dei Angeli, still in the style and spirit of Lorenzo Monaco. It is the last example of Gothic grace in decoration and the use of gold, but his treatment of space, using perspective, makes it a *Quattrocento* work. The *Descent from the Cross*, painted in collaboration with Lorenzo Monaco, has Gothic detail but breathes the spirit of the new humanism with its quest for naturalism, and has a sculpturesque calm inherited from Masaccio. He was the first Italian to paint a recognizable landscape, and also the first to give a sense of nature as a place of enjoyment. He was conscious of, and able to work with, the new understanding of perspective, but always subordinated his technique to the telling of the sacred stories that are the subject of his art. He is "a great artist who deliberately renounced any display of modernity despite his profound understanding of the problems which Brunelleschi and Masaccio had introduced into art" (E. H. Gombrich). Of the three, who are likely to have influenced one another, Brunellesci, born in 1377, was the earliest to paint, but his longer life—he died only four years before Fra Angelico—made him also a contemporary.

In San Marco, from about 1441, Fra Angelico painted a sacred scene in each friar's cell and at the end of every corridor, as an aid to meditation and devotion, and it is this series of frescoes that constitutes the bulk of his work, preserved in its original setting. His purpose is devotional and instructional and his approach simple and narrative, using large areas in a style inherited from Giotto and Masaccio. Subjects include the *Mocking of Christ, Christ in the Sepulchre*, and the *Transfiguration*. Details are kept to a minimum, with none of the "entertaining" extraneous elements usually introduced into devotional works designed for the laity. Many contain figures of a friar and a nun in meditation, enabling the friars and nuns to picture themselves physically contemplating the scenes depicted. The spirit of the paintings reflects the period of calm confidence that settled on the Church in the wake of the Council of Constance in 1429, when for a time all major conflicts seemed to have been resolved. For Fra Angelico, his art was a means of preaching and meditating; his images show people what should be worshipped—in accordance with the Dominican preaching tradition.

While his early style is elegant and static, influenced by the early Florentines as exemplified in the *Coronation of the Virgin,* now in the Uffizi, his later style, which predominates in San Marco, is more naturalistic, with extensive use of *chiaroscuro* and a developing understanding of perspective. His scale also became larger and his compositions simpler as he moved away from detail occupying a major part of his subjects to the absolute plainness of such frescoes as *St Dominic adoring Christ on the Cross.* His Renaissance learning shows in his use of classical architecture, but this is kept to the background, not made central to the composition, as in the *Annunciation,* dating from around 1449, with its accurate representation of the cloister; the *Sacred Conversation* of about the same date has saints diminishing in size according to the laws of perspective.

Outside San Marco, he painted numerous altarpieces, most depicting the Madonna and Child with a group of saints, of the type that was to develop into the theme known as *sacra conversazione.* A typical example, now in the Museo di San Marco, shows the Virgin and Child enthroned, with SS Dominic, Cosmas and Damian, and Mark on their left and SS John the Evangelist, Thomas Aquinas, Laurence, and Peter Martyr on their right: three of the saints are Dominicans, the two evangelists are connected with San Marco, and the remaining three were much venerated by the Medicis of Florence. He was commissioned, probably by Pope Eugenius IV (1431-47), to decorate two chapels in the Vatican; one of these survives, showing scenes from the lives of SS Stephen and Laurence, while the other has been destroyed. In 1447 he began work on a huge fresco cycle of the *Last Judgment* in Orvieto Cathedral, of which he was able to complete only a small part. The "Chronicle of Orvieto," written during his lifetime, called him "a magnificent brother, a master painter, famous above all the painters of Italy." Before he died he was in Rome once more, working on decorations for St Peter's and the pope's private study. Michelangelo later wrote of him, "One has to believe that this good monk has visited paradise and been allowed to choose his models there."

Besides the very considerable investment of time this painting activity must have represented, he played an active part in the affairs of the Order, especially as prior of Fiesole from 1450 to 1452. It is said that Pope Eugenius wished to appoint him archbishop of Florence but that he persuaded the pope to appoint Antoninus instead, preferring the lesser appointment for himself.

By the fifteenth century the devotional quality of his work, or perhaps the prominence of angels in it, had earned him the title of "Fra Angelico," by which he has been generally known ever since. The first Life of him, written by Vasari in 1550, calls him "Fra Giovanni Angelico." In the nineteenth century Ruskin could consider him "not an artist, properly so-called, but an inspired saint." Few, if any, saints can have left such an inspired legacy behind them, and few, if any, artists can have integrated their gift so totally into the ideals of their life. His frescoes represent beatitude, not things in themselves; despite the conventional expression of some figures, their purpose is supernatural.

B. Berenson, *Italian Painters of the Renaissance* (1952), pp. 49-50; E. H. Gombrich, *The Story of Art* (1950), pp. 181-2; *D.Cath.Biog.*, p. 57; H. Osborne (ed.), *Oxford Companion to Art* (1970), pp. 46-7; P. and L. Murray, *The Oxford Companion to Christian Art and Architecture* (1996), p. 71; *N.C.E.*, 1, pp. 502-4; J. Lemaître and E. Lessing, *Florence et la Renaissance* (1992). There are Lives in English by R. Langton Douglas (1902); John Pope-Hennessy (1952). The bulk of his work is still *in situ* on the walls of San Marco in Florence, most of which was converted into a museum at the time of the suppression of religious Orders in the eighteenth century, into which many of his other works have been gathered. There are two frescoes in the chapter house of San Domenico in Fiesole.

BB William Harrington and John Pibush,

Martyrs (1594 and 1601)

William Harrington was born to a gentleman's family of Mount St John, Feklixkirk, in the then North Riding of Yorkshire, in 1566. When he was fifteen, he met Edmund Campion (1 Dec.), who was a guest at Mount St John and who inspired him with the idea of becoming a priest. He was sent to be educated at Douai and entered the college in Reims in September 1582. Two years later he decided to become a Jesuit and moved to their college at Tournai, but he was compelled by ill health to leave and return to England. He was betrayed by one Ralph Miller, who had been a tailor in Reims during William's time there; but perhaps on account of the fact that he was still only eighteen, he was not imprisoned but was returned to the parental home at Mount St John. He spent seven years there and then sailed again for Douai, re-entering the college in Reims in February 1591. He was ordained there in March 1592 by the papal nuncio, Cardinal Filippo Sega, and left for England.

He was at liberty for only about a year, part of it spent ministering in the West Country, before being captured in London at the house of Henry Donne, brother of the poet John Donne. (Henry was imprisoned for harbouring him and died of fever in jail.) He was imprisoned in Bridewell and interrogated in May 1593. About a month later he was moved to Newgate, tried, and condemned to death. He wrote a dignified letter to Pickering, the lord keeper, denying any complicity in plots and any treasonable intentions. This may have been the cause of the delay in carrying out the sentence, in the hope that he might be "turned" to serve the crown. He was finally executed at Tyburn on

18 February 1594 in the usual barbarous manner and is recorded to have "struggled with the hangman" after being cut down alive to be disembowelled and quartered, which Challoner comments on as being only the natural physical reaction rather than any conscious attempt to avoid martyrdom. He has the strange distinction of being the only priest executed for his faith to be accused, after his death, of having fathered a child, an accusation made in the context of such a tissue of lies as not to be worthy of credence.

John Pibush was another Yorkshireman, born in Thirsk in 1567. After spending a year at Douai he entered the college at Reims in 1581, and he was ordained there six years later. He was sent to England on 3 March 1589 and ministered under the aliases of Foster and Gravenor. He was arrested at the Hart Inn at Morton Hendmarsh in Gloucestershire and sent up to London for trial. He was returned to prison at the Gatehouse in Gloucester. On 5 February 1595 there was a mass breakout from this prison: Catholic accounts (such as Challoner) say that Pibush took advantage of this to escape with the others; Protestant (Topcliffe) say that he engineered the escape. Be that as it may, he was careless enough to walk along the highway and was recaptured the following day at Matson, only two miles away.

He was sent up to London again and condemned to death on 26 June, but for some reason he was left to languish in prison for a further six years. His name was on the list of those to be sent to Wisbech Castle in 1599 but was crossed off this list by Lord Chief Justice Popham. He developed tuberculosis in the filthy conditions of the Queen's Bench prison and describes his condition in a moving letter, which has survived (both in its original form and in a translation by Henry Garnet, S.J., into Italian for his general, from which it was translated back again into English). He writes: "Sir, sickness hath made so absolutely a conquest of my bodily health that friends and acquaintance coming to the place where I live, and sitting in my company, have asked, who is he? I have lived reft of holy rites, singled from the society of men, sequestered from my friends, debarred of student's comforts, punished with my company as S. Chrysostom with the soldiers that carried him into exile. Yet eight years' imprisonment and 43 years our common calamity I hope shall not discourage us. For my own part I account mine as but yesterday begun. . . ." At least in the early part of his imprisonment he was badly treated by his fellow prisoners as well as by his jailers, but it seems that in the latter part he was treated less harshly and even allowed to say Mass sometimes.

On 17 February 1601 he was brought to the bar before Popham and simply asked if there was any reason why the original sentence of death should not be carried out. He replied that he had done nothing in his life to deserve such a sentence but was quite willing to die as a Catholic priest. He was executed the very next day at the place in Southwark named St Thomas' Waterings, after St Thomas Becket (29 Dec.).

William Harrington and John Pibush were both beatified on 15 December 1929.

Anstruther, 1, pp. 149-50, 274-5, with refs. to original sources. Also *M.M.P.*, pp. 197, 252-3. The source for the slander against Harrington is Harsnet, *Declaration of egregious Popish Impostures . . .* (1604); those for the circumstances of Pibush's martyrdom are in C.R.S. 5, J. H. Pollen (ed.), *Unpublished Documents relating to the English Martyrs 1584-1603* (1908).

Bd Gertrude Comensoli, *Foundress* (1847-1903)

She was born the fifth of ten children in Bienno, a village in the Val Camonica district near Brescia in northern Italy, on 8 January 1847 and christened Caterina. Her autobiography records her early special devotion to the Blessed Sacrament, before which she declared: "A million times I swear to you, Lord, that I will always be yours, and if I am ever untrue to you, then let me at once die." At the age of fifteen she joined the Institute of St Bartolomea Capitanio in Lovere, but illness forced her to leave after a short time. She then joined the Bienno branch of the Society of St Angela Merici (27 Jan.) and began a fruitful apostolate to the young women of the district.

Her family was poor, living in an area devastated by war and with a declining agricultural output and massive emigration to the United States and Argentina. In order to help them, in 1867 she took a job in domestic service with a Fr Rota, later to become bishop of Lodi. Leaving there after a year, she joined the household of Countess Fè-Vitali in San Gervasio d'Adda in the district of Cremona, where she was to stay for ten years. At the end of this time she made the acquaintance of Fr Francesco Spinelli, and together they planned the foundation of a religious Congregation devoted to the double aim of devotion to Christ in the Blessed Sacrament and the Christian education of girls. In 1879 both her parents died and, free of the need to support them financially, she was free to put her concept into practice. She moved to Bergamo and, with her favourite sister, Bartolomea, and a friend, brought the Congregation into being as "Adorers of the Blessed Sacrament" or "Sacramentines." With the approval of Bishop Camillo Guindani of Bergamo, she, her sister, and another woman were professed, with Caterina, who took the name Gertrude in religion, as their superior, on the octave of the feast of the Immaculate Conception 1882.

The Congregation grew rapidly, largely because it took particular account of the needs of the diocese. Four other houses were opened in the diocese between 1884 and 1887. But it soon ran into trouble: Fr Spinelli, who had helped it originally, quarrelled with Gertrude about the aims of the Congregation and also lost money, leaving it in financial difficulties. The bishop of Bergamo came to the rescue and found the nuns a new house in Lodi, whose bishop (the former Fr Rota, with whom Gertrude had been in service) gave them canonical approval as a Congregation in 1891. The following year they returned to Bergamo to the original house in which they had begun their work. Gertrude spent her last years strengthening the spiritual foundations of the Congregation and open-

ing "Eucharistic cenacles" in several neighbouring towns. In 1906 the Holy
See gave the Congregation definitive approval and formal canonical status.

Gertrude died in Bergamo on 18 February 1903. Her remains were translated to a special chapel next to the town church in 1926. Her cause was
introduced in 1941, and she was beatified in St Peter's by Pope John Paul II on
1 October 1989.

C. Comensoli, *Un anima eucaristica, Madre Gertrude Comensoli del Santissimo Sacramento,
fondatrice delle Suore Sacramentine di Bergamo* (1936). See also *Bibl.SS.*, 4, 129-30; *A.A.S.*
81 (1989), pp. 1055-7; F. Holböck, *Die neuen Heiligen der Katholischen Kirche*, 3 (1994), pp.
149-52.

R.M.
St Agapitus, bishop of Sinai (fourth century)
BB Francis Régis Clet and John Peter Néel, martyrs (1820 and 1862)—see
   "The Martyrs of China," 17 Feb., above.

19

St Quodvultdeus, *Bishop* (439)

Quodvultdeus was bishop of Carthage in the years following the death of St Augustine (d. 430; 28 Aug.). A period of relative tranquillity for the Roman provinces of North Africa in theology and politics was about to come to an end. The majority of the population had converted to Christianity, and though the Donatists were still a force to be reckoned with, they had been forced on to the defensive by state pressure and the theological arguments of Augustine. Then in 429 the situation changed drastically when, led by Genseric, some eighty thousand Vandals, supporters of Arianism, invaded Tangier from southern Spain, initiating a century of persecution for the Church in North Africa.

The Vandals had a reputation for especial savagery toward the Catholic clergy, many of whom considered flight; Augustine tried to rally them by stressing their duty to persevere as long as they had any congregations left, but his words were largely in vain. Peasants fled from the countryside into the larger cities, including Carthage, which were able to hold out longer. Quodvultdeus, who had by then succeeeded Capreolus as bishop of Carthage, lashed out at Christians who still preferred the circus to the example set by the martyrs Perpetua and Felicity (6 March) and those who were even then suffering martyrdom for their faith in the countryside. This, he told his terrified hearers, was the reason for the calamity that had overtaken North Africa, as a punishment by God. In 439 the city fell to the Vandals, with enormous loss of life. Quodvultdeus' life was spared, but he and most of his clergy were banished and put aboard rotting, leaking ships without oars or sails, which somehow managed to reach Naples, where he died soon after.

Quodvultdeus is commemorated in the calendar of Carthage on 8 January, but on today's date in the Roman Martyrology.

The main source for the history is Victor, bishop of Vita, *Historia Persecutionis Wandalicae*, in *M.G.H., Auctores Antiquissimi*, 3, pt. 1, p. 5. See also *Bibl.SS.*, 10, 1334-8. For a continuation of events in Carthage see St Deogratias, 5 January.

St Barbatus, *Bishop* (612-82)

Information concerning Barbatus relies on a Life written in the ninth century, some two hundred years after his death. This makes him a native of Benevento, on the Via Appia some thirty miles north-east of Naples. In the late sixth and early seventh century the Lombards, a central European people who had embraced Arianism, invaded Italy and secured large parts of it, establishing a dukedom somewhat loosely attached to their northern kingdom as far south as Benevento. Here they destroyed the existing bishoprics. By the 660s, however, elements of Catholicism had crept into the Arianism of at least some of the Lombard rulers. Grimoald, duke of Benevento, took the opportunity of a quarrel between the late king Aripert's sons to seize the throne for himself. He was devoted to the Archangel Michael, whose sanctuary on Monte Gargano lay in the duchy of Benevento, and made him patron of his kingdom and nation.

Barbatus, meanwhile, had found even the nominal Christians in the duchy, including Grimoald's son Romuald, who had succeeded to the duchy when Grimoald declared himself king, steeped in superstition, including the veneration of a golden viper. He preached tirelessly against these abuses, praying and fasting equally tirelessly for the conversion of the people, who remained indifferent. Success came in 663, when Grimoald repulsed an invasion from the east led by Constans II, attributing his victory to the intervention of the Archangel Michael. Barbatus had preached that victory would be his and was now able to convince the people. He had the golden viper melted down to make a chalice and felled a sacred tree that had also figured in superstitious rites. The bishop of Benevento, Hildebrand, had died while Constans was laying siege to the city, and Barbatus was elected in his place. As bishop he was able to stamp out pagan practices throughout the duchy; in that capacity he also attended the sixth general council at Constantinople in 680. He died in 682 at the age of seventy.

The Life, dating from not earlier than the ninth century, is in *AA.SS.*, Feb., 3, pp. 139-49; also, in a possibly more correct version, in *M.G.H., Scriptores rerum Langobardum,* pp. 556-63; but see *N.C.E.*, 2, p. 90, which calls the *M.G.H.* version "tendentious." See also *Bibl.SS.*, 2, 770-2; G. Cangiano, "Sulla legenda della 'vipero longobardo' e delle 'streghe,'" in *Atti della Società storica del Sannio* 5-7 (1927-9), pp. 84-96.

St Boniface of Lausanne, *Bishop* (1260)

He was born in Brussels and went at the age of seventeen to study at the university of Paris. He stayed on at the university as a lecturer for seven years after completing his studies but was caught up in the student troubles of 1229-30 (see under Jordan of Saxony; 13 Feb., above), when his students refused to attend his lectures. He left Paris and went to Cologne, where he was appointed to a post in the cathedral school. Two years later he was elected bishop of Lausanne. Perhaps he had learned habits of abrasiveness at Paris: whatever the cause, his denunciation of the weaknesses of the clergy did not make him popular in the diocese. He also offended Emperor Frederick II, who had him attacked and badly wounded. He went to Rome and asked the pope to release him from his office, for which he felt unfit. The pope granted his request, and he retired to Brussels, where he was invited to stay at the Cistercian nunnery of La Cambre. He wore the Cistercian habit, even if he did not take vows, and seems to have acted as a peripatetic bishop without a fixed see, as he is known to have carried out episcopal functions such as consecrating churches and altars during the eighteen years or more that he lived at La Cambre. His reliquary is kept in the church of Notre-Dame-la-Chapelle in Brussels. He was canonized in 1702.

Two short Lives, one of which is almost contemporary, are in *AA.SS.*, Feb., 3, pp. 151-9. Information from contemporary chronicles is used in J. F. Kiechens, *Etude historique sur St Boniface* (1892); A. Simon and R. Aubert, *Boniface de Bruxelles* (1945). See also *Bibl.SS.*, 3, 320.

St Conrad of Piacenza (1351)

As a young married nobleman of Piacenza (in northern Italy midway between Turin and Bologna), Conrad was hunting one day and ordered brushwood to be set alight to drive out the game. The fire burned out of control and devastated neighbouring villages. Conrad, his wife, and the hunting party crept home without admitting their part in the disaster, for which a poor man found gathering firewood was charged, condemned, and sentenced to death. This moved Conrad to confess the truth in order to save the man's life. He was ordered to pay the cost of making good the damage; this accounted for most of his wealth and his wife's dowry. They saw God at work in this great reversal of fortune and resolved to devote the rest of their lives to God's service. They gave what remained to them to the poor, his wife joined the Poor Clares, and Conrad attached himself to a group of hermits. He was only twenty-five years old, and his wife (whose name is not recorded) was even younger.

He lived a life of extraordinary piety, and his fame spread, so that increasing numbers of visitors distracted him from his devotions. To escape them, he sailed to Sicily, where he spent his remaining thirty years as an anchorite, most of the time in the valley of Noto. In Sicily, too, his holiness brought him fame; people suffering from all sorts of complaints flocked to his cell to be cured through his prayers. He died lying before a crucifix praying for the people of Noto and was buried in the church of St Nicholas there, which soon became a popular shrine. He is invoked as patron of hernia sufferers on account of the many cures of ruptures credited to him, an honour he shares with St Catald (10 May), also highly venerated in Sicily. Conrad's cult had been approved by three popes, but there seems to be little evidence for the marvels with which the accounts of his life are filled.

AA.SS., Feb., 3; *Leggendario Franciscano*, 1, pp. 246-54; *F.B.S.*, pp. 127-30; *P.B.*, 2, pp. 593-4, with material from the *Légendaire d'Autun*.

Bd Alvaro of Zamora (c. 1434)

Alvaro is a major figure in the reform of the Dominican Order in Spain. His birthplace has been given variously as either Lisbon or Córdoba, where he spent most of his life, but the new draft Roman Martyrology calls him "of Zamora" (in western Castile on the Duero north of Salamanca) and this is followed here. The precise date of his birth is not known either but was probably 1350. The date of his death has also been given as 1420, which has to be discounted from evidence of his activities, and alternatively as about 1430.

He entered the Dominican convent in Córdoba in 1368, gained a great reputation as a preacher, preaching throughout Andalusia and also in Italy. There he may have met Bd Raymund of Capua (d. 1399; 5 Oct.), who became the chief inspiration for his reform programme. He became confessor and adviser to Catherine (daughter of John of Gaunt) when her husband King Henry II of Castile died, and he helped with the education of her son, King John II. He reformed court life, but political dissension forced him to leave the court and resume his wok as a preacher. His project for a reformed house following strictly the Rule of St Dominic gradually took shape in a mountainous region not far from Córdoba, where he built the foundation known as *Escalaceli,* "Ladder of heaven." This became a major centre of devotion and learning.

He was influential in preventing Castilian support for the Avignon claimant to the papacy, Peter de Luna, who was supported by the King of Aragon and had himself elected as Benedict XIII in opposition to the successive Roman claimants Boniface IX, Innocent VII, and Gregory XII: both Benedict XIII and Gregory XII were eventually declared schismatic by the self-summoned Council of Pisa in 409. Alvaro continued his work of preaching, catechizing, and teaching into his old age. His ascetic practices became more austere; he is said to have spent most of his nights in prayer after returning from long days preaching and begging, since his community relied wholly on alms for its support. A painting in Córdoba shows him crawling on his knees to the chapel of Our Lady of Pity in the monastery grounds, his shoulders bleeding from the discipline, with angels clearing stones from his path. He also built "station" chapels, each representing a scene from Our Lord's passion, and has therefore been credited with originating devotion to the Stations of the Cross in the West, but this had become widespread with the popularity of pilgrimages to Jerusalem, encouraged by indulgences being attached to them in the fourteenth century. He died at an advanced age, and his cult was confirmed in 1741.

Procter, pp. 42-4; Mortier, 4, pp. 210-4. On the history of devotion to the Stations of the Cross see M. Walsh, *A Dictionary of Devotions* (1993), pp. 250-2.

R.M.

SS Maximus, Theodore, and Asclepiodotus, martyrs in Hadrianopolis (Bulgaria) under Maximian (*c.* 310)

St Maris, hermit in Syria (fifth century)

St Rabula the Syrian, abbot in Constantinople (*c.* 680)

Bd George of Lodève, monk of Vabres (diocese of Rodez) and possibly bishop of Lodève (*c.* 877)

Bd Peter of Treja, O.F.M., friar near Ancona (1304)

Bd Elizabeth Bartholomea Picenardi, Third Order of Servites, of Mantua (1468)

20

St Eleutherius, *Bishop* (532)

He was the first bishop of Tournai, in modern Belgium, but even less is known about him than about other bishops of the period, since a major fire in 1092 destroyed most ancient records of his life as well as his relics, and virtually all we are left with is legends. The most extravagant of these tells that a governor's daughter fell in love with him and told him of her love while he, then a young bishop, was at prayer; he fled from her, whereupon she dropped lifeless to the ground. Eleutherius promised to restore her to life if her father became a Christian; he promised, the girl was raised and baptized, but her father reneged on his promise, being converted again only when a terrible plague broke out, which he recognized as punishment for his deceit.

More factual information is that he was born to Christian parents and went to school in Tournai with St Médard (8 June); the two remained lifelong friends. He was appointed bishop in around 486, ten years before the baptism of Clovis I in Reims Cathedral. In 501 he visited Rome to see Pope St Symmachus (498-514; 19 July) and returned there later to obtain confirmation of the orthodoxy of his writings from Pope St Hormisdas (514-23; 6 Aug.). He was known as a zealous preacher and made numerous converts among the Franks in his diocese: the *Vita S. Medardi* claims that he once baptized eleven thousand people in one week, probably at Pentecost. He is supposed to have died from injuries sustained when he was attacked by a group of Arians after saying Mass.

AA.SS., Feb., 3, pp. 190-210; *B.H.L.*, 2, pp. 455-70, lists quasi-biographical materials but without claiming reliability for them. See also *N.C.E.*, 5, p. 265; *Lib. Pont.*, 1, 102-4, 58-61; *D.T.C.*, 4, pt. 2, 2319-20.

St Eucherius, *Bishop* (743)

Eucherius is the subject of an apparently contemporary biography, so, allowing for conventional elements, his life is known with some reliability. He was born in Orleans and became a Benedictine monk in the great abbey of Jumièges in Normandy (then Neustria) in about 714. His uncle, Soavaric, was bishop of Orleans at the time; on his death, the biography states, the senate, people, and clergy of the city sent a deputation to Charles Martel asking his permission to elect Eucherius in his place. Charles, who was then mayor of the palace and effectively ruler of the Franks, gave his permission, and the young man was taken, apparently much against his will, away from monastic tranquillity to fill the vacant see. (It has, however, been pointed out that the episcopal lists of Orleans show two or three bishops between Soavaric and Eucherius.)

He proved an exemplary bishop, but he had been right to fear the ways of the world. Charles Martel, the illegitimate son of Pepin of Herstal, had embarked on a massive campaign of conquest and had only recently overcome the Neustrians. He defeated the Moors near Poitiers in 733 and then occupied Burgundy and Provence. These campaigns had to be financed, and when the confiscated property of his defeated enemies proved insufficient, he turned to Church property, which had increased considerably in the sixth and seventh centuries. In a process of "secularization" he either confiscated property directly or appointed lay officials as abbots and bishops, who then placed the property of their churches at Charles' disposal to equip troops. He was not motivated by anti-religious feeling and indeed saw his victories, especially that over the Moors, as obtained with Christ's help, but the effect on the Church was disastrous, and Eucherius opposed the confiscations vigorously. This opposition was represented to Charles as a personal insult, and he banished Eucherius to Cologne. There he became exceedingly popular on account of his gentleness and piety. Fearing the growth of his influence, Charles sent him to a fortress near Liège, where again his popularity soon spread. The fortress governor eventually allowed him to retire to the monastery at Saint-Trond, near Maastricht, where he is described as spending the rest of his life in prayer and contemplation. A cult had developed certainly by the ninth century. His relics are preserved at Saint-Trond, and he features in the martyrologies of Bede and Rabanus Maurus.

The biography is in *AA.SS.*, Feb., 3, pp. 211-25; see Duchesne, *Fastes*, 2, p. 548 for the episcopal lists of Orleans. See also *Bibl.SS.*, 5, 140-1; *P.B.*, 2, pp. 603-5; *N.C.E.*, 5, p. 621. For the background see Jedin-Dolan, 3, ch. 2, pp. 7ff.

He is sometimes depicted seeeing a vision of Charles Martel in hell, but this legend does not form part of the original biography.

St Wulfric (*c.* 1080-1154)

Wulfric (also Ulric or Ulfrick) has never been formally canonized, and he does not feature in the new draft Roman Martyrology on this day. Nevertheless, he was the subject of a near-contemporary Life by the Cistercian abbot John of Forde Abbey, not far from the Somerset village of Haselbury Plucknett, in which he established himself as a hermit, and seems on several counts worthy of inclusion here.

He was born at Compton Martin in Somerset, eight miles from Bristol, trained for the priesthood, ordained, and appointed to Deverill near Warminster, some twenty miles to the east. Even after ordination his chief loves were hawking and hunting, but he was converted to a more austere way of life in about

1120, by popular account through a chance meeting with a beggar, who told him that he would one day find rest and be numbered among the company of the saints. He returned to Compton Martin as parish priest for some five years and then became an anchorite at Haselbury, which shared its lord of the manor, William Fitzwalter, with Compton Martin. There he built a cell on the north side of the chancel of the parish church, and in this he spent the rest of his life, engaging in such mortifications that "by fasting and scourging he reduced himself to skin and bone," as earlier editions of this work record. He wore a cuirass of chain-mail next to his skin, which was said to be miraculously able to be shortened with a pair of scissors to facilitate the innumerable prostrations in which he engaged.

His penitential way of life was later recounted by a boy named Osbern who served his daily Mass and later became parish priest at Haselbury: he would, we are told, often strip and immerse himself in cold water while reciting the entire Psalter—an action reminiscent of Celtic practice, as were his prostrations. He had no episcopal backing for his way of life but was supported by the Cluniac monks of nearby Montacute. His fame spread and he was widely credited with the gift of second sight and with healing powers. Visitors to his cell included King Henry I (1100-35) and his successor Stephen (1135-54). Henry and his queen, Adela, begged him to cure the knight Drogo de Munci from paralysis, which came about. He foretold Henry's death two years before it took place and greeted Stephen as king even before his disputed accession—though this amounted to no more than guessing, at the time when Adela, Henry I's second wife, had failed to produce an heir. Henry, who had previously exacted support for his daughter Matilda, seems to have recognized Stephen as his heir.

He engaged in practical manual work, copying and binding books and making other articles for use in church services. He died on 20 February 1154, after nearly thirty years of this way of life, and was buried in the cell in which he had lived (the site of the vestry of the present church) despite attempts to claim his body by the monks of Montacute and Forde. Osbern built his tomb there. There was no immediate cult despite his fame during his life, but between 1185 and 1235 "innumerable" miracles were reported and Haselbury became a popular place of pilgrimage. John Gerard records as late as 1633 that his tomb was still standing, but at some point his body was removed for safety to an unmarked grave, whose location is now unknown and where it presumably still remains.

The Life by John of Forde is ed. M. Bell, *Wulfric of Haselbury* (Somerset Record Society, vol. 47, 1933), with introduction and notes and the text of an earlier Life by Jerome Porter, first printed at Douai in 1632. Text also in *AA.SS.*, Feb., 3, pp. 230-5, *s.v.* "Ulric." See also R. M. Clay, *Hermits and Anchorites of England* (1914); D. M. Stenton, *English Society in the Early Middle Ages* (1965), pp. 214-17; *O.D.S.*, pp. 505-6; *Bibl.SS.*, 12, 795.

Bd Thomas Pormont, *Martyr* (1592)

The son of Gregory and Anne Pormont (or Pormort, or Portmore), he was born at Little Limber in Lincolnshire. He studied at Trinity College, Cambridge, and then went abroad to study for the priesthood. He sailed to Rouen, arrived in Reims on 15 January 1581, and was sent on to the English College in Rome, in which he was enrolled in May. He was ordained at the Lateran six years later, and after leaving the college in March 1588 he served Bishop Owen Lewis for a time. (Lewis had been St Charles Borromeo's [4 Nov.] vicar general in Milan from 1580 to 1584 and then returned to Rome, from where he was responsible for the affairs of the college at Reims and those of Mary, Queen of Scots. In 1588 he was consecrated bishop of Cassano in the kingdom of Naples.) Lewis sent him to Milan and so on to England.

In London he met and was befriended by Robert Southwell (21 Feb., below), though he had not been particularly friendly with the Jesuits in Rome. He was sheltered in St Gregory's parish, near St Paul's in London, by a haberdasher named John Barwys, whom he reconciled to the Church. He used three aliases, Whitgift, Meres, and Price. His arrest in July 1591 was the work of a lapsed priest from the English College, William Tedder, who had been arrested at the height of the Armada scare in September 1588 and recanted. Pormont managed to escape but was rearrested in September and imprisoned in the house of the notorious "priest-hunter" Topcliffe himself, where he may well have been tortured, as Topcliffe had—quite illegally—set up a formidable torture chamber in the house. He was tried on 8 February 1592 together with John Barwys, and both were sentenced to death. Barwys obtained a special pardon and was spared; Pormont was executed in St Paul's churchyard on 20 February.

Anstruther, 1, pp. 280-1; *M.M.P.*, p. 186; Stanton, pp. 79-80.

R.M.
St Leo, bishop of Catania (Sicily) (*c.* 780)

21

ST PETER DAMIAN, *Bishop and Doctor* (1007-72)

This prophetic figure of the medieval Church, poet, prose writer, and one of the great reformers in a period of crisis—"calamitous times," even, in the words of the new draft Roman Martyrology—was born in Ravenna, on the Adriatic coast of Italy. The family was large and relatively poor; both his parents died while he was still young, and he was placed in the care of a brother who treated him more like a slave. He was forced to be a swineherd until an elder brother, then archpriest of Ravenna, took him away and took charge of his education, sending him to school first at Faenza and then at Parma. Learning, comprising grammar, rhetoric, and law, proved to be his forte, and in due course he returned to Ravenna as a professor. He adopted an austere way of life, wearing a hair shirt, fasting, and spending long hours in prayer; he would invite the poor to his table and serve them with his own hands.

He resolved to leave the world and embrace a monastic life, and he happened to entertain two Benedictine monks who had followed the reformer St Romuald (19 June) into his foundation at Fonte Avellana in northern Italy. This was a grouping of hermits who lived in pairs, devoting their lives to prayer and *lectio divina*. Peter joined them in 1035 and was soon outdoing the others in austerities: his vigils brought on a near-permanent insomnia, which was cured with difficulty, after which he moderated his hours of watching and praying somewhat. He turned to study of the scriptures and patristic theology, in which he soon became extremely learned. The other hermits agreed that he should take on the direction of the community in the event of the abbot's death. He was reluctant, but the abbot made it a matter of obedience, so he was forced to accept the charge. This was laid upon him in 1043, when the abbot died, though he did not assume the title of abbot, acting rather as prior general and founding five other hermitages, each with a prior who was responsible to him. His first work was a Life of St Romuald, and in it he sets out the ideals that governed the whole of his own life: notably, exaltation of the solitary life and reform of the clergy.

His reputation for personal holiness and the reforming zeal with which he governed his religious houses made him a force to be reckoned with in Rome. He at first supported the papal accession of John Gratian as Pope Gregory VI (1045-6), but his support turned to enmity once it became known that Gregory's election, through the agreed abdication of Benedict IX (1032-45), had been secured by the payment of a substantial sum of money. Henceforth he was concerned with the reform of the process of electing popes, and successive reforming popes employed him in service to the wider Church. Pope St Leo IX (1049-54; 19 Apr.) held synods throughout Italy, at which Peter argued vehemently against simony and clerical marriage. Leo engaged him as theologian in his campaign against simony, but Peter's reflections, contained in his *Liber gratissimus*, did not go as far as to declare simonaical ordinations invalid, as did some of the reformers of the time. He saw a reformed papacy as the key to the reform of the whole Church, and it was Leo who first proposed that the College of Cardinals should be solely responsible for papal elections. In 1057 Pope Stephen IX (1057-8), a reformer in the mould of Leo IX, persuaded him to leave his fastness and appointed him cardinal-bishop of Ostia, the seaport of Rome. This gave the hermit movement an official importance in the Church.

Pope Stephen, foreseeing his coming death, had made the clergy and people of Rome swear not to elect a successor until Hildebrand could return from Germany, but Bishop John of Velletri had himself proclaimed pope as Benedict X. Peter opposed this and refused to officiate at his enthronement, which was carried out by the archpriest of Ostia. Peter held his bishop's office with reluctance, constantly asking Stephen's agreed successor, Nicholas II, another short-reigning pope (1059-61), and then his successor, Alexander II (1061-73), to be released back to his hermitage. Nicholas, however, had an important mission for him in Milan, where a popular reform movement, known as the *Pataria*, was forcing the reluctant urban priests to embrace celibacy. Peter, accompanied by Anselm of Lucca (the future Alexander II), preached the Roman primacy to the less than enthusiastic people of Milan but did manage to restore order and to prevent the *Pataria* from developing into a schismatic reform movement. In 1059 he also took part in the Synod of the Lateran, which proclaimed the right of cardinals alone to elect future popes, largely to prevent the imposition of candidates by emperors.

After Stephen's death Peter backed Alexander's election against that of a candidate supported by Romans and Lombards, who styled himself Honorius II, and composed the *Disceptatio synodalis* for the Synod of Augsburg, which upheld Alexander, in 1062. Alexander, who amongst other strategies extended the concept of a military "crusade" in support of reform against Peter's considered opinion, eventually agreed to his repeated requests to be allowed to return to Fonte Avellana, releasing him not only from his bishopric but from his former supervision of his religious establishments as well, so that he was able to live as a simple monk, but not before he had spent several years playing a central part in reform movements.

He was sent on diplomatic missions as well, including one to Germany when in 1069 Pope Alexander II sent him out of his retirement as his legate to oppose the divorce the emperor Henry IV was seeking from his wife, Bertha of Turin, on the grounds that their two-year marriage had not been consummated. Henry had won over the archbishop of Mainz, who summoned a synod at Frankfurt to pronounce the dissolution of the imperial marriage. But Peter, as papal legate, presided over the synod and persuaded the emperor that he would be acting against the law of God, the canons of the Church, and his own good by proceeding with the divorce. Henry gave way, but he is said to have hated his wife the more as a result. Peter hastened back to Fonte Avellana, where in his last years he turned to making wooden spoons and other useful objects to keep himself occupied when not engaged in prayer or study. Three years later he was sent, again as papal legate, to Ravenna, where the wrongdoings of the archbishop, Henry, had earned him excommunication and split the town into factions. By the time Peter arrived Henry was dead, but Peter was able to bring his former supporters to repentance and to restore peace and order to the city. This was to be his last mission: on his way back to Fonte Avellana he succumbed to a fever and died at Faenza.

His reforming concerns extended to the liturgy, and he fought for the suppression of local rites and the universal extension of the Roman rite. Only the Ambrosian rite of Milan held out against his teaching, adopting no more than certain features of the Roman. His organizational powers ensured the survival of the monastic reform movement begun by Romuald, who had left no written Rule and several of whose communities had quickly disintegrated after his death in 1027. Peter gave the hermit movement a firm theological and organizational base, so that its influence exceeded what might have been expected from its maximum of some ten Congregations. One of his successors, Rudolf, prior of the community at Camaldoli from 1074 to 1089, was to build on his foundations and ensure the rise of the Camaldolese into a major Order based on his principles. These exalted the eremitical life above the cenobitical but did not exclude this; his communities had a monastery as well as hermit cells, but fit disciples were allowed to be hermits from the outset, not after a period of preparation as monks, and the superior had to be a hermit. Peter also sought to extend monastic ideals to the secular clergy, in particular urging canons to respect the ideals of the common life as opposed to owning their own houses and amassing private property. They should endeavour to "imitate the primitive Church," living together and holding all things in common. He defined the term *clericus* as denoting "part and portion of God": being part of God's heritage meant doing as had been done by the original apostolic community. By defining the clerical life as one of community Peter was extending the monastic ideal to the canons regular—an original argument that was to have lasting influence in terms of clerical spirituality.

In his theological and philosophical works Peter openly reacted against his earlier secular learning, declaring grammar to be the work of the devil and all human intellectual endeavour foolishness in the face of the omnipotence and transcendence of God. There was something of rhetoric and more of pastoral concern in this apparently anti-intellectual stance, however. It was designed above all for his hermits, who were to give absolute precedence to the love of

God; it applied less to laypeople and not to the secular clergy, who should have a solid scholarly formation. But all had to maintain the right order, which was the primacy of the spiritual over the secular, and in this sense Peter introduced the idea that philosophy was the handmaid of theology. He was the first to set out the ideal of *sancta simplicitas*, complete detachment enabling knowledge to be used without becoming enslaved by it.

His spiritual writings are addressed mainly to religious, but he addressed several letters to great personages urging repentance, pilgrimage, and detachment from the world, which can be achieved by giving up riches to help the Church. He tells a bishop that he should pray without ceasing: "When you are going from one place to another, or on a journey, or about some necessary business, let your lips continually ruminate something from the scriptures, grinding the psalms as in a mortar, so that they may ever give forth an odour of aromatic plants." To his hermits he taught the ideals of the Desert Fathers and the need to be constantly on watch against temptation; the cell is the place "to make war on the devil"; the "desert" is at once the "dwelling-place of evil spirits" and a place of seclusion and peace. He wrote treatises praising the use of the discipline, but its use should always be accompanied with prayer. He tried to encourage the monks of Cluny to extra disciplines and fasting, but the abbot, St Hugh (28 Apr.), sensibly and humorously invited him to try the life there for himself first: "Eat with us first, and then say whether you think our food needs more seasoning." Peter could be tender as well as harsh, and his devotion to the image of Christ on the cross and the maternal aspects of Mary foreshadowed the *devotio moderna* of the later Middle Ages. Besides his treatises he also wrote hymns, of which the best known is one in honour of St Gregory the Great (3 Sept.), beginning *"Anglorum iam apostolus,"* referring to Gregory's sending of St Augustine (of Canterbury; 27 May) and other monks to convert the English.

Peter was never formally canonized but was declared a Doctor of the Church in 1828 in recognition of his influential preaching and writings in the cause of reform of the Church. His actual date of death was 22 February 1072; he was formerly commemorated with a "double" feast-day on 23 February, but the Calendar reform of 1969 moved his feast-day, as an optional memorial, to 21 February, on which date he is recorded in the new draft Roman Martyrology. In art he is shown in his different roles as cardinal, hermit, and pilgrim.

His Life was written by his disciple John (St John of Lodi; 7 Sept.) and is printed in *AA.SS.*, Feb., 3, pp. 416-27; also in *P.L.*, 144, 113-46. His works are in *P.L.*, 144 and 145; also in *M.G.H.*, "Libelli de Lite Imperatorum et Pontificum in Saeculis XI et XII," 1 (1891). His *Vita B. Romualdi* is ed. G. Tabacco (1957). His poems have been ed. M. Lokrantz (1964); see also A. Wilmart, "Le recueil des poèmes et des prières de S. Pierre Damien," *Rev.Bén.* 41 (1929), pp. 342-57. There is a selection of his works in Eng. trans., ed. and intro. P. A. McNulty, *Selected Writings on the Spiritual Life* (1959). Selected letters in A. Wilmart, "Une lettre de S. Pierre Damien à l'impératrice Agnès," *Rev.Bén.* 44 (1932), pp. 125-46; J. Leclercq, "Inédits de S. Pierre Damien," *ibid.* 67 (1957). Modern studies include, in German, J. Endres, *Petrus Damiani und die weltliche Wissenschaft* (1910); F. Dressler, *Petrus Damiani. Leben und Werk* (1954); in French, J. Leclercq, *Saint Pierre Damien, ermite et homme d'Eglise* (1960); J. Gonsette, *Pierre Damien et la culture profane* (1965); in Italian, *Studi su san Pietro Damiani in onore del Cardinale Cicognani* (1961); in English, J. J. Ryan, *Saint Peter Damian and His Canonical Sources* (1956); O. J. Blum, *St Peter Damian: His Teaching on the Spiritual Life* (1947); *idem*, "The Monitor of the Popes: St Peter Damian," *Studi Gregoriani* 2 (1947), pp. 459-76. For the background see Jedin-Dolan, 3, esp. ch. 42. *O.D.S.*, pp. 393-4; *H.C.S.*, 2, pp. 97-101, 113-4, and elsewhere, with further refs.

ST ROBERT SOUTHWELL, *Martyr* (*c.* 1561-95)

This poet among the English martyrs shares the literary laurels of the English Jesuits with Gerard Manley Hopkins three centuries after him. As a poet, his reputation extends well beyond the Catholic or even religious community; while his verse was not as influential in terms of prosody as Hopkins' was to be, it and his equally lyrical prose works may well have been more influential in changing the temper of an age. Partaking of the literary conventions of his time, it springs directly, nevertheless, from the circumstances and the ruling inspiration of his life: to priesthood and martyrdom.

He was born in the Norfolk village of Horsham Saint Faith, related on his mother's side to the Shelleys of Sussex, where he spent part of his childhood, and was sent to school at Douai. There he embarked on a brilliant course of studies under the Jesuit Leonard Lessius and so made his first contact with the Society. From Douai he moved on to Paris, where he studied under Thomas Darbyshire, who had been archdeacon of Essex in the reign of Queen Mary. He seems to have considered a vocation as either a Jesuit or a Carthusian—which would have enjoined a very different way of life—but at the age of just (or just under) seventeen he announced his intention of joining the Society of Jesus. He was initially refused on account of his age, and his grief at the refusal inspired the earliest of his surviving writings. He laments his exclusion in terms that might seem a little more melodramatic than the cause warranted: "Alas, where am I? Where shall I be? A wanderer in a dry and parched land. . . ."

His exclusion was for a matter of months only, and he was admitted to the Jesuit novitiate at Sant'Andrea in Rome in October 1578. Other writings from the time of his novitiate survive, showing a very clear appreciation of the life and tasks for which he was preparing himself: "How great a perfection is required in a religious of the Society, who should ever be ready at a moment's notice for any part of the world and for any kind of people, be they heretics, Turks, pagans or barbarians. . . ." He was ordained in 1584 and appointed prefect of studies at the English College. Two years later he was sent on the English mission together with his fellow Jesuit Henry Garnet. They arrived a year after it had become high treason for a Jesuit or a priest trained abroad at one of the new seminaries to be in England. Harbouring them was also de-clared a felony. Robert must have been well aware of the likely final outcome of his mission; he would have read the eyewitness account of the execution of Edmund Campion (1 Dec. 1581), the first Jesuit to be martyred in England. He wrote to Fr Robert Persons, disguising the subject matter as a merchant's business letter: "He [Campion] has had the start of you in loading his vessel with English wares and has successfully returned to the desired port. Day by day we are looking forward to something similar of you"—meaning to be sent on the mission and to a martyr's death. From Calais he wrote to the Jesuit general Aquaviva: "Nor do I so much dread the tortures as look forward to the crown. The flesh indeed is weak and profiteth nothing. Yea, while pondering these things it even recoils."

Shortly after his arrival in England he attended a remarkable meeting at Hurleyford House in the Thames valley, which mapped out a new strategy for the survival of Catholicism in England. Held on the feast of St Mary Magdalen (22 July), it was attended by Wiliam Byrd, the court composer, and those present sang a *Missa Solemnis*. Shortly after this Robert preached a sermon on the Magdalen's repentance (identifying her, as usual at the time, with the penitent sinner of Luke 7) to Catholics in the Marshalsea prison in London. He developed this theme in a pamphlet, *Mary Magdalen's Funeral Tears*, which he managed to have published and which was to have a profound effect on the moral climate of the age.

Among the Catholics present to hear him at the Marshalsea was Dorothy Arundell, who recommended Southwell to her relative Anne Dacre, countess of Arundel and Surrey, as a suitable priest to bring her the sacraments occasionally. She was the wife of Philip Howard (19 Oct.), then a prisoner in the Tower, where Robert managed to visit him (and for whom he was to write his *Triumphs over Death* to console him on the death of his half-sister, Lady Margaret Sackville). Robert apparently took the recommendation as an invitation to take up residence at Arundel House in the Strand, a most unsuitably risky place for a Jesuit. A deep friendship developed between him and Anne, and so he began his extraordinary ministry, which was to last for six years, living in a small room in a remote wing of the house and acting so discreetly that his presence was known only to a small number of trusted servants. He spent his days in prayer and writing, emerging at night to minister to Catholics. It was here that he wrote *An Epistle of Comfort*, which he managed to have published in England, most probably with Anne's help: she was, as he wrote, one of those "delicate women who have taken on the courage of men." The basis of *An Epistle of Comfort* was the series of letters he wrote to Philip Howard, later more widely addressed to fellow Catholics persecuted and in prison. His theme is the transience and fickleness of human existence, that "in the midst of life, we are in death"; the comfort is that all are equally brought to the same term: "And so it fares with man's life, he comes into the world with pain, begins his course with pitiful cries and is continually molested with divers vexations; he never ceases running down till in the end he falls into the sea of death. Neither is our last hour the beginning of our death but the conclusion; for then is come what has been long in the coming, and fully finished what was still in the ending."

He ministered outside London as well: at Baddesley Clinton in Warwickshire on one occasion he had a narrow escape when priest-hunters burst in as he was about to say Mass at 5 a.m.; he just managed to hide the vestments and get into the priests' hiding hole.

In response to the Proclamation of 1591 (claiming that Catholics were proscribed for their traitorous intentions only, not for their religion as such), Southwell composed his *Humble Supplication to her Majesty*, a devastating attack on the government claim that there was no persecution on the grounds of religion alone. He summed up his assertion of his co-religionists' loyalty in the words: "We will rather yield our breasts to be broached by our country's swords, than use our swords to the effusion of our country's blood." Despite the secrecy of his existence, he was by now a figure of influence in English literary society. It has recently been argued (by David Lunn) that Southwell was the prime mover in the moral change observable in Shakespeare's work in the period 1591-4, evidenced in the change of tone and subject matter from *Venus and Adonis* to *The Rape of Lucrece*, with its treatment of rape as an allegory for the violation of the soul by mortal sin. Shakespeare had placed himself under the patronage of the earl of Southampton, whom Robert had known from childhood days in Sussex. It was to Southampton that Robert addressed his *Peter's Plaint*, a long narrative of the closing events in the life of Christ put in the mouth of Peter repentant after his denial. In it, he appeals for a moral change: "I move the suit, the grant lies in your hands." *The Rape of Lucrece* could well be the response to this; by the time it was written (1594), however, Southwell was on his way to execution.

The usual practice among Catholic missionaries was to seek not to convert convinced Protestants but to "reconcile" lapsed Catholics to their original faith, and Southwell followed this, combined with the Jesuit policy of concentrating on the aristocracy and influential figures, into which categories both Southampton and Shakespeare would have fitted—though there is no real evidence, despite repeated attempts to prove otherwise, that Shakespeare ever actually embraced, or was reconciled to, Catholicism. For some years Southwell seemed to lead a charmed life in the centre of London, but he was eventually captured, as were so many of his fellow missionaries, through an act of betrayal. The queen's chief pursuivant, the notorious Richard Topcliffe, had exacted an appalling price from the Bellamy family for their part in sheltering young men fleeing after the collapse of the "Babington Plot": two sons were put to death, a third was tortured and exiled, and their sister Anne was raped by Topcliffe in person. Pregnant with his child as a consequence, she was offered an honourable marriage if she would invite Robert Southwell to her house, Uxenden Hall in Harrow; she did so, and he was arrested there.

He was taken to Topcliffe's house in Westminster, equipped as a torture chamber (see Bd Thomas Pormont; 20 Feb., above). The whereabouts of his printing press was discovered, and it was destroyed. He was put ten times to the newly-devised "wall torture"—hanging by manacled wrists from a hook high up on a wall. Topcliffe boasted to the queen: "I never did take so weighty a man, if he be rightly used." Sir Robert Cecil, Elizabeth's chief minister, seeing the effects, declared it "not possible for a man to bear. And yet I have seen Robert Southwell hanging by it still as a tree-trunk and no one able to drag one word from his mouth." Robert himself described the ten tortures as being "each one worse than death." He was then imprisoned in the Gatehouse and the Tower for nearly three years without any charge being brought against him. In the end, he appealed to Cecil that he should be either tried or given at least some measure of liberty. The result of this appeal was that he was brought to trial and condemned for being a priest.

His trial and execution were to prove a turning-point, resulting in the downfall of Topcliffe, a general revulsion against the butchery of hanging, drawing, and quartering, and the start of more diplomatic methods of keeping Catholicism in check. Topcliffe first tried to deny that he had been tortured and then pleaded—as Adolf Eichmann was to do centuries later—that he had only been carrying out orders: "I did but set him against a wall. I had authority to use him as I did. . . . I have the Council's letters to show for it." Robert's reply was simple and devastating in its obvious truth: "Thou art a bad man." Topcliffe then engaged in a shouting match with the judge, who finally ordered him to be silenced. It was the end of his five-year reign of terror. The verdict, though, was inevitable: Robert was to be hanged, drawn, and quartered at Tyburn.

In an echo of Jesus' crucifixion, a notorious highwayman was condemned to be executed with him in order to deflect attention away from the execution of a famous poet, but this only had the effect of swelling the crowd. Robert was dragged, as was customary, to Tyburn on a hurdle but managed to keep his head raised above the mud, so that those in the crowd who had seen many an execution called him "the properest man they had ever seen that came to Tyburn for hanging." He threw his handkerchief to Henry Garnet, his friend and fellow-Jesuit, in the crowd, and Garnet had it by him when he wrote his eye-witness account. He was, after some argument, allowed to make a short speech. He began, "I am come hither to play out the last act of this poor life . . ."; he quoted St Paul: "Whether we live, we live to the Lord, or whether we die, we die to the Lord; therefore, whether we live or die, we belong to the Lord." He then prayed for the queen and for his country and ended, "All you angels and saints assist me." The cart was drawn away and the serjeant moved to cut the rope so that he could be butchered before he was dead. But Lord Mountjoy came forward and pushed the serjeant away, whereupon the crowd began to shout that he should be allowed to hang until he was dead. The sheriff then attempted to cut the rope, but he too was dissuaded by a roar of disapproval from the crowd; the hangman pulled on Robert's legs until he felt the body go limp, then took it down and cradled it in his arms before placing it on the block and severing the head, which he held up with the customary declaration, "Here is the head of a traitor." But the crowd's response was to bare their heads without the usual answering shout of "Traitor!" He was still disembowelled and dismembered, but this marked the end of the butchery of Tyburn.

Robert was a priest and martyr first and foremost, and the prose and poetic works for which he is remembered outside Catholic and even religious circles reflect his life. He wrote using the "conceits" of grammar and expression characteristic of his age and as a poet has often been compared to Philip Sidney. But while Sidney was admired as the perfect gentleman of his day, Southwell was a "treasonable" Jesuit. Yet his works were well known, influential, and admired: "What a famous man and how much beloved was Father Southwell," as Henry Garnet wrote. His lyrics have energy and passion combined with discipline; the best of them are relatively short and direct, with the conceits never taking over from the subject-matter. "The Burning Babe" was much admired by Ben Jonson; "The Virgin Mary to Christ on the Cross" is perhaps the most moving of his lyrics. As prefect of studies at the English College he had thoroughly studied the English language. In the preface to his published poems he declared his aim of turning the secular techniques used in the popular poetry of the age to a divine purpose—as St John of the Cross (14 Dec.), his near contemporary, did with the ballads of the Spanish popular tradition. His intellectual formation in the *Spiritual Exercises* combined with his poetic gifts to work a profound change in the moral climate of England.

Robert Southwell was beatified in 1929 and canonized as one of the Forty Martyrs of England and Wales (25 Oct.) in 1970.

Much of the above is indebted to D. Lunn, *The Catholic Elizabethans* (1997). See also C. Devlin, S.J., *The Life of Robert Southwell* (1956). Southwell's devotional poems, mostly written in prison, were collected under the title *Moeoniae* (1595). His complete works are ed. W. J. Walter (1822); the poems are ed. J. H. McDonald and N. P. Brown (1967); *An Epistle of Comfort*, ed. M. Waugh (1966); citation above from J. Cumming (ed.) *Letters from Saints to Sinners* (1996), pp. 87-9. For the background see H. Foley, S.J., *Records of the English Province of the Society of Jesus*, Series 1, pp. 339ff.; F. Edwards, S.J., *The Elizabethan Jesuits* (1981; Eng. trans. of the first six books of H. More, S.J., *Historia Provinciae Anglicanae Societatis Jesu*, St Omer, 1660); idem, *The Jesuits in England: from 1580 to the present day* (1985), ch. 1. The earliest surviving catalogue of the English College in Rome (1593) lists Southwell as working in London: see M. E. Williams, *The Venerable English College, Rome* (1979). See also *Bibl.SS.*, 11, 1332-4; *O.D.S.*, pp. 439-40.

St Eustathius, *Bishop (c. 338)*

A native of Side in Pamphylia, Eustathius is described as eloquent, learned, and virtuous. He was appointed bishop of Beroea in Syria, and such was his reputation that in about 324 he was elevated to the see of Antioch, which at the time ranked third in order of dignity in the universal Church, after Rome and Alexandria. At the General Council of Nicaea the following year he was received with honour and distinguished himself for his outright opposition to Arianism. As bishop of Antioch he had oversight of neighbouring dioceses, to which he appointed bishops capable of instructing and encouraging their flocks.

His opposition to Arianism brought him into conflict with Eusebius, bishop of Caesarea, the "father of church history" (who does not mention him), whom he accused of distorting the Nicene Creed. This provoked a storm among bishops who still supported Arianism, then finding renewed favour at the imperial court, assiduously cultivated by Eusebius, who persuaded Constantine to depose Eustathius from his see in 330. The see was offered to Eusebius the following year, but he refused it. Eustathius was banished to Trajanopolis in Thrace, but before leaving Antioch he preached to his people with such power that many of them formed a body of "Eustathians," who refused to recognize subsequent bishops appointed by Arians, even though some of these were orthodox. Eustathius died in exile at an unknown date and place.

He wrote copiously, but virtually none of his writings survives. The most important of the works that has been lost was a treatise *Adversus Arianos*, in eight books. Apart from fragments the only surviving piece is an anti–Origenist treatise, *de Engastrimutho*, known variously as *The Witch of Endor against Origen* or *The ventriloquist against Origen*. His theology seems to have been of the Antiochene school, with a more historical and critical approach to scripture than in Alexandria, and this has led him to be suspected of Nestorianism (two separate persons in Christ) and Sabellianism (the Godhead differentiated only by modes or operations, not persons).

The surviving texts and fragments are collected in *P.G.*, 17, 609-1066; there is a more recent collection in M. Spanneut, *Recherches sur les écrits d'Eustathe d'Antioche . . .* (1948); also a critical edition of *de Engastrimutho* in E. Klosterman, *Origenes, Eustathius und Gregor von Nyssa über die Hexe von Endor* (1912). See also R. V. Sellers, *Eustathius of Antioch and His Place in the Early History of Christian Doctrine* (1928); *D.H.G.E.*, 16, 13-23, lists all his works and their provenance and provides a full bibliography; further information and biblio. in *O.D.C.C.*, p. 376.

St Germanus of Grandval, *Martyr* (*c.* 667)

He was brought up as a child by Bishop Modoard (Modoaldus; 12 May) of Trier and at the age of seventeen, inspired by the example of St Arnulf (18 July), who had retired from the bishopric of Metz to a hermitage in the Vosges mountains, asked the bishop's permission to retire from the world. Modoard told him that as an orphan he should seek the king's permission, but Germanus, with three companions, set off to find Arnulf, who received them kindly and suggested that they should join his monastic foundation at Romberg. Germanus sent two of his companions to fetch his younger brother Numerian, still a child, and together they entered the monastery in the Vosges (later famous as Remiremont).

The brothers then moved on to Luxeuil. After some years there the abbot, Walbert, recommended Germanus to Duke Gondo as the best candidate to be abbot of his new foundation at Grandval (or Granfel) in the Val Moutier, a high mountain pass through the Vosges. There was an old Roman road crossing the pass; it had for long been blocked by fallen rocks, and one of Germanus' actions as abbot was to clear these and reopen the road. Two other monasteries were also placed under his charge. Gondo's successor, Cathic, also known as Duke Boniface Kattemund, was of a different temper and oppressed the monks and the inhabitants of the region. Germanus pleaded with him to cease his plunders, and his words seemed to have had some effect, but Cathic's soldiers caught up with him and his prior, Randoald, in the monastery. They stripped them, probably in an attempt to steal their vestments; one of the soldiers ran Germanus through with his lance, while others decapitated Randoald. This took place on the eve of the feast of St Peter's Chair, on which date Germanus and Randoald are jointly commemorated in the diocese of Basle. Their relics were originally interred at Saint-Ursanne but were taken to Berne for safety when threatened by Calvinists in the sixteenth century.

The events of Germanus' life were set down by a contemporary, a monk named Bobolenus. His account is in *AA.SS.*, Feb., 3, pp. 263-5. See also *B.G.*, Feb., pp. 361-2; *P.B.*, 2, pp. 611-14; *Bibl.SS.*, 6, 261-2.

St George of Amastris, *Bishop* (*c.* 825)

This wise, holy, and popular bishop is known from a Greek Life, which tells that he was a late child born, in answer to prayer, to Theodosius and Megetho, who lived at Cromna, near Amastris on the Black Sea. At the age of three he nearly died when he fell into a fire while playing and was left permanently scarred on both hands and one foot. He studied for the priesthood, then decided on complete withdrawal from the world and went into the desert of Mount Sirik, where he met an aged anchorite who undertook to train him in the eremitical life. When the old man was about to die, he advised George not to remain alone but to go to the monastery of Bonyssa, where the monks received him as an old friend even though he was unknown to them.

When the bishop of Amastris died, its people, who had not forgotten George, elected him as their new bishop, sending a deputation to the monastery to inform him of their decision. He refused the office but was carried off by force to Constantinople, to the patriarch, St Tarasius (18 Feb., above). The emperor proposed another candidate for the bishopric, but Tarasius insisted that the people of the diocese should have the final say; they reconfirmed their preference for George, who this time did not refuse, was duly consecrated, and acclaimed by the people.

He was responsible, during the course of his episcopate, for averting an attack by Saracens. Farmers and others living in the countryside had been warned of an impending attack and advised to retreat inside the city walls but could not be persuaded to abandon their homesteads until George went round in person and succeeded in convincing them of the need to do so. The Saracens, seeing that they could not take the city by storm, abandoned the intended attack and withdrew. There is no precise information on the date of George's death.

AA.SS., Feb., 3, pp. 271-83; the complete text of the Greek Life is ed. with intro. by V. Vasilievsky in *Analecta byzantinorussica* 3 (1891), pp. 1-73. See also *Oxford Dictionary of Byzantium*, 2, p. 837; *B.H.G.*, pp. 211-2; *Bibl.SS.*, 6, 533.

Bd Mary Enrica Dominici (1829-94)

She was born near Turin on 10 October 1829 and christened Caterina. In 1850 she entered the Turin house of the Institute of Sisters of St Anne and Providence, where she spent the rest of her life. The Institute had been founded in Turin in 1834 with the aim of educating girls from poorer families.

Her gift of herself to the love of God in the religious life was total; from her youth she felt "an ever-increasing desire to become good and to serve the Lord with a true heart." Her letters and other writings show a child's trust in God as Father of absolute love: she echoed Jesus' *Abba* in her normal form of address to God, *Babbio mio*. "I seemed to rest on the bosom of God, like a little girl sleeping peacefully at her mother's breast: I loved God and would almost say, were it not for fear of exaggerating, that I tasted his goodness."

In 1861 she was elected superior general, a post she held until her death thirty-three years later. Her leadership throughout a period that was always troubled in Italy showed a clear understanding of the needs of the Church and the country and contributed enormously to the development of the Institute. Her spirituality revolved around the concepts of humility and self-giving; her last words to her Sisters were, "I recommend you humility . . . humility." This translated into a life of charity and service to others, including the victims of a cholera epidemic. Pope Paul VI ended his homily at her beatification ceremony, on 7 May 1978, by commending her words "To will what God wills, as God wills it and as far as he wills it" to the reflection of his audience.

N.S.B. 1, pp. 148-50; *Bibl.SS.*, 4, 756-7; *A.A.S.* 70 (1978), pp. 325-8; *N.C.E.*, 17 (Suppl. 2), p. 35, citing *Osservatore Romano* 20 (1978), 1, 8.

R.M.

St Maurice and seventy companions of the Theban Legion, martyrs under Maximian (fourth century)—see 22 Sept.

St James, hermit near Cyrrhus (*c.* 450)

SS Tatulus, Varos, and Thomas, hermits in Armenia (fifth century)

St Zachary, bishop of Jerusalem (*c.* 620)

St Gumbert (Gundebert), monk, founder and first abbot of Sens (*c.* 675)

St Timothy, hermit on Mount Olympus (seventh century)

Bd Noel Pinot, parish priest of Louroux-Béconnais, martyr (1794)—see "Martyrs of the French Revolution," 2 Jan.

22

St Papias, *Bishop* (Second Century)

Papias was bishop of Hierapolis in Phrygia at the beginning of the second century and is known to us from Eusebius, who, however, has a low opinion of his theology. He belongs to the generation who had "listened to the apostles"and is the author of a five-volume work titled *The Sayings of the Lord Explained*, of which only fragments survive, preserved mainly by St Irenaeus (28 June) and Eusebius. Irenaeus tells that he "had listened to John [the Evangelist; 27 Dec.] and was later a companion of Polycarp" (23 Feb., below). He "lived at a very early date," and the new draft Roman Martyrology follows Irenaeus in stating that he had listened to John, but Eusebius points out that in his own preface Papias made it clear that he "was never a hearer or eyewitness of the holy apostles, and tells us that he learnt the essentials of the Faith from their former pupils: 'And whenever anyone came who had been a follower of the presbyters, I inquired into the words of the presbyters, what Andrew or Peter had said, or Philip or Thomas or James or John or Matthew, or any other disciple of the Lord, and what Aristion and the presbyter John, disciples of the Lord, were still saying. For I did not imagine that things out of books would help me as much as the utterances of a living and abiding voice.'"

With Clement of Alexandria he was then a transmitter of the teachings of "the elders," or presbyters—if not the apostles themselves, then members of the early communities of Jerusalem. The second John he mentions in the passage cited above as a "presbyter" rather than a "disciple" is taken by Eusebius as being not the Evangelist but the recipient of the Revelation of the book of that name. Papias goes on to recount miracles and "other stories communicated to him by word of mouth, together with some other unknown parables and teachings of the Saviour, and other things of a more allegorical nature." It is in these that he incurs the contempt of Eusebius: "I suppose he got these notions by misinterpreting the apostolic accounts and failing to grasp what they had said in mystic and symbolic language. For he seems to have been a man of very small intelligence, to judge from his books" (*H.E.*, 3, 39). Despite this, he was influential in the transmission of teaching and stories to those such as Irenaeus, slightly later than him and who "relied on his early date."

He wrote about the composition of the Gospels: Eusebius records him as confirming the account given by Clement of how St Mark the Evangelist (25 Apr.) was persuaded by those who heard St Peter (29 June) preach to write down a summary of the instruction given by Peter: "This, too, the presbyter

[John] used to say. 'Mark, who had been Peter's interpreter, wrote down care-fully, but not in order, all that he remembered of the Lord's sayings and doings. For he had not heard the Lord or been one of His followers, but later, as I said, one of Peter's. Peter used to adapt his teachings to the occasion, without making a systematic arrangement of the Lord's sayings, so that Mark was quite justified in writing down some things just as he remembered them." He also points out that Mark is mentioned by Peter in his First Epistle: "The church in Babylon [Rome], chosen like yourselves, sends you greeting, and so does my son Mark" (1 Pet. 5:13). All that he has to say of Matthew (21 Sept.) is that he "compiled the *Sayings* in the Aramaic language, and everyone trans-lated them as well as he could."

As did Polycarp, Papias rejected the teachings of Marcion (who held that the God of harsh justice of the Old Testament could not be the same as the Father of Jesus Christ) and excluded him from his congregation.

Eusebius, *H.E.*, 2, 15; 3, 36, 39: citations from Penguin Classics revised ed. (1989). Jedin-Dolan, 1, pp. 12, 119, 140, 190. See also J. Daniélou, *The Theology of Jewish Christianity* (1964), pp. 55-64; *Bibl.SS.*, 10, 315-6; *N.C.E.*, 10, pp. 979-80.

SS Thalassius and Limnaeus (Fifth Century)

The little extant information concerning these two hermits comes from the *Philotheus* of Theodoret, bishop of Cyrrhus, who knew them personally. Thalassius was the elder by many years, described as an ascetic of wonderful simplicity and meekness who outshone all his contemporaries. He had made his hermitage in a cave in a hillside south of the Syrian town of Tillima, and there Limnaeus joined him as his disciple. He imposed a long period of com-plete silence on himself in penance for being somewhat free with his tongue.

He then left Thalassius and joined St Maro (d. 433; 14 Feb., above) to complete his training, before becoming a solitary on a neighbouring mountain. He built a rough stone enclosure, apparently with no roof, as Theodoret says that he had "neither house, nor tent, nor cabin," with a door normally kept blocked up and opened only to admit his bishop, Theodoret. He gained a great reputation for healing powers, with crowds flocking to his one window. He also developed a special ministry to the blind and built two houses for them near his own hut. Theodoret records that Limnaeus had been living in this way for thirty-eight years when he composed his history.

There is a French trans. of the *Philotheus*, ed. P. Canivet and A. Leroy-Molighen, 2 vols. (1979): see ch. 12 in vol. 2. The *Philotheus* also tells the story of St Baradates, another hermit of Cyrrhus previously commemorated today but dropped from the new draft Roman Martyrology. See also *Bibl.SS.*, 12, 104-5.

St Maximian of Ravenna, *Bishop* (498-556)

The twenty-eighth bishop of Ravenna, consecrated by Pope Vigilius in 546 and ruling the see for ten years, he was the first bishop in the West to assume the title "archbishop," meaning the head of a group of metropolitans. Starting from a solid financial position and using his considerable vision and his secure position as vicar of both Pope Vigilius and Emperor Justinian, he became one of the outstanding figures of sixth-century Italy. He is known with some precision, since, although his biography by the priest Agnellus was not written until some two centuries after his death, this was able to draw on his own writings.

He was born in Pola in 498 and became a deacon of the local church. The fortunate discovery of a "treasure," made either by him or his father (accounts vary) enabled him to present himself at the imperial court in Constantinople, where he gained the esteem of Justinian. When the bishop of Ravenna died in 545 the inhabitants petitioned the emperor for the *pallium* to be given to the candidate they had chosen as successor, the city then being under the direct rule of the emperor. Instead, Justinian asked Vigilus to consecrate Maximian. Vigilius did so on 14 October 546, but this understandably caused considerable friction between the new bishop and the inhabitants of Ravenna. They saw him as representing an exceptional and intolerable interference in their affairs. He then compounded his position by incuring the displeasure of both pope and emperor by refusing to add his signature to the condemnation of the "Three Chapters." He was forced to camp outside the city as the guest of the Arian bishop of Goti. Gradually, however, his tact and diplomacy—aided, at least according to some sources, by his great wealth—won the people over, and he was allowed to take possession of his see.

The ten years of his episcopate were the golden age of the Church in Ravenna. He completed and consecrated the basilicas of St Michael and St Vitalis, embellished many others, and was entirely responsible for those of St Stephen and probably St John as well as others in his native town of Pola. Most of these were decorated with magnificent mosaics. He also produced a large number of books (mostly now lost): chronicles, descriptions of Ravenna, catalogues of its bishops, and twelve volumes of sermons. He was responsible for a carefully annotated edition of the entire Bible, in which he specified in marginal notes the principles he had followed in adopting a particular reading. Beyond this still, he is credited with a sacramentary on which the Leonine Sacramentary was supposedly largely based. His activities covered the whole of Italy, of which he was effectively primate during the long absences of Vigilius from Rome and Decius from his see of Milan. His eforts were devoted chiefly to restoring harmony and unity among churches divided by the "Three Chapters" schism. His biographer Agnellus says of him that "he welcomed strangers, reclaimed those in error, gave the poor what they needed, and consoled the suffering."

He died on 22 February 556. His remains were interred in the basilica of St Andrew in Ravenna, where they remained till 1809, when the French administration brought in by Napoleon deconsecrated the church; they were then moved into the cathedral.

Bibl.SS., 9, 16-20, with further references. The Life by Agnellus is in *Liber Pontificalis Ecclesiae Ravennatis* (1923), pp. 181-213. See also "Ravenna" in *N.C.E.*, 12, pp. 96-102, with good illustrations.

In the basilica of St Vitalis, which was dedicated in a lavish ceremony attended by the emperor Justinian and his wife, Theodora, he is shown in the great mosaic on the north side of the sanctuary standing next to the emperor, holding a jewelled cross.

Bd Isabel of France (1270)

The daughter of King Louis VIII of France and his queen, Blanche of Castile, Isabel was the younger sister of King St Louis IX of France (1214-70; 25 Aug.). The principal source of information about her is the Life written by the abbess of the monastery she founded at Longchamp, Agnes de Harcourt, who looked after her for the last ten years of her life. As with other accounts of exceptionally pious girls who refused to eat and refused to contemplate marriage, it is impossible at this distance in time to distinguish pathological or psychotic from freely-willed elements in, especially, the austerities attributed to her. Her adolescence seems to have been a complete rejection of the state of life into which she was born: she despised luxury and fine clothes and fasted to the point where her mother despaired of being able to coax her to eat and called in a "holy woman" when Isabel appeared to have brought herself to the point of death—though apparently to prophesy what would become of her rather than to cure her. This woman foretold that she would live but as "dead to the world," which she proved the truth of by rejecting various suitors. Even a letter from Pope Innocent IV (1243-54) urging her to accept King Conrad of Jerusalem for the benefit of Christendom failed to move her; she replied to the pope in such well-reasoned terms that he agreed to allow her to make a vow of perpetual virginity for love of God.

Her brother had succeeded to the throne in 1225 and was an inspiration in his love of the poor and devotion to religion. Isabel used to feed a number of poor people at her table every day and go out to visit the sick and the poor. Louis also later took part in two ineffectual Crusades, on the first of which he was captured in Egypt. This was a harsh blow to Isabel, who supported the cause of recovering the Holy Places by paying the expenses of ten knights. Another obvious influence on her life was St Clare of Assisi (d. 1253; 11 Aug.), both in her personal austerities and in her rule of life. When Isabel's mother died, she resolved to establish a convent for nuns living in accordance with the ideals of the Second Order of St Francis. Louis gave his approval and promised financial help, and leading Franciscans, including St Bonaventure (15 July), collaborated in drawing up a Rule and Constitutions. The foundation was made at Longchamp on the outskirts of Paris (now better known as the site of France's most prestigious horse races, in the Bois de Boulogne) and named the Monastery of the Humility of the Blessed Virgin Mary.

Isabel kept part of her property to enable her to support the foundation financially and continue her assistance to the poor, so she did not take full vows herself, which her damaged health also did not permit. She lived in a part of the building separate from the nuns' cells. This decision was probably also dictated by humility, as she wished to avoid the possibility of being elected abbess. She lived a live of fasting, penance, contemplation, and great devotion there for ten years; before her death she was witnessed in ecstasy by her chaplain, her confessor, and Sister Agnes, who was to write her Life. She died in 1270, in the same year as her saintly brother, who died in Tunis on his way back from his second Crusade. Her cult was confirmed in 1521, and she is numbered among the *beatae* of the Second Order of St Francis, the fourth person in chronological order of date of death to receive this honour (not counting the two saints, Clare and Agnes of Assisi), while her brother, by the same reckoning, is fourth of the saints of the Third Order, though there is no certainty that he ever actually made a profession in the Order.

The Life by Agnes de Harcourt is in *AA.SS.*, Aug., 6, for 31 Aug., pp. 787-808. The Franciscans commemorate her on 8 June with BB Agnes of Bohemia (6 Mar. in the present work, her actual day of death) and Baptista Varani (7 June). See A. Garreau, *Bse Isabelle de France, soeur de Saint Louis* (1943; n.e. 1955); *Bibl.SS.*, 7, 908-9; *Auréole Séraphique*, 3, pp. 89-96; *N.C.E.*, 7, pp. 664-5. On the growth of the Second Order of St Francis see L. Iriarte de Aspruz, *Franciscan History: The Three Orders of St Francis* (1983), pp. 441-7.

St Margaret of Cortona (1247-97)

Margaret, like Isabel of France, is another exponent of extreme penitential practices, prompted by conversion from a life not of luxury but of "sins of the flesh." Her childhood was relatively hard; the daughter of a poor farming family from Laviano in Tuscany, she lost her mother when she was only seven. Her father married again, and she suffered the classic lack of affection from a harsh stepmother, who turned her out of the house at the age of eleven or twelve. Attractive, high-spirited, and naturally pleasure-loving, she took refuge with a young nobleman named Arsenio from Montepulciano, who persuaded her to elope with him, even though he himself was no more than about four-teen years old. As a nobleman he would not have been able to contemplate marrying a farmer's daughter, and she lived openly with him as his mistress for nine years. She was faithful to him and bore him a son, but her position and the considerable style in which she lived caused great scandal in the neigh-bourhood.

One night her lover failed to return from a visit to his estates. The following day his dog ran back alone and led her to the base of an oak tree in the woods, where it began digging. To her horror, she found the murdered body of her lover buried in a shallow pit. She saw—or was persuaded to see: Friar Giunta Bevegnati, who was later to write her "legend," describes it as "the hand of Providence"—this as God's judgment on her way of life, gave away all her possessions, left Montepulciano with her son, and returned to her father's house dressed as a penitent. She was twenty-one years old. Her stepmother refused to admit her. Remembering having heard that the Franciscans at Cortona were known for their kindness to sinners, she went there and was taken to the friars, who became her spiritual guides. Her instincts to punish herself for her past sins led her to public acts of penance: she went to the church at Laviano with a rope round her neck and begged pardon publicly for the scandal she had caused in the past. The friars, especially her confessor Friar Giunta, generally acted as a restraining influence, forbidding her to have herself led through the streets of Montepulciano with a rope round her neck. For her, periods of exaltation alternated with periods of despair; she was convinced that her body could still be the cause of sin, and mistreated it accordingly: "Father," she told Friar Giunta, "do not ask me to come to terms with this body of mine, for I cannot afford it. Between me and my body there must needs be a struggle till death." The friars seem genuinely to have tried to persuade her to abandon her penitential excesses but without success.

She was not a member of a religious community and needed to support herself and her son, who seems to have been drawn into a penitential life without much account taken of his feelings or needs. (He was later sent to school at Arezzo and then became a Franciscan friar.) She began nursing a group of relatively wealthy women in Cortona but then abandoned this comparatively comfortable way of life to live in a cottage in the poorer quarters of the town, nursing the sick poor, living by alms, and giving away the better part of what she received from people's charity. After three years of this way of life, the friars, convinced that she was quite sincere and not acting out of spiritual pride, agreed to her request to join the Third Order of St Francis, the "Order of Penitents." Groups of secular "penitents" had formed in many places, largely as a spontaneous response to the violence and disasters of the age. Their appropriation by religious Orders was part of the Church's effort to keep them within bounds, both physically and spiritually. Many individuals and groups had appealed to St Francis (4 Oct.) to give them direction, and he seems to have responded with an "Exhortation to the Brothers and Sisters in Penance," which exists in two versions and is generally taken as the founding document of the Third Order. Brotherhoods and Sisterhoods of Penance, which claimed various exemptions and privileges within civil as well as ecclesiastical society, almost invariably engaged in charitable works, and Margaret formed a group of Franciscan tertiaries into a nursing community in charge of a project that developed, with assistance from the city council, into the Hospital of St Mary of Mercy. Many such groups earned themselves names that suited their characteristics: there were the *bonomini*, the "good men," who ran the Hospital of St Paul in Florence, and Margaret's became the *poverelle*, the "little poor women."

It was, however, not this practical, achieving aspect of her vocation that won her fame and notoriety during her lifetime and formed the basis of the "legend" on which her canonization was based but rather her self-chastisement and the visions and private revelations that seemed to be her reward for her life of expiation of past sins. She fasted strenuously, slept on bare earth, wore a hair shirt, and adminstered the discipline. Her confessor tells of her direct "colloquies" with Christ, who spoke to her from a wooden crucifix (as to St Francis at San Damiano) and told her she was the "third light" (after Francis and Clare) of the Order, for the Third Order. Word of her revelations inevitably excited envy as well as admiration: rumours that her relations with the friars were not as pure as they should be circulated, bringing contempt on her and restrictions on the movements of the friars. Her response was a more intense prayer life, and in answer to an inner command, telling her that the graces she had received were "not meant for thee alone," she embarked on a more public crusade, calling sinners to conversion in ever-increasing numbers. Her fame spread, helped by accounts of miracles of healing, and people flocked to Cortona from all over Italy and even from France and Spain.

Her health inevitably gave way, though she had sustained her extreme penitential way of life for the space of twenty-nine years and reached the age of fifty. The friars eventually ordered her peremptorily to stop her excesses, but too late. She was acclaimed as a saint on the day of her death, 22 February 1297; the friars claimed her body and the citizens of Cortona immediately began building a church in her honour over a little oratory close to where she died. The Franciscan "Observants" were given charge of the church at the end of the fourteenth century and built an adjoining convent; in the fifteenth the Franciscans were given permission to celebrate her festival in the Order and in the diocese of Cortona, and she was formally canonized in 1728.

The *leggenda* by Giunta Bevegnati is printed in *AA.SS.*, Feb., 3; also ed. L. da Pelago (1793) and E. Cirvelli (1897). There is a full account of it in *Auréole Séraphique*, 1, pp. 272-312, in which Mgr Léon accuses the friars of encouraging her penitential excesses. See also *P.B.*, 2, pp. 618-23. Modern accounts include L. de Chérancé, *Marguerite de Cortone* (1927); M. Nuti, *Marcherita da Cortona: la sua leggenda e la storia* (1923); F. Mauriac, *Margaret of Cortona* (Eng. trans. 1948). See also *Bibl.SS.*, 8, 759-73; *N.C.E.*, 9, p. 201. On the origins and rise of the Third Order see Iriarte, *op. cit.* (previous entry), pp. 477-501, with further bibliog. on pp. 484-5.

The original church, the work of Giovanni Pisano, was demolished in the nineteenth century to make way for a larger structure. A marble sarcophagus from the earlier church by Angelo and Francesco di Pietro (1362) remains, and Margaret's incorrupt body can be seen in a silver coffin dating from 1646 above the high altar. The wooden crucifix supposed to have spoken to her is in a side chapel, and there is a statue of her with the dog that took her to her lover's body. See G. Farnedi, O.S.B., *Guida ai Santuari d'Italia* (1996), pp. 177-8. The library of the adjoining convent contains MS 61, which is probably a copy of the *leggenda* with corrections in the author's hand. She is usually represented contemplating a corpse or a skull with a dog plucking at her robes, but paintings by Tiepolo in the church of San Michele in Isola (Venice) and Lanfranco in the Pitti (Florence) show her purely rapt in prayer without the corpse or the skull.

R.M.
St Concordia, of Rome (third century)
St Athanasius, abbot of SS Peter and Paul in Bithynia, exiled for defending images (826)
Bd Didacus Carvalho, S.J., martyr (1624)—see "The Martyrs of Japan," 6 Feb., above

---

ST POLYCARP (over page)
Blue, gray, white, yellow, and red flames,
brown logs, on silver field.

23

ST POLYCARP, *Bishop and Martyr* (*c.* 69- *c.*155)

Genuine and ancient Acts of martyrs bear witness to a historical sense surviving in the first centuries of the Church amidst a welter of apocryphal writings and legends. In such literature the *Martyrium Polycarpi* occupies an important place. It is a report by the congregation of Smyrna on the death of their bishop in the form of a letter to the Christian community of Philomelium and, through them, to the whole Church. It tells how the pagan population of the town, who had killed a young man named Germanicus during a festival, demanded of the magistrates that all "atheists" should be done away with, and set up the cry, "Fetch Polycarp." Polycarp, who was waiting calmly in a farm near the city, was sought out and brought to trial. Arrested, he refused to deny Christ and was killed by the sword, despite his advanced years, and his body was then burned at the stake, in the town theatre.

Such actions would accord with the general feeling about Christians in the latter part of the second century: there was no general law governing the state attitude to them, but the hostile feelings of pagans gave rise to the view that being Christian was incompatible with the Roman way of life. This made it possible for the authorities to devise a sort of legal maxim that Christianity was a crime in itself. Polycarp himself refers to "persecutions" in his *Letter to the Philippians*, but this cannot be dated with certainty. Such persecutions would tend to be directed against individuals who had angered the populace—as he had—and to be local and sporadic.

Eusebius dates his martyrdom as taking place under Marcus Aurelius (161-80), but this is problematic, and it seems that an earlier date, during the reign of his predecessor Antoninus Pius (138-61), is to be preferred: this was the traditional view before Eusebius wrote. Facts about his earlier life are relatively scarce compared to the detailed account we have of his martyrdom. There is a Life by one Pionius (now held not to be the St Pionius martyred for observing the commemoration of Polycarp's death in about 250; 12 Mar.), which gives him a romantic childhood as a slave boy ransomed by a wealthy lady, but this appears to be fiction. It is agreed that he is one of the "Apostolic Fathers," the generation of bishops who received their teaching direct from the apostles or disciples themselves. Assuming that he was born in about 69, this is possible; he is referred to as a disciple of St John the Evangelist, traditionally regarded as the youngest of the apostles.

He was bishop of Smyrna by about 107, when St Ignatius of Antioch (17

Oct.) met him there during the course of his final journey in chains to Rome, which was to end in his death. He asked Polycarp to take care of his church after his death in one of his seven letters to various churches, which he composed during this journey and which are among the most valuable documents of second-century Christianity. Polycarp himself is known to have written numerous pastoral letters, but besides a short note, only his letter to the congregation at Philippi survives. In this he quotes from the First Letter of John, thereby helping to confirm a relatively early date for this. His own letter was accorded virtually canonical importance and was still being read in churches in Asia at the time of St Jerome (d. 420; 30 Sept.). It provides precious insights into the concerns that seemed urgent to a Christian pastor of the time addressing the faithful of a congregation known to him. He combatted Marcion (see St Papias, 22 Feb., above) for his refusal to accept the God of the Old Testament as the Father of Jesus Christ and is said to have addressed him as "firstborn of Satan" on meeting him in the streets of Rome.

Irenaeus of Lyons (d. *c.* 203; 28 June) knew Polycarp in his youth and in his letter *To Florinus* (upbraiding him for heresy) describes the impression made on him by "the place where blessed Polycarp sat and talked, his goings out and comings in, the character of his life, his personal appearance, his addresses to crowded congregations" (*H.E.*, 5, 20: other versions make this passage refer to "the sanctity of his deportment, the majesty of his countenance, and of his whole exterior," suggesting that Irenaeus' plea to copyists, also recorded by Eusebius, that they should "compare your transcript and correct it carefully by this copy," may not always have been observed). He goes on to describe Polycarp's zeal for orthodoxy: "I remember how he spoke of his intercourse with John and with the others who had seen the Lord; how he repeated their words from memory; and how the things that he had heard them say about the Lord, His miracles and His teaching, things that he had heard direct from the eye-witnesses of the Word of Life, were proclaimed by Polycarp in complete harmony with Scripture. . . . The letters he sent either to the neighbouring churches to stiffen them, or to individual Christians to advise and stimulate them, furnish additional proof of this [how he would have abhorred Florinus' heretical words]."

Irenaeus also describes a last journey Polycarp made to Rome, by then accorded general respect by the Churches of the eastern as well as the western provinces of the empire, at the invitation of Pope St Anicetus to discuss the problem of the date of Easter. This was whether it should be celebrated on the 14th or 15th day of the month of Nisan or on the first Sunday following the 14th day of Nisan. Neither could agree with the other, so they amicably agreed to keep their different practices. Anicetus invited Polycarp to celebrate the Eucharist for the Roman community—which suggests that at least some uniformity in liturgical usage had been agreed by then: "They remained in communion with each other, and in church Anicetus made way for Polycarp to celebrate the Eucharist—out of respect, obviously. They parted company in peace, and the whole Church was at peace, both those who kept the day and those who did not." Irenaeus reinforces the point in his *Against Heresies*: "At all times he taught the things which he had learnt from the apostles, which the Church transmits, which alone are true. These facts are attested by all the churches of Asia and by the successors of Polycarp to this day" (3, 3). Here Irenaeus points up not only Polycarp's role as "Apostolic Father" and the importance of his witness but also his influence on the future transmission of orthodox teaching—"he was a much more trustworthy and dependable witness to the truth than Valentinus and Marcion and all other wrong-headed persons." Because Irenaeus learned from Polycarp, the latter stands at the fountainhead of the transmission of the Faith to western Europe.

The letter from the church of Smyrna recounting Polycarp's martyrdom is partly reproduced and partly summarized by Eusebius. (As his text is now readily available, it is not given at length here.) After telling of the raging persecution in Asia, which Polycarp's martyrdom effectively brought to an end, at least for a while, it recounts how Germanicus, who ignored pleas to consider his youth and virtually drew the lion on to himself and several others, died, and the resultant clamour for Polycarp. The account of him staying calmly in a nearby farm clearly has echoes of Jesus waiting to be betrayed and taken in the garden of Gethsemane, and the whole of the rest of the story provides the basis for the concept of the martyr as identified with Christ, choosing details and using language in a way that echoes the Gospel accounts of the passion. Polycarp offers his captors a supper and goes out to pray alone; the way his prayer is described echoes Jesus' last prayer for all his followers; Polycarp is taken to the city on a donkey: "The hour for departure had come, so they set him on an ass and brought him to the city. The day was a Great Sabbath. He was met by Herod the chief of police, . . ." who questions him in the manner of Pilate and receives the same manner of answer. Herod threatens him with beasts and fire, as Pilate threatened Jesus with his power to crucify him. The crowd behaves in the same way: "The whole mass of Smyrnaeans, Gentiles and Jews alike, boiled with anger and shouted at the tops of their voices. . . ." calling for a lion to be set on him.

Prophetic, visionary, and miraculous elements form a considerable part of the account. Polycarp had had a dream of lying on a burning pillow and accordingly said, "I must be burnt alive." The crowd rushed to collect wood for a pyre and would have nailed him to a stake in the middle, but he said that he had the strength to stay in the fire without this, so they bound him to the stake. But the fire "took the shape of a vaulted room, like a ship's sail filled with wind, and made a wall round the martyr's body" and so failed to consume him. He was therefore killed with a sword-thrust to the neck (in fact, the normal Roman method of execution), whereupon "there came out a stream of blood that quenched the fire, so that the whole crowd was astonished at the difference between the unbelievers and the elect." The Christians were not allowed to take away his body, "though many longed to do this and to have communion with his holy flesh"; the Jews in the crowd are made responsible for this on the grounds that the Christians might "abandon the Crucified and start worshipping this fellow." The body was burned, so that only the bones remained to be taken away as relics: "So later on we took up his bones, more precious than stones of great price, more splendid than gold, and laid them where it seemed right." The letter is careful to rebut the suggestion made by the Jews (which in any case seems a surprising concern for them), claiming that they failed to realize "that we can never forsake Christ, who suffered for the salvation of those who are being saved in the whole world, or worship anyone else. For to Him, as the Son of God, we offer adoration; but to the martyrs, as disciples and imitators of the Lord, we give the love that they deserve for their unsurpassable devotion to their own King and Teacher: may it be our privilege to be their fellow-members and fellow-disciples."

So whatever the derivation or accuracy of some details in this archetypal account of martyrdom, it does show a carefully elaborated theology of Christ's redemptive suffering, of Christian following, and of the due devotion to be shown to the saints. It is also the first certain evidence for the cult of relics. It also furnishes, in Polycarp's final prayer, a new note of confidence in the fact of redemption, a developed Trinitarian theology, and an illustration of how various elements in what were to develop into Eucharistic Prayers had already come together, ending with a doxology and the "Amen" that Christianity had taken over from Judaism:

O Father of Thy beloved and blessed Son, Jesus Christ, through whom we have come to know Thee, the God of angels and powers and all creation, and of the whole family of the righteous who live in Thy presence, I bless Thee for counting me worthy of this day and hour, that in the number of martyrs I may partake of Christ's cup, to the resurrection of eternal life of both soul and body in the imperishability that is the gift of the Holy Ghost. Among them may I be received into Thy presence today, a rich and acceptable sacrifice as Thou hast prepared it beforehand, foreshadowing it and fulfilling it, Thou God of truth that canst not lie. Therefore for every cause I praise Thee, I bless Thee, I glorify Thee, through the eternal High Priest, Jesus Christ thy beloved Son, through whom and with whom in the Holy Ghost glory be to Thee, both now and in the ages to come. Amen.

It was the commemoration of his martyrdom that established the custom of celebrating the anniversary of a martyr's death, seen as the *dies natalis*, the "birthday into heaven": "When, if it proves possible, we assemble there, the Lord will allow us to celebrate with joy and gladness the birthday of his martyrdom, both to the memory of those who have contended in the past, and for the training and preparation of those whose time is yet to come." (This passage may be a later interpolation, but if it is, this merely proves that the commemoration was in existence.) The custom developed first in the East and only later

231

in the West, where the *Depositio martyrum*, the basis of the Roman Calendar, names Callistus (d. 222; 14 Oct.) as the earliest martyr honoured in this way, perhaps because it was only then that the Roman community acquired its own cemeteries and so the legal right to organize a commemorative celebration. In both East and West devotion to martyrdom became, following the example of Polycarp, linked to imitation of Christ: the letter from the church of Smyrna, with its clear parallels with the Gospels, first makes the express connection between Christ and the martyr: martyrs are the authentic disciples and imitators of the Lord, and their finest example is Polycarp.

His feast was celebrated as a "double" on 26 January until the Calendar reform of 1969, when it was transferred to today's date on the basis of the evidence in the original account and recent research that this was the actual day of his death. It now ranks as a "Memorial."

As the previous edition of this work points out (*B.T.A.*, 1, pp. 170-1) at length, the martyrdom of Polycarp raises such important issues that the resultant literature is vast. Discussion has revolved around five main points: (1) the date of his martyrdom; (2) the authenticity of the letter describing it; (3) the authenticity of the letter addressd to him by Ignatius of Antioch; (4) the authenticity of his letter to the congregation at Philippi; (5) how much credence can be attached to his personal relationship with St John the Evangelist and other eyewitnesses to the Lord. On (1), see H. Grégoire, "La date du martyre de Polycarpe," *Anal.Boll.* 69 (1951), pp. 1–38, arguing for the later date of 177; H. I. Marrou, "La date du martyre de S. Polycarpe," *ibid.* 71 (1953), pp. 5–20; E. Griffe in *Bulletin de littérature ecclésiastique* 52 (1951), pp. 170-1; 54 (1953), pp. 178–81; *N.C.E.*, 11, pp. 535-6, suggests the date may have been as late as 169. For (2), the text of the letter is in *AA.SS.*, Jan., 2, pp. 691-707; also in *The Apostolic Fathers*, ed. J. B. Lightfoot (3 vols., 1885; abridged J. R. Hamer, 1 vol., 1891; ed. K. Lake, 1930), with now generally accepted arguments in favour of its authenticity; also in *A.C.M.*, pp. 2–21; Eusebius, *H.E.*, 4, 14–15, cited above from Penguin Classics ed. (1989), pp. 116–23. See also H. von Campenhausen, *Bearbeitung und Interpolationen des Polykarpmartyriums* (1957). Major collections of Acts of the early martys are listed in Jedin-Dolan, 1, pp. 448-9. On (3) and (4) there is a bibliography in *ibid.*, p. 471. Works dealing with points (2), (3), and (4) also tend to confirm the traditional view of (5). An earlier discussion on the authenticity of the Life by Pionius was settled by H. Delehaye, *Les passions des martyrs . . .* (1921), pp. 11–59. On the date of Easter and the development of the liturgy see A. A. McArthur, *The Evolution of the Christian Year* (1953); further bibliog. in Jedin-Dolan, 1, pp. 492-4. On the development of the cult of relics see art. and bibliog. in *O.D.C.C.* (3d ed.,1997), p. 1379; M. Walsh, *A Dictionary of Devotions* (1993), pp. 214-7.

He features in the great procession of male martyr-saints on the right side of the nave of Sant'Apollinare Nuovo in Ravenna, dating from *c.* 561. They carry martyrs' crowns in their hands and are proceeding from the city of Ravenna toward the enthroned Christ with four angels: P. and L. Murray, *The Oxford Companion to Christian Art and Architecture* (1996), p. 420.

St Serenus the Gardener, *Martyr* (*c.* 307)

Serenus was Greek by birth, born in the reign of Emperor Maximian; he left all his possessions to embrace a life of asceticism and prayer, living off the produce of his garden in Syrmium in the province of Pannonia (Mitrovica in present-day Croatia). Persecution broke out against Christians, forcing him into hiding for some months, but he then returned to his garden, where no one knew he was a Christian. He was a good-looking young man and a hard worker so was well regarded by all who came into contact with him, particularly so by the wife of one of Maximian's guards, who progressed from regard to downright advances. He told her that no lady should show herself outside at the dangerous hour of the siesta and that by doing so she was needlessly dishonouring herself and her husband; thus spurned, she wrote to her husband saying he had insulted her.

The husband set out for Syrmium, presented the letter to the governor, and had Serenus brought to trial. At this, he defended himself so well that the lady's husband was convinced that his wife had been at fault and dropped the charge. Serenus was accordingly acquitted and would have been released had not the governor suspected that anyone so scrupulous in such matters must be a Christian. Charged with this and invited to offer sacrifice to the gods, Serenus unhesitatingly professed his faith, refused to sacrifice, and expressed eagerness to die so that "I may have a part in His Kingdom with His saints." His wish was granted, as he was beheaded forthwith.

There may possibly be some historical basis to the above story, which is printed in full in *AA.SS.*, Feb., 3. Some of his relics are claimed by Billom in the Auvergne, where he is venerated as St Cerneuf. He features as the day's "forgotten saint" in the collection by R. Cammilleri, *Santi dimenticati* (1996).

St Ercongota (*c.* 660)

Ercongota (Earcongota, Earcongotha, or Erkongota) belongs to the period of early conversions of the royal family in south-east England, most of whose members became venerated as saints. She was a great grand-daughter of St Ethelbert of Kent (24 Feb., below) and daughter of King Erconbert of Kent and his wife, St Sexburga (6 July), who after her husband's death joined the nuns she had established at Minster on the island of Sheppey and then became abbess of Ely in succession to her sister, St Etheldreda (23 June), who had founded the double monastery there.

Ercongota joined two sainted aunts at the monastery of Faremoûtiers-en-Brie, near Meaux in France: these were St Sethrida (Saethrith, or Saethrid; 7 July) abbess till her death in about 664, and Ethelburga (also 7 July), her half-sister, who succeeded her as abbess. Ercongota died relatively young and so never had a chance to extend the family line of abbesses. As Bede, the chief source of information on all these, remarks: "As yet there were few monasteries [at least for women] built in English territory, and many who wished to enter conventual life went from Britain to the Frankish realm or Gaul for the purpose. Girls of noble family were also sent there for their education, or to be betrothed to their heavenly Bridegroom, especially to the houses of Brie, Chelles and Andelys." Brie here is Faremoûtiers, founded by St Fare (or Fara) in about 617.

Bede says that she "deserves special mention" but can provide no real biography, only "a brief account of her passing to the heavenly kingdom." When she felt death approaching, she visited the cells of all the nuns who were sick, telling them of a vision she had had of men in white robes coming to bear away "the golden coin that was brought here from Kent." She was buried in the nearby church of St Stephen.

She was previously commemorated with her two aunts on 7 July, at least in England, where she seems to have had no separate cult. The old Roman Martyrology mentions only Ethelburga on that day, and a February date was used for Ercongota in Ely and Faremoûtiers, the 21st, and in the diocese of Meaux, the 26th, which suggests that her actual *dies natalis* was around the date now assigned to her in the new draft Roman Martyrology.

Bede, *H.E.*, 3, 8; *AA.SS.*, Feb., 3, pp. 394-5; *Bibl.SS.*, 4, 1309.

St Milburga, *Abbess (c. 715)*

Another member of a royal family well endowed with saints, she was the granddaughter of King Penda of Mercia, the niece of King Wulfhere and the elder sister of St Mildred of Thanet (13 July) and of Mildgyth (local cult on 17 Jan.). Her father was Merewald and her mother St Ermeburga (locally 19 Nov.), princess of Kent and abbess of Minster-in-Thanet, in which office Mildred succeeded her. Her royal uncle and her father helped her to found and endow a convent in about 670 at Wenlock (now Much Wenlock) in Shropshire, of which she became the second abbess. According to the eleventh-century Life of her by Goscelin she was consecrated by St Theodore of Canterbury (19 Sept.).

St Boniface (5 June) in a letter translated into Old English describes a vision of a monk that took place at Much Wenlock during her abbacy. Her testament, preserved by Goscelin, appears to be an authentic list of the very extensive lands close to the Welsh border that belonged to her when she died. Her tomb became the focus of a considerable cult, but the Danes destroyed the abbey, and it was virtually forgotten until Cluniac monks built a new monastery on the same spot in 1079. The new church had a silver casket containing relics of Milburga, with documents describing the whereabouts of her grave as by a certain altar, which could not be found until the monks consulted St Anselm (21 April), who pointed them to the ruins of an earlier church, where they began to excavate. There two boys who were playing fell into a hollow space, which proved to contain her bones.

This story became widely diffused through being described by Otto, cardinal bishop of Ostia, in 1102, the year after the discovery was made. He also described miraculous cures that had taken place at the site, including the healing of lepers and what sounds like delivery from a huge tapeworm. Five churches were dedicated to her; her feast was widely kept and she found her way into the Roman Martyrology. Her bones were re-interred with great ceremony on 26 May 1501—only to be lost again at the dissolution of the monasteries.

AA.SS., Feb., 3, pp. 395-7. Considerable recent research has amended the account given in the previous edition of this work. See *O.D.S.*, p. 340 (also for her two sisters), with refs. to A. Edwards, "An early twelfth-century account of the Translation of St Milburga," in *Trans. Shropshire Archaeol. Soc.* 57 (1962-3), pp. 134-51; H. P. R. Finberg, *The Early Charters of the West Midlands* (1962), pp. 197-224; P. Grosjean, "Saints anglo-saxones des Marches Gauloises," in *Anal.Boll.* 79 (1961), pp. 163-6. The present town of Much Wenlock, between Shrewsbury and Bridgnorth, is built around the ruins of the Norman Wenlock priory. See also *Bibl.SS.*, 9, 479-81; *N.L.A.*, 2, pp. 188-92.

St Willigis, *Bishop* (1011)

This great statesman and eminent churchman was born to humble beginnings in or near the town of Hildesheim, near Hanover in northern Germany. His outstanding intelligence marked him out at an early age for the Church, and he studied for the priesthood, becoming a canon at Hildesheim. This was an age when the German emperors were in effect protectors of the papacy, so when he was recommended by the emperor Otto II's precentor, Wolkold, and consequently appointed imperial chaplain and then chancellor, he was being given a role in the universal Church. Four years later, in 975, Otto nominated him archbishop of Mainz.

Southern Italy came under attack in 976 from Muslims who had invaded Sicily, and Otto, now styling himself emperor of the Romans, took charge of the defence. He was defeated in battle, but the Muslims' leader, Abul Kasim, was killed, and they withdrew. Otto died of a fever in Rome at the age of only twenty-eight in 983, and Willigis crowned his son, not yet four years old, as Otto III in Aachen. The right to crown emperors had been bestowed on him by Pope Benedict VII (974-84) and made him one of the most important personages in the Holy Roman Empire, effectivly governing it together with the empress Adelaide. Otto became a young man of fierce asceticism and piety, cultivating the friendship of austere reformers such as Romuald (19 June) and Adalbert of Prague (23 Apr.) and, with his friend Gerbert of Aurillac, whom he had elected pope as Silvester II, set about the spiritual renewal of the empire, casting themselves as a new Constantine and a new Silvester. But with the emperor permanently in Rome, the pope was forced into a subordinate position, and the situation pleased neither the Germans nor the Romans. Willigis tried to influence Otto III to abandon Italy and concentrate his efforts and forces north of the Alps, but Otto died in 1002 at the age of only twenty-two, without heirs, and his succession was disputed. Duke Henry of Bavaria was eventually able to enforce his claim with Willigis' support, and Willigis crowned him (as King Henry II) at Paderborn together with his wife, Cunegund: both were to become canonized saints (13 July and 3 Mar.). Willigis served his new monarch faithfully, by now as an elder statesman.

It was not, however, for his statesmanship that he was canonized. He lived an exemplary life of prayer, work, charity, and study. The office occupied him till noon, after which he engaged in political business, devoting any free time to study of the scriptures. He daily had poor people fed from his resources and at his table. He was instrumental in spreading Christianity to Schleswig-Holstein, Denmark, and Sweden. He established and consecrated great churches and rebuilt the cathedral of Mainz—only to see it burnt down on the the the very day of its consecration, whereupon he immediately set about a fresh rebuilding, which he was not to live to see completed. He was a considerable patron of the arts, taking as his motto, "By art to the knowledge and service of God."

He became involved, largely through the machinations of a nun named Sophia, a sister of Otto III, in a protracted dispute with St Bernward, bishop of Hildesheim (20 Nov.), over the ownership of the convent and church of Gandersheim, on the boundary between Hildesheim and Mainz. Bernward behaved impeccably throughout, and the dispute was eventually settled in his favour, whereupon Willigis immediately and openly withdrew his claim, handing over his staff as a token of brotherhood and good faith. Bernward's biographer was sufficiently impressed to observe that Willigis died "full of years and of good works." He was venerated as a saint immediately after his death, and a Mass was said on his anniversary in St Stephen's church in Mainz, where he was buried. It is claimed that some of his Mass-vestments survive, but the chalice formerly supposed to be his is of a later date. He was popularized in England in the nineteenth century through the poem by S. Baring-Gould, "The Arms of Mayence," which—anachronistically—describes how he chose a wheel for his escutcheon as a reminder of his father's trade and so his own humble origins, for which he was first sneered at by the burghers of the city and then remembered with pride after his death.

There is a brief summary of his life in *M.G.H., Scriptores*, 15, pp. 734-5. There is no contemporary or early biography, though he appears in the chronicle of Thietmar of Merseburg (976-1018) and in the Hildesheim annals. There is a modern life in German by S. Bruck (1962). *O.D.S.*, pp. 499-500; *Bibl.SS.*, 12, 1122-6; *N.C.E.*, 14, p. 946. For the political and ecclesiastical background see Jedin-Dolan, 3, pp. 210ff., 247ff. (with, surprisingly, no mention of him).

Bd Raphaela Ybarra de Villalonga, *Foundress* (1843-1900)

The Basque foundress of the Institute of the Guardian Angels was born into the wealthy industrialist Ybarra family in Bilbao on 16 June 1843 and christened Rafaela. At the age of nine or ten she was sent to school at Bayonne, in the French Basque country, where she made her First Communion and remained until she was fourteen, when illness forced her to terminate her studies. She was married at the age of eighteen to José Villalonga y Gipulò, also from an industrialist family, and was to bear him seven children. A model wife and mother, she added to her already large family when her sister died in 1875 by adopting her five children. This experience led her to abandon all worldly pretensions and deepen her spiritual life, under the direction of Fr Leonardo Zabala. In 1878, having lost her youngest sister the preceding year, she read St Francis de Sales'

(24 Jan.) *Introduction to the Devout Life*, which she took as her final source of enlightenment and encouragement to lead a purely apostolic life.

In 1879 she began visiting the sick in the hospitals of Bilbao, concentrating her ministrations on young girls who came to the city from the countryside in large numbers and were often sexually and economically exploited, ending up alone and sick. Her mother died in 1883, and she added to her cares by looking after her father until he too died in 1890. In 1885, with her husband's agreement, she took temporary vows of poverty, chastity, and obedience, which she made permanent in 1890. She started a centre to feed unprotected young people, to which some sixty or seventy came every day; she then opened a house to shelter young women, under the umbrella of an association under the name of the Holy Family, which grew so fast that she had to open a larger house. In 1892 she founded a convent of the Daughters of Mary Immaculate, founded by St Vincentia Lopez Vicuna (d. 1890; 26 Dec.), in Bilbao. Her chief concern was to give support to unmarried mothers, for whom she had opened a special centre the previous year. This was followed by another centre for young working women in 1893, while at the same time she reorganized the Association of the Holy Family, giving it a broader role in all sorts of charitable works. In 1894 she opened an orphanage for girls, known as the College of the Guardian Angels, which she entrusted to a new religious Congregation established for this purpose.

In 1898 her husband died, leaving her free theoretically to enter the Institute she had founded herself, as she had planned to do. But a daughter-in-law also died, and she decided instead to take charge of her six children. She was by now beginning to suffer from cancer of the stomach, but she still laboured at developing the organization of her Congregation and finding a permanent home for it. She died on 23 February 1900, mourned by thousands whom by now she had helped in the most practical ways and who regarded her as their mother. She had used her wealth and position entirely for others, seeing the problems a rapidly industrializing society with its concomitant flight from rural areas could cause, especially for young people, and taking direct steps to remedy its worst effects. She turned her intense spirituality outward to some of the most helpless victims of a society largely lacking in social conscience, becoming a Mother Raphaela of Bilbao in much the same way as and a century before Mother Theresa of Calcutta. She was beatified by Pope John Paul II on 30 September 1984.

N.S.B. 1, pp. 247-9, citing *Osservatore Romano* 44 (1984), pp. 6-7; *D.H.G.E.*, fasc. 146-7, 583-4.

R.M.
SS Antoninus, Moseus, and Antioch, hermits in Syria (fifth century)
St John Theristus ("the harvester"), of Calabria (eleventh century)
St Milo, bishop of Benevento (Campania) (*c.* 1070)

24

ST ETHELBERT OF KENT (560-616)

The first Anglo-Saxon king to be converted to Christianity, Ethelbert (Aethelberct, Aedilberct, or Edilbertus), was the third *bretwalda*, or overlord, of England, with a titular if not an effective rule extending over all England south of the river Humber. He married, sometime before 588, the Christian princess Bertha, daughter of King Charibert of Paris. A condition of the marriage was that she should be free to practise her religion and bring over a chaplain with her. This was Bishop Liudhard (formerly venerated at least locally as a saint himself on 7 May), who officiated in an old converted church which he dedicated to St Martin. He has been credited with a major part in the conversion of Kent, but it seems that in fact his role was limited to some possible influence on Ethelbert's eventual conversion.

In 597 Pope St Gregory (the Great; 3 Sept.) sent St Augustine (of Canterbury; 27 May) and his companions to evangelize the English. They landed on the Isle of Thanet and sent a message to the king explaining their purpose in coming; Ethelbert asked them to remain on the island until he came to hear what they had to say. "After some days," Bede then relates, "the king came to the island and, sitting down in the open air, summoned Augustine and his companions to an audience. But he took precautions that they should not approach him in a house; for he held an ancient superstition that, if they were practisers of magical arts, they might have opportunity to deceive and master him." The monks came carrying a silver cross and at Ethelbert's command "preached the word of life to the king and his court." Ethelbert reacted with considerable caution, telling them: "Your words and promises are fair indeed; but they are new and uncertain, and I cannot accept them and abandon the age-old beliefs that I have held together with the whole English nation." But he promised to treat them fairly, as they had come from so far; he gave them a house in Canterbury and permission to preach and win converts. "At length," Bede says, Ethelbert himself was converted, after which the monks had "greater freedom to build and restore churches everywhere." His conversion is generally dated to Whitsunday of 597; Bede's comment that it was twenty-one years before his death would produce a date of 595 and cannot be correct. The later date of 601, when Gregory wrote to him would seem more probable. He was then pleased to see more converts being made but would not apply any sort of compulsion on his subjects to accept Christianity, since he himself had been taught that Christ must be accepted freely, though he favoured converts, as being now his fellow-Christians.

In 601, Pope Gregory sent him a letter and gifts. Parts at least of the letter, it must be said, are hardly eirenic in tone: "Press on with the task of extending the Christian Faith among the people committed to your charge. Make their conversion your first concern; suppress the worship of idols, and destroy their shrines. . . . And when you have thus cleansed your subjects from their sins, you will bear the load of your own sins with greater confidence before the judgment seat of God." Ethelbert gave Augustine land for his episcopal see in Canterbury and also built a monastery outside the city, dedicated to SS Peter and Paul but later called St Augustine's when it was dedicated by Augustine's successor, Laurence (2 Feb.). He also helped Augustine to arrange a meeting with the "bishops and teachers of the Britons," then still not under the influence of the Roman Church, to attempt—unsuccessfully—to persuade them to adopt the Roman calculation of the date of Easter and other customs. He was influential in bringing about the conversion of King Sabert of the East Saxons, who ruled under his overlordship as *bretwalda*. The capital of their province was London, and Ethelbert founded the first church dedicated to St Paul there, which later developed into St Paul's Cathedral. He made Mellitus (24 Apr.) first bishop of London and also founded the episcopal see of Rochester (then Hrofescaestir, after an early chieftain named Hrof), and Augustine, with Ethelred's support, appointed Justus first bishop there. Ethelbert gave the new sees of London and Rochester many gifts, and further endowed that of Canterbury.

Besides his support for the Church, Ethelbert conferred secular benefits on the nation. He was the first Anglo-Saxon king to introduce a code of law; Bede, with his enthusiasm for things Roman, states that this was based on Roman law, but in practice it resembled the Salic law of King Clovis of the Franks. One of the first provisions of this was to lay down severe penalties for those who stole church property. This was in contravention of Gregory's enactment.

Ethelbert died on 24 February 616 after a reign of fifty-six years and was buried beside Bertha in the side-chapel dedicated to St Martin in the monastery of SS Peter and Paul in Canterbury. His death proved a great setback to the Church, as his son Eadbald, besides indulging in flagrant sexual immorality, abandoned the Faith. A candle was kept burning in front of Ethelbert's tomb up to the time of the Reformation, though the cult was unofficial and confined to Canterbury until the Middle Ages. His commemoration in the Roman Martyrology was and is on today's date, but in England his feast was formerly celebrated on the 25th or 26th to avoid a clash with that of St Matthias, whom the Calendar revision of 1969 moved to 14 May.

The principal source for his life is Bede, *H.E.*, 1, 25-6 and 32-3; 2, 2-3 and 5. On his laws and the early Canterbury charters see D. Whitelock, *E.H.R.*, 1, pp. 357-9; W. Levison, *England and the Continent in the Eighth Century* (1946), pp. 174-233. On the dating of his conversion, N. Brooks, *The Early History of the Church of Canterbury* (1984). See also *AA.SS.*, Feb., 3, pp. 474-84; *Bibl.SS.*, 5, 116-8; *N.C.E.*, 5, p. 566; *O.D.S.*, pp. 162-3, with further bibliog. on the above aspects and on his cult.

Bd Robert of Arbrissel, *Abbot* (*c*. 1047-1117)

A doctor of the university of Paris and a vigorous reformer, Robert suffered severe criticism for his actions during his lifetime, probably more for rumoured than actual deeds. He has, on the other hand, been rated as one of the major figures of his day and as one of the "most astonishing saints the Church has produced" (Mgr Guérin), one who has no need of miracles to prove his sanctity, for which his life is sufficient evidence—which perhaps suggests French pressure for his canonization and Vatican resistance to it.

He was born into a relatively poor family in Brittany; his parents were deeply pious, and his father became a priest and his mother a nun. After his schooling in Brittany he went on to the university of Paris and duly received his doctorate. He was then appointed vicar to the bishop of Rennes in Brittany by the chancellor to the duke, Silvester de la Guierche. In this office he exercised wide secular powers and found that unpopular decisions were delegated to him. When Silvester died, he was left with many enemies and no family to protect him. He was forced to leave his native land, apparently when his reforming zeal became too much for the bishop in 1093. After a period spent teaching in Angers, he became a hermit in the forest of Craon in Anjou. He was part of a widespread current of reform of monastic life issuing in new Congregations and came into contact with other ascetic figures such as St Bernard of Tiron (25 Apr.), who founded the abbey from which the Benedictine Tironian Congregation arose, and Bd Vitalis of Savigny (16 Sept.), who founded the abbey of Savigny (which also developed its own Congregation, later absorbed into the Cistercians) and made several journeys to England.

His spell as a hermit in Craon produced (after some wanderings in the company of women of dubious reputation), in 1099, a monastic foundation on the borders of Poitou and Anjou that was to develop into the famous monastery of Fontévrault. This became a double monastery, with both nuns and monks under the rule of the prioress (Petronilla de Craon, widow of Baron de Chemille and Robert's patron), on the lines of those developed at Whitby and elsewhere in earlier centuries. In the eleventh century this responded to a growing development and intensification of spiritual life among women. The nuns at Fontévrault lived a contemplative life according to the Rule of St Benedict. Their material needs were supplied by the work of lay brothers, while a community of male religious living according to the Rule of St Augustine celebrated the liturgy and administered the sacraments to them. Robert had recognized a need and devised a way of meeting it, but the double monastery, unsurprisingly, gave rise to rumours, expressed in surviving letters from Bishop Marbod of Rennes and Abbot Geoffrey of Verdun, now accepted as authentic. Robert rather than Petronilla was the target of the attacks: he was accused of harbouring prostitutes and women giving birth out of wedlock and of even more heinous crimes. The most vituperative accusations were made by Godfrey of Vendôme, who, however, later withdrew them. Despite this, various popes supported the foundation, which soon spread to other houses, becoming an Order in its own right with over a thousand nuns and almost as many monks.

Robert was responsible for the conversion of many prominent persons, notably Bertrada, daughter of Simon de Montfort. She had left her husband, Fulk of Anjou, and formed a liaison with King Philip I of France. Robert dissuaded her from this, and she eventually became a nun at Fontévrault. This remained one of the major religious foundations in France until it was dissolved at the time of the French Revolution.

Robert died at the priory of Orsan in 1116 or 1117. He has never been formally beatified, despite processes begun in the seventeenth and the nineteenth centuries, but he is included as Blessed in the new draft Roman Martyrology with the note that he is venerated in diocesan calendars, and the fact that in his monastery even the monks obeyed the abbess is recorded.

The sources are Lives by Baldric (d. 1130) and Andrew, a monk of Fontévrault and a disciple of Robert: in *AA.SS.*, Feb., 3, pp. 598-621, they date from a time when the critical letters were thought inauthentic. See *P.B.*, 3, pp. 4-16, for Guérin's enthusiastic appraisal. There is a study in German by J. von Walter, *Die ersten Wanderprediger Frankreichs* (1903); this was accused in *Anal.Boll.* 23 (1904) of a "manque de sérieux," perhaps showing that the extreme variations in appreciation of him continued for a long time. The most complete work is R. Niderst, *Robert d'Arbrissel et les origines de l'ordre de Fontévrault* (1952). See also *N.C.E.*, 12, p. 528; *H.C.S.*, 2, pp. 142, 156, 260. On the developments of new Orders in the period see P. Schmitz, *Histoire de l'ordre de Saint-Benoît*, 6 (1949), pp. 250-8. There is a substantial notice in *H.S.S.C.*, 6, pp. 229-32.

Bd Constantius of Fabriano (1481)

At first sight he seems a figure of such untouchable holiness as to be beyond serving as an ideal, let alone an example, for other mortals, but this impression may derive from local attempts to keep him, and therefore eventually his relics, in a particular town. So he is credited with gifts of miraculous healing powers and second sight and with an outstandingly holy childhood. But the most authoritative account of his life lays more stress on his theological attainments and reforming actions within the Friars Preachers, whom he joined at the age of fifteen.

He was probably clothed by Bd Laurence of Rippafratta (28 Sept.), a reformer, able biblical scholar, and master of Fra Angelico (Bd John of Fiesole; 18 Feb., above). He took part in the reform of the priory of San Marco in Florence, which he would have known at a time when Fra Angelico's frescoes were glowing fresh on the walls, and rebuilt the friary at Ascoli, where he then lived till his death, despite the pleas of the people of Fabriano that he should return there. His renowned holiness during his lifetime seems to have gone with a somewhat depressive temperament; he constantly doubted whether his actions were pleasing to God and recited the office for the dead every day. He was given a public funeral at the expense of the town council, which regarded his death as a "public calamity." His cult was confirmed in 1821.

The account in Mortier lays most stress on his learning and reforms.

Bd Josepha Naval Girbés (1820-93)

In many ways a typical *beata* of the nineteenth century with a deep devotion to the Virgin Mary, Josepha lived an outwardly uneventful life, dogged by persistent ill health, entirely devoted to the well being of others. She was born on 11 December 1820 in Algemesí, in the archdiocese of Valencia in eastern Spain. At the age of eighteen she took a vow of perpetual virginity, though without intending to enter a religious Order, and under the direction of her parish priest dedicated herself to the care of young girls. She opened an embroidery workshop in her home where girls could learn a trade and at the same time receive instruction from her in Christian virtue. She joined the Association of St Vincent de Paul (founded by Frederick Ozanam, beatified in August 1997; 8 Sept.), active in promoting the welfare of the poor, and became known for her effectiveness in reconciling those involved in family and local feuds.

Her health had been delicate from childhood and worsened into a combination of the chronic illnesses endemic at the time, all of which she bore with great patience. The main characteristics of her life were simplicity and the practice of evangelical poverty: through sacrificing her own needs she was able to supply those of others. She was mild in temperament but with a core of toughness that made her resolute in correcting the faults of those around her. She died in her home village of Algamesí on 24 February 1893 at the age of seventy-three. The informative process inquiring into her holiness was begun by the diocese of Valencia in 1950, her cause was introduced in 1982, and she was beatified by Pope John Paul II on 25 September 1988. At the ceremony he praised her witness as a single woman at a time when it was not easy to be one outside a religious Order, a witness that made her an example of the apostolate of the laity to be promoted by the Second Vatican Council: "sharers in the priestly, prophetic, and kingly functions of Christ . . . they carry out their own part in the mission of the whole Christian people with respect to the Church and the world" (*Lumen Gentium*, 31). He summed up her character and her life of sacrifice by referring to 1 Corinthians 9:22: "To the weak I became weak, so that I might win the weak. I have become all things to all people, that I might by all means save some."

There is a Life by B. Asensi Cubells, *Biografía de la sierva de Dios Josefa Naval Girbés* (1975). *Bibl.SS.*, Suppl. 1, 959-60. F. Holböck, *Die neuen Heiligen der katholischen Kirche*, 3 (1994), pp. 66-8.

R.M.
St Evetius, martyr in Bithynia under Diocletian (303)
St Peter *cubicularius*, martyr under Diocletian (303)
Bd Mark dei Marconi, Hieronymite friar of Mantua (1510)

25

St Nestor, *Bishop and Martyr* (251)

Nestor was bishop of Magydus in the Roman province of Pamphylia during the reign of the emperor Decius (249-51). After a period of mainly peaceful co-existence between the empire and Christianity during the first part of the third century, Decius came to power determined to re-establish what he saw as the tarnished brilliance of the Roman State by renewing persecution of Christians. He sent out an edict requiring all citizens to sacrifice to the Roman gods, apparently intending to secure a mass return to the old pagan observance rather than to initiate a perscution of Christians. Everyone was required to produce a *libellus*, or certificate of having sacrificed, by a certain date, under pain of being imprisoned and tortured. The measure was extremely effective, and the numbers of Christians who sacrificed far exceeded the number of those who stood firm, as Cyprian of Carthage (16 Sept.) and Dionysius of Alexandria (17 Nov.) amongst others attest. Pollio, governor of Pamphylia, saw the harshness with which he enforced this edict as the means to gain the emperor's favour.

In all provinces there were those who stood firm, and in Pamphylia their leader was Nestor. He sent many of his people to hide in places of safety but himself waited calmly in his house for the inevitable arrest. He was highly respected by pagans as well as by his own flock, and when he was taken before the magistrate, the whole court rose to its feet and gave him a place of honour in which to sit. The magistrate tried to persuade him to sacrifice quietly, but he insisted that he knew only the laws of God, not those of the emperor. He was sent before the governor and again treated at first with respect, but he remained equally inflexible. He was cruelly tortured on the orders of Pollio, having his sides torn with iron hooks, and when he insisted that he would be ever with his Christ, he was ordered to suffer the same fate and was accordingly crucified. According to his Acts, of which the original Greek has been lost, pagans knelt with Christians to pray as he died.

There is a Latin version of his *acta* in *AA.SS.*, Feb., 3, generally agreed to be ancient, though not reliably contemporary. P. Franchi de' Cavalieri gives another Greek account in *Studi e Testi*, 22, pp. 97ff. See also *Bibl.SS.*, 9, 825-7; *Oxford Dict. of Byzantium*, pp. 161-2. On the persecution under Decius see Jedin-Dolan, 1, pp. 222-6, with further references. See also the entry for Pionius, 12 Mar., in the present work.

St Caesarius of Nazianzen (*c.* 329-69)

Caesarius was the brother of Gregory of Nazianzen (2 Jan.), and it is from the latter's funeral oration on his death that that most of the information about him derives. He received his education at Alexandria, studying oratory, philosophy, and above all medicine. After further medical studies in Constantinople, he was known as the foremost physician of his age. He refused initially to settle there but was ordered back by the emperor Julian the Apostate (361-3), who made him his chief physician and exempted him from the consequences of his edicts against Christians. He was then, as he was for most of his life, a catechumen only. His father, who was bishop of Nazianzen, and Gregory persuaded him to resign, though he took up the same post again under Julian's successor Jovian, who ruled for a year only. Jovian's successor, Valens, eastern emperor from 364 to 378, appointed him keeper of the privy purse and treasurer of Bithynia.

In 368 he narrowly escaped death during an earthquake at Nicaea, which persuaded him to seek baptism and then renounce the world, and on his death the following year he left all his possessions to the poor. His funeral was a great Christian celebration, with both his parents present. It seems unlikely that he would be regarded as a saint but for his family connections, but Baronius added his name to the Roman Martyrolgy, and he is still included in the new draft.

Gregory's funeral oration, *In laudem Caesarii*, is in *P.G.*, 35 (*Orat.* 7), 765B; also in *AA.SS.*, Feb., 3, pp. 501-7. See also *N.C.E.*, 2, pp. 1048-9.

St Walburga, *Abbess* (779)

A nun at the double monastery of Wimborne in Dorset, daughter of Richard of Wessex and Wunna, and sister of SS Willibald (7 July) and Winnibald (18 Dec.), Walburga was one of the many Anglo-Saxon religious of both sexes who joined St Boniface (5 June), who was also her mother's brother, in his crusade of evangelization of Germany. She had come to Wimborne as a child to the monastic school—when such schools provided virtually the only sources of education for women, while the double monastery afforded women some protection in a violent age. At Wimborne she trained under Tatta (also locally venerated as a saint), whom Boniface asked for nuns to found a convent in newly evangelized parts of Germany. In 750 Tatta sent her and others to St Lioba (28 Sept.), who had also been a nun at Wimborne, had been sent to help Boniface in 748, and had established a convent at Tauberbischofsheim (on the river Tauber, some twenty miles south-west of Würzburg), where Walburga spent her first two years in Germany and where she became skilled in medicine.

Winnibald had established a large double monastery, the only known one of its kind in Germany, at Heidenheim (some fifty miles east of Stuttgart), and summoned Walburga to govern the nuns while he governed the monks. He died after suffering protracted ill health in 761, and Walburga was appointed superior over both nuns and monks by her elder brother, Willibald, who had by then been appointed by Boniface to be first bishop of Eichstätt (in Bavaria, halfway between Munich and Nürnberg). There is no contemporary biography of her, so we know virtually nothing about her rule (though the new draft Roman Martyrology claims that she ruled *optime*, very well). Her appointment over both men and women reflected the English pattern exemplified at Wimborne and Whitby: the nuns were generally of high birth, while the monks or brothers were there primarily to supply their physical needs, so having a woman as overall superior was mainly a reflection of their superior social status.

Winnibald's relics were translated to Eichstätt in 776 and interred in the church of the Holy Cross there. When Walburga died in 779, her body was first interred at Heidenheim but transferred the following year to lie beside that of her brother. From there she took on an extraordinary posthumous career as miraculous healer, owing to an aromatic fluid with undoubted healing properties which flowed—and indeed still flows each year—from a fissure in the rock on which her tomb stands. This caused her remains to be inspected in 893 and widely dispersed, some going to other places in Germany and the Rhineland, some to Flanders, and others to France, thereby spreading her cult to these countries and giving rise to legendary accounts of her presence in at least Flanders. In France, Charles the Simple dedicated a shrine to her in his palace chapel and declared her patron of his kingdom. The fluid is known all over the world as St Walburga's Oil.

In Germany variants of her name are Wilburga, Warpurg, and Walpurgis, and the latter, in conjunction with a feast of the translation of her relics observed on 1 May seems to have produced the unlikely and inappropriate association of this English West Country nun and the witches' sabbath of *Walpurgisnacht* (later universally known through Wagner's music), at which witches were supposed to revel at Blocksberg in the Hartz mountains. This association with a spring fertility rite may also have given rise to her being represented in art holding three ears of corn, though this is ascribed in her hagiology to her having cured a girl afflicted with a voracious appetite with three ears of corn—and she had studied medicine. The most probable explanation for the association and the attribute seems to be that her name resembled that of the earth goddess Walborg. She is more usually shown with a crown and sceptre and a phial of oil, for the healing fluid from her tomb.

Texts of relatively late Latin Lives are in *AA.SS.*, Feb., 3, pp. 511-72; also, ed. Holder-Egger, in *M.G.H., Scriptores*, 15, pt. 1, pp. 86-106. For the Anglo-Saxon missions to Germany see W. Levison, *England in the Continent in the Eighth Century* (1946); C. H. Talbot, *The Anglo-Saxon Missionaries in Germany* (1954); E. S. Duckett, *The Wandering Scholars* (1959), ch. 10; further bibliog. in D. H. Farmer (ed.), *Benedict's Disciples* (n.e. 1995), p. 117. See also this chapter for the sociology of double monasteries. *O.D.S.*, pp. 485-6; *Bibl.SS.*, 7, 876-7.

There are churches dedicated to her all over Europe and also in America, and abbeys, towns, and villages are named after her in Germany and elsewhere. She is often shown in paintings with her canonized brothers, or with her parents, as in a sixteenth-century wall-painting at Schloss Maihingen. Earlier representations show her as a simple nun, but from the fifteenth century she is depicted as an abbess. One of the earliest representations is an eleventh-century wooden bust in which she holds a crown, sceptre, and apple. The present church in Eichstätt, which contains her tomb, is baroque, dating from 1706. She is patroness of the diocese of Eichstätt and, at least locally, of midwives, builders, and domestic animals.

St Gerland of Girgenti, *Bishop* (1100)

His life has been reconstructed from various sources and traditions, and little is known of him with any certainty beyond that he was born in Besançon in Burgundy and became bishop of Girgenti in Sicily. He is supposed to have been of Norman blood, related to Counts Robert Guiscard and Roger II, who reconquered Sicily from the Arabs in the eleventh century. They would have brought their relative over and entrusted him with various ecclesiastical appointments. He was apparently so horrified by the behaviour of the conquerors that he returned to Burgundy with the intention of becoming a hermit. But Count Roger summoned him back to Sicily, where he was consecrated bishop of Girgenti by Pope Urban II (1088-99). He rebuilt the cathedral, which had been devastated by the Saracens, and is said to have held colloquies with Jews and Arabs, many of whom he converted and baptized, but through the force of gentle persuasion and nothing harsher. He died after returning from a visit to Rome. The cathedral at Girgenti is dedicated in his name.

The various accounts are collected in *AA.SS.*, Feb., 3., pp. 595-8; *Anal. Boll.* 57 (1939), pp. 105-8, has an article by T. White, Jr., on "La date du mort de S. Gerland." See also *Bibl.SS.*, 6, 324-5; *P.B.*, 3, pp. 25-7.

Bd Sebastian Aparicio (*c.* 1502-1600)

The life of this peasant from the north-western Spanish province of Galicia, spanning nearly a hundred years and two continents, is at once unique and, in its rags to riches progress combined with deep religious fervour, paradigmatic of the era of the Spanish conquest of Latin America. He was the son of poor parents and spent his childhood minding sheep. When he was fifteen his parents sent him to wealthier Castile as servant to a widow lady. She apparently attempted to seduce him; he ran away from her and found new employment as valet to a wealthy gentleman of Salamanca. His heart, however, was in the countryside, and he returned to sheep farming after a year and worked at this for a further eight years—with some success, as he managed to make enough money to provide dowries for his sisters. This must have made him a relatively attractive marriage proposition himself, but he fled from the prospect, this time to the New World.

He arrived in Mexico and settled in Puebla de los Angeles (to become known throughout the Catholic world as the setting of the Third General General Conference of Latin American Bishops in 1979). He initially worked as an agricultural labourer, but was obviously a person of more entreprenurial bent and developed his own business carrying merchandise and letters between Zacatecas and Mexico City. This showed him the need for better roads, and so he set about building them, becoming wealthy in the process. Among his constructions was the main highway from Mexico City to Zacatecas, which is still in use. But he lived most austerely and devoted his wealth to charitable purposes, including lending money at no interest to farmers. His reputation grew among Spaniards and Indians, and he was often invoked to settle disputes between them, with both sides always respecting his decisions.

In 1552 he retired from his business, bought a property near Mexico City and once again worked the land, this time breeding cattle. He finally consented to marry at the age of sixty, perhaps because he felt he could now do so without giving way to temptations of the flesh; his first wife, a poor girl whose family had entreated him to marry her, died quite soon; he married again, and again his wife died. Both marriages were, by mutual consent, never consummated. He was now seventy-two years old, and he became dangerously ill. He unexpectedly recovered, saw this as a warning from heaven, gave all his possessions to the Poor Clares, became a Franciscan tertiary, and then entered the Observant Franciscan convent in Mexico City as a novice. From there he was sent first to Tecali and then to Puebla, where he joined a large community. His fervour, humility, and obedience were exemplary despite his advanced age, and he was to live for a further twenty-six years, mainly employed in going round the countryside with an ox cart to beg for food. Animals obeyed his slightest whispered command, and he was said to have miraculous powers over them and to be accompanied by angels on his travels.

He died at the age of ninety-eight and was beatified by Pope Pius VI on 17 May 1789. His body rests in a glass tomb in a chapel adjoining the Franciscan church in Puebla.

P.B., 3, pp. 32-3; *F.B.S.*, pp. 124-6; *Auréole Séraphique*, 1, pp. 313-9. On the Franciscans in Mexico see L. Iriarte de Aspruz, *Franciscan History* (1982), pp. 325-9; M. A. Puente, "The Church in Mexico," in E. Dussel (ed.), *The Church in Latin America, 1492-1992* (1992), pp. 217-29, with further bibliog.

Bd Frances Anne Cirer Carbonell, *Foundress* (1781-1855)

Francisca-Ana was born on 1 June 1781 in Sansellos on the island of Mallorca, the daughter of a poor peasant farmer named Juan Cirer and his wife, Juana, *née* Carbonell. She was baptized on the day of her birth. Her mother died when she was still young, and she begged her father, in vain, to allow her to follow a religious vocation. When he also died, she joined a community but, on the advice of her confessor, continued to live in the family house, where she was already engaged in works of charity, especially curing the sick. She realized that the house was destined to become the core of a new religious family: that of the of Sisters of Charity of St Vincent de Paul.

On 7 December she and a group of companions were permitted to take the veil. She added "of the Virgin of Sorrows" to her name. She remained a prudent and exemplary superior of the little community till her death. Taking St Vincent de Paul (27 Sept.) as her model, she ministered to the needy of every sort but gave most attention to the poorest. She died of a stroke during Mass on 25 February 1855, just after receiving Holy Communion. The local populace turned her funeral into that of a saint. Her cause was introduced in 1940, and she was beatified on 28 November 1989.

Bibl.SS., 5, 1010–11; *A.A.S.* 33 (1941), pp. 126–8; and 81 (1989), pp. 569–70, for the address on the occasion of her beatification.

BB Aloysius Versaglia, *Bishop and Martyr* (1873–1930), and Callistus Caravario, *Martyr* (1903–1930)

These two martyrs in China are the first two martyrs of the Salesians of Don Bosco (St John Bosco; 31 Jan.). They belong to a later period than the Martyrs of China considered on 17 February, above, and though they inherited much of the same history, merit separate consideration here. They died in a period marked by continued feuding between local warlords, the rise of the Kuomintang government of Sun-Yat-Sen and then Chiang-Kai-Shek, the birth of the Chinese Communist party, its initial alliance and then break with the Nationalists, and the continued "imperialist" protection of foreign interests and nationals in China.

Aloysius (Luigi) Versaglia was born in Olivia Gessi, near Pavia in the Lombardy region of Italy, on 5 June 1873. Don Bosco sent him to study at his Valdocco "Oratory" in Turin when he was twelve. At that stage his great passions were mathematics and horses, and he told his parents that he was going to study there not to become a priest but to be a veterinary sugeon. He had counted without the extraordinary charism of Don Bosco, however; he changed his mind and joined the Salesians four years later, making his simple profession on 11 October 1889. He studied for a doctorate in philosophy from 1890 to 1893, was ordained in 1895, and spent ten years as superior and novice-master of the new Salesian seminary at Genzano, near Rome. In 1905 the bishop of Macao appealed to the Salesians for missionaries. Aloysius had always longed for a missionary summons; he was appointed leader of the first Salesian missionary expedition to China, setting sail on 7 January 1906 and based initially in Macao. There he was put in charge of a small orphanage, which he transformed into a highly respected school with two hundred pupils and a spiritual centre for the whole town.

A secularizing revolution in Portugal in 1910 deprived the religious of their school, at least for a time, and the bishop sent him into China, on the Heung-Shan mission, between Macao and Canton. This was also the year of the downfall of the Chinese "Heavenly Empire," which gave way to a republic plunged into civil turmoil. Aloysius organized residences, schools, and hospitals; he trained catechists and dreamed of a wider mission entrusted to the Salesians alone. This was to come about in 1918, when the superior of the College of Foreign Missions in Paris persuaded the pope to split the apostolic vicariate of Kwangtung (Canton and surrounding area) into two, entrusting the northern portion, with its centre at Shiu-Chow (where Matteo Ricci had landed in 1589), to the Salesians. New missionaries were sent from Turin: their leader brought Aloysius a fine chalice as a present from the superior general of the Salesians in Turin; he took it in his hands and recalled a dream Don Bosco had had—that the Salesian mission in China would grow when a chalice was filled with blood: "It is that chalice you have brought me; it is my task to fill it," he said. In 1920 the area was constituted an "autonomous apostolic vicariate," and Aloysius was the obvious person to take charge of this. He was consecrated bishop on 9 January 1921 in the cathedral of Canton.

He took charge at a dangerous time, which made his presentiment of a martyr's death entirely probable of fulfilment. The Kuomintang government of Sun-Yat-Sen had not succeeded in unifying the country, and local warlords still ruled in the north. The apostolic vacariate straddled the north-south divide. Sun-Yat-Sen appealed to the newly-formed Communist party for help; its ideology had inherited violent anti-foreign feeling from the Boxers. In such conditions, nevertheless, Aloysius over the next nine years built elementary, secondary, and tertiary schools and colleges, a cathedral, orphanages, and a seminary for Chinese candidates to the priesthood. The continued development of a native clergy was the outstanding missionary achievment of the 1920s, and Aloysius played a leading part in it. The bishop undertook endless and exhausting pastoral visitations throughout his territory, and the number of Christians trebled. Monsignor, later Cardinal, Constantini, then representative of the Holy See in China, was to say of him: "He was the best type of missionary bishop: simple, courageous, inspired by the apostolic fervour stemming from a deep communion with God and seeking nothing other than God's reign and glory. Father and brother rather than commander, and so deeply loved and obeyed by missionaries and faithful, from whom he asked no more than he himself had done or was prepared to do."

Callistus (Callisto) Caravario was born into a working-class family in Cuorgnè in Piedmont on 8 June 1903, was educated by the Salesians, and joined the Order, taking his first vows on 19 September 1919. In 1922 he met Bishop Versaglia when the latter made a visit to Turin and promised him that he would rejoin him in China. He was sent on the China mission in October 1924. His first appointment was in Shanghai, where the Salesians had opened a school for orphans; there he learned English, French, and Chinese, began to study theology, and prepared children for baptism. The city was attacked by Nationalist-Communist militia in 1926, and his superior sent him away for safety to the island of Timor in the Indonesian archipelago, then a Portuguese colony. The Nationalists broke with the Communists in 1927, taking charge of Shanghai. After spending two years teaching and studying on Timor, Callistus returned to China, saying that he would die a martyr's death there; he was ordained by Aloysius Versaglia in Shanghai on 18 May 1929 as a priest for the vicariate of Shiu-Chow. Thereafter the bishop and priest worked in close collaboration for what were to prove the last eight months of Callistus' life. He was sent to join another priest in the distant mission station of Lin-Chow in a ministry caring for 150 converts and two schools, one for boys and one for girls. He was back in Shiu-Chow on 13 February 1930, when Bishop Aloysius asked him to accompany him on a pastoral visit to Lin-Chow. They were never to get there; Aloysius knew the risks but declared that if they were to wait until the passage was safe, they would never leave.

On 24 February the bishop and priest with others, including two male Chinese teachers, a sister of each of these, and a young woman catechist destined for the Lin-Chow mission, embarked by boat on the Pak-Kong River. The three young women were Mary Tong Su-lien, aged twenty-one, returning home to inform her parents of her decision to become a nun; Pauline Ng Yu-che, aged sixteen; and the catechist, Clare Tzen Tz-yung. The presence of these attractive young women on the boat was to play a decisive part in the subesquent course of events.

The previous year, Chiang-Kai-Shek had defeated a Communist force under General Chang-Fat-Kwai, whose soldiers were roaming the countryside living by brigandage. The bishop's junk, after a day's journey, happened on a band of river pirates, who regularly operated on the river and generally let missionaries pass unharmed. But this group had been joined by some soldiers from the defeated Communist army, who had been indoctrinated with anti-foreign and anti-Christian attitudes. They demanded $500 to allow the boat to proceed, threatening to shoot its occupants if this was not paid. Aloysius and Callistus protested that they were missionaries, who had usually been treated with respect, but the soldiers called them "European devils" and boarded the junk. There they found the young women and tried to drag them off to rape them. (It is possible that one of them may have been a rejected suitor of Mary Tong.) The bishop and priest stood in the doorway of their cabin to prevent this but were knocked to the ground with rifle-butts and bamboo canes.

They were all dragged on to the river bank, where Aloysius and Callistus were bound and shoved into a clump of bamboo. The women were asked why they wanted to follow the missionaries to their death; they were told that the Communists were going to destroy the Catholic Church and that they should follow them instead. Callistus made a last attempt to save them, offering to send money, but the soldiers replied that they no longer wanted the money, only to kill them because they belonged to the hated foreign religion. Aloysius begged them to kill him only, as he was old, and to spare the young, but to no avail. The brigands shot him and Callistus, battering in their skulls and putting out their eyes after they were dead. The two teachers were sent on their way on the junk. Their sisters and the catechist were taken off into the mountains. They were freed three days later by soldiers of the Nationalist army and told the whole story, declaring that Aloysius and Callistus had given their lives for them. The soldiers had paid some local villagers to bury the two bodies, which were recovered two days later. They were given an honourable burial in Shiu-Chow on 13 March. The two martyrs were regarded locally as heroes by both Christians and non-Christians because they had died to defend the women. The evidence of the specifically anti-Christian motives of the soldiers was sufficient for the Vatican to decide that they had died for the Faith; both were beatified by Pope John Paul II on 15 May 1983.

N.S.B. 1, pp. 202-9, with photographs; V. Schauber and M. Schindler, *Heilige und Namenspatrone im Jahreslauf* (1992), pp. 79-80, also with photographs. For the background see bibliog. to "The Martyrs of China," 17 Feb., above.

R.M.
SS Daniel and Verda, martyrs in Persia under King Shapor II (344)
St Rheginus, bishop of Thessaly and martyr (355)
St Aldetrudis, O.S.B., abbess of Maubeuge (Belgium) (526)
St Donatus, bishop in Dalmatia (*c.* 811)
Bd Adelhelm, O.S.B., abbot of Engelberg (Switzerland) (1131)
St Avertanus, O.Carm., monk of Lucca (Tuscany) (*c.* 1386)
Bd Laurence Pe-Man, martyr (1856)—see "The Martyrs of China," 17 Feb., above.

26

St Porphyry of Gaza, *Bishop* (353-421)

St Porphyry is the subject of a near-contemporary Life ascribed to Mark, his deacon, which not only sheds light on his character but provides valuable information about the final collapse of paganism in the Christian East. Acording to this, Porphyry came from Thessalonika in Macedonia. When he was twenty-five, he abandoned "the world," like so many of his contemporaries, and spent five years as a monk in the desert of Skete. He returned to Palestine and spent a further five years as a hermit in a cave near the river Jordan. Forced to abandon this after being crippled by illness, he returned to Jerusalem, where he made daily visits to the Holy Places with the help of a walking-stick and where Mark first met him, being immediately impressed with his devotion.

Mark offered to help him up some steps, which was refused, but won his confidence, so that he was entrusted with the task of travelling to Porphyry's family estate in Thessalonika to sell it so that the money could be given to the poor. He accomplished this mission and returned to Jerusalem with the money three months later. He found Porphyry transformed, restored to full health, and listened in amazement to his account of being asked by Christ in a vision to carry his cross, which he did for "some way," awaking to find himself free from all pain, as he had been ever since. The money from the estate was distributed among the poor of Jerusalem, and Porphyry, having thus deprived himself of any income, learned to dress leather and make shoes, with which he earned a small subsistence. Mark was skilled at copying books, from which he earned more, but Porphyry refused his offer to share his earnings, reminding him that St Paul earned his living from his trade as tent-maker.

When Porphyry was forty years old, in 393, the bishop of Jerusalem ordained him priest and gave the great relic of the Holy Cross into his care. Three years later he was elected bishop of Gaza without his knowledge. Ordered to Caesarea on the pretext that John, the bishop there, wished to consult him on various problems in scripture, he was at first reluctant to go, but another vision told that Christ wished him to "marry . . . a wife, poor indeed and lowly, but of great piety and virtue." Uncertain what this might mean but determined to obey the will of God, he set out, accompanied by Mark. In Caesarea, at the instigation of the bishop he was effectively kidnapped by the townspeople of Gaza, forcibly consecrated as their bishop, and made to undertake an arduous three-day journey there over roads which the local pagans had broken up and strewn with logs and thorns to prevent his coming.

In Gaza, he was accused by the pagans of bringing a drought on the area, their god Marnas having foretold that his arrival would portend calamity. No rain fell for two months after his arrival, and the pagans gathered in the temple of Marnas (sensitively spared from destruction by Emperor Theodosius I for its architectural beauty) to pray; the Christians organized a rival fast and procession to the church of St Timothy, outside the town walls. They found themselves locked out and redoubled their prayers for rain. The heavens opened, and the pagans, convinced, opened the gates with cries of "Christ alone is God! He alone has overcome!" Many conversions followed, but those who remained pagan saw their influence decreasing and brought in measures to debar Christians from trade and public office. Porphyry appealed to the emperor for permission to destroy the remaining pagan temples, which was granted, largely through the advocacy of St John Chrysostom (13 Sept.) and Empress Eudoxia after first Mark and then he had made journeys to Constantinople. On their return, a statue of Venus apparently fell down as the procession of welcome passed. Eight temples, including that of Marnas, whose beauty was no longer considered adequate reason to spare it by the zealous Christians, were burned down, and houses were ransacked for idols, which were destroyed. Many pagans were converted, but others resisted and caused a riot in protest, in which Porphyry was almost killed.

He built a cruciform church on the site of the temple of Marnas, himself carrying stones and, with his clergy and flock, helping to dig the foundations. The church was consecrated in 408 and named the Eudoxiana after the empress, who had sent marble and other precious materials from Constantinople. Porphyry spent the remaining thirteen years of his life in the zealous discharge of his pastoral duties in Gaza, renowned above all for his generosity to the poor.

AA.SS., 3, pp. 649-66, prints a Latin version only of the Life by Mark the Deacon; Eng. trans. by G. F. Hill (1913); original Greek text with French trans. and commentary by H. Grégoire and M. A. Kugener (1930) claiming that Mark is not in fact the author, but that it was written some twenty-five years after his death. *Anal.Boll.* 59 (1941) contains a Latin version of a Georgian Life in which the writer claims that Christianity was brought to Gaza without the violence associated with St Cyril in Alexandria. See also *P.B.*, 3, pp. 35-8; B.G., Feb., pp. 434-41; *N.C.E.*, 11, p. 54.

St Victor the Hermit (*c.* 610)

It is unlikely that Victor (Vittré, in French) would have found his way into the Roman Martyrology were it not for St Bernard (20 Aug.), who, in the words of the previous editors of this work, "seems simply to have made himself the mouthpiece of vague local tradition." He did so in the form of a sermon in which he used Victor as a peg on which to hang a vision of the communion of the saints in heaven with those still left on earth: "It is not a land of oblivion in which Victor dwells. Heaven does not harden or narrow hearts, but it makes them more tender and compassionate; it does not distract minds or alienate them from us; it does not diminish but increases affection and charity; it augments capacity for pity."

The few facts attaching to his life seem to be that he was born in the diocese of Troyes and became a hermit at Arcis, near Plancy-sur-Aube in the Champagne region of France. He is credited with the conversion of many sinners through the shining example of his life. His remains were transferred to the Benedictine monastery of Montiéramey, and it was through the monks there that he achieved his cult, as they asked Bernard to draw up an office in his honour, which he did, including a hymn he composed himself.

Bernard's sermon is in *AA.SS.*, Feb., 3, pp. 669-74.

Bd Robert Drury, *Martyr* (1607)

Robert is reported to have come from a gentleman's family of Buckinghamshire. He followed the path of those who wished to study for the priesthood to Reims, where he arived on 1 April 1588. After two years' study there he was sent on to the English College in Valladolid, where he arrived in September 1590; he was ordained priest there by the bishop of León.

He was sent on the English mission in 1605, sailing from Seville. He is one of the joint signatories of a letter written on board ship to the students of the English College in Rome, urging them to bury differences that had arisen among them. In England, where he used the aliases of Brown and Hampden, he was lodged in the second house managed by Anne Line (27 Feb., below), through the agency of Fr John Gerard, S.J., and stayed there at least until 1598 and perhaps until Anne was herself martyred in 1601.

He became involved in differences of opinion among the Catholic clergy in England arising at a time when persecution was abating, and he was actually suspended from his office on 17 December 1600 for supporting the appeal against the archpriest at Wisbech. He evaded any clash with the civil authorities and was never forced to leave the country. Persecution, however, intensified once more in the wake of the Gunpowder Plot in 1605, and he was arrested when it seemed to be dying down again, on 10 February 1607, together with another priest, William Davies (not the martyr of the same name commemorated on 27 July), in the house of a Catholic family, the Stansbys, in London. All the inhabitants of the house were questioned, but only the two priests were taken away. They were clapped into irons in Newgate Prison, examined, and condemned for being priests. They were offered a reprieve if they would take the Oath of Allegiance, but both refused.

The night before he was executed, Robert wrote an account of his arrest, imprisonment, and trial; this document was completed with an account of his execution. He and William Davies were both dragged to Tyburn on hurdles, but Davies was reprieved at the last minute, perhaps on account of his advanced age, and banished instead. Robert was hanged, drawn, and quartered on 26 February 1607. There was some confusion as to whether he was a Benedictine monk, arising from the publication of *A true report of the arraignment and condemnation of a popish priest named R. Drewrie*, which describes him as "having put on after the manner of the benedictine friars beyond the seas a new suit of apparel, being made of black stuff . . . and a black new stuff's priest's gown or cassock." This was a misunderstanding never shared among Catholics, though there was also some confusion in Catholic circles over whether or not he had become a Jesuit just before his execution. This was denied by a priest named John Mush, no friend of the Jesuits, in a letter dated 13 May 1607: "Mr Hampden [Robert's alias] died with great edification of all classes of men. The jesuits say (though falsely) that he had been admitted to their society two days before his martyrdom. You should understand that this is certainly fiction, for Mr Hebborn [Anthony Hebburn, 1567-1611, a priest of the same anti-Jesuit persuasion] was with him the greater part of the night before his passion and was his confessor."

Anstruther, 1, pp. 104-5. Drury's own account is preserved in the Royal Archives in Brussels, *Papiers d'Etat et de l'Audience*, reg. 365, folios 183-7. The *True report . . .* is reprinted in *Harleian Misc.* 3, p. 38. John Mush's letter to A. Champney is in the Vatican Archives, Nunz. Ing. 19, folio 24. On the controversy surrounding the prisoners in Wisbech Castle see T. G. Law, *The Archpriest Controversy* (1896); more briefly, F. Edwards, S.J., *The Jesuits in England: from 1580 to the present day* (1985), pp. 24-5.

R.M.
St Gelasius, martyr (297—but probably St Genesius the Comedian, 25 Aug.)
St Faustinian, second bishop of Bologna (fourth century)
St Macrobius, bishop and martyr in Egypt (fourth century)
St Agricola, bishop of Nevers (*c.* 594)
St Andrew, bishop of Florence (ninth or tenth century)

27

St Julian and Companions, *Martyrs* (250)

The brief reign of the emperor Decius (249-51) was marked by a renewed outbreak of persecution, motivated, at least according to Eusebius, by Decius' hatred of his predecessor, who was sympathetic to Christians, and whose son, also Philip, was even said to be a Christian. Eusebius, as he generally does, quotes his source in full: this is a letter from Bishop St Dionysius of Alexandria (bishop from 247 to 265; 17 Nov.) to Bishop Fabius of Antioch, describing the ordeals suffered by those who were martyred at Alexandria under Decius. (This is the same letter that describes the sufferings of "the wonderful old lady Apollonia; see 9 Feb., above.)

After lamenting the fact that so many fell away from the faith in the face of threats and torture, Dionysius describes those who stood firm, among whom was an old man named Julian, so crippled with gout that he could not stand, let alone walk. Two friends had to carry him to his trial; one of these renounced his faith and was released, but the other stood firm with Julian and was condemned. They were "taken right through the city, which as you all know is immense, mounted on camels and whipped while perched aloft. Finally, while the whole population milled around, they were burnt up with quicklime." Julian's companion was named Cronion (Eunus in Latin) "but nicknamed Goodfellow." The insults heaped on them by the mob roused a soldier who was standing by to protest; he in turn was arrested and brought to trial, so "Besas the gallant warrior of God . . . having fought like a hero in the great war for the Faith, was beheaded."

According to Dionysius, their deaths were followed by those of "another man, of Libyan stock," named Macar (a variant form of the first word of each Beatitude), and Epimachus and Alexander, who had been "in prison a long time endur[ing] numberless agonies from scrapers and whips" and were thrown into the pit of quicklime. These three, however, have not found their way into the new draft Roman Martyrology. Through a mistranslation of Eusebius into Latin, when Besas' name (which appears late in a somewhat strange sentence construction) was omitted, one St Agatho has, for 7 December, but he has been shown to be the same as Besas, given a name out the martyrologist Ado's head.

Eusebius, *H.E.*, 6, 41. See Quentin, pp. 449, 462, 611, 658, for the Agatho-Besas confusion.

St Baldomerus (*c.* 660)

Baldomerus (also variously Galmier, Garmier, Germier, Baudemir, or Waldimer in French) was a locksmith in Lyons. He lived devoutly and austerely, giving away all he could afford—and sometimes what he could not afford, such as the tools of his trade—to the poor. He greeted everyone he met with an "arrow-prayer"—*In nomine Domini gratias semper,* "In the name of God, let us give thanks always."

Viventius, abbot of Saint-Just, came upon him when he was at prayer and was deeply impressed by his devotion; he entered into conversation with him and was even more impressed by his knowledge of the scriptures. He offered him a cell in the monastery, where he devoted himself to a life of contemplation, and much against his will, he was ordained subdeacon by Bishop Gundry. Wild birds would come and feed out of his hand at monastery meal times: he exhorted them with another "arrow-prayer" to "take your refreshment and always bless the Lord of heaven." Mgr Guérin describes him as "true, sincere, obliging, affable, ready to do all the good that lay in his power, inviolably pure in soul and body." The truth is, though, that very little reliable material exists on which to build a life story. Because of his trade he was sometimes venerated as the patron saint of locksmiths and represented in art with pincers and other tools of his trade.

AA.SS., Feb., 3, pp. 688-9; *P.B.,* 3, p. 52, cited above; *D.H.G.E.,* 19, 907-11, devotes more than three columns to him; *Bibl.SS.,* 2, 725-6.

St Anne Line, *Martyr* (*c.*1565-1601)

Anne was born around 1565 at Dunmow in Essex, the daughter of William Heigham, gentleman, and his wife—fervent Calvinists. Before she was twenty she had become a Catholic together with her brother William. For this she and her brother were disinherited. She married Roger Line from Ringwood in the New Forest (Hampshire), who was also a disinherited convert. He was imprisoned for attending Mass and eventually forced into exile in Flanders, where he died in 1594. Anne was left virtually destitute and suffering from continual ill health in the form of violent headaches and "inclinations to dropsy." Despite this she determined to devote the rest of her life to helping her hunted co-religionists.

She offered her services to the Jesuits and was asked to take charge of the large house of refuge in London organized by Fr John Gerard, S.J. This operated safely for two or three years. Anne, despite her poor health, ran the finances of the houses, organized tours and other safe houses for the priests who passed through, and even found time to teach children and to work at embroidering vestments. Without joining an Order, she took voluntary vows of poverty, chastity, and obedience in order to make her dedication more complete. After Gerard's escape from the Tower in 1587, however, the house came under suspicion, and she was forced to move. The new residence was also tracked down by the authorities; on Candlemas Day (2 Feb.) of 1601 Fr Francis Page, S.J., had just vested to say Mass for an unusually large group when pursuivants broke in. Anne and others were arrested, though Fr Page managed to escape.

She was brought to trial on 26 February 1601 before Lord Chief Justice Popham at the Old Bailey, charged under Statute 27 Elizabeth with harbouring a priest. The principal evidence brought against her was the altar found in her house. She was so ill at the time that she had to be carried to the court in a chair. Despite this and despite the failure of the prosecution to prove its case in any sense that might be deemed juridically valid, Popham directed the jury to find her guilty, and she was sentenced to die the next day. She spent her last night in prayer and was taken to Tyburn to be hanged on 27 February 1601. There she kissed the gallows and prayed till her last moments. She was beatified in 1929 and canonized by Pope Paul VI as one of the Forty Martyrs of England and Wales in 1970 (see 25 Oct.), one of three laywomen in the group.

M.M.P., pp. 257-9; *Bibl.SS.*, 8, 55-6; *N.C.E.*, 8, pp. 771-2; 17 (Suppl. 2), p. 36; *O.D.S.*, pp. 299-300; John Gerard, ed. P. Caraman, S.J., *The Autobiography of a Hunted Priest* (1952; 2d ed., 1956); M. O'Dwyer, *Blessed Anne Line* (pamphlet, 1961).

BB Mark Barkworth and Roger Filcock, *Martyrs* (1601)

Mark Barkworth, venerated as the first English Benedictine martyr, and Roger Filcock, a Jesuit priest, were executed immediately after Anne Line (above). Mark kissed the hem of her dress and her hand as she hung from the gallows, saying, "Thou hast got the start of us, sister, but we will follow thee as quickly as we may" (otherwise reported as, "Ah, sister, you've got ahead of us but we'll soon catch you up").

Mark Barkworth was born near Searby in Lincolnshire in 1572. A Protestant by birth and education, he was apparently told by a woman reputed to be a seer that he would end his life on the scaffold. This so shocked his parents that they sent him to study at Oxford University. There is, however, no record of his attendance there. He embarked on travels on the Continent and visited the seminary at Douai, where he embraced the Catholic faith and entered the college, probably in the autumn of 1593, matriculating at the university the following year. Because plague was rife, he was sent on to the English College at Valladolid in Spain, where he was ordained in the summer of 1599 and sent on the English mission. He had become friendly with the Benedictines in Valladolid, apparently the leader of a group of students who had considered joining the Order, to the displeasure of the Jesuits who ran the English College. He left Valladolid as a secular priest but on the way to England visited the abbey of Hirache in Navarre and there received permission to profess himself a member of the Order if in danger of death.

He lodged in England under the alias of Lambert but was soon arrested and imprisoned in the Bridewell Prison. He is said to have told a Genoese priest, Hortensio Spinola, that he had received a vision of St Benedict, who told him that would die a martyr and a monk. He was tried for being a priest and condemned to death by a jury that included three apostates who had probably been fellow-students of his and so knew that he was a priest. No independent witnesses were called. He had somehow acquired a Benedictine habit and tonsured his head in the Benedictine manner, using the pivilege granted him in Spain. It has been suggested that Anne Line and these two priests were executed with haste as this was the day on which Elizabeth's former favourite, the earl of Essex, was executed for treason, and the Catholics were used to distract public attention away from an unpopular decision. Barkworth was described as "a man of stature tall and well proportioned showing strength, the hair of his head brown, his beard yellow, somewhat heavy-eyed." He addressed the crowd to remind them that Pope St Gregory had sent Benedictine monks to evangelize their heathen ancestors, claiming that he was dying "as a Catholic, a priest, and a religious of the same Order." His body was quartered in the usual barbarous manner but not exposed to public view; it was reclaimed by Catholic onlookers and part of it was discovered in a reliquary of crimson damask in the study of John Cotton in Hampshire in 1613. It had been given to him by his chaplain, George Jetter.

Roger Filcock came from Sandwich in Kent and studied at the seminaries of Douai and Valladolid. He arrived at Douai on 15 June 1588 and was one of the first group of ten students to be sent on to the newly-acquired college in Valladolid. He left for there on 29 September 1590 and was ordained there as a secular priest. He wanted to join the Jesuits, but the superior, Fr Henry Garnet, judged it more prudent that he should prove his mettle on the English mission for some time before being admitted. He sailed for England from Bilbao, via Calais, in December 1597. After he had worked in England for two years, Fr Garnet received him into the Society. He was due to undertake his Jesuit novitiate in Flanders, but before he could go there he was arrested. He was imprisoned in Newgate and brought to trial on 23 February 1601. No evidence was brought against him, but he was sentenced to death for high treason. Mark Barkworth wrote of him as "always one of my chiefest and dearest friends, as well formerly when he was at liberty as now in prison. A man exceedingly humble and of extraordinary patience, piety, and charity."

As he watched Barkworth die, Filcock cried out, "I desire to be dissolved and to be with Christ."

See Bede Camm, O.S.B., *Nine Martyr Monks* (1931), pp. 1-44; *M.M.P.*, pp. 253-7; *D.N.B.*, 18 (1889), p. 438 (Filcock). Anstruther, 1, pp. 21-2, 116.

St Gabriel Possenti (1838-62)

He was born the eleventh of thirteen children of a distinguished lawyer who held a succession of official posts in the Papal States and was christened Francesco. Several children died in infancy, and their mother died when Gabriel was four. His father had been appointed registrar of Spoleto and sent Gabriel to the Jesuit college there to be educated. He was a bright student and by all accounts a cheerful youth with a reputation of being something of a "ladies' man"—*damerino*. As the previous edition of this work comments, it comes as something of a relief to find no account of the precocious piety or self-mortification associated with so many nineteenth-century candidates for canonization attached to his childhood. He was later, in letters, to accuse himself of being a great sinner, but this is likely to be an exaggeration brought on by the fervour of his novitiate.

He was twice dangerously ill, and he vowed that if he recovered he would enter religious life, a vow that went unfulfilled the first time but was eventually fulfilled the second. After debating whether to join the Society of Jesus, he eventually, with the approval of his Jesuit masters, opted for the Passionists. The trigger for this seems to have the death of his favourite sister from cholera. He entered the Passionist novitiate in September 1856, taking the name Gabriel-of-Our-Lady-of-Sorrows in religion. The rest of his short life was one of scrupulous attention to duty and the needs of others in every tiny action—redeemed from excessive piety by his unfailing cheerfulness. This is a constant theme in the testimonies for his beatification.

After only four years in religion he developed symptoms of tuberculosis. He bore the relentlessly advancing disease with patience and a determination not to accept any special dispensations. Shortly before his death he destroyed the notes he had made on his inner spiritual life, thereby perhaps depriving later generations of a male equivalent of the *Story of a Soul*, as he resembled St Thérèse of Lisieux (1 Oct.) so closely in his normal childhood, cheerful disposition, and death from tuberculosis at the age of twenty-four.

He died very peacefully in the early morning of 27 February 1862 at Isola di Gran Sasso in the Abruzzi. He was beatified on 31 May 1908 and canonized by Pope Benedict XV on 13 May 1920.

There are Lives by N. Ward (1904); A. della Dolorosa (1920), the official publication for his canonization; E. Burke, *Happy Was My Youth* (1961); G. Poage, *Son of the Passion* (1962).

Bd Mary Deluil-Martiny, *Martyr* (1841-84)

She was born in Marseilles in southern France on 28 May 1841. Her father, Paul, was an eminent lawyer in the town; her mother's name was Anaïde Marie Françoise de Salliers. A devout child, she felt a vocation to the religious life soon after being confirmed. She was invited by the foundress of the "Guard of

Honour of the Sacred Heart of Jesus" to join her in the monastery of the Visitation in Bourg-en-Bresse. She developed this into a Congregation, moving the nuns to Belgium in 1863. She was clothed, together with four companions, by her spiritual director, Mgr Van den Berghe, in a modest house in Antwerp.

She wanted her nuns to participate in a special way in the expiatory prayer of the Church and instituted a continual rota of prayer before the Blessed Sacrament, with nuns taking each other's place every half hour. She laid more emphasis on inner mortification and obedience than on external practices. The Society adopted the Rule of St Ignatius, to which she made some modifications to bring it into line with contemporary needs. The Constitutions in this form, for what became the Daughters of the Heart of Jesus, were approved by Cardinal Dechamps, archbishop of Malines, in February 1876. She took perpetual vows in 1878, the year that a church entrusted to the Daughters was consecrated in Antwerp. Another house had been opened in Aix the previous year, and a third was added near Marseilles the following year, which was to house the novitiate.

Here, on Ash Wednesday, 27 February 1884, she was attacked by the convent gardener, Louis Chave, who was fanatically anti-religious. She died from her wounds, being heard to exclaim, "I forgive him . . . for the work . . . for the work!" She was originally buried in the family cemetery; her remains were then moved first to the convent cemetery and then, in 1906, to Belgium, where they lie in the crypt of the church of the Sacred Heart in Antwerp. Her cause was introduced in 1921, and she was beatified by Pope John Paul II on 22 October 1989.

Bibl.SS., 5, 547; Anon., *La madre Maria di Gesù Deluil-Martiny, fondatrice della Società delle Figlie del Cuore di Gesù* (1955).

R.M.
St Honorina, martyr in Normandy (fourth century)
SS Basil and Procopius, monks, defenders of images (741)
St Hippolytus, abbot and bishop of Loudun (*c.* 770)
St Gregory, monk in Armenia (*c.* 1005)
St Luke, abbot of St Saviour's in Sicily (1149)

28

ST OSWALD OF WORCESTER, *Bishop* (992)

Oswald was of Danish descent and came from a military family. A nephew of St Oda, or Odo, archbishop of Canterbury from 942 (d. 959; 4 July), and of Oskytel, archbishop of York, he received his early education from Oda. He was a canon of Winchester Cathedral for some years before becoming a monk. He then crossed over to France to study at Fleury-sur-Loire (which claims the relics of St Benedict; 11 July) and took the Benedictine habit there. It would have been there that he gained his knowledge of French, Roman-orientated, ecclesiastical administration. Oda several times invited him to return to England, but he would not do so until he heard news that his uncle was dying, when, in 958 or 959, he returned as a priest and a monk.

He came to the notice of St Dunstan (19 May), appointed archbishop of Canterbury in 960, whose fruitful collaboration with King Edgar (king of Wessex from 959 to his death in 975) did so much to reform the Church in England, largely through the instrumentality of the monastic Order and the replacement of secular canons by monks in strategic cathedrals. On Dunstan's recommendation, King Edgar appointed him bishop of Worcester in 961. From there he founded the monastery of Westbury-on-Trym, near Bristol, the following year, initially with twelve monks. In 969 he reformed the cathedral chapter of Worcester. Local tradition has it that he did so by building a church of St Mary near the then cathedral church of St Peter, staffed by monks, which so outshone the cathedral that the townspeople deserted the latter and flocked to the former. The canons, deprived of their congregation, were obliged to follow them and join the monks, whereupon St Mary's became the cathedral church. Recent historical research, however, has called the gradualness of this process into question and suggested that he may have acted more abruptly, as Ethelwold (1 Aug.) had done at Winchester in 964 and Wulsin (8 Jan.), also appointed on Dunstan's recommendation, was to do at Sherborne in 998. Oswald established a great musical tradition at St Mary's and, together with Dunstan, Ethelwold, and his own later successor St Wulfstan (19 Jan.), was one of the great forces for keeping the flame of learning alight in England before the Norman invasion.

In 971 he built the great monastery of Ramsey in Huntingdonshire, on an island in the marshes formed by the floodplain of the river Ouse. Most of the monks from Westbury were transferred there and it in turn became the founding house of the abbeys of Pershore and Evesham in the Severn valley. His first biographer tells that Ramsey was his favourite place of residence. He enhanced its intellectual status by bringing men of learning over from the Continent, including Abbo of Fleury (13 Nov.), mathematician, astronomer, and one of the foremost scholars of his day, who spent two years at Ramsey Abbey, from 985 to 987. His teachings there did much to advance the movement of monastic reform, and his influence can be seen in the writings of Byrthferth of Ramsey, one of the great intellectuals of the eleventh century and possibly Oswald's first biographer.

From 972 to 1016 (and briefly in 1040 and 1061, when the pope abolished the practice) the see of Worcester was combined with that of York. Oswald was promoted to the archdiocese of York in 972 but retained the see of Worcester at the king's request and with the pope's permission. This plurality can be seen to sit a little awkwardly with the strict reforms he imposed on his clergy. F. M. Stenton has suggested that the reason for the combination was that the see of Worcester, part of the southern province, was rich and powerful—as it continued to be until well after the Reformation as evidenced by the magnificence of the bishop's palace at nearby Hartlebury Castle, home of the bishops of Worcester for over a thousand years—whereas York, the capital of the northern province, was poor and turbulent. One reason for the choice of Oswald as archbishop of York may have been that, being of Scandinavian descent but strongly loyal to Edgar, he was seen as a man to unite the northern and southern provinces. Oswald certainly built up the wealth of Worcester through the acquisition of large tracts of land, and he may well have been unwilling to abandon the luxuriance of his holdings in the fertile Severn valley altogether for the relative wastelands of northern Britain. Nevertheless, the Life possibly by Byrhtferth stresses his special love for the poor, and he was certainly widely revered for his sanctity during his lifetime.

He continued to adminster his two dioceses until he died, building churches, acting as judge, and visiting his monasteries. His last visit to Ramsey was made in 991, the year before his death. The tower had fallen down, causing extensive damage to the church, and his visit was for a ceremonial reopening of the church. After a magnificent Mass and a great banquet he bade his monks there farewell, sensing that it was probably a final farewell. He spent his last winter at his beloved cathedral of Worcester. It was his habit each Lent to wash the feet of twelve poor men each day, and he was able to carry on with this practice till Leap Year Day, when he died after kissing the feet of the twelfth and pronouncing a blessing. His death is said to have produced "such lamentations that merchants left their bargaining and women their distaffs and their weaving" (Hill and Brodie).

The contemporary Life, on which all accounts except those by Florence of Worcester (1, 141) and William of Malmesbury (*Gesta Pontificum*, R.S. 52, 1870, pp. 247-50) depend, is ed. J. Raine, in *Historians of the Church of York*, 1 (R.S., 1879), pp. 399-475; there is a further Life, by Eadmer in *ibid.*, 2 (1886), pp. 1-59, which is abridged in *N.L.A.*, 2, pp. 252-60. See also *AA.SS.*, Feb., 3, pp. 755-62; *Bibl.SS.*, 9, 1296-7; *N.C.E.*, 10, p. 811, Stanton, pp. 89-90; *D.N.B.*, 14, 1217-19. Citation above from R. Hill and C. Brodie, "From 627 to the Early Thirteenth Century," ch. 1, in G. E. Aylmer and R. Cant, *A History of York Minster* (1977). *O.D.S.*, pp. 370-1, with further refs.

St Romanus of Condat, *Abbot* (*c.* 460)

The founder of the monastery of Condat in the Jura mountains, between France and Switzerland, first went to the region as a hermit at the age of thirty-five. He took with him a few tools and some seeds and settled in a precipitous place at the confluence of two rivers, the Bienne and the Alière. His aim was to emulate the Desert Fathers in austerity, and he took with him copies of Cassian's *Institutes* and *Conferences*, based on the teachings of the Desert Fathers, as his guide. He perhaps failed to realize that although the desert can be cold at night, the air there is dry, which it is not between rivers in the Jura, and he was eventually obliged to modify some of his initial austerities out of consideration for the climatic difference. But he and his community ate no meat, allowed themselves milk and eggs only on occasions, and dressed in wooden clogs and animal skins.

He was joined first by his brother Lupicinus (21 March), then by their sister and a growing number of other recruits. With their help he built the monastery of Condat, followed by another at nearby Leuconne and then a convent for the women at La Beaume, where the village of Saint-Romain-de-la-Roche now stands in his honour. He made a pilgrimage to the reputed spot of the martyr-dom of St Maurice and the Theban Legion (22 Sept.), now Saint-Maurice in the Valais, and is reputed to have healed two lepers on the way. News of this miracle reached Geneva, through which he had to pass, so that the bishop and all the townspeople turned out to greet him. He died in around 460 and was buried, at his request, in his sister's convent. He was succeeded as abbot of Condat by Lupicinus, who survived him by twenty years and was held to be much harsher in his rule.

Some early Lives place their commemoration on the same day, together with Eugendus (1 Jan.), later abbot of Condat, and sometimes others, but the previous edition of this work and the new draft Roman Martyrology assign the two brothers to separate dates, and this is followed here. Romanus is also (with Bd Daniel Brottier) one of only two saints commemorated today every year: the others, including Oswald (above), have their *dies natalis* on 29 February and are now commemorated on that date in leap years, simplifying a more complex system current to the previous edition of the Roman Martyrology.

L. Duchesne established the authenticity of the Lives of Romanus, Lupicinus, and Eugendus in "La Vie des Pères du Jura," *Mélanges d'archéologie et d'histoire*, 18 (1898), pp. 3-16. The text is in *M.G.H., Scriptores Merov.*, 3, pp. 131-53.

St Hilarus, *Pope* (468)

Hilarus, born in Sardinia the son of a certain Crispin, succeeded St Leo the Great, pope from 440 to 461 (10 Nov.) and was to prove a worthy successor. Leo's attempts to impose his concept of the universal primacy of the papacy on the Eastern Church had been decisively rejected by a combination of Emperor Theodosius II and Bishop Dioscorus of Alexandria at the so-called "Robber Synod" of Ephesus in 449. His legates were maltreated and barely escaped with their lives. Hilarus was one of these legates; he protested against the treatment of Flavian of Constantinople, for which he was so threatened that he had to take refuge in the tomb of St John the Evangelist (27 Dec.). He recorded his experience in a letter, still extant, to the future empress St Pulcheria Augusta (10 Sept.), describing how the violence of Dioscorus had prevented him from coming to Constantinople. Leo expressed his admiration for him in a letter to Theodosius II: "We have been informed, not from an unreliable source but rather by a most faithful narrator, our deacon Hilary, of the events that have occurred. He, not to be forced to sign [the decree upholding Eutyches], took to flight. . . ."

Still a deacon, he was unanimously elected to succeed Leo in 461. He attributed the fact that he had been able to escape to Rome with his life to the intercession of St John and in thanksgiving built three chapels in Rome, one dedicated to St John the Evangelist in St John Lateran, adjoining the baptistery; one dedicated to St John the Baptist (29 Aug. and 24 June), to whom he extended his gratitude; and one to the Holy Cross. The first two are still standing, with the mosaics he commissioned, and over the door of the first is the inscription: *Liberatori suo beato Iohanni evangelistae Hilarus episcopus famulus Christi*, "Hilarus, bishop and servant of Christ, to his liberator, blessed John the Evangelist." He also restored and embellished many churches as well as building public baths at Verano, outside the city walls, and two libraries.

He set out his agenda at the beginning of his pontificate: "I shall provide for universal concord among the priests of the Lord: so that none may be concerned with himself alone, but all may take care to obtain the things that are of Christ." In effect, he was largely concerned with strengthening church discipline and adminstration, which meant supporting the authority of bishops in some areas and curbing their excessive use of their powers in others. He summoned a Roman council in Santa Maria Maggiore in 465, at which many bishops from Italy, some from Africa, and a few from Gaul were present. Hilarus used the council to confirm existing norms with regard to access to Holy Orders, reiterating the ban on remarried widowers, men who had married widows, those lacking education, and those with physical defects.

In Gaul he intervened to uphold the unity of the episcopate under the authority of the metropolitan, Leontius of Arles, conferring wide new powers on him. He was faced with a fresh problem over relations with the Arian Germans; he was eventually forced, after previously protesting successfully to the emperor, to admit a community of them to establish itself in Rome and build their own church there; this later became the church of Santa Agata dei Goti. Several of his letters to bishops have survived. In all things he strove to maintain "the domination and primacy of the Holy, Catholic, and Apostolic See" (*Liber Pontificalis*).

He died on 29 February in the leap year 468 and was buried in the church of St Laurence at Verano next to the bodies of Popes SS Zosimus (417-8; 26 Dec.) and Sixtus III (432-40; 28 Mar.), Leo's immediate predecessor.

Lib.Pont., 1, pp. 242-8; *Bibl.SS.*, 7, 737-53; *N.C.E.*, 6, p. 1113; *O.D.P.*, p. 45. Some of his letters to bishops are in *P.L.*, 58, 11-31.

Bd Antonia of Florence (1472)

Antonia was born in Florence, married at a young age, and lost her husband a few years later. Resisting her parents' attempts to persuade her to remarry, she dedicated herself to the religious life and was one of the first postulants to enter the convent of regular tertiaries of St Francis founded in Florence in 1429 by Bd Angelina of Marsciano (15 July). This was the fifth of Bd Angelina's foundations; the first had been made at Foligno in 1397, and a year after her entry Antonia was transferred there as superior in recognition of her exceptional merits. Here she worked directly under the guidance of the foundress for three years and was then sent to take charge of a recent foundation at Aquila, in the Abruzzi, where again she showed her holiness in charitable works.

She found, however, that the rule of the regular tertiaries was not strict enough for her. She told St John of Capistrano (23 Oct.), who was visiting Aquila, of her desire for a stricter way of life, and he arranged for her to transfer, with eleven of her nuns, to the newly-built monastery of Corpus Christi, where they embraced the original Rule of St Clare (8 Aug.) in all its austerity. The house soon proved too small for the numbers who flocked to join the community and had to be enlarged to accomodate over one hundred nuns. Antonia called poverty the "Queen of the House" and showed unfailing humility and kindness in her dealings with her nuns. She ruled for seven years, through a series of personal difficulties caused by ill health, vestiges from her past life in the shape of a son who dissipated his entire inheritance and a gaggle of quarrelsome relatives, and difficulties in her own spiritual life. She then resigned her position as superior and devoted the remainder of her life to prayer. She was reported often to be seen rapt in ecstasy and sometimes showing more startling physical phenomena, such as levitation and a halo of fiery light around her head. She died in 1472 and was buried with full ceremony; the bishop, magistrates, and all the people of the town insisted on bearing the costs of the service. Her relics are preserved in Aquila, where those of St Bernardino of Siena (20 May) and Bd Vincent of Aquila (7 Aug.) also lie. She was beatified in 1847.

F.B.S., pp. 150-2; *Auréole Séraphique*, 2, p. 36, *Bibl.SS.*, 2, 74-5; *N.C.E.*, 1, pp. 643-4.

Bd Daniel Brottier (1876-1936)

Daniel was born at La Ferté Saint-Cyr, in the diocese of Blois, on the river Loire between Orleans and Tours and showed a desire to become a priest from an early age. He was encouraged in this by his parents and by a priest who arranged for him to enter the diocesan seminary. He was ordained on 22 October 1889 and then spent three years teaching at the Free School in Pontlevoy.

He longed for wider horizons, however, and joined the missionary Congregation of the Holy Spirit. They sent him to Senegal, West Africa, where he spent eight years in labours that took a severe toll of his health. This obliged him to return to France, to his great regret, but he continued to exercise his mission by raising funds for the building of the new cathedral in Dakar, the capital of Senegal. On the outbreak of the First World War in 1914, though in secular France priests were subject to drafting into the army, he was exempted from conscription on grounds of poor health; he was one of the first priests to enroll as a volunteer chaplain and spent over four years at the front. He flung himself into the most dangerous situations, ministering to the suffering and dying wherever he could. Almost miraculously he survived in positions where the average life expectancy was measured in weeks rather than months. Totally careless himself of his personal safety, he attributed his survival to the protection of St Thérèse of Lisieux (1 Oct.), to whom he had a great devotion and to whose protection he had been specially vowed by the vicar apostolic of Senegal. He survived fifty-two months at the front without a wound.

In 1923 the cardinal archbishop of Paris asked the Holy Spirit Fathers to loan him Fr Brottier to help in his planned restoration of the Orphan-Apprentices project in the Paris suburb of Auteuil. Daniel succesfully established the project and spent the last thirteen years of his life ministering to orphaned and abandoned children, whom he likewise vowed to the protection of St Thérèse, with the same devotion he had previously shown on the African mission and in the trenches. He died on 28 February 1936 and was beatified by Pope John Paul II in Paris on 25 November 1984. His orphanage at Auteuil continues to flourish, as does the cathedral of Dakar, which was completed in 1916, twenty years before his death.

N.S.B. 2, pp. 232-3; *A.A.S.* 76 (1984), pp. 1029-31.

R.M.

Bd Augustus Chapdelaine, priest of Paris Society of Foreign Missions, martyr (1856)—see "The Martyrs of China," 17 Feb., above.

Alphabetical List of Entries

(Names are listed for those saints and blessed who have entries in the main body of the text. Those listed in the RM paragraph at the end of each day are omitted.)

Consultant Editors

DAVID HUGH FARMER. Former Reader in history at the University of Reading. Author of *St Hugh of Lincoln* and other biographical studies of saints. Author of *The Oxford Dictionary of Saints*. General consultant editor.

REV. PHILIP CARAMAN, S.J. Author of numerous biographies of saints and chief promoter of the cause of the Forty English Martyrs (canonized in 1970). Consultant on English Martyrs.

JOHN HARWOOD. Librarian of the Missionary Institute in London and course lecturer on the Orthodox churches. Consultant on Eastern and Orthodox saints.

DOM ERIC HOLLAS, O.S.B. Monk of St John's Abbey, Collegeville, Minnesota, and director of the Hill Monastic Manuscript Library in Collegeville, where he also teaches theology at St John's University. General consultant, U.S.A.

PROF. KATHLEEN JONES. Emeritus Professor of Social Policy at the University of York. Author of many books and articles on social policy and mental illness. Honorary Fellow of the Royal College of Psychiatrists. Translator of *The Poems of St John of the Cross* (1993). Consultant on social history and abnormal behaviour.

DOM DANIEL REES, O.S.B. Monk of Downside Abbey and librarian of the monastery library. Bibliographical consultant.

DR RICHARD SHARPE. Reader in diplomatic history at the University of Oxford. Author of *Medieval Irish Saints' Lives* (1991), *Adomnán of Iona. Life of St Columba* (1995), and numerous articles on Celtic saints. Consultant on this subject.

REV. AYLWARD SHORTER, W.F. Long experience of African Missions and author of many books on the subject. Former President of Missionary Institute, London, now Principal of Tangaza College, Nairobi. Consultant on missionary saints.

DOM ALBERIC STACPOOLE, O.S.B. Monk of Ampleforth Abbey. Fellow of the Royal Historical Society. Secretary of the Ecumenical Society of Our Lady. Editor of several works, including *Vatican II by Those Who Were There* (1985). Engaged on a study of St Anslem. Consultant on feasts of Our Lady.

DOM HENRY WANSBROUGH, O.S.B. Monk of Ampleforth Abbey, currently Master of St Benet's Hall, Oxford. Member of the Pontifical Biblical Commission. Author of numerous works on scripture and Editor of the *New Jerusalem Bible* (1985). Consultant on New Testament saints.

SR BENEDICTA WARD. Anglican religious. Lecturer at Oxford Institute of Medieval History. Author of numerous works on hagiography, spirituality, and mysticism. Consultant on Middle Ages and age of Bede.